Public Speaking

Preparation & Presentation in a Digital World

Virginia McDermott
The Nido R. Qubein School of Communication
High Point University

Rachel A. Wegter
Coastline Community College/Golden West College

Adaptation of
Public Speaking: Choices for Effective Results, 6e
by: **Gail Mason, Mark Butland, John J. Makay**

Kendall Hunt Book Team

Chairman and Chief Executive Officer Mark C. Falb
President and Chief Operating Officer Chad M. Chandlee
Vice President, Higher Education David L. Tart
Director of Publishing Partnerships Paul B. Carty
Senior Editor Lynnette M. Rogers
Vice President, Operations Timothy J. Beitzel
Assistant Vice President, Production Services Christine E. O'Brien
Senior Production Editor Mary Melloy
Senior Permissions Coordinator Renae Horstman
Senior Cover Designer Heather Richman

Coast Learning Systems Book Team

Andrew C. Jones, Chancellor, Coast Community College District
Loretta P. Adrian, President, Coastline Community College
Dan C. Jones, Administrative Dean, Office of Learning & Information Technologies
Lynn M. Dahnke, Director of Marketing & Product Development
Judy Garvey, Director, Instructional Media Design & Production
Meg Yanalunas, Instructional Designer
Wendy Sacket, E-Media & Publishing Project Coordinator
Marie Hulett, Production Coordinator

Cover design by Don Vierstra; cover images © iStock, Inc., and Shutterstock, Inc.
All Shutterstock images used under license from Shutterstock, Inc.

Kendall Hunt
publishing company

www.kendallhunt.com
Send all inquiries to:
4050 Westmark Drive
Dubuque, IA 52004-1840

Dedication

To my students and colleagues, all of whom have made me a better teacher and a better person.

—Virginia McDermott

To my parents and first teachers, Rex and Laura, brother, Seth, and husband, Tyler; your love and support in my life is a magnificent blessing.

—Rachel A. Wegter

Brief Contents

Contents

Preface

Every person has a distinct voice that deserves to be heard. Incorporating the principles of public speaking will help students to develop that voice into a potent instrument of influence, productivity, and interpersonal significance. *Public Speaking: Preparation and Presentation in a Digital World* focuses on how to present yourself and your messages in a way that increases the odds of being heard and getting what you want in an efficient and ethical manner. While the primary focus is on the more formal presentations life brings to us in the workplace, at school, and in the community, this textbook also contains effective strategies for less formal venues of public speaking, such as conference calls, emails, social media, status updates, text messages, and face-to-face conversations.

Public Speaking: Preparation and Presentation in a Digital World is available **in print** or as an **eTextbook**. It was created to work in tandem with the 14-lesson online course produced by Coast Learning Systems. Whether it is used in an on-ground classroom, a hybrid, or fully online, the textbook will link students to the many "public faces" they need to recognize and communicate effectively with.

Textbook Objectives

Public Speaking: Preparation and Presentation in a Digital World has been designed as a college introductory (100) course on public speaking. It will satisfy the general education requirements for a two-year or four-year degree in higher educational institutions.

This textbook was written to accomplish five overall objectives with the general purpose of developing public speakers who can think clearly and reason soundly. Two additional concepts are threaded throughout the text and help to build the students' awareness of and responsibility toward cultural diversity and what it means in public speaking and how technology today impacts the developing public speaker. After reading this textbook and completing the activities assigned by their instructor, students will be able to:

- **Apply the principles, skills, and processes of public speaking in preparation of a speech by performing audience analysis, developing appropriate purpose and thesis statements, conducting topic research using appropriate resources, applying relevant critical thinking and effective reasoning skills, creating an outline for the speech, developing the speech in an appropriate format, using effective language, and incorporating content that supports the purpose/thesis, and creating appropriate presentational aids.**
- **Apply the principles, skills, and processes of public speaking in the delivery of a speech by effectively integrating verbal and nonverbal skills, using presentational aids when appropriate, using an appropriate delivery style (e.g., extemporaneous, impromptu, speaking from manuscript), and adapting a previously prepared speech to suit unexpected changes in audience, venue, and so forth.**
- **Analyze and critique written and oral speeches.**
- **Use technology effectively in the preparation and delivery of a presentation.**
- **Prepare and deliver oral presentations that appropriately reflect ethical considerations and appreciation of culturally and ethnically diverse audiences.**

By equipping students with the necessary knowledge and skills, this textbook will prepare students to make intelligent choices tailored to meet the needs of the varied public speaking situations they will encounter throughout their lives.

Textbook Organization

Public Speaking: Preparation and Presentation in a Digital World contains 14 chapters that are presented in three distinct units within the textbook, allowing instructors to customize the course to suit their individual teaching preferences.

Unit 1—Communicating: Strategies for Dynamic Delivery

Chapters 1 through 4 provide an overview of the basic principles of public speaking, including coverage of such topics as overcoming public speaking apprehension, strategies for audience analysis, ethical considerations, and communicating with diverse audiences.

Unit 2—Creating: Speechwriting Tactics for Powerful Presentations

Chapters 5 through 9 explore the many facets of preparing a speech and explain how research, supporting evidence, organizational patterns, and memorable language help you structure relevant material to suit your chosen topic and engage the attention of your audience.

Unit 3—Connecting: Adapting Your Speech for Diverse Audiences and Situations

Chapters 10 through 14 focus on speaker-audience connections involved in informative and persuasive speaking, describe speaking on special occasions, and explore the particular applications of public speaking as part of group presentations.

Textbook Features

Public Speaking: Preparation and Presentation in a Digital World includes a number of features designed to make learning easier and more productive.

Each chapter begins with clearly defined learning objectives so that students are aware of what they are expected to learn over the succeeding pages. The objectives are phrased in terms of not just what students will understand, but how they will be able to demonstrate their understanding after completing each chapter.

Online course references appear throughout each chapter to refer students and to describe what examples, activities, and concepts are contained in the accompanying online course.

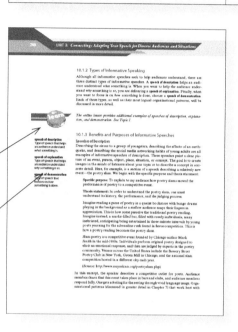

Key terms are highlighted, with formal definitions appearing in the margins for easy reference.

The **principles of public speaking** are shown in action by incorporating narrative examples and extracts from speeches that relate directly to students' actual life experiences.

High-quality photographs and illustrations bring to life key concepts in ways that help students link concepts to effective delivery.

A series of "aside" boxes illustrate examples of noted speeches, offer advice on giving effective, successful speeches, and provide helpful insights for students.

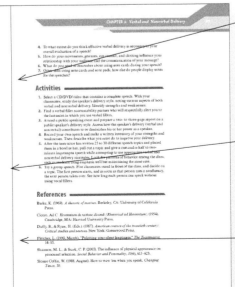

Finally, at the end of each chapter, a succinct summary capsulizes the material presented followed by a list of review questions to test student understanding of the material and flag any areas in which further study might be needed.

Key terms are repeated along with the page number where they were defined. Students will be able to go back and review definitions before moving on to the next chapter.

Also at the end of each chapter, Questions for Reflection and Activities allow students to discuss and demonstrate their knowledge of the key concepts.

Acknowledgments

Enormous thanks and appreciation are expressed for the contributions of the following key individuals, without whose input and dedication, this textbook and its accompanying online course would have not been possible.

Lead Academic Advisors

Virginia McDermott, Ph.D., High Point University, NC

Rachel A. Wegter, M.A., Coastline Community College, CA

Members of the National Academic Advisory Team

The following scholars, teachers, and practitioners helped focus the approach and content of each chapter to ensure accuracy, academic validity, significance, and instructional integrity.

Cara Cotellese, Ph.D., Kutztown University, PA

Alycia Ehlert, Ph.D., Volunteer State Community College, TN

Angela Grupas, Ed.D., St. Louis Community College-Meramec, MO

Sandra King, Ph.D., Ann Arundel Community College, MD

Joshua Levenshus, M.A., Coastline Community College, CA

Virginia McDermott, Ph.D., High Point University, NC

Alma Martinez-Egger, M.S., Tarrant County College Trinity River Campus, TX

Kristen Ruppert-Leach, M.A., Southern Illinois University, IL

Michelle Imani Scott, Ph.D., Savannah College of Art and Design, GA

Andrea Thorson, Ed.D., Bakersfield College, CA

Rachel A. Wegter, M.A., Coastline Community College, CA

Many thanks go to Meg Yanalunas of Coast Learning Systems for instructional design and quality assurance, as well as coordination of this textbook and its accompanying course content.

Special thanks are extended to our textbook authors and content developers for the online course, Ginny McDermott and Rachel A. Wegter, for their significant contribution, review, and scrutiny of content over each chapter, including the creation of many exercises and examples that engage the student and enhance their learning. We also appreciate the contributions of Frank Selinsky, who provided invaluable assistance with editing this textbook.

Very special thanks go to the dedicated members of the Coast Learning Systems eMedia & Publishing team headed by Judy Garvey, who managed the coordination, design, and production of this textbook: Marie Hulett, Wendy Sacket, and Thien Vu.

Additional thanks go to Marie Hulett of Coast Learning Systems, who spent tireless hours researching and acquiring images and permissions for the photographs and illustrations that appear in this textbook.

We also thank all staff members of Kendall Hunt Publishing, Higher Education Division, for their hard work and dedication and help in making this textbook happen, especially David Tart, Paul Carty, Lynne Rogers, Mary Melloy, Renae Horstman, Angela Willenbring, and Georgia Botsford.

Last, but certainly not least, we wish to thank members of the Coast Community College District and Coast Learning Systems, especially our Board of Trustees, Chancellor, President, and our Executive Dean of Instructional Systems Development, for their support.

We especially thank the many individuals who so graciously supplied us with and allowed us to use many interesting photographs in this textbook.

About the Authors

Virginia M. McDermott (Ph.D., University of Illinois) is an Associate Professor of Communication at High Point University, where she teaches graduate and undergraduate courses in strategic communication, including communication campaign development and persuasion. Her research examines how problematic events change the nature of relationships and conversations, how communication facilitates coping, and how communication campaigns can be used to address health disparities and social inequities. Her recent publications include an article in *Communication Theory* and a chapter in *Emerging Perspectives in Health Communication: Meaning, Culture, and Power* (2008). Virginia has extensive experience in organizational training and specializes in seminars on how to develop a positive organizational environment.

Rachel A. Wegter (M.A., California State University, Long Beach) is an award-winning Communication Studies instructor at both Golden West College and Coastline Community College; she teaches a variety of communication-based courses including honors public speaking, small group dynamics, literature and communication, voice and articulation, journalism and mass communication. She has extensive instructional design experience in both traditional and distance learning formats, is a featured academic in the film documentary *Accidental Icon: The Real Gidget Story*, and directs speech and debate and journalism programs at a large urban high school. As a speech expert, Rachel specializes in public speaking and interview coaching, new media strategies for effective online instruction, military education, business communication, team building, the International Phonetic Alphabet, and on-camera delivery. Her conference presentations reflect her interest in how technology has challenged and transformed the face of communication, and she enjoys helping individuals of all backgrounds and levels of experience to find their authentic voice. In her spare time, Rachel loves spending time with her family, watching silent films, shopping for antiques, and playing with her peek-a-poo pup, Jethro, in Seal Beach, California.

This textbook is an adaptation of *Public Speaking: Choices for Effective Results*, sixth edition (2012), written by the respected authors John J. Makay, Mark Butland, and Gail Mason.

Gail Mason, Ph.D., has retired as Professor in the Department of Communication Studies at Eastern Illinois University, where she taught courses in public speaking, conflict management, organizational communication, intercultural communication, and women's studies. After receiving her master's degree from Washington State University, Gail worked for the extension program at the University of Missouri-Columbia and taught public speaking on campus. After finishing her Ph.D. at Indiana University, she taught graduate and undergraduate courses at Central Michigan University, the University of Arkansas at Little Rock, and the University of Maryland European Division. Her publications and conference presentations reflect an ongoing interest in pedagogy as well as a life-long love of international travel.

Mark Butland, M.A., has taught public speaking at Texas State University, Baylor University, McLennan County Community College, and Austin Community College, where he currently serves as Professor of Speech Communication. In addition to his 20 years of teaching experience, Mark is a professional speaker and workshop trainer. Mark is an active member of the National Speakers Association, a professional speakers association that focuses on the art and business of speaking, and the American Society of Training and Development, a professional trainers association. Insights and lessons from the trenches enliven and inform his academic perspectives on public communication. While on faculty at Austin Community College, Mark served as founder and coordinator of the college Honors Program from 1997 to 1999, was a pioneer in distance learning and has received recognition and awards for his excellent teaching. He has published scholarly research in instructional communication and has written instructor's manuals in interpersonal communication and public speaking. Mark received his B.A. and M.A. at Texas State University.

John J. Makay, Ph.D., is currently Professor Emeritus in the Department of Interpersonal Communication and the School of Communication Studies at Bowling Green State University. His teaching experience includes courses and seminars at the graduate and undergraduate levels. He has served as a department chair and as director of the School of Communication Studies at BGSU. He was the director of the basic course in public speaking at the Ohio State University for 16 years, and he has taught public speaking at Purdue University, The Pontifical College Josephinum, The State University of New York at Geneseo, Bowling Green State University, and Owens Community College in Toledo, Ohio. Dr. Makay has authored, edited, and co-authored a number of books in communication and his work has appeared in national, regional, and state communication journals and at international, national, regional, and state conventions. He currently resides in Maumee, Ohio.

About the Instructional Designer

Meg M. Yanalunas, MSE, is an educational media designer for Coastline Community College, where she routinely has the roles of instructional designer for online learning, project management, and management of virtual teams that support projects for Coastline. She also supports the development and training for the college learning management system, Seaport3, and its faculty users.

Her professional background includes working in higher education, corporate, and healthcare systems. Typically working with leadership, she has developed and deployed enterprise-wide training and professional development for administration, faculty, and staff around the topics of quality tools and processes, team building, developing engaging online courses for higher education, and designing and delivering effective needs assessments. She has been honored to present at both national and international organizations on a variety of topics. She is one of the authors of "A Case Study of a Project-Management-Centered (PMC) Approach to Knowledge Management in Online Learning Environments," published by IRMA in 2007.

In her "real life," Meg adores her very humorous family (immediate and extended) who keep her on her toes, gardening outdoors, visiting inland lakes, most things Michigan, and dreaming of adopting a dog-friend soon that is at least partially Labrador.

Communicating:

Strategies for Dynamic Delivery

Chapter 1
Public Speaking for Success

Chapter 2
Public Speaking Apprehension and Listening Strategies

Chapter 3
Verbal and Nonverbal Delivery

Chapter 4
Audience Analysis, Adaptation, and Presentation Ethics

Chapter

1

Learning Objectives

After reading this chapter and completing the online activities for this lesson, you will be able to:

1. Relate public speaking to everyday life.
2. Discuss the elements of the communication process.
3. Apply the steps to develop a speech.

Public Speaking for Success

At a Glance

INTRODUCTION

Reflect for a moment about the time you joined your first online social network. Perhaps it was Facebook, Twitter, or LinkedIn. You were likely excited about it. There was an audience out there online with whom you wanted contact. You may not have given it much thought, but as you set up your profile, shared information about yourself, and even selected pictures to showcase, you were crafting a message that was intended to shape how people see and respond to you. It was intentional communication aimed at a desired result.

You have been presenting yourself and your ideas your entire life. At a young age, you likely brought interesting treasures to show and tell (**FIGURE 1.1**). Maybe you wanted to share your jewelry box, a new video game, some special trading cards, or a favorite stuffed animal with your kindergarten classmates. You did not realize this was a public speaking event; you may not have even known what the term "public speaking" was, but you were probably engaging in it naturally because you were discussing something you loved.

© 2012 Lorelyn Medina. Shutterstock, Inc.

FIGURE 1.1 For most people, the opportunity to engage in public speaking begins early in life.

Today, you probably engage in public speaking more than you realize. Being a server at a restaurant, working in customer service, or even teaching Sunday School to small children requires you to express yourself to an audience in an effective manner. Because there is a greater purpose than the "speech" itself (e.g., doing the job well enough to earn tips, clearing up issues to secure return customers, or keeping kids entertained), public speaking in everyday situations as mentioned above is usually less daunting than the speeches delivered in class. In this course, we want to help you find a way to channel the same energy and naturalness you have in your everyday speaking experiences into your more formal presentation opportunities. Speaking effectively with an audience can be a powerful experience and mastering public speaking can propel you in desirable directions!

This textbook focuses on how to present yourself and your messages in a way that increases the odds of getting what you want in an efficient and ethical manner. You have a distinct voice, and incorporating the principles of public speaking will help you to develop that voice into a potent instrument of influence, imagination, productivity, and interpersonal significance. Though our primary focus will be on the more formal presentations life brings each of us, many of the ideas we develop may be applied to other, less formal messages you create and share, such as status updates, text messages, conference calls, emails, and face-to-face conversations.

This first chapter lays a foundation for the rest of our textbook by helping you see how vital and relevant public speaking is to several aspects of your life. We introduce a model that helps clarify the parts of the communication process and how the parts interact to enhance, and sometimes challenge, our communication effectiveness. Then we turn our attention to the steps to take to create your first speech.

1.1 Public Speaking in Your Life

Public speaking can be a powerful skill. People who wish to present new information, to advocate for a particular position, or persuade an audience to take action need to know the tools of the trade. We can use our public speaking skills to defend the oppressed, clarify our own position on an issue, and convey our passion on a subject. As we write this textbook, the United States is still engaged in military action in the Middle East. In the midst of national and international tensions and military actions, public speaking serves as a powerful force for taking action, resolving disagreements, persuading adversaries, and keeping audiences informed. Power is inherent in effective public speaking—power to communicate facts and emotions, convictions and attitudes, and values and beliefs—in a way that leaves a lasting, and often unequaled, impression on the audience.

1.1.1 How Communication Relates to Power, Creativity, and Decision Making

Public speaking is also a creative activity that includes both mental and physical aspects. The mental dimension involves connecting thoughts and ideas in an original or innovative manner while centering on the audience's needs and interests. Delivering the speech is the physical aspect of the creative process, which includes knowing how to visually connect with the audience, where to pause, when to place emphasis, how to use appropriate gestures and body movement, the strategies behind communicating ethically, and expressing self-confidence. Your unique voice and style can be honed so that each creative choice you make is a reflection of your personality and presence. Effective speakers have learned the art of public speaking and are able to design and deliver a speech that resonates with listeners through careful word selection, organization, supporting material, appropriate eye contact, and meaningful gestures. This art is audience-centered, and its core is the message.

Public speaking is also a decision-making process. While taking your public speaking class, you will have to determine your interests, analyze your audience, decide where to look for information, figure out the best way to organize your information, make decisions about word choice, and decide how to deliver your speech

FIGURE 1.2 Public speaking skills help you to build healthy interpersonal relationships with friends, family members, and romantic partners.

most effectively. This practice and experience not only will enhance your speaking skills but also will strengthen your ability in daily life to think on your toes, plan clearly with limited time, and produce a worthy outcome that is the result of a quality thought process.

Finally, public speaking contributes to your interpersonal satisfaction. Being able to successfully say what you mean, articulate complex emotions, and argue a position while maintaining respect are skills that enhance our relationships with family, friends, classmates, significant others, and those with whom we come into contact as a result of our jobs. Often, the trials in our lives stem from some form of interpersonal turmoil and, although strong public speaking skills will not entirely prevent this difficulty, they will help you say what you intend to say the first time.

1.1.2   Public Speaking Is a Valuable Activity

You may be asking yourself, "What profits can successful public speaking bring to my life?" We know that you may be nervous about presenting in public, but you will really benefit from learning this information. Becoming a more competent speaker has a two-fold payoff: it benefits both the speaker and the audience. When you develop self-confidence in front of an audience, learn how to make the best use of the time allowed, and embrace the opportunity to express what you know and how you feel, you are reaping the personal benefits of public speaking. Being able to genuinely and memorably entertain your listeners, effectively and respectfully convey an opinion, and enlighten and open others' minds to a new concept are tangible benefits for the audience. Consider these three real-life examples in the box on the next page.

Public speaking skills are important for success in school, career advancement, and for increasing self-confidence. They are the gift that keeps on giving since they

What's in It for *ME*?

- Chad, a young veteran who had recently returned to school, always knew he enjoyed expressing himself. After a few weeks in a public speaking course, he began to understand that his natural flair for humor and vivid storytelling could be implemented into skillful and captivating speeches that grabbed the audience and made them listen. His newfound excitement about public speaking has propelled him to want to pursue a career in communication that will allow him to use his speaking skills to engage and entertain.

- Alicia, an admittedly shy public speaking student, was getting ready to apply for jobs in the pharmacology field. Although she had performed well on her speeches in class, she knew that a high-stakes face-to-face interview might throw her for a loop and challenge her composure. After conferencing with her professor to discuss ways she could strategically use her new public speaking skills to do well in an interview, she applied for a variety of positions and began to prepare. She approached her opportunities with confidence and was offered the position following the first interview she attended; she attributes this success to her public speaking experience and preparation.

- Claudia proudly announced to her class that what she was learning in her public speaking course had been instrumental in raising her level of personal achievement. She had set out to obtain community sponsors for a breast cancer awareness charity that she and her friend had started. Her speech to an audience of Rotary International club members persuaded them to make a contribution of $1,000 to their cause. A Rotarian told Claudia that her heartfelt, honest, and effective presentation was key to their decision to support her charity.

are applicable to all areas in our lives. Learning to communicate in a public setting is valuable for many reasons, including the six identified below.

1.1.3 Public Speaking Influences Success in College

Since you are currently in college, it makes sense to note that the first reason to learn and practice the essentials of public speaking is because they may influence your success in higher education. On a basic level, public speaking is a required course at many academic institutions, so doing well is imperative to your overall success on your degree path. However, even if the course is not a requirement, oral presentations in English, philosophy, political science, and art are common occurrences and all considered public speaking events. Normally, part of your grade is based on your presentation skills; in turn, honing those skills is a wise and beneficial choice.

In addition to making presentations in your classes, any involvement in extracurricular activities may also be influenced by your ability to speak in public. If you are comfortable expressing yourself and possess the skills to address an audience, it will be possible to run for student body president, to present your point during an organizational meeting, to discuss a grade discrepancy with a professor, to be part of a film criticism workshop, or to even be a participant on a competitive speech team.

1.1.4   Public Speaking Teaches Critical Thinking Skills

A second reason for studying public speaking is that it teaches critical thinking—the application of the principles of reasoning to your ideas and the ideas of others. Generally, teachers of all subjects are concerned that students learn to think critically. Some argue that of all the skills you will learn in college, and thereafter, none is more important than critical thinking. **Critical thinking** enables you to evaluate your world and make choices based upon what you have learned. It is the intellectual tool necessary to make crucial decisions at work ("Should I recommend or discourage the hiring of this prospective employee?"), at home ("Should I start a family before I have a stable career?"), and in your roles as a consumer and citizen ("Should I believe this Mac vs. PC commercial or do my own independent research?"). The critical thinking skills required to answer these questions can be developed, in part, through public speaking.

Below are five ways you use critical thinking every time you prepare a speech:

1. **Choose Appropriate Speech Topics.**

   Although you are encouraged to let your own interests guide the selection of speech topics, evaluating different subjects based on their significance to you and your audience is key. For example, as a car buff, you may decide that although a speech describing how to supercharge a car's engine would be suitable for a group of auto mechanics, it could be too technical for your public speaking classmates. To stay within your area of interest, then, you may decide to inform your classmates about simple and inexpensive strategies they can use to improve fuel economy (like ensuring proper air pressure in tires, regular oil changes, or reducing drag). As everyone in your audience is probably a driver, this topic could be more relevant and applicable to your listeners.

2. **Research Your Topic.**

   You must decide what kinds of supporting material, or evidence, best enable you to express your views and develop your arguments. Questions to ask include the following: What evidence is available and necessary? What support is credible and relevant? Should I use quotations, examples, statistics, analogies, or a combination of these, as well as other forms of support? What and how should I present visually? These decisions will ultimately affect your credibility as a speaker.

3. **Organize Your Presentation.**

   The order in which you present your ideas reflects the clarity of your thinking. Careful critical thinking will help you to avoid "jumping all over the place" and instead will ensure that you convey your content clearly and logically. Your audience is more likely to comprehend what you say and give importance to your message if you have organized your information in a way that best serves your purpose for speaking.

4. **Build, Advance, and Assess Arguments.**

   You must know how to construct lines of reasoning for both informative and persuasive purposes. **Reasoning** is the process of using known and believed information to explain or prove other statements less well understood or accepted. Instead of letting a gut reaction or strong emotions guide your decisions, thinking critically requires you to explore arguments in active, organized, and purposeful ways.

---

critical thinking
Type of thinking that enables you to evaluate your world and make choices based upon what you have learned.

reasoning
The process of using known and believed information to explain or prove other statements less well understood or accepted.

5. **Choose Appropriate Language and Style of Expression.**

Language choices are based on how much your audience already knows about your subject, their familiarity with specialized vocabulary, and the unique constraints of the occasion. It would be inappropriate, for example, to use slang while accepting a prestigious academic award or addressing professionals at your workplace. Think about how you would respond to your classmate who started her speech with the following:

I had a friend from high school named Steven. A few weeks ago, I found out that he was sent to jail. He was out in Los Angeles with his best friend, drinking and celebrating his acceptance into USC grad school. At the end of the night, they stopped at a gas station. They both got out of the car, and he went inside to get change for the gas while his friend was on his phone near the back of the car. After pumping gas, Steven got into his car and quickly reversed to leave the gas station and felt a thud hard behind his car. He soon realized that he had just hit his best friend who fell to the ground and hit his head. His friend died on the spot. This is a true story of someone who drank, thought he was okay to drive, and ended up accidentally killing his best friend.

Most people think they can drink and drive after a few hours. They assume their blood alcohol content (BAC) is below the legal driving limit of 0.08 percent. But how do you really know that you're okay to drive unless you have your own Breathalyzer? You don't really know, so you guess. That is why if you even have one drink of alcohol, you should not get behind the wheel. This issue hits home with many of us because we have been in a situation where we have had a drink and decided to drive. Or we have been passengers in a vehicle where the driver has had a drink. And some of us might even know someone who has a DUI or has been in an alcohol-related accident. Today I'm going to talk about why our current DUI law doesn't work, propose a new law, and explain why the new law would improve our lives.

The way that Janet addressed the class, from her language, use of emphasis, and execution of pauses to her reference to a life-altering experience, had an impact on her listeners. After reading this introduction, you might think, "Wow! It would be horrendous to accidentally kill someone," or "I would NEVER drive while under the influence," or "Yeah. I lost someone to drunk driving. I can personally relate to this serious issue." Some students may reflect on their own experiences with drinking. Others may think of friends or relatives they know who have problems with alcohol dependency. Still others may focus more on the speaker and wonder how it must be to deal with such a situation. In turn, because Janet started her speech with carefully selected language that set a serious tone and detailed a powerful personal example, the audience became emotionally engaged and intellectually focused on the topic at hand, drunk driving.

As you can see, critical thinking is necessary to the development of an effective speech. Critical thinking is also important in your role as **listener**. A listener perceives through sensory levels and interprets, evaluates, and responds to what he or she hears. Critical thinking skills are essential as you listen to and evaluate the messages of other speakers. Being able to articulate what is working and what is not working in a speech is vital to the process; instead of merely stating, "I didn't like it, it was boring," or "That was a fantastic speech," having the skills to communicate

listener
One who perceives through sensory levels and interprets, evaluates, and responds to what he or she hears.

Get That Job: Strategies to Consider When Preparing for an Interview

Rachel A. Wegter, one of the authors of this textbook, privately coaches individuals who want to gain an advantage in job interviews. Since public speaking skills are inextricably linked with interview performance, knowing how to use your oral communication skills effectively is paramount to interview success. Consider using these strategies to maximize your own interview performance.

1. Dress the part.

Make sure to select a classic, well-fitting outfit for the interview—no jeans, T-shirts, or athletic shoes! A nice pair of slacks and a dress shirt or blouse, a pencil skirt and blouse with a cardigan (all in dark, basic colors with no patterns) are strong choices. Keep hair off of your face (so you don't accidentally fidget with it) and wear shoes that are dressy but comfortable (no teetering in heels unless you can completely handle them). For women, light makeup to look polished and bring out natural beauty includes mascara, a bit of blush, and some neutral lip-gloss or lipstick.

2. Practice your handshake.

When meeting your interviewer, you should always clearly introduce yourself and give a firm and confident handshake. Extend your hand, look into their eyes, and smile as you "pump" the shake three times or so. Practice with friends or family in advance to get honest feedback!

3. Arrive early.

You do not want to be rushed and stressed, so give yourself ample time to get to your destination. Have two copies of your resume (and a copy of your completed application, just in case) as well as a pen so you are prepared if you have to fill something out on the spot. Be sure your cell phone is silenced.

4. Prepare for potential questions.

Search the Internet for a list of potential interview questions and come up with answers to them in advance. For example, "What are your strengths?" Weaknesses? What can you bring to the job? How do you work with people? How would you handle this problem? Greatest lesson learned? What is your availability? Why do you want to be considered for this position? They probably won't all be asked, but you want to be prepared. Have some reasonable questions about the job (e.g., "What is the most rewarding part of

the precise elements that contributed to the speech's overall strengths or weaknesses is important. As an audience member, your analysis will focus on several factors, including the purpose and organization of the speech; whether the speaker has accomplished his or her goal to persuade, inform, or speak appropriately on a special occasion; whether he or she has satisfied your needs as an audience member; how effective the speaker's delivery style was, and so on. When you are able to recognize the pros and cons of a speech, you are also able to apply those observations to your own speech performances by avoiding what you dislike and embracing what you find particularly compelling. As your critical thinking skills develop, you will be able to say effectively what you mean as well as assess another speaker's effectiveness.

1.1.5 Public Speaking Skills Influence Career and Community Success

A third reason to study public speaking is that your public speaking skills may influence your success in career and community settings. With the fluctuation of

the job?" and "What does a typical shift entail?") on hand so that if and when the interviewer asks you if you have any questions, you actually do.

5. Be mindful of nonverbal communication.

During the interview, maintain comfortable eye contact, lean forward in your seat, cross your legs (if in a skirt, especially), nod and smile occasionally when the interviewer makes a good point, gesture naturally when speaking and keep verbal fillers to a minimum. Be as physically relaxed as you can be—rigidity and excessive nerves are easily perceived so warm up (e.g., deep breaths and visualization) beforehand if you need to.

6. Strive to make whoever is in the room comfortable.

Focusing on the well-being of others will help you to spend less time dwelling on your own nerves (if present) and create a calm environment. Remember, it must be sincere and genuine!

7. Thank the interviewer.

Express gratitude at the end of the interview and gently ask when they will be notifying applicants of their decision—this shows interest and personally gives you a timeframe to consider when anticipating feedback.

8. Follow up.

Send a brief thank you email after the interview, the day of, that conveys gratitude for the opportunity to interview, states appreciation for learning more about the company/job, and closes with a phrase like "looking forward hopefully to hearing from you in the near future" (hopeful and interested, but not entitled or demanding). This leaves an immediate, lasting, and classy impression.

©2012 Yuri Arcurs, Shutterstock, Inc.

A firm handshake conveys confidence.

the economy, the job market has become increasingly competitive. In light of this sobering reality, it benefits public speaking students to know that the number one skill that employers overwhelmingly seek in prospective hires is communication-based (www.quintcareers.com). The ability for an employee to listen, write, and speak effectively is coveted by employers; these skills are strongly rooted in public speaking since being an audience member is focused on critical listening, speech development involves clear writing skills, and delivering a presentation uses confident speaking. Although these skills are invaluable *before* securing employment because they can help you to have a successful interview experience, they also prove necessary *during* employment as they are generally a part of the daily demands of most jobs. Public speaking skills are an essential part of most professional inter-actions, including sales presentations, campaigns for public office, teaching and training programs, the presentation of research findings at conventions, committee meetings, employee recruitment campaigns, and award ceremonies. People who are articulate and engage in good conversations have clear advantages. Furthermore, upward movement in the corporate hierarchy may depend on your ability to speak to groups at business conferences and at public presentations. People involved in business, politics, and community activities, as well as members of the clergy who promote their ideas also promote themselves and what they represent, whether this is their intention or not. Few professionals can avoid public speaking, so knowing how to best express yourself is vital to your employment health and well-being.

1.1.6   Public Speaking Skills Are Key to Leadership

A fourth reason public speaking is valuable is that it is an integral part of the leadership process. In his book, *The Articulate Executive* (1996), corporate communication consultant Granville Toogood discusses the relationship between effective speaking and coming across as a leader. He advises, "You've got to be able to share your knowledge and information (perhaps even your vision) with other people. It is not in any job description, but you've got to be a translator (explaining the law or technology to neophytes, for example), a teacher, and, eventually, a leader. The only way you can ever be a leader is to learn to speak effectively" (p. 10).

A skill all leaders tend to possess is the ability to appear before audiences with well-prepared speeches and deliver them with authority, sincerity, enthusiasm, and self-confidence. However, using your voice to influence and inspire can be achieved both formally and informally. For a true leader, the conversation that you have with one individual is just as important as the speech you share with thousands. People want a leader who is clear, sincere, honest, and charismatic; public speaking focuses on these very attributes.

1.1.7   Public Speaking Skills Complement Technology

A fifth reason we find public speaking skills important is that they complement technology. Through Internet access, we can access millions of facts, but those facts may not be as impressive without the added human element. Speeches are supported by computer-generated graphics, supporting material is discovered on electronic databases, and images can easily be projected while a speech is being delivered.

The "mega churches" in Protestant Christianity rely greatly on graphics and other technology to put forth their message (Wolfe, 2005, p. 76). Upon entering a large room that can seat approximately 1,000 people, individuals may find themselves facing up to six large video screens and a stage with a half-dozen musicians in place. The main speakers have microphones clipped on, replacing the traditional microphone at the pulpit. In the midst of this multimedia and technologically supported stage, the audience is addressed by the main speaker.

Additionally, such forms of technology-mediated communication as social networking, emails, text messaging, podcasts, streaming video, and blogging have expanded public speakers' options for expression in both their personal and professional lives, enabling them to access and communicate with an enormous audience with the click of a button. Skype and other video conferencing applications allow individuals otherwise separated by thousands of miles and differing time zones to meet and interact in "virtual" meetings and even job interviews; consequently, the rising popularity of these technological mediums creates public speaking opportunities in situations that were once limited by space and time.

1.1.8 Public Speaking Is Part of Our Democratic Tradition

Public speaking is a part of our democratic tradition. This is the final reason why public speaking is important. The drive for change often begins with the spoken word. Indeed, since America's early federal period, when the First Amendment to the U.S. Constitution guaranteed certain freedoms, public speaking has served an important purpose in our democratic processes and procedures. Citizens have gathered in our nation's capital to listen to abolitionists, suffragettes, and individuals who support the civil rights movement, the women's movement, and the environmental movement. We have witnessed peace marches, antiwar demonstrations, and animal rights protests.

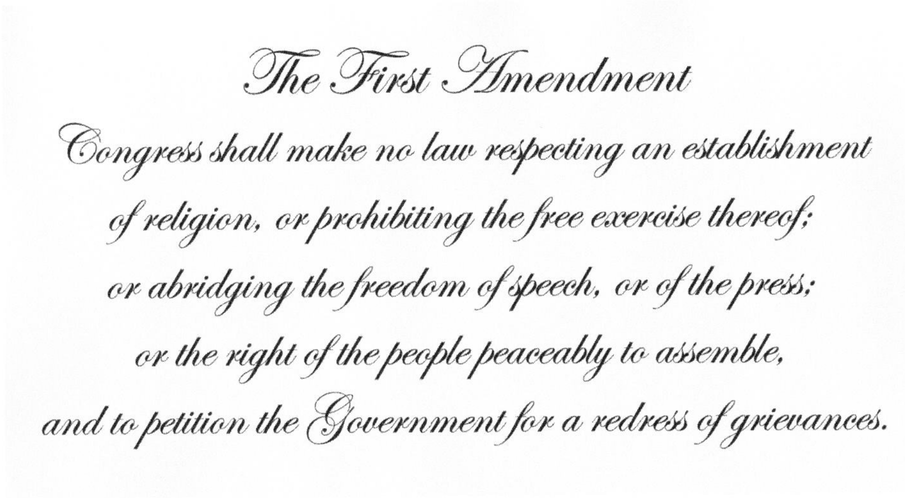

The First Amendment

Congress shall make no law respecting an establishment of religion, or prohibiting the free exercise thereof; or abridging the freedom of speech, or of the press; or the right of the people peaceably to assemble, and to petition the Government for a redress of grievances.

Illustration: Courtesy of Marie Hulett.

FIGURE 1.3 These sacred words from the First Amendment to the U.S. Constitution represent power and protection for every public speaker.

As you speak to your classmates, keep in mind that your speeches are rhetorical opportunities to show your understanding of and commitment to an idea and your ability to communicate your thoughts and feelings to others. If you use your public speaking class as a training ground to develop and refine your skills as a communicator, these learning experiences will serve you well throughout your life. Moreover, the confidence you develop here will allow you to freely speak up in other areas of your life.

1.2 Public Speaking and the Communication Process

Communication is the creation of shared meaning through symbolic processes. You communicate your thoughts and feelings to your audience with the intent of generating knowledge and influencing values, beliefs, attitudes, and actions. Often, your purpose is to reach mutual understanding. As you speak in public, you will use the shared symbols of communication to achieve a specific purpose.

communication
The creation of shared meaning through symbolic processes.

The speeches you deliver will fall into three general categories: *to inform*, *to persuade*, and *to entertain*. Sometimes, you may want to share information and create a clear understanding with an audience. Other times, you may want your audience to change their attitudes and/or follow a different course of action. On special occasions, your task may be to entertain, inspire, or celebrate. Each of these main categories will be treated in subsequent chapters to explain fully what is required for success and effectiveness. No matter what type of speech you deliver, your speaking objective is to elicit a response from your audience by sharing meaning with them.

1.2.1   Elements of the Communication Process

Because the act of communication is intrinsic to our everyday experience, it can be easy to overlook that it is a complex interaction comprised of many distinct parts. As both a speaker and an audience member, you will find it is beneficial to understand how these parts interface to create shared meaning. The communication process involves at least ten elements: sender, receiver, message, feedback, encoding, decoding, channel, noise, occasion, and cultural context. These elements are discussed briefly here, but they will be explored in more detail throughout this textbook.

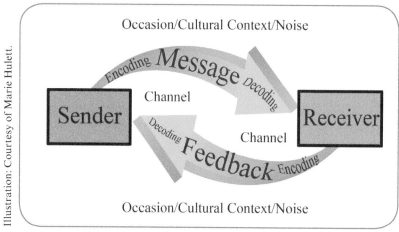

Illustration: Courtesy of Marie Hulett.

FIGURE 1.4 The Communication Model is composed of interdependent elements that work together to create shared meaning.

sender
The one who conveys a message to an intended audience.

static variables
Those things that remain stable from speaking situation to speaking situation.

dynamic variables
Variables that are subject to change, like the decision you make about a particular speech, your appearance and word choice.

Element 1: Sender/Receiver.

Each speaker brings something unique to the occasion; as the **sender**, you convey a message to an intended target. As the speaker, you may have an interesting perception of an issue because of static and dynamic variables. **Static variables** are those things that remain stable from speaking situation to speaking situation. These include biological aspects such as race, gender, and age. Experience and knowledge are also considered static, since you do not change your experience, knowledge, and health based on the speaking situation. **Dynamic variables** are variables that are subject to change. They would include decisions you make about a particular speech, word choice, the structure you choose to support your points, your mood and energy level, and aspects of appearance that are easily changed (clothing, hair, accessories). In your role as a speaker, remember two things:

First, your image makes a statement. Always keep this in mind. As a speaker, your presence is shaped by your reputation, your appearance, what you say, and how you say it. So, before you even open your mouth, the image your audience has of you will be formed by the clothing or accessories you wear, and with each comment you make, the image becomes stronger and more pronounced and will, in part, determine how your audience responds to your message overall. In turn, select clothing and accessories that do not distract or detract from your message (e.g., ill-fitting garments, shirts with graphics or writing on them, or noisy shoes or jewelry); your physical image should not precede your oral content! When you speak, your words and style of delivery communicate your involvement with your topic, so select your content carefully and practice your presentation in advance. Your listeners will need only a few moments to pass judgment on your confidence, knowledge, integrity, and skill.

Second, the speaker and the audience both have needs. The speech is about you AND your audience. Through the communication exchange, speakers seek from their audience a response that can satisfy certain needs. Depending upon the situation, speakers need to be understood, to have influence, to bring about action, to be liked, or to be respected. For example, a common practice among financial advisers is to invite clients and potential clients to evening seminars where informative sales presentations are made. The speakers' needs are to produce results in the sale of their financial products and services. After the presentation, the successful speaker will meet the needs of his or her audience, which in this case involves helping clients meet both immediate and long-term financial needs.

In our model, whether you are speaking or are a member of the audience, you are always playing the dual role of sender and receiver; this **transactional communication** process asserts that as a communicator, you are simultaneously sending and receiving messages. As sender, the speaker initiates the message in public speaking. The impact of the speech is affected by whether or not the receivers find the speaker to be believable, trustworthy, competent, sincere, and confident.

For example, if audience members are receiving a lethal dose of PowerPoint overload, they will likely send messages of boredom through yawns, murmurs, and possibly nodding off. An effective speaker who has **rhetorical sensitivity** is acutely aware of the speech setting and audience behavior, monitors this audience reaction, or feedback, and adjusts appropriately. In this secondary sense, the sender is also a receiver.

Element 2: Receiver/Sender.
In the communication process, the **receiver** is the target of the message. In public speaking, the receiver is the collection of individuals gathered to hear the speaker. We underscore the primary importance of the receiver or audience in public speaking situations. An effective speaker focuses on having some meaningful impact on his or her receivers. Listeners (receivers) bring their own frames of reference, which are influenced by the same variables found in the speaker: race, gender, age, health, personality, knowledge, experience, and so on. These variables influence how the audience responds to a speaker's message.

Although audience members may hear every word a speaker says, they can miss shades of meaning or may attribute meanings that have little or nothing to do with the speaker's intent. Because the potential for misunderstanding always exists, it

transactional communication
The process of simultaneously both sending and receiving messages.

rhetorical sensitivity
The speaker's ability to be aware of the speech setting and audience reactions and adjust accordingly.

receiver
The target of the message.

is critical to plan every speech with your audience in mind. In the classroom, use terms your classmates can understand and use examples that touch their lives. Use language that they understand and find engaging but not offensive.

Both the speaker and members of the audience share the responsibility of achieving mutual understanding. As such, listening as a necessary skill is mentioned frequently in this textbook. As Ron Hoff, a consultant and author on speech making, explains, "By coming to your presentation, by simply showing up, your audience is expressing a need for help, counsel, wisdom, inspiration—maybe even something that can change its life. . . . If truth be told, the audience arrives on the scene with the ardent hope that the presenter knows something that it does not" (1988, p. 9).

Listening to the speaker and interpreting the speaker's message is the receiver's primary role in the communication process. However, it is important to remember that receivers send messages nonverbally while the speaker presents his or her message (**FIGURE 1.5**). Receivers nod, clap, laugh, yawn, talk to each other, text message, check their watches, frown, and smile. All of these behaviors communicate something to the speaker. It is important to avoid distracting the speaker, but much of the receiver's feedback is relevant. The audience may send cues to the speaker that it is time to wrap up, that the speech is very funny, or that something is confusing. The receiver is not a passive participant in the communication process.

© 2012 James Francis, Shutterstock, Inc.

FIGURE 1.5 Speakers need to be aware of their receivers' feedback and adjust accordingly.

Element 3: Message.

message
The content being conveyed by the sender.

The **message** is what is communicated by the speaker and perceived by the audience. Public speaking is a meaning-centered process. Theorists have long recognized that the *essence* of the message lies not only in what the speaker intends but also the meaning ascribed to the message by the listeners. A speaker may intend to send a certain message, such as knowledge about a film, but may also send an unintentional message, such as superiority or a faulty memory. Likewise, a speaker may choose to send a message via video-blog, only to later discover that audiences bore more easily when watching streaming video.

With technological mediums at our disposal, the nature of synchronous and asynchronous messages should be considered. A **synchronous message** is relayed in real time, with both the sender and the receiver experiencing the content as it is delivered. A speaker delivering a speech to a live audience in the same room or an instant message session occurring online (even if participants are in different time zones around the world) are examples of synchronous messages. In contrast, **asynchronous messages** deal with a time gap that does not allow real-time delivery or feedback. For example, in your public speaking course you may be asked to deliver a speech to a video camera. Then, that speech gets uploaded to your computer and when your instructor watches the speech, he or she will not be experiencing it live. Another common example of asynchronous messaging is email. Though crafting a note and sending it off may feel instantaneous, the recipient may not respond immediately. In turn, asynchronous feedback, however accurate and useful, is delayed.

synchronous messages
Content relayed in real time, allowing receivers to respond immediately.

asynchronous messages
Content delivered with a time gap that prevents real-time delivery or immediate feedbacks.

The time it takes for content to be conveyed and processed is not the only variable with messages. Interpretation, based on an audience's perceptions and experiences, also affects the outcome. Although one hundred people may listen to the same speech, each individual will come away with his or her own interpretation of what the speaker said. Although we may share the same language, we do not share identical experiences. Consider the following example:

> Angry students have gathered in a residence hall lounge to hear their protest leader. A meeting was called to express frustrations over a new college ruling declaring two freshmen residence halls off-limits to persons of the opposite sex after 9:00 p.m. Violators are to be expelled from the dorm. Most of the residents are in attendance, and the primary spokesperson in opposition to the ruling is one of the residence hall presidents, who is about to learn what it is like to be at the center of a conflict. She stated initially:

> *We are here today as responsible adults, although the administration insists on treating us like children; we are here today because we do not want an anonymous college official behaving like our parent. As a matter of fact, our parents never asked for this either. We are old enough and smart enough to know when others have stepped over the line that divides guidance from interference.*

As the hall president continued, she called upon her fellow students to respect the privacy and personal values of their roommates. Some listeners perceived her remarks as too authoritative, while others questioned why she labeled the school's decision as too parental. The process is one of give-and-take between a speaker and the audience. While the residence hall president spoke, members of her audience listened to her remarks, attributed meaning to them, and responded based upon their own attitudes, values, and beliefs. Near the end of the meeting, a petition was placed on a table in the back of the room, and members of the audience lined up and began signing their names.

The need to speak, listen, and respond was considerably important to the speaker and her audience. She responded to the feedback from her audience. A fundamental task of the speaker's message is to maximize understanding—clarity is imperative. You are challenged to make your speech as clear as possible—through your words,

encoding

The way in which a message is packaged so that it is best received.

decoding

The act of unwrapping the message and assigning meaning to it.

slang

The specialized vocabulary of "stigmatized" groups, such as criminals or teenagers.

jargon

The technical language of professional subgroups, like doctors and lawyers.

cant

Refers to the specialized vocabulary of nonprofessional groups, such as truck drivers and construction workers.

argot

A collective term that encompasses the specialized vocabulary of all subgroups.

lines of reason, and delivery. The message is constructed from your knowledge, feelings, and additional research.

Elements 4 and 5: Encoding and Decoding.

The way in which we package the message (both verbally and nonverbally) so that it is best received constitutes **encoding**. For example, if you want to ask your boss for a raise, it is unwise to storm into her office while she is on the phone and tell her that you are the best employee the company has ever had and they would be fools to not increase your pay. Although your message would indeed be received, it would certainly not be *best* received. To achieve a positive response, you would likely knock on the door, ask whether it was good time to ask a question, make sure that your boss is in a pleasant mood and then express your commitment and pleasure in working for the company, followed by a polite request for her to consider giving you a raise. Your selection of words, tone, and timing all work together to create an encoded message that has a fighting chance of being understood and responded to favorably. **Decoding** is the act of unwrapping the message and assigning meaning to it. In the example above, your boss's act of decoding would probably deem your first encoded request as rude, arrogant, and presumptuous, while the second request could be decoded as respectful, timely, and worth considering.

These elements are central for a public speaker as well. If you want to convince your audience to consider the value of home schooling, bashing the public school system (which probably most of your audience has attended) or attacking teachers is a poor use of encoding. Instead, discussing the merits of educating a child at home, highlighting standardized test trends, and sharing anecdotal evidence will allow an audience to decode your message more favorably and perhaps see the merits of an alternative education format without feeling like the status quo (public schooling) has been disrespected or brutalized.

Word choice is equally important in the encoding process; using slang or technical language will set a tone for your listeners that may work to your advantage or challenge your credibility. For example, calling an audience of females "broads"

What Do You Mean?

According to Fred Jandt (2009) in his book on intercultural communication, the specialized vocabulary of subgroups has been called slang, cant, jargon, and argot.

- **Slang** has been used to refer to the specialized vocabulary of "stigmatized" groups, such as gangs, drug dealers, and prostitutes, as well as teenagers. Examples include "jump in," "trick," "a-boot," "getting glassed," "tight," "crunk," and "sick."

- **Jargon** has been used to refer to the technical language of professional subgroups, such as doctors and lawyers. Examples include "in vitro," "pro bono," "subcutaneous," and "tort."

- **Cant** refers to the specialized vocabulary of blue collar professional groups, such as truckers, lumberjacks, and construction workers. Examples include "alligator," "bear in the air," "barber chair," "river pigs," "lapjoint," and "turnkey."

- **Argot** has become more recognized as a term that encompasses all of the above examples. In other words, argot is the specialized language of a particular group.

or "chicks" (which constitutes slang) could potentially be so offensive that your audience may not choose to listen to the rest of your message. Conversely, choosing technically advanced jargon such as "dyspnea on exertion" (which really means "shortness of breath with activity") or "deep venous thrombosis" (which is a fancy term for a "blood clot") when discussing common medical problems in a speech might heighten your credibility, as long as the common definition is also provided to enhance shared understanding.

Element 6: Channel.

The **channel** is the medium through which the message is sent. In the previous example, the message was sent from speaker to audience through face-to-face communication. Students could respond nonverbally, displaying disagreement or agreement and understanding or confusion through their facial expressions and body movement. In our wired and wireless society, a speaker's message can be sent by a variety of channels, including a public address system, radio, television, the Internet, recordings, cell phones, and text messages.

In spite of the improved quality of video and undeniable utility of technology-mediated communication mediums, one of the richest channels for communication is still face-to-face. When you are in the same room with a speaker, you have the advantage of experiencing the speaker firsthand and are in a strong position to judge the intangible qualities, including the speaker's honesty, ethical stance, commitment to the topic, trustworthiness, and sincerity. However, those qualities *can* be communicated through eye contact, gestures, and the speaker's voice. Technology-mediated communication, especially video, does allow for such elements to be conveyed. As a speaker, it is essential to make the most of whatever channels you have at your disposal, and as an audience member, it is wise to consider the channels being used before drawing conclusions about the speaker and his or her message.

Element 7: Feedback.

In the public speaking transaction, **feedback** refers to the messages the audience sends back to the speaker. Feedback may be immediate or delayed. **Immediate feedback** is instantaneous and may range from laughter, nods, and applause to verbal comments, the rolling of eyes, and even boos. A speaker may choose to ignore the feedback or he may change his message in response to the feedback. For example, if the audience looks confused, you may want to slow down, elaborate more fully, or give additional examples. Immediate feedback may be difficult for some speakers to interpret accurately at first, but with practice it becomes easier as rhetorical sensitivity increases.

Delayed feedback may come in the form of letters, emails, phone calls, formal evaluation, or votes. For example, it was discovered that a politician had plagiarized much of a speech delivered in a local campaign. A report of the incident was noted in the local newspaper, and the politician lightly dismissed his use of someone else's words without acknowledgment. Subsequently, a letter was written and sent by an irate citizen to the editor of the newspaper. The published letter was a form of delayed feedback. In a public speaking class, delayed feedback may occur when a classmate tells you that your speech on the merits of blood donation prompted him to give blood three weeks after your initial presentation.

channel
The medium through which the message is sent.

feedback
In public speaking, this refers to the messages the audience sends back to the speaker.

immediate feedback
Feedback that is instantaneous and may range from laughter, nods, and applause to verbal comments, the rolling of eyes, and yawns.

delayed feedback
Type of feedback that is time-lapsed and may come in the form of letters, emails, phone calls, formal evaluation, or votes.

Element 8: Noise.

Noise is anything that interferes with the communication process. In an ideal world, noise would not exist, but it does exist, and you as a speaker will benefit from understanding its nature and being able to identify its many forms. It is only in its acknowledgment that noise can be combated. Noise can be physical, physiological, psychological, or semantic.

Physical noise includes anything within the environment that distracts the speaker or listeners. Examples include cell phones going off, the microphone not working well, people talking in class, students kicking chairs or clicking pens, people talking outside the classroom, thunder, noisy cars, a loud air conditioning unit, and lights that make buzzing sounds. Physical noise does not actually have to be heard to be considered noise. The classroom may be too cold, the lights may too dim, the listener may be seated too far from the speaker, or the room may have distracting artwork. Generally, some physical noise always exists, and both speaker and listeners are aware of physical noise. As a speaker, you may choose to lightly verbalize your awareness of the noise (e.g., "Wow, that thunder is definitely not shy.") to clear the air and help to keep the audience focused on your message.

Physiological noise is present when our senses fail us in some way. If we have hearing loss, or have poor vision, for example, we might become frustrated when we cannot hear or see adequately. Likewise, a speaker may grapple with physiological challenges of stuttering, lisping, or tics beyond their control. Maybe the formation of cataracts has diminished the ability to read note cards in the dim lighting often accompanying public speaking. When our senses fail us, typically they are accompanied by another kind of noise as well, that being psychological. Our mind sends us silent, distracting messages of frustration that are challenging to ignore.

Psychological noise occurs within the individual's mind. The speaker could be having a bad day and is not happy to be there; it may be near lunchtime and the listeners are thinking about how hungry they are. The speaker may be thinking about a fight she just had with her boyfriend, and another listener may be thinking about

noise
Anything that interferes with the communication process. Noise can be physical, physiological, psychological, or semantic.

physical noise
Anything within the environment that distracts the speaker or listeners, including cell phones ringing, a loud truck driving by, or a buzzing light fixture.

physiological noise
Interference with the communication process that occurs when our senses fail us in some way, like poor vision or hearing loss.

psychological noise
Interference with the communication process that occurs within an individual's mind, including stress about a relationship, a poor exam score, or financial worries.

© 2012 Wavebreakmedia ltd., Shutterstock, Inc.

FIGURE 1.6 Personal concerns or ill health are examples of noise that can affect the way your audience processes your speech.

the project that is due next period. Understanding psychological noise is more difficult than understanding physical, physiological, or semantic noise. It is easy to tell that the auditorium is cold or that there is too much noise in the hallway. It is not possible to see or hear what affects people psychologically. Sitting in the same row may be a person who is happy to be there, another who is distracted by relationship problems, and a third who is worried about his or her future career. As a speaker, strive to be sensitive to the diverse needs and emotions of your audience. As a listener, do your best to deal with psychological noise by writing down your concerns (this allows many to "table" the issue for a later moment without risk of forgetting its importance) or having a conversation with a trusted friend or family member. In either role, try to develop a system that enables you to focus on the here and now, as this ability is expected in professional settings.

Semantic noise refers to a disconnect between the speaker's words and the listener's interpretation. This disconnect may result from the use of inappropriate or offensive words, misunderstanding or misinterpretation, or disagreement on the meaning of words. Your professor may use vocabulary that you do not know or a speaker may use culturally specific words that aren't in your repertoire. For example, an audience member might be confused by the use of the phrase *pro bono* (which, in Latin, refers to an attorney who takes a case without payment), instead, believing it to be a misplaced but favorable reference to the lead singer of the band U2. Additionally, when hearing the term *euthanasia* (otherwise known as assisted suicide), a member of the audience may think the speaker is talking about kids in Asian countries, which could prove completely perplexing in the greater context of the speech! To plan for this potential noise as a speaker, make sure to offer synonyms or brief definitions for challenging words so the audience gets the opportunity for correct interpretation. To manage this noise as a listener, instead of fixating on the lack of understanding (which can lead to checking out and shutting down), write down the word or words that you do not know and seek clarification for them at a later time. You can either look them up in a dictionary or online, or ask the speaker what they meant after the speaking occasion has concluded.

Element 9: Occasion.

The situation for public speaking is often referred to as the **occasion** and is comprised of the time, place, event, and traditions that define the moment. Before a speech begins, an audience already has an expectation of what they would like to hear from you. At a recent college commencement ceremony, the usual speakers gave their speeches in the five-to-seven minute range. Then it was time for the invited speaker to present. She spoke for twenty-five minutes about her background and experience. After about ten minutes, audience members started shifting in their chairs. After twenty minutes, the audience's annoyance was clear to everyone but the speaker. The invited speaker failed to recognize that the commencement ceremony is an occasion designed to focus on the students graduating, not the illustrious experience of the guest speaker. She violated their expectations and lost the listening audience because she did not consider the demands of the occasion carefully.

Physical surroundings also help define the speaking occasion. As a speaker, you should know in advance whether you are speaking to five people or several hundred and whether you will be speaking from an elevated platform or from an easy

semantic noise
The disconnect that can exist between the speaker's words and the listener's interpretation.

occasion
The situation for public speaking comprised of the time, place, event, and traditions that define the moment.

chair surrounded by an audience of listeners also seated in easy chairs. Be aware of the order of your speech in the day's events. Are you the first or last speaker? Is your speech scheduled right before or after lunch? Knowing the circumstances surrounding your speech will help you prepare better to meet the needs of the occasion with an appropriate presentation. For example, if your speech is scheduled at the end of the day, a short speech is always more appropriate than a long one, since your audience members are likely fatigued and eager to get home.

Element 10: Cultural Context.

Every speaking occasion operates within a broader cultural context that affects the entire experience. **Culture** is defined in terms of norms, the rules people follow in their relationships with one another; values, the feelings people share about what is right or wrong, good or bad, desirable or undesirable; customs accepted by the community of institutional practices and expressions; institutions; and language. Culture often determines the common ground between speaker and audience.

As a speaker, it is important to realize that cultural differences exist between audiences. As U.S. markets expand throughout the world, and the global village is but a mouse click away, Americans need to understand that different countries view speaking situations differently. For example, China is a hierarchical society, and the senior member of a delegation meeting with Chinese contacts should do the talking. In their book about business customs around the world, Morrison, Conaway, and Douress (2001) write that senior executives in a delegation often do the talking, and "junior members do not interrupt and only speak when spoken to" (p. 75). Russians, they claim, "expect walkouts (during negotiations) and dire proclamations that the deal is off" (p. 319). Regarding Japanese culture, the authors purport that, "A persuasive, positive presentation is compatible with Japanese culture—a high-pressure, confrontational approach is not" (p. 229).

Cultural similarities and differences exist not only between nations but also between co-cultures that exist within our own population. Therefore, adaptation is necessary. A university hired a new president who was familiar with the corporate culture of a large business organization. When he sought to impose standards mostly from the culture from which he had come, there was considerable opposition to his efforts. Finally, at a faculty meeting, one department chair stood up, faced the new president, and declared: "With all due respect for your new position, you need to understand that this is a different culture than the one you have worked in, and what you found to be successful rules there are not going to work here." (For more information on co-cultures, see the sidebar "Co-cultures: Different but Equal").

An effective speaking style in the United States may not be viewed as such by members of a different culture. If we want to be successful speakers, knowledge of our audience's cultural norms is crucial. Failure to adapt can result in a loss of credibility, and prevent you from achieving the purpose of your speech.

As speakers, we need to be aware of those aspects of communication we have some influence over, and those we do not. Clearly, it is in the speaker's best interest to address the issue of noise. This may include closing doors, not allowing cell phones, making sure the equipment works, being aware of cultural differences, choosing words carefully and thoughtfully, and possibly providing examples for concepts that might be difficult for the audience. Although we cannot change things like

culture

A society's shared and socially transmitted ideas and perceptions of the world as defined in terms of norms, the rules people follow in their relationships with one another; values, the feelings people share about what is right or wrong, good or bad, desirable or undesirable; customs accepted by the community of institutional practices and expressions; institutions; and language.

Co-cultures: Different but Equal

Chances are, even if you subscribe to a defined culture, you probably identify with other cultures as well. For example, you may be Latina by ethnicity, which possesses its own earmarks of culture ranging from language and food to gender expectations and religious preference. However, you may also like punk music and be a longshoreman at a local port. With such diverse interests, with which culture do you end up identifying most? In the past, one interested in punk music might be considered a part of the "punk subculture" and those who work at the port have their own labor union-oriented subculture, however, today, co-cultures make it possible to be a part of many cultures simultaneously.

Whereas some define the term *subculture* as meaning "a part of the whole," in the same sense that a subdivision is part of—but no less important than—the whole city, other scholars reject the use of the prefix "sub-" as applied to the term *culture* because it seems to imply being under or beneath and being inferior or secondary. As an alternative, the word **co-culture** is suggested to convey the idea that no single culture is inherently superior to other coexisting cultures (Orbe, 1998).

Each country has a dominant culture, although in every culture there are internal contradictions or polarities. According to Samovar, Porter, and McDaniel (2007), co-cultures are defined as "groups or social communities that exhibit communication characteristics, perceptions, values, beliefs, and practices that are sufficiently different to distinguish them from other groups and

© 2012 Igor Kovalchuk, Shutterstock, Inc.

Like this young woman, most of us identify with many co-cultures, including our ethnic background, personal interests, and careers.

communities and from the dominant culture" (p. 11). Co-cultures can be based on race, ethnic background, gender, age, sexual orientation, abilities or disabilities, profession, legality (drug culture or "underworld"), and so on. Since we can be members of a dominant culture and one or more co-cultures simultaneously, we are afforded the richness of a true multicultural experience.

whether someone in our audience is hungry or battling with distracting thoughts, effective delivery still may help minimize some psychological noise.

Finally, do not forget that the eight elements of the communication process are also relevant in a mediated situation, such as a videoconference, live streaming of a speech, or recording a speech for later playback. The online speaker or speaker presenting in some other mediated situation needs to create a background conducive to listening, and take care to avoid external noises, such as noises in the hall or construction noise outside. Since the channel is mediated, video should be clear, and care should be taken to make sure the speaker can be heard and seen. Taping a

co-culture
Conveys the idea that no one culture is inherently superior to other coexisting cultures.

speech in your dorm room with all of your "stuff" around can be distracting, just as having a stationary camera might not be effective. We provide more suggestions in Chapter 13 on communicating in an electronic world.

Understanding the transactional communication process and its elements will enable you to effectively analyze and incorporate these elements into your first speech.

1.3 Steps in Speech Development

Imagine you are to give a speech in 30 minutes. Where do you begin? Without an understanding of the proper process, many individuals would panic or freeze with this task at hand. Even the most comfortable communicator might be overwhelmed with the steps necessary to create their speech. However, once you see the process of speech development as a series of reasonable, achievable steps, the experience becomes entirely manageable. Although this textbook is designed to give you detailed instructions on every step of the process, the following is a brief overview of the five steps to embrace when planning your own speech.

Determine Your Purpose, Audience, and Setting.

Finding a direction for your first presentation can be both exciting and daunting. Understanding your purpose for speaking is a great start. Once your purpose has been determined, consider what type of audience to whom you will be speaking. What are their needs, interests and existing levels of knowledge? Then, clarify the setting of your speech. What size is the room you will be in, at what time of day will you speak and what does the audience know about you before you begin to share? Figuring out this vital information at the start will set the tone for the work you do with developing content and practicing delivery!

Select the Topic.

Choosing a topic should be a reflection of your speaking purpose, your interests, and the audience's needs and knowledge. Brainstorm to come up with all possible ideas and then narrow your options based on the constraints of the speech. Make sure that you are comfortable and committed to whatever topic you decide upon; remember, if you are not interested in your topic, this disinterest is contagious, and your audience will probably not be engaged as well!

Plan and Organize Your Message.

general purpose
In a speech, the general purposes are to inform, persuade, and entertain or inspire.

specific purpose
The precise response a speaker desires from his or her audience.

thesis statement
Premise that focuses on what you want to say and generally includes your speech direction as well as your main points.

Upon selecting your topic, systematically determine your **general purpose** (Are you informing, persuading, or entertaining your audience?), create your **specific purpose** (which is what you want your audience to get out of your speech), and craft your **thesis statement** (which should reflect both your specific purpose as well as the main body points of your speech). Establishing these important elements early on in your speech preparation process will help to lay the groundwork for smooth and seamless speech writing. From its inception, make sure that your speech is on its way to possessing a sense of beginning, middle, and end, reflected by a distinct introduction, body, and conclusion. For more information on how to develop these elements, consult Chapter 5 on speech preparation. As a guide, consider the following example below:

TOPIC: Tap Water Benefits

GENERAL PURPOSE: To persuade

SPECIFIC PURPOSE: To persuade my audience to drink tap water in place of bottled water.

THESIS STATEMENT: I propose that every American give up bottled water, and drink tap water instead for three reasons: tap water is as clean as bottled water; the bottles themselves drain our natural resources, and bottles can be toxic.

Note how the thesis statement above clearly and succinctly states the speaker's position on the issue and also highlights the main points to be discussed in the body of the speech ("Tap water is as clean as bottled water," "The bottles themselves drain our natural resources," and "Bottles can be toxic."). Once your main points are finalized, choose an organizational strategy that will work best with your intended content and start researching for supporting material and begin outlining your speech. Chapter 6 provides you with excellent details on the research process, while Chapter 7 skillfully covers organization and outlining.

Thoughtfully Choose Language.

The language you choose to use for your speech has the potential to captivate your audience, keep them moderately engaged, or even repulse them. Select words that enhance your personal voice as well as your credibility as a knowledgeable speaker, while simultaneously achieving clarity and understanding. Simply put, aim to use language that represents the best version of yourself—it should be genuine, sincere, enlightening, and polished. For more information, refer to Chapter 9—it gives guidance on language strategies to enhance every type of speech.

Rehearse Your Speech for Maximum Delivery Impact.

Preparing quality speech content is essential; however, the value of practicing your content must not be overlooked. Rehearsal time will give you the opportunity to refine your delivery, that is, the way in which you verbally and nonverbally convey your speech material. Your eye contact, gestures, posture, vocal variety, articulation, pronunciation, energy, and avoidance of verbal fillers during a presentation communicate just as much, if not more, than your intended words. The only way to master these elements, which will lead to a more comfortable and composed performance, is to rehearse many times over before speaking in front of your audience. Time yourself, deliver your speech to friends and family or in front of a mirror, and practice the handling of your notes and/or presentational aids. All of these efforts will collectively work together to provide you and your audience with the best possible speech experience. Chapter 3 explores the basics of delivery and provides you with strategies to make your speech natural, enjoyable, and successful.

FIGURE 1.7 Rehearsing your speech in front of a mirror will give you a sense of what your audience will see when you formally deliver your presentation.

FIGURE 1.8 Because public speaking can take many forms in life, gaining presentation skills will be to your benefit.

As this chapter has demonstrated, pursuing a skill set in public speaking is a valuable and useful endeavor. The content you will learn both in this textbook and in the online course will rigorously prepare you for a variety of speaking styles and situations. You have the power to make this experience a positive one. Embrace the knowledge provided with focus and energy and view each communication moment you experience, from asking a question in class, sending out a text message or filming a video and uploading it to YouTube, to speaking to a group of children at church, posting a status update or accepting an award at work, as opportunities to hone your public speaking skills and become the effective communicator you are meant to be.

Chapter Summary

Public speaking can be a powerful tool that is also a creative activity and a decision making process. It is a valuable activity that influences success in college, teaches critical thinking skills, influences career and community success, is a key to leadership, complements technology, and very importantly, is part of our democratic traditions.

Public speaking is an audience-centered activity that has one of three purposes: to inform, to persuade, or to entertain. In order to help you understand that communication is a complex process, we discuss the following ten elements of communication: sender/receiver, message, encoding, decoding, channel, receiver/sender, feedback, noise, occasion, and cultural context. Once you understand the communication process and its elements, you are ready to incorporate your analysis of these elements in your speech.

Additionally, this chapter provides a brief overview designed to help you with your first speech. We offer five steps for preparing to speak include: determine purpose, audience, and setting; select the topic; plan and organize your message; thoughtfully choose language; and rehearse your speech for maximum delivery impact.

Learning the skills associated with public speaking will provide you with many benefits in your personal, professional, and community experiences.

Key Terms

argot, 18

asynchronous messages, 17

cant, 18

channel, 19

co-culture, 23

communication, 13

critical thinking, 8

culture, 22

decoding, 18

delayed feedback, 19

dynamic variables, 14

encoding, 18

feedback, 19

general purpose, 24

immediate feedback, 19

jargon, 18

listener, 9

message, 16

noise, 20

occasion, 21

physical noise, 20

physiological noise, 20

psychological noise, 20

reasoning, 8

receiver, 15

rhetorical sensitivity, 15

semantic noise, 21

sender, 14

slang, 18

specific purpose, 24

static variables, 14

synchronous messages, 17

thesis statement, 24

transactional communication, 15

Questions for Reflection

1. Considering your personal career goals, how are public speaking skills likely to help you in achieving your goals for the future?
2. What are the ethical implications of "public speaking power"? Can you think of instances in history when an individual's public speaking power was used for a negative aim? A positive aim?
3. Think of some of the major institutions in society, including, among others, government, schools, the judicial system, and organized religion. What role do public speakers play in each of these settings and what do you see as their strengths and their weaknesses?
4. How potent do you think the First Amendment is today? Would you rather have the personal right to offend, or the right to not be offended?
5. Why is it important to consider the elements of occasion and cultural context when developing your speech? How might your approach to convincing people to vote change based on these two elements?
6. How have technological mediums contributed to social impatience and preference for synchronicity in communication experiences? What does this say about the value of asynchronous communication mediums?
7. What factors should you keep in mind when choosing a topic and framing a purpose for speaking?
8. Discuss with member of your class what is understood to be the relationships between a speaker's link to a topic, choice of a purpose, amount of information available, and the needs of the audience.

Activities

1. Think of someone in the public eye whom you admire as a public speaker and write an essay describing why you have chosen to write about this person as a speaker.
2. Prepare, in detail, a written statement about how you think public speaking will benefit you personally and professionally.
3. Design and detail a model of communication as you understand the key elements.
4. See how many examples you can list of slang, jargon, and cant. How many of these words do you use in your everyday life?
5. Describe a time when you had to adapt to individuals that were culturally different from you. How did you change your communication?
6. Take an inventory of what you believe to be your own strengths and weaknesses as a public speaker and establish goals as well as expectations you intend to pursue as you participate in this course.
7. Make a list of the basic steps in preparing your first speech for class. Study your list to see how it relates to the steps featured in this chapter.

References

Hoff, R. (1988). *I can see you naked: A guide to making fearless presentations.* Kansas City, MO: Andrews and McMeel.

Jandt, F. E. (2009). *An introduction to intercultural communication: Identities in a global community* (6th ed.). Thousand Oaks, CA: Sage Publications.

Morrison, T., Conaway, W. A., & Douress, J. J. (2001). *Dun & Bradstreet's guide to doing business around the world* (2d rev ed.). Paramus, NJ: Prentice Hall.

Orbe, M. (1998). *Constructing co-cultural theory: An explication of culture, power, and communication.* Thousand Oaks, CA: Sage Publications.

Samovar, L. A., Porter, R. E., & McDaniel, E. R. (2007). *Communication between cultures* (6th ed.). Belmont, CA: Thomson Wadsworth.

Toogood, G. N. (1996). *The articulate executive.* New York: McGraw-Hill.

Hansen, R. S., & Hansen, K. (2011, January 9). What do employers *really* want? Top skills and values employers seek from job-seekers. Retrieved on August 30, 2011, from http://www.quintcareers.com/job_skills_values.html.

Wolfe, A. (2005). *The transformation of American religion: How we actually live our faith.* Chicago: University of Chicago Press.

Chapter

2

Learning Objectives

After reading this chapter and completing the online activities for this lesson, you will be able to:

1. Identify communication apprehension.
2. Discuss the importance of listening.
3. Become a better listener.

Public Speaking Apprehension and Listening Strategies

At a Glance

INTRODUCTION

"At a funeral, the average person would rather be in the casket than giving the eulogy." When Jerry Seinfeld said this, he was commenting on surveys that indicate that for most Americans, a fear of public speaking ranks higher than a fear of death (Song, 2004). When confronted with an audience ready to listen to you speak, perhaps you would rather be somewhere else. Well, you are not alone. Most of us get nervous when speaking before an audience. In this chapter, we will explain how communication apprehension affects presenters (and how it may even be beneficial to you) and identify strategies for managing your apprehension. We will also present guidelines for developing your listening skills, which not only will help you succeed in college and in your chosen profession but also will make you a better audience member.

Did you know…

> The famous actor, Laurence Olivier, frequently vomited before stage performances. Although he was a world-renowned Shakespearean actor, producers would place a bucket in the wings for him to use before going on stage.

> Singer Carly Simon would panic before performing in front of audiences. She was so nervous performing at President Bill Clinton's fiftieth birthday party that she asked the orchestra's horn section to spank her; the trumpet player stopped just before the curtain came up.

> Actress Nicole Kidman has admitted to panicking while on set. She would start shaking and have trouble breathing. Her then-husband, actor Tom Cruise, would talk her through her stage fright.

FIGURE 2.1 Many famous people experience debilitating stage fright. They have also learned how to manage their apprehension.

It's true. Each of these instances was shared in Susan James's 2008 ABC News/Health story about anxiety and stage fright. Importantly, these performers also found ways to ways to make their anxiety work for them. We will take a closer look at fear responses and help you learn how to listen closely to your body and regain control. With a bit of preparation and a few pointers, your nervousness can actually propel you toward a confident, energized delivery style.

Another obstacle we face is listening carefully to others. Most of us think we are pretty good listeners, but studies paint a very different picture. It turns that out our ears are overworked and undertrained. Listening is an important skill for all of us to master and improvements are easily gained. Ironically, those most in need are the least likely to listen. The second part of this chapter will help you hone your hearing and enhance your listening abilities.

So, we arrive at the theme that unifies this chapter: overcoming obstacles. Most of us know we can do a better job of listening. We can benefit from improved listening to our own internal states, like nervousness, as well as to what others are saying. Yet, often we stay in denial, ignoring these problems rather than seeking solutions. Careful application of your attention and effort will make you a much more confident speaker and competent listener.

2.1 Communication Apprehension and Strategies to Manage It

What Is Communication Apprehension?

Fearful of public speaking? You are not alone. Scholars have defined the natural fear or anxiety of communicating in various settings as **communication apprehension** and the fear specific to speaking in public as public speaking apprehension (also called **glossophobia**). For many college students, public speaking is their greatest fear (Bodie, 2010). Take, for example, a student who liked to be called Gator. Gator was a sophomore at a large university in Texas. He was one of those cool, quiet students who was liked by everyone. Gator was confident when speaking one-on-one or in small groups but was petrified at the prospect of giving a speech. He dressed up, Texas style, for his first speech—a nice Polo shirt, khaki shorts, and boat shoes. From the start of his speech, Gator's nerves got the better of him—his knees were literally knocking together (which, because he was wearing shorts, everyone could see). About two minutes into the speech, Gator stopped speaking and asked to be excused. The instructor asked the rest of the class to work on a separate assignment for a few minutes. When she walked out of the classroom, Gator was standing there with tears in his eyes. He explained that it was too much for him, and he was going to drop the class. Rather than accept his drop slip, his instructor asked him what his worst fear was. He replied, "that I will mess up and everyone will laugh at me." When his instructor asked whether he had messed up, he said, "Yes." Then she asked, "Did everyone laugh at you?" He went still and said, "No, they were all looking at me and nodding. No one was making fun of me." "Well," said his instructor, "it seems as if you've experienced your worst nightmare and it wasn't so bad. What do you think will happen if you try your speech on Wednesday?" Gator thought for a second and then said, "Well, I couldn't do worse. Will you let me try again?"

communication apprehension
The natural fear or anxiety of communicating in various settings.

glossophobia
The fear specific to speaking in public.

© lineartestpilot, Shutterstock, Inc, modified by Marie Hulett.

FIGURE 2.2 Approaching a microphone or a podium can generate apprehension, but this anxiety is something you can learn to manage.

His instructor said, "Of course, but I recommend that you wear long pants." Gator was back in class on Wednesday, made it through his entire speech, and earned a "B" on the speech. Gator gave three more speeches in that class, and in each speech he was more comfortable and confident. Although he may never want to jump on the stage in front of 1,000 people, Gator became a competent public speaker. More important, he did not let his fear stop him from trying.

The reason that public speaking apprehension is especially problematic, unlike a fear of snakes (also called ophidiophobia), is that speaking and presentation skills are linked to success. According to a study by the American Society of Personnel Administrators (Curtis, Winsor, & Stephens, 1997), communication has been ranked first for decades in a list of factors employers are looking for, followed by such things as your resume, specific degree held, and letters of recommendations. People with strong speaking and presentation skills are also promoted faster (Harrell & Harrell, 1984). In sum, those who confidently speak up tend to get ahead in life.

2.1.1   Symptoms of Communication Apprehension

The intensity of discomfort most people feel when giving a speech varies widely from person to person, but the physiological and psychological symptoms are largely universal. To some degree, almost everyone giving a presentation experiences one or more of the following symptoms:

TABLE 2.1 Apprehension Symptoms

Rapid pulse	Shaky hands	Shallow breathing
Dry mouth	Stammering	Dizziness
Increased sweating	Quivering or cracking voice	Feeling jittery
Speaking too quickly	Increased blinking	Nausea
"Butterflies" in the stomach	Flushing and heat flashes	Loss of concentration

© 2012 Balazs Justin, Shutterstock, Inc.

FIGURE 2.3 When you look at this picture, how do you feel? However you feel, it's normal. Pictures like this may also help people overcome their nervousness by helping them visualize stepping onto a stage and getting ready to present.

Sound familiar? These are the manifestations of our autonomic nervous system when in "fight or flight" mode. These adaptive reflexes have enabled our species to rise to challenging situations for eons, yet they clearly pose an obstruction for some speakers today. For some, speaking in public can be an exciting, adrenaline-producing activity, but for others, it is a scary experience. Most of us find ourselves somewhere between these extremes; we can survive speaking but wish it were easier.

Although public speaking apprehension is normal, scholars who examine public speaking anxiety distinguish two types: **trait apprehension** and **situational apprehension**. The trait perspective proposes that some people are generally more anxious about public speaking than others; regardless of the situation, they just feel nervous and anxious about speaking in front of others. The situational perspective proposes that apprehension is "a fleeting and speech specific reaction exhibited as psychological, cognitive, and behavioral responding" (Bodie, 2010, p. 77). Regardless of the root cause of your apprehension, however, there are some things that may increase your sense of nervousness:

trait apprehension
The perspective that some people are generally more anxious about public speaking than others.

situational apprehension
The perspective that apprehension is a short-term reaction to specific contexts.

The autonomic nervous system is the part of our nervous system that controls bodily functions that we do not consciously direct (e.g., breathing and digestion). When we experience fear, our bodies automatically prepare us for action. For some, the fear associated with public speaking triggers a defensive response in their bodies.

- Little to no preparation or practice
- Repeating negative thoughts to oneself
- No experience with public speaking
- A hostile audience
- A prior, bad experience with public speaking

You can imagine how each of these events might increase someone's nervousness. However, you should also know that your public speaking course is designed to minimize or negate each of these issues. You will be given plenty of time to prepare (except for impromptu speeches, but those can be fun), you will gain experience, you will have a supportive audience (the second half of this chapter will focus on listening to and showing support to the speaker), and you will develop positive experiences with public speaking. If it makes you feel better, in all the years the authors of this textbook have taught public speaking, not one student has died and only one has had a heart attack. (Well, it wasn't really a heart attack. The student was in his 80s and got so nervous that he set his pacemaker off and passed out. He recovered and delivered his speech the next class period. If he can do it, you can, too).

The online lesson will provide you with skills for minimizing negative thoughts and will help you practice specific strategies for you to manage your feelings of apprehension.

Look more closely at the symptoms of public speaking apprehension listed in TABLE 2.1—increased pulse, sweaty palms, and butterflies in your stomach. Do you notice that these are the exact same symptoms you have when you are excited? It is not the symptoms that are the problem, it's how we interpret and manage the symptoms. Sometimes and for some people, public speaking apprehension creates an enthusiasm that propels them to a strong delivery style.

It is possible for your feelings of apprehension to be an asset to you. Although these feelings may never go away completely, they can be managed and harnessed to provide an invigorating delivery style; they may also prompt you to prepare more and practice more.

Short-Term Stress

Public speaking apprehension can be beneficial to your health! Short-term stress (scientifically referred to as "acute time-limited stressors") like public speaking can trigger a variety of changes in your immune system. Two researchers, Suzanne Segerstrom and Gregory Miller, analyzed 319 studies involving almost 19,000 people. Their results, published in 2004, indicate that some stress can be a good thing. They wrote: "reliable effects on the immune system include increases in immune parameters, especially natural immunity … this effect is consistent with the view that acute stressors cause immune cells to redistribute into the compartments in which they will be most effective" (p. 610). In other words, the stress you experience while giving your speech might be good for you.

2.1.2 Strategies to Manage Your Nervousness

"I puke quite a lot before going on stage. Though never actually on stage. But then, the bigger the freak-out, the better the show."
—Singer Adele on preconcert jitters (2011)

Chances are, you will experience, or have already experienced, some communication apprehension. However, we can provide some help. One thing to consider is that a major symptom of communication apprehension is a physiological reaction. Most people experience three stages of physiological arousal immediately before and during the first few moments of a speech.

The *anticipatory stage* takes place in the minutes before the speech—heart rates zoom from a normal resting rate of about 70 beats per minute to between 95 and 140.

The *confrontational stage* is typically at the beginning of the speech, when heart rates jump to between 110 and 190 beats per minute. This stage usually lasts no more than thirty seconds and gives way to the final stage.

The *postconfrontational stage* is when the pulse returns to anticipation levels or lower.

The physiological effects experienced in stage two are so strong that speakers may not perceive the decrease in their pulse (Motley, 1988). For this reason, make sure you have planned and rehearsed a strong beginning for your message. If you can get through the first 30 seconds to a minute, you will regain your wits for the rest of the speech.

You may recall people's advice about your fear—suggestions such as imagining your audience in their underwear (guaranteed to make you blush), look above their heads (guaranteed to make you aloof) and drink plenty of water (guaranteed to make you wet). These suggestions don't work because they don't effectively treat the problem: your fear itself. But researchers over the last several decades have found and refined new approaches to reduce stage fright. There are cognitive, behavioral, and communication strategies you can use before your speech and during your speech.

Cognitive Strategies: How you could think about the situation.

Behavioral Strategies: What you could physically do about your anxiety.

Communication Strategies: Ways you could express yourself.

TABLE 2.2 Speech Techniques

Before Speech Techniques			During Speech Techniques		
Cognitive	**Behavioral**	**Communication**	**Cognitive**	**Behavioral**	**Communication**
Visualization	Exercise	Practice	Focus on audience	Use movement	Use visual aids
Systematic desensitization	Relaxation	Talk it out	Segment	Smile	Include the audience
Reframing	Planning	Write it out	Eliminate perfectionism	Script your actions	Keep on talking

We will review one strategy from each category—cognitive, behavioral, and communication—for managing your apprehension before and during your delivery of a speech. The other techniques will be explained in your online lesson.

Strategies for Controlling Public Speaking Apprehension

Cognitive Strategy Before a Speech: Reframe Your Thoughts. Changing the frame on a portrait changes the way the picture looks; how we react to an event is determined by how we interpret it. **Reframing** is the cognitive process of reinterpreting the meaning of an event. One of the authors of this textbook has a really large dog that barks, jumps, and lunges toward the door when the postal carrier arrives. The reason? She loves Dale the mailman and thinks all postal carriers are there to give her a treat. If the substitute postal carrier has spoken to Dale or previously has been to the house, he or she just smiles and usually gives the dog a treat. If the postal carrier is unfamiliar with the house, he or she jumps backs and looks alarmed. How the postal carrier interprets the dog's actions—aggression or aggressive affection—influences his or her reaction. How you interpret a public speaking event—terrifying or challenging—will influence how you feel about the speech.

Reframing is similar to **cognitive restructuring (CR)**, a cognitive therapy to help people cope with anxiety by redefining what they are afraid of (Wilcox, 1997). In its simplest form, you find strategies to replace negative self-talk with more realistic statements. For example, your thought that "I am going to really make a fool out of myself in this speech" would be replaced with something more realistic and less catastrophic, like "I have prepared, and I'll do just fine, and it will all be over before I know it."

When you hear the phrase "public speaking," what other words do you associate with it? If you look at the column below, you will see many of the common words people use to describe their feelings and thoughts.

reframing
The cognitive process of reinterpreting the meaning of an event.

cognitive restructuring (CR)
A cognitive therapy to help people cope with anxiety by redefining what they are afraid of; this therapy has successfully reduced people's fears of public speaking.

TABLE 2.3 Descriptions of Public Speaking
Awkward
Challenge
Embarrassing
Nervous
Self-conscious
Worried
Wound-up

Can you reframe the feelings to a more positive interpretation? For example, feeling self-conscious—very aware of your thoughts, feelings, actions, and how people are viewing you—is a negative frame. Self-awareness—very aware of your thoughts, feelings, actions, and how people view you—is a positive frame. Self-consciousness and self-awareness are cognitively and physiologically similar, but our reaction to them is influenced by our framing.

The online lesson has a Reframing Flash Cards Activity in Lesson 2, Topic 1.

FIGURE 2.4 Is the glass half full or half empty? It's all in how you look at it. How you frame, or cognitively interpret, a situation will influence how you react.

© 2012 Myroslav Orshak, Shutterstock, Inc.

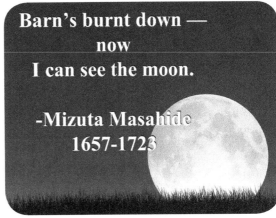

Barn's burnt down —
now
I can see the moon.

-Mizuta Masahide
1657-1723

© 2012 Sergey B. Nikolaev, Shutterstock, Inc.; modified by Marie Hulett.

FIGURE 2.5 This quotation from Mizuta Masahide, a seventeenth-century Japanese poet and samurai, demostrates that he was clearly a master of reframing.

The online lesson will help you use **visualization** to reduce your apprehension. According to the USA Swimming website (2010), there are two components of imagery: control and vividness. Coaches first teach swimmers to control their imagery (e.g., picture the perfect start to the perfect race rather than the slow start that the athlete is working on). Second, coaches help the swimmers to make their images "clear, vivid, and as close to reality as possible" (for example, picture how you stand at the start, feel the temperature of the water, smell the chlorine, hear the sound of the starting pistol, and sense the elation of winning). Visualization is pretty easy to master, and after a few practices, the swimmers can visualize the perfect race and "see and feel themselves responding to any adverse situations." What are the vivid elements you should incorporate in your visualization?

visualization
A technique by which a person creates powerful mental images of successful performances in order to reduce nervousness.

Swimmers on starting blocks.

© 2012 Gert Johannes Jacobus Vrey/ Shutterstock.com, Shutterstock, Inc.

Behavioral Strategy Before a Speech: Relax. Deep breathing has a calming effect on the body and mind. The authors of this textbook have used this technique personally, and we find our students have used it with success as well. You can do this as you are waiting to speak—take a deep breath and hold it for a moment. Repeat 3 to 5 times. It also helps to take a final deep breath after you get in front of the audience and just before you speak. Try it!

Communication Strategy Before a Speech: Practice! Practice sharpens your presentation and builds confidence. Start with a sound speech plan and then rehearse the speech aloud by yourself. Then practice in front of others to get the feel and response of an audience. If possible, record your speech and watch it yourself. One of the first things you will notice is that you do not look as nervous as you feel. If your instructor has provided you the grading rubric, use it while watching your speech.

Cognitive Strategy During a Speech: Focus on Your Message and Your Audience, not Yourself. Keep your mind on your message and the best way to convey it to your audience. Always think of your audience as being on your side. Once you see your role differently, you will feel more comfortable. Researchers discovered that when most people deliver a speech, they think of what they do as a "performance." Because of this, we become obsessed with trying to deliver speeches like a famous speaker or trained actor might. This added pressure increases our anxiety levels even more. If we can change our ideas about our role as a speaker, we can reverse this process and actually reduce our stage fright. Begin the shift in your mind by placing emphasis on communicating your message to your audience through your presentation rather than performing for them.

Behavioral Strategy During a Speech: Release Tension Through Assertive and Animated Delivery. Here is where a nervous speaker may be caught between a rock and a hard place. Being nervous can inhibit your delivery, but assertive and animated delivery can provide a release from pent-up tension. So, if you are prepared to speak, you have practiced speaking out loud, and you focus on your audience, you will be able to gesture, use eye contact, and move—all means for releasing nervous energy.

illusion of transparency
A speaker's sense that their anxiety is more apparent than it really is.

Communication Strategy During a Speech: Keep Talking. An important strategy about how to express yourself during the speech is to keep talking—"fake it 'til you make it" so to speak. People nervous about speaking in public often fear that everyone can see how nervous they are, so they get even more nervous about how nervous they look and start to stumble during the speech. However, most people are better at concealing their nervousness than they think. This is called the **illusion of transparency**—a speaker's sense that his or her anxiety is more apparent than it really is (Savitsky & Gilovich, 2003). When you are nervous, you are so aware of the tension in your body that it's easy to think that everyone can see how you feel. The good news is that most observers aren't skilled at detecting how others' feel, so it's likely that you're the only one to know. During the speech, if you keep talking, even if it means looking at your notes, you will start to feel better. From experience, we can tell you that the first few minutes are the hardest, so "fake it" for bit—the audience won't know.

We encourage you to try several of these suggestions during your first speech. You may not overcome your fear of speaking, but you might reduce it and be able to use your nervous energy productively. Keep in mind, nothing substitutes for preparation and practice; the more you practice, the more you learn, and the greater the likelihood of success. Ultimately, your goal is to channel this nervous energy into public speaking with self-confidence.

It's perfectly normal to feel nervous before giving a speech; almost everyone experiences some symptom of communication apprehension—sweaty palms, flushed face, or loss of concentration are common. Public speaking apprehension is the natural fear people have about presenting in front of audiences. There are two types of apprehension—trait and situational—but the feeling of nervousness is made worse by lack of preparation, limited experience, and repeating negative thoughts. There are a variety of cognitive, behavioral, and communication strategies speakers can use to manage their nervousness before and during a speech. One important technique is reframing, in which a speaker tries to think about the event differently; public speaking is simply an opportunity to tell a group of people about something that interests you. One important thing some people need to reframe is listening skills. In public speaking, listening isn't just to help you learn something; it is also a way for you to show support for the speaker.

2.2 The Importance of Good Listening Skills

> *"You know, it's at times like this when I'm trapped in a Vogon airlock with a man from Betelgeuse and about to die of asphyxiation in deep space that I really wish I'd listened to what my mother told me when I was young!"*
>
> *"Why? What did she tell you?"*
>
> *"I don't know! I didn't listen!"*
>
> —Douglas Adams, *The Hitchhiker's Guide to the Galaxy* (1979)

Public speaking is an audience-centered process. Decisions made throughout this process, from topic selection to delivery, should focus on your listeners. One way to improve your chances of success is to develop better listening skills. These skills are essential for two different but complementary reasons:

1. By understanding how an audience listens and recognizing the barriers to effective listening, you will be able to develop and deliver speeches that have the greatest chance of communicating your intended meaning.

2. By understanding the factors affecting listening, you will be able to monitor your own listening habits and more effectively evaluate and criticize the speeches of others, including those of your classmates. There is a direct relationship between the quality of your listening and the quality of your speaking. *Good speakers use what they hear to analyze and respond to the needs of their audience, as well as to present information in a way that promotes communication.*

FIGURE 2.6 The Chinese character for *listen* includes the characters for ear, eyes, heart, and undivided attention. The character, and the importance of good listening, are included on the U.S. State Department's diplomacy website.

The root word of *audience* is "audi-," as in audible, and means, "to hear." It is the speaker's job to make sure the audience hears; it is the audience's responsibility to listen. It may sound as if we're playing a word game by referring to hearing and listening as separate acts. Well, they are separate acts. Hearing is a physiological process; listening is a psychological process. Hearing just happens; listening requires effort. Hearing what someone said is only the first step to listening.

Despite the amount of time we spend hearing other people speak, our ability to retain what we hear is limited. For more than 50 years, communication researchers have known that we do not remember most of what we hear. According to communication professor Ralph G. Nichols, a pioneer in listening research, immediately after listening to a speech, we can recall only half of what was said. After several days, we can recall only about 25 percent of the speech (Nichols, 1961). This research was conducted more than half a century ago—do you think our listening skills have improved? Given the multitasking many of us engage in, we speculate that 50 percent may be an optimistic number.

Listening skills are important, and good listening skills will benefit you in many ways. First, good listeners are more likely to learn something. Have you ever tried to listen to someone explain a process (e.g., directions, a recipe, fixing a computer problem), while also trying to watch television, text, or play a game with a child? Did you get it all right? Listening to process information requires that we attend to what the other person is saying; we really can't multitask the way we think we can. Second, good listening skills help you build relationships. Reflect on your romantic relationships. How many times have you heard, "Are you listening to me?" If you're like us, you've heard it, and said it, too many times to count. Your personal relationships and professional ties will be enhanced if people know you take the time and energy to listen to them. Finally, good listening doesn't just enhance romantic relationships—it also enhances your relationship with your audience. We imagine

FIGURE 2.7 Standing there and hearing someone talk is not the same as listening.

© 2012 CREATISTA, Shutterstock, Inc.

that you like people who are respectful of you and listen to you when you speak. Speakers will like you if you listen (and look like you're listening). Also, in our society, we often adhere to a norm of reciprocity—you do something for me, and I will do something for you. If a speaker knows you're listening, he or she will be more likely to listen to you when it's your turn to speak.

2.2.1 Consequences of Poor Listening

Reasons Audiences Stop Listening

Many people think of listening as a simple task that involves sitting back and giving the speaker your attention. As the following interchange suggests, listening is more complicated than it appears. As public speakers, we hope our message and

Poor Listening	
Speaker	**Listener**
Around forty years ago, at about this time of year, I—and a whole lot of other committed students—spent a solid week—day and night—in the offices of our college president. Needless to say, we hadn't been invited.	*Here I am again—listening to another speaker who says he stormed his college administration building in the 60s. This must be a popular topic on the college speaking circuit. Maybe this guy will be different from the other three middle-aged radicals I heard, but I doubt it…* *The least they could do is turn up the air conditioning. It's so hot I can hardly breathe, let alone listen.*
We were protesters and proud of it. We were there because we believed the Vietnam War was wrong. We were there because we believed racism was wrong. We were there because we believed that women should be given the same opportunities as men.	*These guys keep talking about how they know the way and how we're all wrong… I wonder what he does for a living. I'll bet he hasn't saved any lives lately or helped the poor. He probably earns big bucks giving speeches on campus telling us how horrible we are… He looks like he spends a lot of time cultivating his hippie look. He must have slept in those clothes for a week. These guys all look the same.*
Were we victorious? For about ten years, I thought so. Then something happened. The signs were subtle at first. Haircuts got shorter. The preppie look replaced torn jeans. Business became the major of choice.	*He's harping on the same old issues. Doesn't he know the Vietnam War is ancient history; that women have more opportunities than they ever had—I wish I could earn as much as Katie Couric … I guess I'll have a pizza for dinner. I should have eaten before I came. I'm really hungry.*
In a flash—it happened that quickly—these subtle changes became a way of life. Campus life, as I knew it, disappeared. Revolution and concern for the oppressed were out, and conservatism and concern for the self were in.	*Of course we're interested in business. Maybe he had a rich father who paid his tuition, but I don't. I need to earn money when I graduate so I can pay back my student loans.*
From the point of view of someone who has seen both sides—the radical, tumultuous sixties and the calm, money-oriented eighties, nineties, and the new century—students of today are really forty-year-olds in twenty-year-old bodies. They are conservative to the core at the only time of life when they can choose to live free. I am here to help you see how wrong you are.	*Who does he think he is—calling us conservatives? I'm not a bigot. When I believe something is wrong, I fight to change it—like when I protested against ethnic cleansing overseas and flag burning right here.* *I wonder when he'll finish. I've got to get back to the dorm to study for my marketing exam. He just goes on and on about the same old things.*

meaning will be understood. As audience members, we may have other things on our minds—distractions, preconceived notions, prejudices, misunderstandings, and stress—and the message we receive may be much different from the message sent. The speaker (left-hand column on page 43) is an elderly activist from the 1960s. The listener (right-hand column) is a 24-year-old student.

2.2.2 Barriers to Effective Listening

You may see a bit of yourself in the "Poor Listening" sidebar example. Maybe you do not have this internal dialogue frequently, but most of us experience this occasionally. So, *why do we stop listening?* There is no single answer to this question, but the six reasons listed below may strike a familiar chord. We stop listening when:

1. *There is too much information*
   Information overload is a term used to describe the difficulty we have processing information when there is too much information. Think about when you go to a new city and need to find a place to eat—you look online and find 52 restaurants close by. Too many to pick from, isn't it? When too much is going on (or a speaker is giving us too much information to follow), many of us disengage. (Heck, one of the authors of this textbook owns almost 200 pairs of shoes, but she typically wears the same 15 to 20 pairs. Who has the time and energy to think through 200 shoes when putting together an outfit?)

2. *There is not enough information*
   We can think much faster than someone can speak. Most people can say 120 to 180 words per minute. That may seem like a lot, but it's only two to three words a second. The actors on audiobooks usually speak at 150 to 160 words per minute. Most listeners can, however, process around 500 words per minute. This **speed differential** is exacerbated if the speaker is a "slow talker." If the speaker is not conveying enough information, the listener's mind may wander. In the next section, we will give you some techniques to stay focused.

speed differential
The difference in the rate of normal speech and the speed with which we can process information.

3. *We are distracted*
   Our environment determines how well we can listen. During the process of writing this chapter, one of the authors of this textbook was teaching a class and the classroom started to shake. Few individuals living on the East Coast of the United States truly expect to experience an earthquake, but in August of 2011, the epicenter of a 5.9 earthquake was located in the state of Virginia. No matter how fascinating the instructor was (and she was certainly fascinating), the students were too distracted to listen to her speak. In the above example, the temperature distracted the listener in the "Poor Listening" sidebar. Many people are distracted by the speaker's verbal fillers (e.g., um, uh, like, you know). If you know you are getting distracted, try to eliminate the distractions and refocus.

Does your rate of speech matter? Yes, if you want your audience to listen to you. The online lesson will help you determine your rate of speech and offers you an opportunity to assess the verbal fillers in your speaking style. See Topic 2 in your online course.

4. *We have preconceived notions*

   Before the speaker in the "Poor Listening" sidebar above opened his mouth, the listener had already decided what the speaker stood for based on the speaker's appearance and on a stereotype of what sixties radicals stood for. Although in this case he was right—the speaker's views conformed to the listener's preconceived notions—he may be wrong about other speakers.

5. *We jump to judgment or conclusions*

   Few women earn as much as Katie Couric. Yet the listener in the "Poor Listening" sidebar based his reaction to the speaker's message on the premise that if one member of a group can succeed, all can. His prejudice prevented him from seeing the truth in the speaker's words. Additionally, although the speaker identified continuing social ills, the listener did not share his concerns. From his point of view, much more was right with the world than the speaker admitted—a perspective that reduced the listener's willingness and ability to consider the speaker's message.

6. *There are too many issues with technology*

   When audio or visual quality is poor, listeners sometimes feel justified in tuning out. If you're listening to a speech and the PowerPoint slide continuously flickers, you may be tempted to look away and stop listening. Conversely, if there is too much technology—the presenter has a slide with too much text and is also showing a video, you may simply focus on the technology and not the information. We need, however, to focus on what is important: the speaker.

As audience members, we know our purpose is to listen, think critically, and retain the central idea of the message. But think about what *you* do as you listen and why you stop listening. You may consciously or unconsciously tune the speaker out. You may focus on minor details at the expense of the main point. You may prejudge the speaker based on appearance. You may allow your own emotional needs and responses to distort the message, and so on. Later, we will provide specific tips for improving your listening skills, but first, we will discuss the elements of listening.

2.3 Becoming a Better Listener

2.3.1 How to Listen without Judgment

John Kline, a senior executive and Academic Provost for Air University, regularly asked his students to rate their own listening skills. On a scale of 1 to 10, with 10 being the highest, the average score students give themselves is a 7.5. He then asks students to rate their group members' listening skills—the average rating is a 4.1. Clearly, students think listening is a problem, but they think it is someone else's problem.

Think back to a time when, in an argument with a family member or friend, you responded with, "I hear you!" You *heard* them. It is possible, though, that you did not *listen* to them. Put this way, you can see there is a difference between hearing and listening.

FIGURE 2.8 Just because someone said something does not mean the audience listened to them.

FIGURE 2.9 Listening requires more than just hearing the words—we have to concentrate on what the other person is saying and what they are trying to say.

Hearing is the physical ability to receive sound; listening is a more complex process. Although listening seems to be instantaneous, it consists of several identifiable stages: sensing, interpreting, evaluating, and responding (see **FIGURE 2.10**) (Steil, 1983). We move through these stages every time we listen, regardless of the situation. We may be part of a formal audience listening to a paid speaker, we might be engaged in a conversation with a friend, or we might be home alone, listening to "zombies that go bump in the night." Listening can take place on several different levels characterized by different degrees of attention and emotional and intellectual involvement. At times, we only partially listen as we think about or do other things; other times we listen with complete commitment. The following is an elaboration of the four stages of listening.

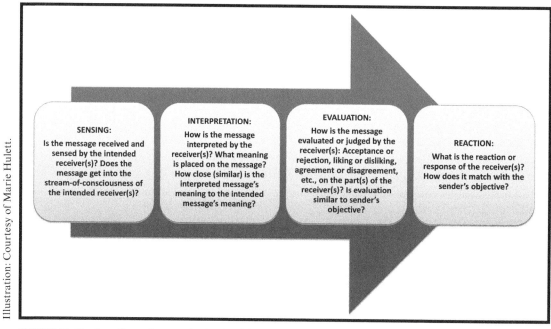

FIGURE 2.10 The Four-Stage Communication Model.

2.3.2   The Four Stages of Listening

Listening Starts When You Sense the Information from Its Source

Listening begins with sensing someone wants to communicate with you. Although people equate the start of listening with hearing, people with hearing impairments also sense when someone wants to communicate. Sight is also a factor, since the speaker's gestures, facial expressions, and use of presentational aids communicate intent.

As anyone who has tried to listen to a speech over the din of a car siren or people talking in the hall will realize, obstacles can—and often do—interfere with reception. Noise is anything that interferes with the clear reception of a message. It's easy to understand how loud neighbors, a stuffy room, an uncomfortable chair, and even your cell phone could hinder your listening, but it's less obvious when the noise is within us. Some internal noise is temporary: hunger, sleepiness, and thinking about looming deadlines. Other internal noise, however, may consistently prevent us from fully listening: preconceived notions, bias, and disinterest. At times, a remedy is possible. The speaker, for example, can ask audience members to move closer to the front, silence their phones, and resist texting, and audience members can find more comfortable seats. When nothing can be done about noise, put yourself in the position of the speaker. Then work hard to ignore any remaining noise so you can listen to the message.

© 2012 Mat Hayward, Shutterstock, Inc.

FIGURE 2.11 When you're in a large audience, there are many distractions that make it difficult to concentrate on the speaker.

Listening Involves the Interpretation of Messages

A second critical element in listening is interpretation, the phase in which you attach meaning to the speaker's words. As a listener, it is important to keep in mind that words have different meanings to different people and that we interpret words based on subjective experiences.

Our ability to interpret what we hear is influenced by emotional and intellectual barriers that get in the way of the speaker's intended message. We may hear specific words that offend us, or we find a statement or message repugnant. These barriers are forms of semantic noise or psychological noise. Novelist David Leavitt explains how emotional barriers prevented him from dealing with the topic of AIDS many years ago. Leavitt, who is gay, found any mention of AIDS so threatening that he shut off his ability to listen:

> *The truth was that AIDS scared me so much I wanted to block it out of my mind. When AIDS came up in a conversation, I'd change the subject. When a frightening headline leaped out at me from the pages of the newspaper, I'd hurriedly skim the article, and, once assured that it described no symptoms I could claim to be suffering from myself, turn the page. Only later... did I recognize the extent to which I was masking denial with self-righteousness (Leavitt, 1989, p. 30).*

In this case, the psychological mechanism of denial caused the listening obstruction. A college student who is $140,000 in debt as a result of loans and maxing out credit cards may consciously "tune out" a classmate's persuasive speech on credit card debt in order to avoid thinking about the future. An expert on public health can hardly sit still as he listens to a lecture on lead paint removal. After a few minutes, he realizes that he and the speaker have completely different views on removal procedure costs and safety. Instead of listening to the rest of the information, he fumes over this difference of opinion.

Whether emotional and intellectual barriers are the result of an unwillingness to deal with real-world problems, a refusal to take advice, or a difference of opinion, the result is the same: Listening is obstructed, interpretation skewed, and effective communication prevented.

Listening Involves Evaluating the Message

Evaluation requires that you assess the worth of the speaker's ideas and determine their importance to you. You must decide whether you share the speaker's point of view and, if not, why not? If you perceive a speaker as trustworthy, competent, reliable, highly regarded by others, dynamic, sociable, and similar to you, you will likely evaluate them positively than when we see them in negative or less acceptable ways.

It is a mistake to assume that we judge these messages solely on their own merits. Instead, our assessment is influenced by how the message fits into our value system. This results from "the human preference for maintaining internal consistency among personal beliefs, feelings, and actions" (Friedman, 1986, p. 13). We agree with messages that are consistent with other beliefs we have, and we disagree with messages that conflict with our beliefs.

cognitive dissonance
The psychological theory by Leon Festinger that argues that we seek internal consistency between attitudes and behaviors.

This tendency was first described by psychologist Leon Festinger (1957) in his theory of **cognitive dissonance**. Essentially, the theory argues that we seek internal consistency between attitudes and behaviors. If we do not like a colleague and that person acts badly, we experience consistency between attitude and behavior. If someone we do not like acts in a sincere, friendly manner, we experience inconsistency.

When inconsistency exists, we experience mental stress. To reduce the stress, we are forced to change one or more of our attitudes or behaviors so that the inconsistency is reduced or eliminated. For example, assume you are a school board member who holds a high opinion of the school superintendent, until he angrily tells you to "Shut up!" during a meeting. You may experience dissonance because

FIGURE 2.12 Cognitive dissonance describes the uncomfortable tension that may result from having two conflicting thoughts (cognition) at the same time or engaging in behavior that conflicts with one's beliefs.

you cannot reconcile your previous esteem for this person with your new feelings of being disrespected. Dissonance disappears when your overall impression is consistent. In this case, you have a choice. You can either rationalize the inappropriate behavior and go back to having a high opinion of the school superintendent ("He was under a lot of stress; he didn't mean it"), or you change your opinion of the person ("Someone who behaves this way in a formal meeting should not be leading our district"). Thus, as listeners, we are comfortable with information consistent with what we already know; we accept ideas more readily if they are linked to our values and commitments.

To preserve psychological balance, we often reject conflicting ideas and retain our original point of view. According to Friedman (1986), this rejection can take many forms, including the following.

Shoot the messenger. If you are a member of a college club, you may reject the notion that any club found guilty of a hazing violation should be banned from campus. You may criticize the speaker as uninformed or as someone who was never in a club like yours himself.

Rally 'round the flag. Listeners who disagree with a speaker's message may seek the support of others who share their point of view—in this case, other club members. Shared support provides comfort and reassurance. However, it does not necessarily mean that you are right.

What the speaker says is not what you hear. Although the speaker may focus on hazing violations that put fraternity pledges in physical jeopardy, you hear him say that all violations—even minor infractions—should result in any club being banned.

Convince yourself that the speaker's message has nothing to do with you. Even when opinions collide, you may convince yourself that you and the speaker are talking about two different things. You decide that the club issue does not really have any bearing on your club because he is primarily concerned with fraternities' hazing.

Don't think about it and it will go away. If, as a fraternity member, you took part in several unpleasant hazing incidents, listening to the speech may force you to question what you have done. To avoid the emotional discomfort that goes with this soul-searching, you may unconsciously block messages with which you do not agree.

Although these methods may seem extreme, we all rely on one or more of them at one time or another. As active listeners and supportive audience members, it is important that we consider how our prior experiences affect our ability to listen and respond.

Listening Involves Responding to the Speaker's Message

Feedback is also part of the listening process. In a conversation, the roles of listener and speaker change regularly. As the listener, you can interrupt the speaker, ask questions, and engage in nonverbal behavior such as maintaining eye contact, touching, or hugging. At the mass media level, you may respond positively to a television series by watching it weekly or by purchasing a product that is advertised during the commercial. Listeners in a public speaking setting provide feedback in a variety of ways: laughing, smiling, nodding in agreement, cheering, clapping, booing, or questioning the speaker after the presentation is over. Listeners also provide feedback on a less conscious level, such as yawning, looking around the room, or whispering to the person next to them.

Effective speakers rely on and encourage feedback from their audience. They watch carefully for messages of approval or disapproval and adjust their presentations accordingly. We discuss audience feedback in detail in Chapter 4 on the connection between the speaker and the audience.

© 2012 wavebreakmedia ltd., Shutterstock, Inc.

FIGURE 2.13 A smiling and clapping audience provides good feedback to the speaker.

2.3.3   Strategies for Improving Listening Skills

Fine-tune Your Listening Skills

As a skill, listening is notoriously undervalued. How much formal instruction did you have when learning to read? How many instructors have taught you to write? Your reading and writing skills, in part, determined your placement in college: the SAT and GRE both have reading and writing sections. Now, review your entire educational career. How many classes focused on listening? How many instructors had listening assignments? Did your parents teach you to listen or just expect you to know how to listen? Because most of us are born with the ability to hear, we assume we know how to listen. That, however, is not true. Listening is a skill, and like any skill, it needs instruction and practice. In this section, we explain how you can improve your listening skills—and, therefore, the chances of meaningful communication—by becoming conscious of your habits and, when necessary, redirecting your efforts.

Below, you will see a table of cognitive, behavioral, and communication strategies for improving your listening skills. We will review one strategy in each category.

TABLE 2.4 Strategies for Improving Your Listening Skills

Cognitive Strategies	Behavioral Strategies	Communication Strategies
Commit to listen	Eliminate noise	Show that you're listening
Listen without judgment	Take notes	Monitor your nonverbal communication

The online lesson covers the other strategy in each category and will help you develop these important skills. See Topic 3 in your online course.

Cognitive Strategy: Commit to Listen

Preparation is critical, especially when you have other things on your mind. Plan to make the effort to listen even before the speech begins, deliberately clearing your mind of distractions so you are able to concentrate on the speech. Here are a few specific strategies that will help you commit to listening:

- Don't tune out subjects you don't think you're interested in.
- Try and see the topic from the speaker's perspective.
- Ask yourself: How can I apply this information?
- Listen as though you will have to present the same information later. Think about how hard you listen when you know you will be tested on it; commit to listening that carefully to the speaker.

Behavioral Strategy: Eliminate Noise and Distractions

This step is more difficult than it sounds, for it often involves overcoming emotional, intellectual, and physical barriers to listening. Some distractions are more easily dealt with than others. Does what you see outside the window distract you? Do you look at the door every time someone walks by? Do you keep one eye on your phone in case you get a text message or someone updates her Facebook status? If you know you can be easily distracted, eliminate the distractions: move away from the window or door and put your phone where you can't see it. Although dealing with distractions is never easy, you can try to put them aside so you can focus on the speaker and the speech. This task will become easier if you view listening as a responsibility—and as work. By considering listening as more than a casual interaction, you will be more likely to hear the message being sent.

Minimizing our internal noise, such as bias and preconceived notions, is more difficult. Many of us need help in recognizing our listening "blind spots." As you communicate with your classmates about each other's speeches, try to determine whether the message you received from a speaker was the same message they heard. If it was not, think about what the topic means to you; try to identify any reasons for your misunderstanding. Sometimes an entire audience misses the point. If a question-and-answer period follows the speech, you can question the speaker directly to make sure you have the right meaning.

FIGURE 2.14 We are faced with many distractions. Some we carry with us, like cell phones. Sometimes, the distraction is about what may be happening somewhere else. Good listeners work to eliminate distractions.

Communication Strategy: Show That You're Listening

One of the worst things about lecturing to 200 or more students is that some of them believe they cannot be seen because there are so many in the audience. So, they talk to their neighbors, toss notes to their friends, slouch low in the seat, put their heads on their desks, or tuck into the cover of the hoods on their sweatshirts. What these students do not know (surely you are not one of them!) is that we can see you and we want you to be engaged in the listening process.

Let speakers know that you are listening. Even in a large lecture hall, the speaker is aware of the audience and will establish eye contact with members of the audience. As an audience member, be engaged; lean forward in your chair, nod your head, and smile, as appropriate. This kind of participation will force you to focus your attention on the speaker and the speech. Providing feedback at the various stages of a speech can be hard work, requiring total involvement and a commitment to fighting distractions.

Active listening skills will enhance your personal and professional relationships. By actively listening, you show the speaker respect and demonstrate support. Often, however, we need to also evaluate the message. Our final piece of advice about developing listening skills: Be the kind of listener you want listening to you.

The online lesson will explain what **critical listening** *is and how to examine evidence, assess a source's credibility, analyze rhetorical strategies, and analyze reasoning. See Topic 3 in your online course.*

active listening
Type of listening where a person focuses exclusively on the speaker and the message.

critical listening
Listening with the need to assess, evaluate, and judge the merits of the ideas and propositions.

Chapter Summary

Public speaking apprehension is difficult to avoid and poses a problem for most speakers. Recognizing the symptoms of your fear and taking appropriate action to minimize negative consequences of fear will make you a better speaker. We offered suggestions to help you control your public speaking apprehension, but your goal is ultimately to make your nervousness work for you, giving you an animated, excited delivery style.

Good listening skills are important for two reasons. First, by understanding the listening needs of your audience, you have a better chance of developing and delivering successful speeches. Second, an understanding of the factors affecting listening will enable you to monitor your own listening habits and help you to evaluate the speeches of others. Studies have shown that although we spend a great deal of time listening, most of us are not good listeners. Listening is a complex activity that involves four separate stages: you sense the information from its source through the physiological process of hearing; you interpret the message by attaching your own meaning to the speaker's words; you evaluate what your hear by judging the worth of the speaker's message and deciding its importance to you; and you respond to the speaker's message through feedback.

You can improve your listening skills by using cognitive, behavioral, and communication strategies. Specifically, commit to listening, minimize distractions, and use nonverbal communication to show your attentiveness.

Key Terms

active listening, 53

cognitive dissonance, 48

cognitive restructuring (CR), 38

communication apprehension, 33

critical listening, 53

glossophobia, 33

illusion of transparency, 40

reframing, 38

situational apprehension, 35

speed differential, 44

trait apprehension, 35

visualization, 39

Questions for Reflection

1. What factors should you keep in mind when choosing a topic and framing a purpose for speaking?
2. Discuss with members of your class what is understood to be the relationships between a speaker's link to a topic, choice of a purpose, amount of information available, and the needs of the audience.
3. Although degrees of speech tension vary from speaker to speaker, most inexperienced speakers share common feelings of discomfort. What can you do to minimize your feelings of apprehension and make your nervous energy work *for* you rather than against you?
4. What role do our emotions play in listening, and how are they related to our ability to think about and analyze a message? Can we suspend our feelings while listening to a speaker? Why or why not?
5. Why is preparation important in listening? How would you prepare to listen to the following?
   a. a speech on a topic about which you have strong, negative feelings
   b. a political campaign speech delivered by a candidate you support
   c. a speech on a crisis that affects your life
   d. a lecture on a topic that interests but does not excite you

6. From a listener's point of view, what is the relationship between the content and delivery of a speech? How does a dynamic delivery influence your opinion of the speaker's message? Compare this to your reaction to a flat, uninspired delivery.
7. Discuss the art of criticism as it pertains to public speaking. Why do so many people define criticism only in negative terms? Think of several well-known public speakers and evaluate the content and delivery of their messages.

Activities

1. Take an inventory of what you believe to be your own strengths and weaknesses as a public speaker and establish goals as well as expectations you intend to pursue as you participate in this course.
2. Make a list of the basic steps in preparing your first speech for class. Study your list to see how it relates to the steps featured in this chapter.
3. Prepare and deliver a five- to six-minute informative speech. Draw the topic from your own experiences or interests and not from one of your college courses.
4. Attend a lecture, political event, or religious service with the intent of monitoring your own listening behavior. What barriers to listening do you notice as you attempt to follow the speaker's message?
5. Listen to a controversial speech in person or what it on video. Then, with the stages of listening in mind, jot down your thoughts and feelings at different times in the speech.
6. Write a brief paper (one to three pages) about a successful listening experience. Be certain to explain what made the experience successful for you.

References

Adams, D. (1979). *The hitchhiker's guide to the galaxy.* New York: Harmony Books.

Adele. (2011, September 26). Loose talk: What the stars said this week. *US Weekly,* Issue 867, 22.

Bodie, G. D. (2010). A racing heart, rattling knees, and ruminative thoughts: Defining, explaining, and treating public speaking anxiety. *Communication Education, 59,* 70-105.

Curtis, D. B., Winsor, J. L., & Stephens, R. D. (1997). National preferences in business and communication education. *Communication Education, 38,* 6–14.

Festinger, L. (1957). *A theory of cognitive dissonance.* Palo Alto, CA: Stanford University Press.

Friedman, P. G. (1986). *Listening processes: Attention, understanding, evaluation* (2nd ed.). Washington, DC: National Education Association.

Harrell, T. W., & Harrell, M. S. (1984). Stanford MBA Careers: A 20 year longitudinal study. *Graduate School of Business Research Paper No. 723.* Stanford, CA.

James, S. D. (2008, April 30). Not so vain: Carly Simon's panicky past. ABC News/Health. Retrieved from http://abcnews.go.com/Health/SummerConcert/story?id=4754440&page=1#.TsKzA3Fd7Ro

Kline, J. A. (1996). *Listening effectively.* Maxwell Air Force Base, AL: Air University Press.

Leavitt, D. (1989, July 9). The way I live now. *The New York Times Magazine,* 30.

Motley, M. T. (1988). Taking the terror out of talk. *Psychology Today,* 46–49.

Nichols, R. G. (1961). Do we know how to listen? Practical helps in a modern age. *Speech Teacher, March,* 118–24.

Savitsky, K., & Gilovich, T. (2003). The illusion of transparency and the alleviation of speech anxiety. *Journal of Experimental Social Psychology, 39,* 618–625.

Segerstrom, S. C., & Miller, G. E. (2004). Psychological stress and the human immune system: A meta-analytic study of 30 years of inquiry. *Psychological Bulletin, 130,* 601-630.

Song, S. (2004, July 19). Health: The price of pressure. *Time* (online). Retrieved from http://www.time.com/time/magazine/article/0,9171,994670,00.html

Steil, L. K. (1983). *Listening: Key to your success.* New York: Random House.

U.S. Department of State. (n.d.). *Diplomacy in action: Active listening.*

USA Swimming (2010). Imagery & visualization. Retrieved from http://www.usaswimming.org/ViewMiscArticle.aspx?TabId=1781&Alias=Rainbow&Lang=en&mid=7901&ItemId=4959

Williams, J. R. (1998). *Guidelines for the use of multimedia in instruction.* Proceedings of the Human Factors and Ergonomics Society 42nd Annual Meeting, 1447–1451.

Chapter

3

Learning Objectives

After reading this chapter and completing the online activities for this lesson, you will be able to:

1. Know the various methods of delivery and when they are best used.

2. Understand the purpose and goals of verbal and nonverbal delivery.

Verbal and Nonverbal Delivery

At a Glance

INTRODUCTION

Have you ever wondered why you want to listen to certain people and not to others?

© 2012 Monkey Business Images, Shutterstock, Inc.

FIGURE 3.1 A strong delivery style helps to increase audience focus and attention.

delivery
The verbal and nonverbal strategies a speaker can use when conveying his or her message to the audience.

Chances are the speaker's ability to captivate or bore his or her audience can be reduced to a single factor: **delivery**, which involves the vocal and physical elements a speaker can use when presenting a speech. Although the message that a speaker chooses to construct and convey is certainly important, it is often the quality of the performance that remains with you long after you have forgotten the content of the message. To simplify, the *way* you engage in public speaking—specifically, your style of delivery—often makes the most lasting impression.

Words alone are not enough to make audiences want to listen to a speech. You probably have encountered brilliant individuals from all walks of life: scientists, police officers, mathematicians, lawyers, politicians, engineers, even professors—who seem to have difficulty truly connecting with their audience. No matter how knowledgeable they are in their field of expertise, something is missing and the audience is left feeling like an afterthought. Maybe they are too stiff or come across as awkward or detached; perhaps they attempt to "be your best friend" or talk down to you. In poor delivery situations, it is as if there is an imaginary wall between the speaker and the audience and both parties are only partially aware of each other's existence. Tragically, a speaker's weak delivery usually ends up being much more memorable than whatever content he or she intended to share.

Delivery can enhance your credibility as a speaker. That is, we tend to want to watch and believe speakers who express their content in a warm, natural, competent, and committed manner. Your ability to communicate information, persuade, and entertain effectively is influenced by the manner in which you present yourself to your audience. A successful delivery style should work *for* you, not against you.

FIGURE 3.2 When dynamic delivery is lacking, audience members may have a tendency to "check out."

3.1 Methods of Delivery

The reason we study delivery is that understanding the appropriate way to deliver your message will help the audience receive the message you intend. One of the most basic elements of delivery is the type of speech style a speaker chooses to use. Though you may find comfort in one style more than the other, you will have an opportunity to explore different methods of delivery during your public speaking course. Each of the four methods we discuss are appropriate in certain situations. As a speaker, you will benefit from being aware of your audience and the occasion when choosing the method of delivery that is most appropriate and effective. It is vital that you think about performance guidelines like how much time you have to prepare and speak, who is listening, and what you hope to achieve when selecting a method of delivery. In any given situation, there are four types of speech styles that you can employ: **speaking from manuscript**, **speaking from memory**, **extemporaneous speaking**, and **impromptu speaking**.

3.1.1   Speaking from Manuscript

Because this delivery style involves writing out your speech and reading it word for word, there is a fine line between speaking from manuscript and simply reading to an audience. When executed properly, a manuscript speech is an excellent choice for occasions when the message must be precise to convey meaning and avoid misunderstanding; we see this style frequently reflected in company apologies, speeches by politicians, official statements by legal officials, or anything that will become archived for public record. Today, speaking from a manuscript is commonly achieved with a teleprompter as well. We will cover how to effectively work with a teleprompter later in Chapter 13.

speaking from manuscript
Reading the speech verbatim.

speaking from memory
Committing the entire speech to memory and delivering it without the aid of notes.

extemporaneous speaking
A method of delivery that involves a combination of speech practice and the use of carefully prepared notes to guide the presentation.

impromptu speaking
Usually a short speech delivered at the spur of the moment with little preparation time.

The online lesson also covers the use of a teleprompter to deliver speeches. See Topic 1.

To make a speaking from manuscript situation work for you, it is key to understand that the audience tends to naturally tune out speaking events that seem too scripted or impersonal. The good news is that you can apply certain delivery techniques, detailed below, to help your manuscript speech have a more memorable impact.

Pay special attention to preparing the written text.

If you cannot read what you have written, you will struggle through delivery. To help with clarity and ease of delivery, type your manuscript, make sure you choose a large enough font to see without squinting, and double-space your document so that you do not lose your place.

Practice.

The key to successful manuscript speaking is a great deal of practice in as many settings as possible. Don't settle for a few practice rounds in an empty room; make notes on your draft that indicate pauses and changing in pacing, work in front of a mirror, and then try delivering your speech to friends and family. Getting an authentic reaction and feedback from a live audience, no matter how informal the setting, is invaluable. The goal is to practice enough that you are not visually dependent on the manuscript—the less you need to look down at each sentence, the more eye contact you can establish with your audience. Eye contact should be more than an occasional glance up; you should think about making the glance down at your notes the exception to the rule!

© 2012 Picsfive, Shutterstock, Inc.

FIGURE 3.3 Although notes can be a valuable resource for speakers, they must be accompanied by practice and familiarity.

Express yourself naturally, capably, and personably.

Think about what you want to emphasize and vary the pitch of your voice to avoid being monotone; varying pace and infusing emotional tones and energy into the manuscript speech bring it life and help you to combat *sounding* like you are reading. Make sure to clarify difficult to pronounce words in advance and make phonetic notes in your manuscript if you still need help. Finally, let yourself shine through—your distinct personality and a level of warmth, both physically and verbally, will help the audience to tune in to your message.

3.1.2   Speaking from Memory

At the start of public speaking classes each semester, there are students who are under the erroneous impression that each of their speeches must be memorized. This mindset is undeniably terrifying for a new speaker. We can probably all think of a time where our minds went blank during a performance—maybe it was in the midst of our monologue in the sixth grade play or perhaps during a choir solo. Either way, forgetting content that we have "memorized" is nothing short of a nightmare—while our heart rate races and we break into a sweat, life begins to pass in slow motion as we strategize for a graceful exit plan that may or may not materialize. This nightmare becomes reality on a regular basis in public speaking classes. Since speaking from memory is a potential form of speech delivery in public speaking courses, students who memorize their speeches might find themselves struggling if they have not taken the necessary precautions.

Although memorization is not required in many situations, there are times when having your speech memorized is beneficial. For example, when you know you will be receiving an award or recognition, memorization may be a useful delivery tool to convey a heartfelt sentiment. Special occasions, such as *briefly* toasting the bride and groom or delivering a graduation speech, are also opportunities for delivering a memorized speech while relaying a personal touch. Memorization enables you to write the exact words you will speak without being forced to read them. By doing so, it's easier for you to establish eye contact with your audience, which is a fantastic asset for a speaker. Eye contact helps you to connect, create interest, and relay emotion! If you find yourself in a situation where memorization is necessary, consider the following five performance guidelines.

Start memorizing the speech as soon as possible.

You do not want to delay the process so that you are under a severe time constraint. *The night before does NOT work!* Make sure you have ample time to work on the memorization aspect of your delivery. Even experienced professional speakers have to work hard to remember their content.

Memorize small sections of your speech at a time.

Do not allow yourself to become overwhelmed with the task. *Memorizing small sections* of your speech at a time will help minimize the chance that you will forget your speech during the delivery. Try writing out your speech a few times; many students who competitively speak attest to the effectiveness of this process. Remember that some people can memorize speeches more easily than others, so work at your own pace.

Try a mnemonic device—"ROYGBIV," "FANBOYS," "HOMES."

Mnemonic devices have been used since the ancient Greeks and Romans had to rely on their memories to deliver the history, culture, and tradition of their preliterate society. In Cicero's work, *Ad Herennium*, the power of the memory as an aid to speaker is explored. It is believed that a speaker can access an "artificial memory" that is trained by practice and discipline. Some useful mnemonic devices include the **loci method**, where a speaker assigns various main points to rooms of a place in which they are familiar and simply mentally "walks around" from room to room, letting each room trigger the next part of the speech and the **striking images principle**, which encourages speakers to assign vivid characteristics (they are easier to remember) to ideas they wish to convey.

Mnemonic devices will be covered in greater detail in the online course material. See Topic 3.

loci method

Involves a speaker assigning/associating each main idea (from the speech) to a part of a place they know well (like their house).

striking images principle

Idea that speakers should assign vivid characteristics to ideas they wish to convey in their speeches.

Determine where you need pauses, emphasis, and vocal variety.

Vocal variety can help you to *avoid sounding robotic or monotone*, which are tones that can crop up in memorized speeches. You want to convey the appropriate tone for your speech: enthusiasm, excitement, anger, expertise. You can achieve this by emphasizing certain words, speaking faster or more slowly, and increasing or lowering your volume and/or pitch.

Avoid looking like you are trying to remember the speech and plan for everything.

As instructors, sometimes we can *see* speakers trying to remember the words, as if they had a motherboard in their head, trying to access the right file. Speakers might look up, look to the side, or simply look pensive as they try to "retrieve" the information. Try focusing your attention toward the audience instead. Even if you chose this tactic, it is important *that some form of speech notes are nearby* to aid in recovery should you lose your train of thought.

3.1.3   Extemporaneous Speaking

Strong extemporaneous speaking, which is often the focus and goal of most speech classes, involves preparing well and practicing in advance but NOT reading verbatim or delivering from memory. It is the quintessential combination of structured preparation and natural delivery.

Extemporaneous speaking has many advantages. In particular, because notes are not so heavily relied upon, you can maintain a personal connection with your listeners and respond to their feedback in the midst of your speech. Not relying on notes allows for a looser delivery and improves your eye contact, allowing you the greatest level of flexibility. You can adjust your choice of words and decide what to include—or exclude—in your speech *while speaking*.

Speaking extemporaneously means that your word choice is *fresh*. Although you know the intent of your message in advance, you choose your exact words as you are delivering your speech. The result is a natural, conversational tone that puts you and your audience at ease. Certainly, as you practice your speech, key words or phrases will remain with you, and the more you practice, the more likely you are to commit a particularly fitting word or phrase to memory. Extemporaneous speaking also enhances your freedom to gesture as you would in conversational speech. With both hands free (you can gesture with notes on the podium or note cards/technological device in one hand), you can move about and emphasize key points with natural gestures. Consider the following guidelines as you prepare for your extemporaneous speech:

Prepare carefully.

There is a sense of peace when you know that you have done everything necessary to convey intelligent and interesting content. In turn, when preparing an extemporaneous speech, use the same care you would use when developing a written report. Choose your purpose, develop your core idea, research your topic, organize your ideas, and select the language and presentation style that is most appropriate for your audience.

Create an outline and speaker's notes.

A well-crafted outline is a great deal like using a road map for a cross-country trip. As soon as you know your destination, or core topic idea, you can chart your way there with city stop offs (or main points and sub-points). Outlines allow you to see the big picture and not lose sight of the end goal; they also allow you to develop enough supporting material to reach your time limits. You will learn more about outlines in a later chapter. Once a workable outline has been fleshed out, you can select whatever information you will need to reference in the actual speech to form your **speaker's notes**. Today, speaker's notes can take a variety of forms, ranging from neatly constructed note cards to key word outlines to smartphone programs. Regardless of the medium that you choose, your speaker's notes should be clear, concise, and easy to use.

speaker's notes
One note option for speakers—they provide guidance for the speaker, do not reveal nerves the way that paper does and they are portable and easy to manage.

The online course material explores the types of notes used in public speaking in greater detail. See Topics 2 and 3.

Note Card Construction

- Write or type neatly on ONE side only
- Group or cluster main ideas
- Double space
- Numbered at top right hand corner (in case they are dropped!)
- 4 to 5 lines per card on one side only
- Try not to have more than 4 cards for any speech

Guidelines for Other Note Types

- Prepare them in an easy-to-read font
- Highlight or underline important information for verbal emphasis
- Be highly selective with what you include—choose just basics to trigger your memory rather than everything!
- Keep it simple and know how to access your information (if in an electronic format)

Checklist for Handling Notes

Note Cards:

- Hold note cards in nondominant hand only (frees dominant hand for more natural gesturing)
- Cards should be off to side at eye level
- Bring cards to front to switch, then "break" and return to position (this is visually explained in the online course!)

Other Note Types:

- Notes can be kept on podium but should not bring the speaker's eyes down for extended periods of time
- Do not read PowerPoint slides (or similar materials) to the audience
- Practice with your notes ahead of time to achieve fluidity

Use your notes as a prompter NOT a script.

Notes enable you to keep your ideas in mind without committing every word to memory. Notes also make it possible to maintain eye contact with your listeners. You can glance around the room, looking occasionally at your cards, without giving anyone the impression that you are reading your speech.

3.1.4   Impromptu Speaking

Impromptu speaking involves little to no preparation time, and the speech is generally brief. Although some speakers may initially find this style to be intimidating, there is a significant benefit to being able to think on your toes and say something articulate. Arguably, some of the most important moments in life are impromptu: a job interview, a confrontation with a good friend, a conversation with your future mate. In these situations, which can have profound effects on the course of our lives, we do not have the luxury of using prepared notes or practicing many times over. Chances are, you are already employing effective impromptu speaking in many areas of your life. You don't rehearse before ordering at a restaurant or asking a professor a question in class. Imagine how ridiculous it would look to rifle through note cards when asking out the object of your affection or glancing at a key word outline when requesting a raise from your boss. This is why it is vital to train your mind for how to handle these impromptu instances competently with grace and strength, both inside and outside of the classroom.

In a public speaking class, many instructors include impromptu speaking opportunities throughout the semester. In particular, it is helpful for students to give a brief impromptu speech at the beginning of the semester just to get on their feet and face the audience. Instructors generally feel that the more opportunities students have to present, the more comfortable students will feel in the speaking environment. It is important to note that although you may not prepare in the traditional sense, impromptu speaking definitely benefits from a mental preparation process that any speaker can learn to embrace. Next are several suggestions that will help you organize your ideas.

Be persuasive.

To avoid simply listing obvious facts, make sure that your speech as a sense of beginning, middle, and end. During the brief planning phase (this can be done in about a minute), impromptu speakers should:

- Choose a position to argue
- Decide on an attention getter
- Determine two to three points to support the position
- Create a summary and creative close (usually tied to the position and attention getter)
- Make sure to commit in spirit and delivery (e.g., take advantage of eye contact and gesturing)

The online lesson will explain more about how to make this planning process work for you when preparing to deliver impromptu speeches. See Topic 1.

Focus your remarks on the audience and occasion.

Depending on the type of impromptu speech you find yourself needing to deliver, it might be useful to remind your listeners of the occasion or purpose of the meeting. For example, "We have assembled to protest the rise in parking fines from $10 to $25." When unexpectedly called to speak, talk about the people who are present and the accomplishments of the group. You can praise the group leader ("Michelle's done so much to solve the campus parking problem"), the preceding speaker, or the group as a whole. You may want to refer to something a previous speaker said, whether you agree or disagree, such as "The suggestion to organize a petition protesting the fine increase is a good one." The remarks give you a beginning point, and a brief moment to think and organize your comments.

Use examples.

Be as concrete as possible, such as "I decided to become active in this organization after I heard about a student who was threatened with expulsion from school after accumulating $500 in unpaid parking fines." Examples make your speech personal and help the audience to instantly want to tune in. Keep in mind that as an impromptu speaker, you are not expected to make a polished, professional speech—everyone knows you have not prepared. But you are expected to deliver your remarks in a clear, cogent manner.

Do not try to say too much. Do not apologize.

Instead of jumping from point to point in a vague manner, focus on your specific purpose. When you complete the mission of your speech, turn the platform over to another speaker. Never apologize. Your audience is already aware it is an impromptu moment, apologizing for the informality of your address is unnecessary. You do not need to say anything that will lessen your audience's expectations of your speech.

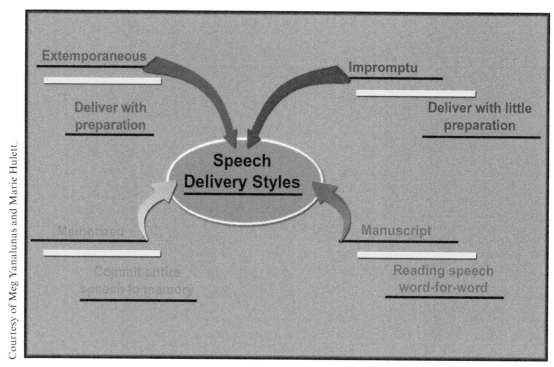

Courtesy of Meg Yanalunas and Marie Hulett.

FIGURE 3.4 Consider the four delivery style options when crafting your own speech.

volume
How loudly or softly you talk.

pitch
The frequency of sound waves in a particular sound–specifically, level, range, and variation.

rate
The number of words spoken per minute.

pauses
Intervals of silence between or within words, phrases, or sentences.

emphasis
Stressing certain words or phrases to draw attention.

pronunciation
Involves saying a word in an acceptable manner.

articulation
The act of speaking clearly, precisely, and intelligibly; your verbalization of distinct sounds.

3.2 Goals of Verbal and Nonverbal Delivery

Let's face it, some people are just more compelling to watch and listen to than others. Television shows like *American Idol* and *America's Got Talent* are constantly touting the fact that some individuals possess a certain "X Factor"—a characteristic that generally means the unknown factor or unexplainable thing that adds a certain value to a person or performance. In speech, the "X Factor" can be boiled down to delivery elements; understanding what the elements are, both verbally and nonverbally, and how to use them in an effective manner. This is essential for you as a successful public speaker who would like to set yourself apart from the crowd.

3.2.1   Natural Delivery Tactics/Aspects of Verbal Delivery

Your voice is an instrument that contributes to the meaning of language. Using your voice to connect with the audience is key to maximizing your potential as a speaker. When presenting in public, consider the following aspects of vocal delivery: **volume**, **pitch**, **rate**, **pauses**, **emphasis**, **pronunciation**, and **articulation**.

Volume
Volume, plainly stated, is how loudly or softly you speak. If your audience cannot hear you, your speech, unfortunately, is a waste of time. In turn, in a performance situation, direct your voice to the last row in the audience—if they can hear you, so can everyone else. In order to do this effectively, it is important to understand how volume works: the loudness of your voice is controlled by how forcefully air is expelled through the trachea onto the vocal folds. This exhalation is controlled

by the contraction of the abdominal muscles. The more forcefully you use these muscles to exhale, the greater the force of the air, and the louder your voice.

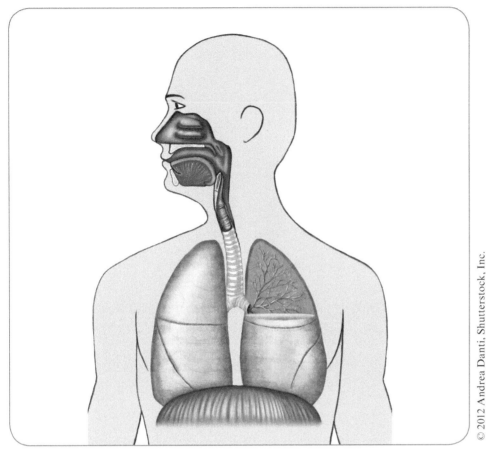

FIGURE 3.5 With the exhalation of breath, your diaphragm forces air through the larynx (which contains your vocal chords and glottis), producing sound and varying pitch and volume.

Do not mistake shouting for projection. Shouting involves forcing the voice from the vocal folds, which is irritating to the folds. Projecting is powering the sound to come from the abdominal area. Straining your voice will only make you hoarse. Instead, work on your posture and breathing from the diaphragm.

Diaphragmatic breathing is detailed further in the online course. See Topic 2, as well as Topic 1 of the online lesson on Public Speaking Apprehension and Listening Strategies.

Use volume to add interest and variety to your speech. Maybe you want to add a bit of humor to your introduction of a speaker. Using a "stage whisper," you could say something like, "And if we all clap very loudly, we can coax him on to the stage." On his television show, Dr. Phil McGraw uses volume effectively by getting loud when he thinks people should be annoyed by what is happening and speaking softly when he is showing amazement or sharing a startling fact. Increasing volume at certain times during your speech will draw attention to your point, and having variety, in general, will help keep interest.

Do not talk to the podium. If you have your notes on the podium and your head is bent, the audience will not be able to hear. Don't talk to your notes. Look up and speak to your audience.

© 2012 AISPIX, Shutterstock, Inc.

FIGURE 3.6 Relaxed and natural delivery involves appropriate vocal pitch and speech rate.

Pitch

Pitch refers to your vocal range or key, the highness or lowness of your voice produced by the tightening and loosening of your vocal folds. The range of most people's voices is less than two octaves. Your goal should be to operate within a natural and comfortable pitch that is neither too high nor too low.

Vary your pitch. Variety adds interest to your presentation and helps you to avoid a monotone and robotic style. When you do not vary the pitch of your voice, you risk putting your listeners to sleep.

Use your voice potential. Take advantage of the fact that your voice has incredible range. To add color, lower the pitch of a word or phrase you want to emphasize. Resist the temptation to raise your voice too much at key points.

Rate

Speech rate, or the number of words spoken per minute, can convey a great deal about you as a speaker: how comfortable you are, how much you've thought about the audience, and how seriously you'd like to be taken can all be revealed by how quickly or slowly you choose to speak. On the average, Americans' rate of speech ranges from 120 and 160 words per minute. Keep in mind, our normal rate of speech may be acceptable within our own region or culture, but when speaking to a culturally diverse audience, we may need to speak more slowly.

Nervousness may affect your normal pattern. When practicing alone, you may be relieved when you find that in timing your speech you are just over the minimum time required. However, under the pressure of giving a speech, you may find yourself speeding up ("The faster I talk, the faster I'll finish.") or slowing down. Rate is also affected by mode of delivery. If you read a manuscript rather than speak extemporaneously, you may find yourself running a verbal road race.

Choose an appropriate rate. Your rate of speech should be consistent with the ideas being expressed and for the context. For example, it makes sense that a sportscaster announcing a basketball game speaks faster than a sportscaster at a golf match. Also, if you are using several terms that might not be known to your audience, you want to slow down as you mention those terms.

Vary your rate of speech. By changing your rate, you can express different thoughts and feelings. You may want to speak slowly to emphasize an important point or to communicate a serious or somber mood. A faster pace is appropriate when you are telling your audience something they already know (many speeches include background information that sets the scene) or to express surprise, happiness, or fear.

Pauses

Pauses are known as intervals of silence between or within words, phrases, or sentences, and can be helpful for a variety of reasons. Some speakers talk nonstop until, literally, they run out of breath. We can probably all think of a time when our body forced us to breathe or swallow because we weren't giving ourselves a chance to do so naturally. Others will pause every three or four words in a kind of nervous verbal chop that can make the audience frustrated and tense. Still others, particularly those who read their speeches, pause at the wrong times—perhaps in the middle of an important idea—making it difficult for their listeners to follow.

When executed properly, pauses can add color, expression, and feeling to your speech; they should be used deliberately to achieve a desired effect. Pauses serve multiple purposes.

- They communicate self-confidence, power, and control, delivering the nonverbal message that you are relaxed enough to stop talking for a moment.
- They help listeners digest what you are saying and anticipate what you will say next.
- A significant pause also helps you move from one topic to the next without actually telling your listeners what you are doing.
- A pause signals *pay attention*. This is especially true for long pauses lasting two or three seconds ... they truly punctuate an important point. According to Don Hewitt, producer of the CBS news program *60 Minutes*, "It's the intonation, the pauses, that tell the story. They are as important to us as commas and periods are to the *New York Times*" (in Fletcher, 1990, p. 15).
- Pauses can help you to avoid verbal fillers (e.g., "um," "uh," "like," and "you know"); if you briefly pause in silence instead of using a verbal filler, you have a better chance of maintaining composure and credibility. One of the authors of this textbook had a professor in college who exemplified this principle beautifully; although he used pauses to catch his thought or refocus, he never once used a verbal filler!

Tie your pauses to verbal phrasing. To a speaker, a phrase has a different meaning than it does to a writer. It is a unit you speak in one breath in order to express a single idea. Each pause tells your listeners you are moving from one thought to the next. Pausing when you introduce a new idea or term gives your listeners time to absorb what you are saying. It helps listeners keep up with you.

Use pauses to change the pace and add verbal variety. Pauses can be an effective tool speakers use to keep attention or to draw attention to a particular thought or emotion. Pause just before you speed up or pause just before you slow down. In both cases, the pause indicates to the audience that something is going to happen.

Extend pauses when displaying a visual. This tactic enables your audience to read the information on the visual without missing your next thought. It is important to pause after the display, not before it. Try pausing for two or three seconds.

Emphasis

You can use emphasis to draw attention to a specific word or phrase. It involves stressing certain words or phrases. It can add weight to what you say, and make a particular word or phrase more noticeable or prominent. An emotion can be highlighted through the use of emphasis. Emphasis is a nonverbal way of saying, "Listen to this!"

Think about how many ways you can say "Come in." Depending on how they are said and how they are accented by nonverbal behavior, these words can be:

TABLE 3.1 Verbal Emphasis	
A friendly invitation	(from one friend to another)
A command	(from a supervisor to an employee)
An angry growl	(from a mother with a headache to her teenage son who has already interrupted her five times)
A nondescript response	(to a knock at your office door)

These changes give meaning to a word or phrase. By singling out a few words for special attention, you add color to your speech and avoid monotony. Emphasis can be achieved by using different techniques.

Change your volume and pitch. Whether you choose to speak more loudly or more quietly, you draw attention to your speech through contrast. A quieter approach is often a more effective attention-grabber. When you speak in a monotone, you tell your listeners you have nothing to emphasize. When you vary the pitch of your voice, you let them know that what you are saying is important.

Pause when changing your speaking rate. A change of pace—speeding up or slowing down—draws attention to what will come next; pausing can do the same.

Use emotion. Emphasis comes naturally when you speak from the heart. When you have deep feelings about a subject—domestic abuse, for example, or the need to protect the environment from pollution—you will express your feelings emphatically. Anything other than an impassioned delivery may seem inadequate.

Eliminating Verbal Fillers

Verbal fillers, or nonfluencies, are meaningless words that interrupt the flow of our speech. We may use them unintentionally, but we need to work consciously to avoid them. Nonfluencies are also known as filled pauses or vocal fillers. As previously stated, pauses can work *for* you, but nonfluencies distract your listeners. These include: "uh," "um," "like," "you know," "so," and "okay." If your economics professor says "okay" after every concept presented, or your history professor adds "uh" or "um" after every thought, it can cause you to lose focus and for the professors to lose credibility. After learning about verbal fillers, one student related that she kept track of her English professor's nonfluencies. She counted 57 "ums" and "uhs" over the course of a one-hour class meeting. Here's the thing with verbal fillers—once you tune into them, they cannot be ignored! Nonfluencies are verbal debris; they add nothing to the content of your speech, and they also annoy an audience. As a speaker, avoid them.

Throw out other types of speaking distractions as well: giggling, throat clearing, lip smacking, and sighing. These interrupt the flow of speech and may also irritate the audience. As you give speeches during this term, think about any habits you have that may distract your audience. We do not expect you to be perfect, but striving to improve your speaking ability is a realistic goal.

Be aware of your speech patterns. Many people do not realize they use fillers. If you have been videotaped, listen for them as you watch your speech. Or, you can record your own phone conversation on a tape recorder or on your computer. You can also ask friends to identify them when they hear you use fillers, or ask your teacher or classmates to keep track of nonfluencies.

Have you noticed two central themes throughout this discussion of vocal delivery? The first is to *practice*. It is important to practice your speech so it flows smoothly. Practice pronouncing unfamiliar words so they come easily to you when you give your speech. The second theme is *vocal variety*. Try varying pitch, rate, and volume to keep the audience's attention. Create interest in your speech, and stress key words, phrases, and thoughts. You have something relevant to share with your audience. You want to make it easy for them to understand you, and you want to keep them interested from start to finish.

Pronunciation

Pronunciation involves saying a word in an acceptable manner; mispronunciation, in turn, is not knowing how to say a word and, as a result, saying it incorrectly. Sometimes speakers simply do not know the word and mispronounce it; other times, a word is mispronounced because of dialect differences among speakers. For example, politicians, or their detractors, sometimes reference "nucular" weapons (sounding like new-cue-ler) instead of the correctly pronounced, "nuclear" (noo-klee-er). People also present "axed" instead of "asked," and talk about the "Eye-talians" and the citizens of "Eye-raq." Mispronouncing a word or name can certainly challenge your credibility as a speaker. It is, therefore, important check and confirm the pronunciation of unfamiliar words before presenting and practice difficult words until mastery is achieved. We can take a cue from newscasters in this area. Chances are, they wouldn't know how to masterfully pronounce the names of the current president of Iran, Mahmoud Ahmadinejad, or of the famed footwear designer, Christian Louboutin, without careful practice!

verbal fillers
"Nonwords" and phrases like "um," "uh," "like," and "you know" that disrupt the flow of speech and challenge speaker credibility; *also known as nonfluencies, filled pauses, or vocal fillers.*

Confirm correct pronunciation. The dictionary provides reliable pronunciation cues; however, if you have difficulty translating the pronunciation spelling, there are a variety of resources on the Internet that have an audio component so that you can hear the correct pronunciation of a word in the voice of an actual human. Use your favorite search engine to find these resources using the following search words: dictionary, pronounce, pronunciation audio.

Do not comment on your pronunciation. Do not say, "or however you pronounce that" or "I cannot pronounce that." We are likely to forgive regional differences, but our credibility will be reduced if our listeners see we have made little or no effort to determine the correct pronunciation.

Practice the pronunciation of difficult words. You do not want to stumble or draw attention away from the point you are making. Just like learning a foreign language, it may take several efforts to pronounce a word correctly. So practice the word several times over a span of time.

Articulation

Articulation refers to the production of sound and how precisely we form our words; in turn, a person who articulates well is someone who speaks clearly and intelligibly. In this fast-paced world, the serious pursuit of articulation might seem like a lost art. Many of us probably have grandparents who still place a value on articulation—perhaps they've told you not to slur or mumble, maybe they complain that your music has lyrics that they cannot understand. This obvious "generational gap" in the area of articulation is further demonstrated in film—try watching a film from the 1940s—Cary Grant and Rosalind Russell speak at the speed of light without dropping a single syllable because the studio system at that time hired elocution coaches to make sure their actors spoke with great clarity, both on and off screen. Today, film actors who mumble their way through their lines in Hollywood blockbusters are often, sadly, just as unintelligible when giving interviews on television. Who can forget Sylvester Stallone's slurring in real life (not just in the *Rocky* installments), Ozzy Osbourne's incessant ramblings, or Joaquin

© 2012 DFree, Shutterstock, Inc.

FIGURE 3.7 For some, Sylvester Stallone has become nearly as famous for his unclear speech patterns as he is for his talent in the entertainment industry.

Common Lazy Speech Examples

Instead of "tuh"…say "to" or "too"

Instead of "dontcha"…say "don't you"

Instead of "wanna"…say "want to"

Instead of "fer" or "fur"…say "for"

Instead of "gonna"…say "going to"

Instead of "Innernet"…say "Internet"

Instead of "samwich"…say "sandwich"

Instead of "wha" or "huh"…say "what"

Phoenix's bizarre blathering on *The Late Show with David Letterman*? In these cases, their inarticulate manner spoke much louder than their intended message. Whether you are delivering a formal speech or simply engaging in conversation with your peers, careful articulation can help you to be a more effective communicator.

In order to adequately articulate, your words need to be crisp and clear. The listener should be able to distinguish between sounds and not be confused. Often, "lazy speech" can creep into our talking without us even realizing it. Leaving off the "g" in words like "going," "driving," and "shopping" is common in American culture. Saying "I wanna," "I coulda," and "I hafta," or "tuh" instead of "to" are other examples of sloppy articulation that can challenge your credibility.

Think "consonants, vowels, breath." Articulation can be broken down into these three simple components. First, make sure that you pronounce each consonant crisply. Then, devote your energy to saying each vowel with its true vowel sound (we often carelessly replace true vowel sounds with the universal "uh"). Finally, make sure your breath feels like a consistent stream of air letting you flow from one word to the next.

Work to eliminate bad habits. Reflect on your own articulation. Do you speak clearly? Do you mumble? Do you have certain words that you mispronounce? Do you leave the endings off words? Make a conscious effort to think about articulation.

Try the tongue twisters below; once you feel like you've spoken each one clearly, then increase your speed and try again without compromising clarity!

1. A big black bug bit a big black bear, made the big black bear bleed blood.
2. The treatise on the Antarctic was definitely not accessible to the non-native speakers residing in Washington.
3. Toy boat. Toy boat. Toy boat.
4. Denise sees the fleece. Denise sees the fleas. At least Denise could sneeze and feed and freeze the fleas.
5. Clean clams crammed in clean cans.
6. Which witch watched Willy watch Wanda wash windows.
7. Red leather yellow leather.
8. The queen in green screamed.

3.2.2 Aspects of Physical Delivery

Your physical delivery may convey professionalism or lack thereof. It can convey self-confidence or nervousness. Your delivery communicates enthusiasm or relative boredom, sophistication or incompetence. The ways you gesture, move, look at people, and dress say a great deal about you. *You are your own public relations representative!* More important, these elements leave a lasting impression that affects the speaker-audience connection. Although mastering the art of nonverbal communication will not guarantee your speaking success, it will help you convince your audience to pay attention. The areas of physical delivery for you to consider are **eye contact**, **gestures**, **facial expressions**, **posture/movement**, and **appearance**.

Eye Contact

No other aspect of nonverbal behavior is as important as eye contact, which is the connection you form with listeners through your gaze. You engage your audience

eye contact
The connection you form with listeners through your gaze.

gestures
Using your arms and hands to illustrate, emphasize, or provide a visual experience that accompanies your thoughts.

facial expressions
The movement of the eyes, eyebrows, cheeks, and mouth to communicate affect or feelings.

posture
The relative relaxation or rigidity and vertical position of the body.

movement
The physical shifts from place to place.

appearance
Your physical nonverbal presence established through clothing choice, accessories, piercings, tattoos, and hairstyle.

© 2012 takayuki, Shutterstock, Inc.

FIGURE 3.8 Establishing eye contact when speaking increases audience attentiveness and adds an authentic and genuine element to a speaker's delivery style.

by drawing them in through eye contact. Sustained eye contact can communicate confidence, openness, and honesty. It suggests you are a person of conviction, you care what your listeners are thinking and feeling, and you are eager for their feedback. Making eye contact with your audience is a way for you to express nonverbally, "I acknowledge that you are there and I want you to understand me."

When your eye contact is poor, you may be sending unintentional messages that the audience interprets as nervousness, hostility, being uncomfortable, or lack of interest. The audience may think you have something to hide or that you are not prepared.

In the process of writing this textbook, one of the authors attended a recognition ceremony where several honorees gave brief speeches. One speaker began by looking at her notes, then made eye contact with the audience, looked back at her notes, and then appeared to look at something on the wall to her right. She repeated these behaviors throughout her speech. After a while, audience members began looking up at the same spot on the wall. The speaker admitted to being nervous before her speech. Clearly, this nervous tic distracted her audience.

Sometimes students only look at the instructor during their speech. Do not do this! It makes teachers uncomfortable, and you are deliberately excluding the rest of the audience. Also, some student speakers ignore half the class by looking at the right side or the left side of the class only.

Anchors of the nightly news or reality show emcees are looking straight at you. As a result of television, eye-to-eye contact is what you expect from every speaker; it is the norm. When a speaker looks away, we sense that something is wrong or feel like we are being ignored. We offer the following five performance guidelines for reflection.

Distribute your gaze evenly. Work on sustained eye contact with different members in the audience. Avoid darting your eyes around or sweeping the room with your eyes. Instead, try maintaining eye contact with a single person for a single thought. This may be measured in a phrase or a sentence. It may help to think of your audience as divided into several physical sectors. Focus on a different person in each sector, rotating your gaze among the people and the sectors as you speak.

Look and lock. Strive for actual eye contact. Often, speakers will send their gaze over the audience without locking eyes with individual audience members—this is not as effective as making an authentic connection eye to eye. Just keep the connections brief—looking at one person for too long (more than a second or two) can seem creepy or imposing.

Glance only briefly and occasionally at your notes. Do not keep your eyes glued to your notes. You may know your speech well, but when you are nervous, it may feel safer to keep looking at your notes. However, this is counterproductive.

Do not look just above the heads of your listeners. Although this advice is often given to speakers who are nervous, it will be obvious to everyone that you are gazing into the air (and missing the point!).

Gestures

Gestures involve using your arms and hands to illustrate, emphasize, or provide a visual experience that accompanies your thoughts. Before we discuss the importance of gestures, body movement, and eye contact, we have a story about Jeffrey, a student who returned to school to complete his communication degree after three years of working in advertising. He prepared a speech with his audience's needs in mind and his specific purpose was to explain how the history of punk music has affected today's music industry. He began by playing an audio clip of The Clash's "Rock the Casbah" (1982), and then continued:

> *Many of you have heard this song countless times, perhaps on the radio, in a club, or dissected in a remix. But did you know that this song is more than just a catchy tune? It is one of countless recordings that have created a legacy for the punk music style, helping a subculture become mainstream and giving millions of listeners their first taste of punk music. Today I will talk with you about how punk music's history has had an impact on the current world of popular music by exploring the influence of three seminal punk bands: The Clash, The Sex Pistols, and The Ramones.*

Opening with a recognizable audio clip is a fantastic attention getter. Also, college students are generally into music, so the exploration of how the punk style relates to some of their favorite bands of the present is both relatable and relevant for the audience. Although Jeffrey's message was effective, his delivery was stiff and uncomfortable. He grasped the lectern for dear life, as if he were afraid to move from his spot. When he did employ the use of his body, he motioned his hands and arms awkwardly, forcing them to move rather than letting them express his message naturally. Since both verbal and physical discomfort can be contagious, his listeners responded by becoming restless and uncomfortable themselves. During the post-speech criticism, one audience member explained what she was feeling: "You looked so wooden that I had trouble listening to what you were saying, which is amazing since I really like punk music to begin with!"

© 2012 S_L. Shutterstock, Inc.]

FIGURE 3.9 When you are holding notes, or even a microphone, use your free hand to gesture naturally. "Talking with your hands" infuses life and energy into your presentation.

Jeffrey's problem was a lack of natural gestures and body movement, which his audience could not ignore despite the inherent interest of his speech. Natural gestures tell an audience that you are comfortable and self-confident. As an outlet for nervous energy, they actually help you feel more at ease. Gestures encourage an enthusiastic presentation. If you put your body into your speech through movement and gestures, it is difficult to present an unnatural speech. Gestures also have a positive effect on breathing; fluid and intentional movement can help you to relax the muscles that affect the quality of your voice.

Gestures are especially important when you are speaking to a large audience. People in the back rows may not be able to see the changes in your facial expressions, and gestures may be their only way of seeing your involvement with your speech.

You can tell whether your gestures are effective by checking where your listeners are looking. If they are focusing on the movement of your arms and hands instead of your face, your gestures are a distraction rather than a help. If this situation occurs, reduce the amount of gestures during the rest of your speech. Think about the following three guidelines as your practice using gestures.

1. **Use natural gestures.** Your gestures should reinforce both the ideas in the message and your own personality. Stand straight, with your arms bent at the waist and your hands relaxed, so you are ready to gesture. Pay attention to the position of your elbows. If they hang stiffly at your sides, your gestures will look shortened and artificial. To move your hands and forearms freely, make sure there is plenty of room between your elbows and your body. Avoid looking as though your upper arms are velcroed to your body.

2. **Gesture purposefully.** Ideally, gestures should be meaningful and enhance your message and should arise from genuine purpose or emotion. For example, if you were trying to persuade people to donate blood, you might want to give your audience three reasons for doing so. When you say, "three reasons," you can hold up three fingers. When you say, "First," hold up one finger, and then when you say, "Second," hold up two fingers. You get the picture. These gestures are meaningful because they serve as an organizational guide. They tell your audience where you are in your speech. The same thing is true if you were giving an after-dinner speech in which you were trying to convince your audience to stop complaining. You could put up one or both hands in the "stop" position when you say, "Stop complaining" to your audience. This is meaningful because it emphasizes your assertion.

3. **Gesture appropriately.** Gestures should be timely. You do not want to hold three fingers up before or after you say "three reasons," but *as* you are saying it. You do not want arms flailing around as you speak; they should match what you are saying. Appropriate gestures are timely, and they should make sense within the context of your message. If you are speaking before a large audience, gestures are bigger and, generally, more dramatic. Those same gestures may look awkward and exaggerated in a smaller environment.

3.2.3 Pitfalls in Speech Delivery

Actions That Inhibit Gesturing

The preceding three guidelines are designed to help you gesture effectively. The authors of this textbook have close to 100 years of combined experience grading student speeches, and we have noticed several actions that reduce the overall effectiveness of a student's speech and/or distract the audience. As you deliver your speech, try to avoid the following:

TABLE 3.2 Actions That Inhibit Gesturing.

Clasping your hands together.	It makes gesturing impossible except if you are willing to raise both hands at once.
Hugging your body.	It makes you look as though you are trying to protect yourself from assault.
Clasping your hands in the "fig leaf" stance.	Holding your hands together at your crotch is another protective position, and it may be distracting.
Locking your hands behind your back.	That position may encourage you to rock back and forth. This "at ease" military stance is not appropriate for the classroom.
Putting your hands in your pocket.	This restricts movement and may encourage you to play with change in your pocket or something else that will make sound and distract your audience.
Grasping and leaning into the lectern.	Some students do this for support when they are nervous. You can touch the lectern; just do not hold it in a death grip. Free your hands so you can gesture. Release your energy through your movement.

Posture and Movement

Remember the second problem related to Jeffrey's delivery? He appeared glued to the lectern. After a while, his listeners got tired of watching him remain static. Jeffrey's mistake is typical. Like many speakers, he failed to realize that an active speaker can encourage an active response from an audience but an immobile, hunching speaker can leave listeners wanting more. When you hold yourself with composure and move from one place to another while you speak, your listeners are more likely to keep their eyes on you. Movement has an additional advantage of helping to release your nervous energy. It can work against you, however, if you look like a collapsed house, a pacing animal in a cage, or if your movement has no purpose (like rocking, swaying, or fidgeting). Embracing an appropriate posture, or position of the body, can provide you with the foundation for natural and relevant movement. In other words, posture and movement are inextricably linked. Think about the following four guidelines of physicality as you prepare your speech.

1. **Find your base.** You should maintain openness, which involves keeping your hands free to move at will; your arms and legs or feet are not crossed or intertwined and your body is facing toward the audience. Much like a strong but flexible tree, your weight should be equally distributed, with both feet on the ground and a naturally upright head.
2. **Move naturally.** Relax and use movement reasonably. Do not pace back and forth like a caged lion or make small darting movements that seem panicked or involuntary.
3. **Tie your movements to your use of visual aids.** Walk over to the visual as you are presenting it and point to its relevant parts. Walk back to the lectern when finished. Make sure your movement is fluid—aim for graceful and smooth movements that reflect that you are in control of your body.
4. **Be prepared.** Your instructor and the speaking environment will influence the opportunities for physical movement. Your instructor may allow or prohibit you from speaking behind a lectern or podium. In informal situations, it may be appropriate to walk through the aisles as you talk. In a small room,

you can walk around without a microphone and still be heard. In a large room, you may need the help of a wireless microphone. Be prepared to adapt to your instructor's rules and the speaking environment. Remember that movement is a way for you to connect with your audience, get them involved, and keep their attention.

Appearance

Although we know that it is unfair to "judge a book by its cover," wearing inappropriate clothing or accessories can distract or offend those with whom we interact, compete with the message being sent and challenge our credibility. Standards for appearance are influenced by culture and context. Americans visiting the Vatican will find that shoulders and knees should be covered in order to gain entry. It is okay for students to wear baseball caps outside, but in some contexts, it may be offensive to keep one on inside. In high school, you may have violated the student conduct code by wearing something that was deemed inappropriate. You might have been eager to graduate simply to free yourself from restrictive dress codes but probably have discovered that the professional world has its own expectations. Although some businesses allow more casual attire, others expect classic, tailored clothing and footwear. As rhetorical theorist Kenneth Burke (1969, p. 119) reminds us, your clothes make a rhetorical statement of their own by contributing to your spoken message.

Left: © 2012 wavebreakmedia ltd. Shutterstock, Inc.; Right: © 2012 Rene Jansa. Shutterstock, Inc.

FIGURE 3.10 Since audience members likely will see you before they hear you deliver the contents of your speech, appearance is an unavoidable factor in speech delivery. In turn, be well groomed and select apparel that is classic, flattering, and professional so that your appearance complements, rather than competes with, your message.

Your choice of shoes, suits, dresses, jewelry, tattoos, hairstyle, and body piercings should not isolate you from your listeners. If that occurs, the intent of your speech is lost. Garments and accessories are an extension and reflection of ourselves and should be carefully selected prior to presentations. We offer the following guidelines for appearance, but the bottom line is, *do nothing to distract from the message.*

Your appearance should be in harmony with your message. Communication professor Leon Fletcher (1990) describes a city council meeting addressed by college students pleading for a clean-up of the local beaches. Although the speeches were clearly organized, well-supported, and effectively presented, the unkempt physical appearance of the speakers conflicted with their message. They wore torn jeans, T-shirts, and sloppy sandals. Their hair looked ungroomed. The city council decided to take no action. Several months later, the same issue was brought before the council by a second group of students, all of whom wore ties and sport jackets—symbols of the neatness they wanted for the beaches. This time the proposal was accepted (p. 14).

Although no one would tell you that wearing a certain suit or dress will make your listeners agree with your point of view, the image you create is undoubtedly important. Research on employment interviews suggests that "physical appearance and grooming habits are factors in the hiring process" (Shannon & Stark, 2003, p. 613).

Be clean and appropriately dressed and groomed. In your public speaking class, your shoe choice is not likely to create a stir. However, your audience expects that you will be clean and appropriately groomed. Keep cosmetics tasteful and hair off of your face (you are much less likely to fidget with it!). Your instructor may provide you with specific guidelines regarding your appearance on the day you speak. A general guideline is to be modest and slightly more formal than your audience.

Avoid clothing and accessories that detract from your message. If the audience focuses on your appearance, your speech loses effectiveness. Wearing a baseball cap, a skullcap, or having your sunglasses perched on top of your head is usually frowned upon. The audience wants to see your eyes, and you should not ignore the possibility that your instructor views most hats as outdoor, not indoor, wear.

Do not wear shirts that have writing or graphic designs on them. It is probably not wise to give a persuasive speech on the day you wear a T-shirt with "I'd rather be texting" on it. One of the authors of this textbook had a male student who chose to wear a T-shirt with a half-dressed woman in a provocative pose. Clearly, this apparel choice did not work for him. In fact, it ended up harming his overall effectiveness and credibility. Whether what is written on your T-shirt is witty or offensive, it takes focus off the message.

Certain types of jewelry or other accessories can make noise when you naturally gesture—make sure to keep your accessories simple to avoid this distraction. Also, check your shoes to make sure your laces are tied or that the high heels you've selected to wear are sturdy enough to withstand some natural movement in front of your audience.

Some students may need the following gentle reminder: Your instructors, and probably many of your classmates are not interested in seeing your belly, rear end, undergarments, or *any* type of cleavage. And a note to the females—if you wear a tight shirt or a short skirt, and you tug or pull on it, you draw attention to yourself, not what you are trying to say. At the end of the day, make sure that clothing is conservative, fits well, and is tasteful as to reflect the professional and credible you.

Speech Delivery and Disabilities

Speaking with a disability or to audience members who have disabilities may require some thinking ahead. The World Heath Organization defines the term **disability** as follows: *Disabilities is an umbrella term, covering impairments, activity limitations, and participation restrictions. An impairment is a problem in body function or structure; an activity limitation is a difficulty encountered by an individual in executing a task or action; while a participation restriction is a problem experienced by an individual in involvement in life situations. Thus disability is a complex phenomenon, reflecting an interaction between features of a person's body and features of the society in which he or she lives.*

Speaking to Audience Members with Disabilities:
An effective speaker needs to anticipate the kind of challenges his or her audience members may face. It is imperative that speakers understand that not every disability is visually identifiable. Accommodation considerations for audience members with disabilities include:

- Visual/presentational aids—should be explained for those who are visually impaired
- Volume—should invite audience members to let you know if you need to speak louder
- Seating arrangements—those with particular impairments may want to sit in front or back
- Pacing—cognitive impairments can make rapid speech pace difficult to process
- Gesturing—should be balanced with the vocal elements for visually impaired
- Providing breaks during longer presentations—sometimes students with less identifiable disabilities (e.g., irritable bowel syndrome) need to step outside
- Sensitivity, empathy, and tact should be infused into every presentation; just because no one has identified themselves as having a disability does not mean that those with disabilities are not present

Speaking with a Disability:
When an individual, with a disability, delivers a speech, there are few issues he or she may want to consider. They include:

- Deciding what role (if any) the disability will play in the speech—it can be used to inspire a story of overcoming challenges or take a back seat to other speech objectives.
- Working with the disability—words and voice can have a huge impact, even if movement is restricted; identify any required electronic adaptations necessary to deliver the speech, get an advance feel for the speech setting, identify any perceivable obstacles (including the podium) that may limit range of motion, and plan accordingly.
- Disclosing the disability—as mentioned above, some disabilities are not easily detected. If you have a disability that might affect require you to sit or stand in a manner inconsistent with standard expectations, you may want to share that with the audience to avoid being perceived as overly relaxed or unprofessional.

Chapter Summary

Delivery involves the method as well as vocal and physical elements selected by the speaker to most effectively convey the message; it is often what can challenge or enhance the overall success of the speaker. The four methods of speech delivery are memorization, manuscript speaking, extemporaneous speaking, and impromptu speaking. Each method is appropriate in varying circumstances. Following the guidelines for the method you choose will enhance the effectiveness of your speech. In this chapter we focus on extemporaneous speaking, a method in which you prepare the content of your speech in advance, but speak from carefully prepared notes. Impromptu speaking involves speaking without lengthy preparation.

Nonverbal communication is an important part of delivery. Your vocal and physical delivery affects your presentation. Aspects of vocal delivery include articulation, pronunciation, volume, rate, pitch, pauses, and emphasis. Guidelines for effective vocal delivery are provided. In addition, an effective speaker has relatively few nonfluencies. Aspects of physical delivery include gestures, physical movement, eye contact, and appearance. A good speaker will use nonverbal delivery to capture and maintain the attention of the listeners and plan for accommodations involving those with disabilities.

Key Terms

appearance, 75

articulation, 68

delivery, 60

emphasis, 68

extemporaneous speaking, 61

eye contact, 75

facial expressions, 75

gestures, 75

impromptu speaking, 61

loci method, 64

movement, 75

pauses, 68

pitch, 68

posture, 75

pronunciation, 68

rate, 68

speaker's notes, 65

speaking from manuscript, 61

speaking from memory, 61

striking images principle, 64

verbal fillers, 73

volume, 68

Questions for Reflection

1. Why is extemporaneous speaking generally the most appropriate form of delivery? Under what circumstances are manuscript reading, memorization, and impromptu speaking appropriate?
2. In which situations have you engaged in impromptu speaking? How would you approach similar situations differently in light of what you have read in this chapter?
3. What would you say is the difference between a public speaking event where you have memorized a speech and a theater performance where the script has been memorized?

4. To what extent do you think effective verbal delivery is necessary to your overall evaluation of a speech?
5. How do your movements, gestures, eye contact, and clothing influence your relationship with your audience and the communication of your message?
6. What do you need to remember about using note cards during your speech?
7. Other than using note cards and note pads, how else do people display notes for the speeches?

Activities

1. Select a CD/DVD/video that contains a complete speech. With your classmates, study the speaker's delivery style, noting various aspects of both verbal and nonverbal delivery. Identify strengths and weaknesses.
2. Find a verbal filler accountability partner who will respectfully alert you to the instances in which you use verbal fillers.
3. Attend a public speaking event and prepare a two- to three-page report on a public speaker's delivery style. Assess how the speaker's delivery (verbal and nonverbal) contributes to or diminishes his or her power as a speaker.
4. Record your own speech and make a written inventory of your strengths and weaknesses. Then describe what you must do to improve your delivery.
5. After the instructor has written 25 to 30 different speech topics and placed them in a bowl or hat, pull out a topic and give a one-and-a-half to two-minute impromptu speech while attempting to use appropriate verbal and nonverbal delivery strategies. Look for patterns of behavior among the class, such as students using emphasis well but maintaining the same rate.
6. Try a group speech. Five classmates stand in front of the class, and decide on a topic. The first person starts, and as soon as that person uses a nonfluency, the next person takes over. See how long each person can speak without using vocal fillers.

References

Burke, K. (1969). *A rhetoric of motives*. Berkeley, CA: University of California Press.

Cicero. Ad C. *Herennium de ratione dicendi (Rhetorical ad Herennium)*. (1954). Cambridge, MA: Harvard University Press.

Duffy, B., & Ryan, H. (Eds.). (1987). *American orators of the twentieth century: Critical studies and sources*. New York: Greenwood Press.

Fletcher, L. (1990, March). "Polishing your silent languages." *The Toastmaster*, 14–15.

Shannon, M. L., & Stark, C. P. (2003). The influence of physical appearance on personnel selection. *Social Behavior and Personality, 31*(6), 613–623.

Sloane Coffin, W. (1988, August). How to wow 'em when you speak. *Changing Times*, 30.

Chapter

4

© 2012, Andresr, Shutterstock, Inc.

Learning Objectives

After reading this chapter and completing the online activities for this lesson, you will be able to:

1. Recognize how being audience-centered is a critical factor in public speaking.

2. Adapt your communication to different audiences and situations.

3. Identify guidelines for ethical considerations in speaking to audiences.

Audience Analysis, Adaptation, and Presentation Ethics

At a Glance

INTRODUCTION

Have you ever been in the audience when someone talked about something that fascinated him or her but really bored you? How do you feel when a friend assumes you know more about a topic than you really do? Two students, Liz and Sarah, had to deal with similar issues. At the end of the second week of their public speaking course, Liz and Sarah approached their instructor, Mr. Wyckoff. Liz asked, "Why do you use so many baseball examples? I know it's the national past-time and all that but neither of us care for the sport." "Yeah," Sarah added, "we don't get all the references, and to be perfectly honest, we lose interest and start tuning you out." Mr. Wyckoff, surprised that the whole world did not share his enthusiasm for baseball, explained, "Oh, I've loved baseball since I first played T-ball, and I've umpired for the last 10 years. But thanks for the heads-up. I'll work on variety—assuming there are other sports." Mr. Wyckoff learned an important lesson about assuming things about this audience and adjusted to his lectures, used examples that related to his audience, and received more positive reinforcement from his class as a whole.

Whether in an auditorium, a boardroom, or a classroom, it's important to understand key characteristics of audiences. First, audience members are often egocentric and want to know "What's in it for me?" That is, they want to understand how your topic relates to them, what they can learn from your speech, or how they can take action that will, in some way, enhance their lives. Second, audiences generally have short attention spans, so get to your point quickly. Finally, people come with their own set of assumptions and biases and are diverse in composition. So, it is important that you adapt to their needs. If you show your audience you understand their needs and help them achieve their goals they will want to listen. Being audience-centered is critical in creating effective presentations.

© 2012 wavebreakmedia ltd., Shutterstock, Inc.

FIGURE 4.1 "This is SO boring!"

However, you also have to be sure that your presentation follows ethical guidelines—adjusting to your audience does not give you the right to mislead them or misinform them. In fact, caring about your audience implies that you want to treat them well and give them the best information you can. These issues, audience analysis, audience adaptation, and ethics, lie at the heart of this chapter.

How do you prepare and deliver a speech that will get your audiences' attention and convince them to listen? Begin by learning as much as you can about your listeners so you can identify and focus on their concerns.

4.1 Being Audience-Centered

An audience is any collection of people who will listen to your speech. When we talk about audience in this chapter, we are usually talking about the people in the room with you. However, frequently there are other audiences that you need to consider.

The online lesson covers the various audiences you need to consider: primary and secondary audiences, present and distant audiences, now and later audiences, and even the same person at two different times. So, when you try to understand your audience, you may need to think about more than the people in the room. See Topics 1 and 2.

Thinking about your intended audience before you start writing your speech will give you a stronger, more tailored presentation that your audience will be more likely to listen to. This will help you because during your speech you will feel the energy and enthusiasm that a receptive and captivated audience exudes and you will probably perform better. In essence, if you are audience-centered, both you and your audience benefit.

Audience Analysis Acronym

When preparing a speech, there is a lot you need to know about your audience. This acronym identifies some of the key questions you need to ask yourself.

A-nalysis: Who are my audiences? How many will be there?

U-nderstanding: What is their knowledge of the subject?

D-emographics: What is their age, sex, educational background?

I-nterest: Why are they there? Who asked them to be there?

E-nvironment: Where will I stand? Can they all see and hear me?

N-eeds: What are their needs? What are your needs as the speaker?

C-ustomized: What specific needs do you need to address?

E-xpectations: What do they expect to learn or hear from you?

Modified from Lenny Laskowski, LIL Seminars. Used by permission.

DO YOUR RESEARCH!!

Jon Favreau, born in 1981, assumed his position as President Obama's speechwriter in January of 2009.

Jon Favreau, born fifteen years earlier in 1966, is an actor, director, and producer. You may know him as the director of the 2008 movie, *Iron Man*, or as one of the boyfriends of the character Monica Geller on the popular television show, *Friends*.

Courtesy of The Official White House Photostream.

Barack Obama and Jon Favreau in the Oval Office.

When doing research, it is important to check your assumptions. When reading about Obama's speechwriter, one of the authors of this textbook assumed that the Jon Favreau mentioned was the director of *Iron Man*. Imagine how awkward that would be if that mistake made it into a presentation about speechwriting. So, be sure to always check your facts.

Courtesy of Edgar Maritano.

Actor-producer-director Jon Favreau.

4.1.1   Know Your Audience

Jon Favreau, who is credited with incorporating Obama's campaign slogan, "Yes we can," assumed the position of Director of Speechwriting when President Barack Obama took office. Before being hired, the then-presidential candidate asked, "What is your theory of speechwriting?" Favreau admitted:

"I have no theory. But when I saw you at the [2004] convention, you basically told a story about your life from beginning to end, and it was a story that fit with the larger American narrative. People applauded not because you wrote an applause line but because you touched something in the party and the country that people had not touched before. Democrats haven't had that in a long time." (quoted from Richard Wolffe, *Newsweek*, January 6, 2008).

Favreau's observation serves to confirm that Obama's approach to the 2004 speech was audience-centered. The speech "touched" people, both those at the convention and those watching the proceedings on television.

In discussing the primaries, Favreau shared his impression of Obama's campaign speech:

> *The message out of Iowa was one of unity and reaching out across party lines. We knew we were going to do well with independents, young people and first-time voters. We knew the message was similar to what he said at the 2004 convention.*

© 2012 Paolo Vairo, Shutterstock, Inc.

FIGURE 4.2 Barack Obama delivering a speech.

In creating a message of "unity and reaching out across party lines," Favreau identifies the targeted audience characteristics: independents, young people, and first-time voters. Obama's success in the primaries as well as the general election confirms his ability during that campaign to analyze his audience effectively.

You need not be a presidential speechwriter to understand your audience. All speakers can create a sketch of their listeners by analyzing them in terms of key demographic and psychographic characteristics. **Demographics** are used to describe the sociological categories of your audience. These include:

demographics
Used to describe the sociological categories of your audience.

TABLE 4.1 Demographic Categories		
Age	Education level/ Knowledge	Religious background
Biological sex	Occupational group	Political affiliation
Race/ethnicity	Socioeconomic status	Geographic identifiers

psychographic analysis
An analysis that provides a profile of an audience based on individual characteristics rather than group characteristics. Psychographics identify behaviors, such as lifestyle choices, attitudes, beliefs, and values.

psychographics
The study and classification of listeners/ audiences according to their behaviors, interests, aspirations, attitudes, beliefs, and values.

homogeneous
Of the same or similar nature or kind (e.g., "a tight-knit, *homogeneous* society").

heterogeneous
Diverse in character or content (e.g., "a large and *heterogeneous* collection").

When thinking about your audience, you may also want to consider a psychographic analysis. A **psychographic analysis** provides you with a profile of your audience based on individual characteristics rather than group characteristics. **Psychographics** identify behaviors, such as lifestyle choices, attitudes, beliefs, and values. Although the type of psychographic analysis you would conduct depends on your topic, you want to ask questions or assess answers to statements that help you understand what motivates your audience. Some psychographic statements (answered on a seven-point scale) one of the authors of this textbook used to understand teenagers were:

- Knowing that I am physically safe is important to me.
- I like to buy the best of everything when I go shopping.
- I like doing things that are new and different.

Information that emerges from demographic and psychographic analyses helps you create a mental picture of your audience and is the raw material for a successful speaker-audience connection (Woodward & Denton, 2004). Additionally, if you've completed your audience analysis, you might want to let the audience know what you know about them—show them that you did your research on them. Depending on your general and specific purposes, certain demographics and psychographics may be more important than others. In most cases, you won't know this information, so you have to ask your audience. Later in this chapter, we will provide you some strategies to learn more about your audience.

4.1.2   Using Audience Analysis to Create a Speech

An audience analysis helps you to think about the link between your speech (topic, main points, support material) and your audience characteristics. One of the first things you need to know is if your audience is **homogeneous** (they share many similar characteristics) or **heterogeneous** (have few similar characteristics). If you have a homogeneous audience, you may have an easier time finding examples they can relate to. If your audience is heterogeneous, you will need to include a variety of appeals and examples.

When you are thinking about your audience, don't just think about their characteristics—think about your characteristics and how you might be perceived as well. Whether you are male or female, 19 or 49, from New Jersey or from Texas may affect how the audience perceives you and responds to your message.

One of the authors of this textbook, Ginny McDermott, had been asked to facilitate a workshop on managing conflict in the workplace. The employees were told that a professor from the University of New Mexico would arrive the following week. However, the employees thought that Jimmy McDermott was coming (in a later chapter, we will talk about the importance of pronunciation). So, when Ginny arrived, the audience was surprised—they had pictured a 50-something, white-haired male who wore glasses and had a beard. Instead, a 30-something, redheaded female with no glasses or beard was standing in front of the room.

How do you think this affected Ginny? Her audience? What would you do if you found yourself in a similar situation?

Depending on the speaking situation, detecting demographics might be easy. First, you may make some assumptions about the audience as a whole. If you were asked to give a presentation on job interviewing, think about the demographic differences between high school students and MBA graduates.

Second, you may have the opportunity to observe the audience in advance and learn first-hand what their demographics are. Third, you could interview someone who knows the audience well. Finally, a fourth strategy involves creating a simple audience analysis survey that you can adapt. Later in this chapter, we will cover types of questions you might use to uncover demographics. Whether through knowledge of the group the audience represents, direct observation, interview, or survey, it is important to gain insight into your audience before you constructor your speech. Some key demographics are identified below.

Demographic Analysis
Age

Ask yourself, "How does my age potentially impact my audience's perceptions of me?" "How does their age potentially impact their perceptions of my topic?"

Making Demographics Work for You

Vicky was enraged about proposed tuition increases and decided to speak to the college's board of trustees about the issue. Knowing that the board members were, on average, 30 years her senior, Vicky used examples and illustrations appropriate for their age demographic, including a brief reference to the GI Bill and the Great Society, as well as an impassioned anecdote about a sharecropper family whose son would change the world for migratory farmers: Cesar Chavez. Vicky's message was better received because her audience could identify with her examples. Her tactic was unexpected and appreciated by an audience who thought they were about to hear a whining diatribe with little real substance. Vicky was able to make age-related assumptions work in her favor and serve her ultimate goals for speaking.

When taking into consideration your age and the age(s) of your audience, we suggest the following:

- *Avoid assumptions about the average age of your audience.* If you read the "Do Your Research!!" sidebar, you saw that President Obama's speechwriter was younger than 30 when he got the job. Your audience will likely include people from a wide range of age groups, so don't think that just because your audience is college students, they will all be 18 to 23.

- *Focus on your speech, not your age.* In many cases, there is no reason to bring attention to your age. Doing so may detract from your message.

A political consultant and strategist, LB, who wants to stay anonymous because her candidate is running for office, started working in politics while in her 20s. "When I first started offering communication training, my clients, potential political candidates, and the staffers, always seemed surprised to see a young woman," said LB. "I knew they were inclined to discount me, based just on my age, but I was certain I could help them." So LB, who'd been a public speaking instructor in graduate school, used her skill to surprise the audience. "My first challenge was to establish my credibility, and I did that by communicating my message clearly and confidently. Once I demonstrated that I 'walked the talk' so to speak, they were more inclined to listen to my advice about how to prepare and deliver a speech." Her clients may have reacted differently if she had made excuses for her age.

- *Avoid "dating yourself" with references or language.* When talking to teenagers, be sure they can relate to your examples. If you are addressing a group of middle-aged executives, do not assume that they know what college students are thinking. Avoid purposefully using slang or phrases that might come off as sounding patronizing and condescending.

Biological Sex

Although men and women communicate much more similarly than they communicate differently (Canary & Hause, 1993), some topics may have broader appeal to men, while others may be of greater interest to women. For example, although a topic on breast-feeding may be important and interesting to all members of your audience, some men may feel excluded.

One of the authors of this textbook, Mark, was asked to speak to a group of insurance sales associates. He had assumed that men made up the vast majority of his audience (bad assumption and stereotype). He soon learned that the audience was going to be made up almost entirely of women. He adjusted his presentation to include a review of the research on women in financial industries and sales. By changing his focus to address his audience's specific concerns, rather than just the information on the current challenges being faced in the insurance industry, his audience was much more involved. Imagine if Mark had delivered the speech written for the all-male audience—all of his examples and images featured men—he could have easily estranged his audience.

Noninclusive Language versus Inclusive Language

Noninclusive language privileges one viewpoint or experience. When preparing your speech, be sure to use language that includes everyone.

Speaker says...	Better to say...
You guys all know...	*Everyone here knows…*
We need people to man the front desk	*We need people to staff the front desk*
Who wants to be chairman of the committee?	*Who wants to chair the committee?*

One suggestion we have related to the demographic of gender is to structure your speech so you are inclusive. Avoid unfairly categorizing or stereotyping members of the audience. For the most part, speakers should avoid relying on the masculine pronoun and find ways to include men *and* women in their audiences.

Also, while we do not identify sexual orientation as one of the key demographics, it is closely related. Every audience will likely contain members who are gay, lesbian, bisexual, transgendered, questioning, and heterosexual. Maintaining this awareness by using sensitive and inclusive language and examples goes a long way toward fostering greater understanding of your message.

Race and Ethnicity

Long ago, the image of the United States as a melting pot gave way to the image of a rainbow of diversity—an image in which African Americans, Hispanics, Asians, Greeks, Arabs, and Europeans define themselves by their racial and ethnic ties as well as by their ties to the United States. Although most of us can grasp the concept of **race**, which is about shared biology, understanding **ethnicity** is somewhat more difficult. Ethnicity is about shared culture, heritage, and even language. Within this diversity are beliefs and traditions that may be different from your own. It is important that you understand these differences and do not assume that everyone in your audience has the same background or experiences as you or as each other.

As you develop your speech, we ask that you avoid invoking stereotypes related to race, ethnicity, or nationality, even if these groups are not present in your audience. Even when couched in humor, such comments are deeply offensive, potentially hurtful, and unethical. Appreciation of different people and ways can help you avoid several critical errors in your speech. Any of these gaffes will surely compromise the connection you are trying to create.

Understand also, that **ethnocentrism**, which is the belief that one's own culture is superior to other cultures, is evident when we express a bias for the way we do things. Unfortunately, some individuals who might be identified as ethnocentric have little experience with other cultures. You should try to avoid being offensive or unfair by examining your language usage as well as the examples, stories, and illustrations you are contemplating incorporating into a speech.

race
Major division of humankind, having distinct shared biology and understanding.

ethnicity
The fact or state of belonging to a social group that has a common national or cultural tradition, heritage, and even language.

ethnocentrism
Belief in the superiority of one's own ethnic group.

A Latino speaker recently noted in his opening comments to a largely Anglo Midwestern audience, that he was pleased to be the lone representative from the "real south." His comment brought both laughter and an appreciation for his unique point of view. He made the most of an obvious contrast with his audience (ethnicity) by addressing it quickly and with humor. Notice, though, that he left it at that and did not continue to talk about it. Going too far with racial and ethnic comments can create more tension and discomfort. Noting the obvious is welcomed by audiences, as long as it is handled with deftness and tact.

Education Level/Knowledge

Are the members of your audience high school or college graduates, experts with doctorates in the field, or freshmen taking their first course? Knowing the educational level of your audience will aid in the construction of your message. If you're speaking to elementary students about Queen Elizabeth I, you can safely assume they need to be provided with some historical background. But to a group of European historians, such information would not be necessary. However, don't assume just because your audience members have college degrees that they are experts on your topic—you need to determine how much they know.

In addition to determining what type of background information or explanation is needed, another consideration is language. You want to speak *to* your audience, not over their heads or at such a basic level that you sound condescending. Use jargon they will understand. To avoid losing your audience's attention, be aware of their level of knowledge regarding your topic.

Occupational Groups

You may find an occasion where you are speaking to a specific occupational group, such as teachers, students, doctors, lawyers, union representatives, miners, or factory workers. Occupational information can often tell you a great deal about listeners' attitudes. An audience of physicians may be unwilling to accept proposed legislation that would strengthen a patient's right to choose a personal physician if it also makes it easier for patients to sue for malpractice. A legislative speaker might need to find creative ways to convince the doctors that the new law would be in the best interests of both doctors and patients.

Knowledge of what your listeners do for a living may also tell you the type of vocabulary appropriate for the occasion. If you are addressing a group of newspaper editors, you can use terms common to the newspaper business (e.g., below the fold, lead, copy) without bothering to define them. Do not use job-related jargon indiscriminately, but rather, use them to your advantage to create a bridge to the audience. By showing you know the correct jargon, you demonstrate your credibility and the audience may relate to you more positively.

Our suggestion regarding occupational groups is to avoid too little analysis or too much analysis of the importance of occupational affiliation to your audience members. When you ask people to describe themselves, what is the first thing they say?

It might be, "I'm a white female," "I'm a gay activist," "I'm the mother of four young children," or, "I'm a lawyer." Some people define themselves by their occupation; others view their jobs as a way to feed a family and maintain a reasonable lifestyle. By determining how important the occupational group characteristic is to your audience, you can create an on-target message that meets their needs.

FIGURE 4.3 Understanding an audience is a speaker's crucial first step. if a speaker needed to address this audience of protesters in Wisconsin, what audience characteristics would he or she need to assess?

Socioeconomic Status

Depending on the situation, it may be difficult to determine whether members of your audience earn more than $100,000 a year or less than $30,000. However, this demographic characteristic may influence how you develop your speech and create common ground with your audience. When Rabbi Harold S. Kushner talks to groups about his book, *When All You've Ever Wanted Isn't Enough* (2002), he learns the group's socioeconomic status in advance. He explains:

> *Generally, if I'm addressing affluent business executives, I concentrate on the downside of economic success and on the spiritual nature of affluence. When the group is less affluent, I talk about learning to cope with economic failure and with the feeling of being left behind.*

This statement illustrates how one person adapts to his audience based on socioeconomic status. Knowing whether or not the economic situation has changed recently for your audience or whether or not there is likely to be another change soon may influence your approach to your topic. For example, when speaking to a group of incoming freshmen at a public university in 2011, it might be wise to spend more time on financial aid than a speaker would have in 2001. Topics such as welfare, socialized medicine, and Social Security will be approached differently based on whether your audience comes from a wealthy background or one of poverty.

Religious Background

According to the 2005 *Newsweek* article, "Where We Stand on Faith," many people in the United States consider themselves spiritual and religious (*Newsweek*, September 6, 2005, pp. 48–49). Suppose your topic is in vitro fertilization, one of medicine's generally effective techniques to help infertile couples have children. Your presentation goes well, but the faces of your listeners suggest you hit a nerve. Without realizing it, you may have offended your audience by failing to deal with the religious implications of this procedure.

Speakers seldom intend to offend their audiences. However, when it comes to religion, speakers can offend unwittingly. Please consider that religious beliefs may also define moral attitudes. When addressing issues such as abortion, premarital sex, birth control, gay marriage, and gays in the military, speakers risk alienating their audience. By no means are we suggesting you avoid such topics. However, failing to acknowledge and address the religious beliefs of your listeners when your speech concerns a sensitive topic sets up barriers to communication that may be difficult to overcome.

Political Affiliation

In an election year, our interest in political affiliation is heightened. However, whether you consider yourself to be a Libertarian, member of the Tea Party or the Green Party, or whether you are a mainstream Democrat or Republican, political affiliation may influence how you respond to a given speaker. If you are fundraising for the homeless, you will probably give a different speech to a group with liberal beliefs than to a group of conservatives. Consider these variations of a message based upon political affiliation:

To a group of political liberals:

We are a nation of plenty—a nation in which begging seems as out of place as snow in July. Yet our cities are filled with poor citizens who have no food or lodging. They are the have-nots in a nation of haves. I ask for your help tonight because we are a nation built on helping one another escape from poverty. No matter how hard you work to cement your own success, you will never achieve the American Dream if one person is left on the streets without a home.

To a group of political conservatives:

It is in your best interest to give money to homeless causes. I'm not talking about handouts on the street but money that goes into putting a roof over people's heads and into job training. In the long run, giving people dignity by giving them a home and training them for productive work will mean fewer people on welfare and lower taxes. Is it a leap of faith to see this connection or just plain common business sense?

Acknowledging political differences has been important in America since it was formed. You will not compromise your values when you accept the fact that political differences exist. Rather, you will take the first step in using these differences as the starting point for communication.

We cannot stress enough that all members of a particular party do not share the same attitudes, beliefs, and values. Find out how to connect to the diversity of your audience. Your speech as a conservative Republican addressing a group of conservative Republicans will sound different than when addressing an audience that represents the Republican spectrum.

Geographic Identifiers

We have a variety of ways we can discuss geographic identifiers. Among them are directional differences, for example north/south or east/west. Think how an audience comprised largely of people from the Deep South might vary from an audience of individuals from the Northwest. We might look at upstate vs. downstate. For example, Illinois is divided into two general areas, Chicago and Downstate, or the area south of Chicago. This also alludes to the geographic identifier of "urban" vs. "rural." You may have an audience that all live in the same community, or you may have an audience that represents a number of communities. Yet another geographic identifier may relate to terrain, such living near the mountains, lakes, oceans, or as one of the authors of this textbook, Gail, describes herself, living near corn and bean fields and being a "flatlander."

We suggest that understanding geographical identifiers and making reference to them as well as focusing your message as much as possible on their geographical areas of concern will enhance your message's impact and your credibility with the group. You may need to adapt your message to accommodate not only differences in language, speech rate, and references but also specific interests and issues.

Do you think people from different parts of the United States perceive things differently?

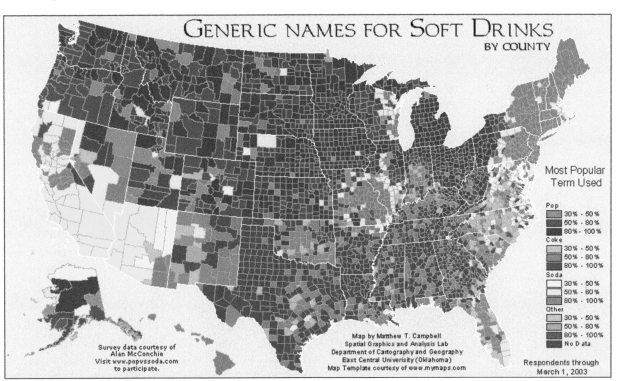

Courtesy of Gregory Plumb, East Central University.

FIGURE 4.4 Within the United States, there are vast differences in the way people talk. As you can see, soft drinks are called different things in different places. It's soda in New Jersey but Coke in Texas—even if you want a Sprite.

4.2 Psychographic Analysis

Psychographics refer to the behaviors, interests, attitudes, beliefs, and values of your listeners. Although an analysis of demographic characteristics, the first stage of audience analysis, will give you some clue as to how your listeners are likely to respond to your speech, it will not tell you anything about the speaking occasion, why people have come together as an audience, how they feel about your topic, or about you as a speaker. This information emerges from the second stage of analysis, psychographic, and centers on the speaking situation specifically.

4.2.1 Behaviors

Your lifestyle choices say a lot about you. Do you walk, bike, drive, or take public transportation to work? Perhaps you avoid driving because walking and biking are more "green" and viewed as more healthy. If you choose to be a city dweller, living in a twenty-second story studio apartment, you probably have less inclination to experience nature than if you opt to live on a fifty-acre farm in Vermont. If you put in twelve-hour days at the office, your career is probably more important to you than if you choose to work only part-time. Behavioral choices are linked to the attitudes, beliefs, and values of your listeners.

In addition to how your audience members spend their time, you will also want to consider the constraints that audience members may have.

The online lesson identifies some individual challenges (for example, auditory and visual challenges), technological challenges, and situational constraints. See Topic 1.

4.2.2 Interest Level and Expectations

Discovering the interest level in your topic and your audience's expectations also helps you adapt to your audience. Interest level often determines audience response. High school seniors are more likely than high school freshmen to listen to someone from the financial aid office at the local college discuss scholarship, grant, and financial aid possibilities. People who fly frequently are less likely to pay attention to the flight attendant's description of safety procedures than individuals who have seldom flown. We tend to pay attention to things that are timely and that we know will affect us.

Robert Waterman, Jr., coauthor of the very successful book *In Search of Excellence*, indicates he spends a day or two before a speech observing his corporate audience at work. What he learns helps him address the specific concerns of his listeners (Kiechel, 1987).

The online lesson identifies audiences with different interest levels, ranging from audiences who are knowledgeable about the topic but members disagree with the specific viewpoints the speakers advocate to those who are informed and favorable toward you and your topic. See Topic 1.

4.2.3　Attitudes, Beliefs, and Values

Attitudes are predispositions to act in a particular way that influence our response to objects, events, and situations. Attitudes tend to be long lasting but can change under pressure. They are often, but not always, related to behavior. Understanding your audience's attitude toward your topic will help you to create examples and select your supporting material. If your audience has a largely unfavorable attitude toward environmental conservation, your speech on recycling needs to address that.

Beliefs represent a mental and emotional acceptance of information. They are judgments about the truth or the probability that a statement is correct. Beliefs are formed from experience and learning; they are based on what we perceive to be accurate. To be an effective speaker, you must analyze the beliefs of your audience in the context of your message. For example, if you are dealing with people who believe that working hard is the only way to get ahead, you will have trouble convincing them to take time off between semesters. Your best hope is to persuade them that time off will make them more productive and goal-directed when they return. By citing authorities and providing examples of other students who have successfully followed this course, you have a chance of changing their mind-set.

Values are deep-seated, abstract judgments about what is important to us. Values separate the worthwhile from the worthless and determine what we consider moral, desirable, important, beautiful, and worth living or dying for.

An audience of concerned students that values the importance of education might express this value in the belief that "a college education should be available to all qualified students" and the attitude that "the state legislature should pass a tuition-reduction plan for every state college." If you address this audience, you can use this attitude as the basis for your plea that students picket the state capitol in support of the tuition-reduction plan. Understanding your listeners' attitudes, beliefs, and values will help you put your message in the most effective terms.

4.3　Accessing Audience Information

In order to adapt your message to a particular audience within a specific situation, you need to gather information. There are many ways to gather data about your audience, ranging from passive strategies (observing the audience and making educated guesses) to very active strategies (survey the intended audience, interview the intended audience, and interview the person who selected you as the speaker).

The online lesson briefly reviews these strategies, but in this chapter you can read more about surveys and interviews. See Topic 1.

4.3.1　Conducting a Survey

A **survey** is a data collection method. A **questionnaire** is the tool used in survey research—it is a compilation of questions. You develop a questionnaire to survey a group of people.

attitudes
Predispositions to act in a particular way that influence our response to objects, events, and situations.

beliefs
A mental and emotional acceptance of information; judgments about the truth or the probability that a statement is correct.

values
Socially shared ideas about what is good, right, and desirable. They are deep-seated, abstract judgments about what is important to us.

survey
A data collection method in which information or opinions are gathered for the purpose of analysis.

questionnaire
A compilation of questions used to conduct survey research.

For audience analysis, doing a survey can help you determine the specific demographic and psychographic characteristics of your listeners as well as their perceptions of you and your topic. It can also tell you how much your listeners know about your topic and the focus they would prefer in your speech.

sampling
The act, process, or technique of selecting a representative part of a population for the purpose of determining parameters or characteristics of the whole population.

Sampling is the process of selecting and asking questions of some members of the whole group. Whether you survey all your classmates, sampling every fourth person in your dorm, or calling selected members of your audience to ask them questions, you can find out important information about your audience relatively quickly. In addition, and depending upon the age of your intended audience, online survey creation and response tabulation companies now make it easier to poll a group of people via the Internet.

The first step in conducting a survey is designing a questionnaire that will help you get the information you need. Three basic types of questions are most helpful to public speakers: fixed-alternative questions, scale questions, and open-ended questions (Churchill, 1983).

fixed-alternative questions
Questions with limited responses to specific choices, such as age, education, and income. Fixed-alternative questions can offer many different responses, or they can offer only two alternatives, such as yes/no. Such questions help you analyze the attitudes and knowledge of your prospective listeners.

Fixed-alternative questions limit responses to specific choices, such as age, education, and income. Fixed-alternative questions can offer many different responses, or they can offer only two alternatives, such as yes/no. These questions help you analyze the attitudes and knowledge of your prospective listeners. Here is an example of a fixed-alternative question focusing on attitudes:

> *Do you think all professional athletes should be carefully tested for drugs and steroids? (Choose one)*

- Professionals should be carefully tested for drugs and steroids.
- Professional athletes should be tested for the use of drugs and steroids in selected sports.
- Professional athletes should never be required to test for drugs and steroids.
- No opinion.

This type of question is easy for the audience member to answer, and easy for you to tabulate and analyze. Further, because you ask each person the same question, you can be fairly sure that if you asked the same question a second time, you would get the same answer. Fixed-alternative questions also provide standardized responses. For example, if you just asking people, "How many times a week do you eat out?" you may receive answers like "regularly," "rarely," "every day," and "twice a day." Interpreting these answers is more difficult. Instead, you should supply possible responses, such as "every day," "4 to 5 times a week," "2 to 3 times a week," "1 to 2 times a week," or "less than once a week."

The disadvantage of using fixed-alternative questions is that it may force people to respond to a question when they uncertain or have no opinion, especially if you fail to include "no opinion" as a possible response.

scale questions
A type of fixed-alternative question that asks people to respond to questions set up along a continuum.

Scale questions are a type of fixed-alternative question that asks people to respond to questions set up along a continuum. For example:

How often do you vote?

Always   Regularly   Sometimes   Seldom   Never

or

How much do you agree with this statement: People should be required to spay or neuter their pets.

Strongly Disagree   Disagree   Neutral   Agree   Strongly Agree

The disadvantage of the scale question is that it is difficult to get in-depth information about a topic. Additionally, people might answer even if they don't know anything about the topic.

In an **open-ended question**, audience members can respond however they wish. For example:

> *How do you feel about a twelve-month school year?*

> *Why do you think the Japanese sell so many cars in the United States?*

A variety of answers are possible for these questions. In response to your question about extending the school year, one respondent may write, "Keep the school year as it is," while another may suggest a workable plan for extending the year. Because the responses to open-ended questions are so different, they can be difficult to analyze. The advantage to these questions is that they allow you to probe for details; you give respondents the opportunity to tell you what is on their minds. The next page lists a few guidelines for constructing usable questions.

open-ended questions
Questions that let audience members respond however they wish.

4.3.2 Observe and Interview

You may find that the best way to gather information about a prospective audience is to assume the role of an observer. If you are to deliver a speech on weight control to a former smokers' support group, you could attend a meeting to determine how many members believe they are overweight and how much weight they have to lose. Then ask several people whether their weight problem is the result of their efforts to stop smoking or if they were overweight at other times in their lives. Similarly, if you are delivering a speech to corporate executives on ways to improve their written communication, ask for samples of letters, memos, and reports they have written in order to be personally familiar with their writing skills and styles.

The interviews you conduct during this process are likely to be less formal than the style of interview you use to gather information about your speech topic. When questions occur as you watch a group in action, ask people their thoughts and feelings. Their responses will help you analyze audience need.

Analyzing your audience is a critical step in developing your speech. You develop speeches to be delivered to audiences, so you have to know who will be listening to you and what they already know, think, and feel about your topic. The more you know about your audience's demographics and psychographics, the easier it is to select material, decide main points, and choose visual aids. And, of course, the more you know about what they think about your topic, the better prepared you will be for questions. You can learn about your audience in different ways—observe them, create and distribute a survey, or conduct some interviews.

Guidelines for Survey Questions

Avoid leading questions. Try not to lead people to the response you desire through the wording of your question. Here are two examples of leading questions:

- *Do you feel stricter handgun legislation would stop the **wanton killing** of innocent people?*
- *Do you believe able-bodied men who are **too lazy** to work should be eligible for welfare?*

These questions should be reworded. For example, "Do you support stricter handgun legislation?" is no longer a leading question.

Avoid ambiguity. When you use words that can be interpreted in different ways, you reduce the value of a question. For example:

How often do you drink alcohol?

Frequently   Occasionally   Sometimes   Never

In this case one person's "sometimes" may be another person's "occasionally." To avoid ambiguity, rephrase the possible responses to more useful fixed-alternatives:

How often do you drink alcohol?

More than once a week

At least once a month

Not more than once every six months

Never

Ask everyone the same questions. Because variations in the wording of questions can change responses, always ask questions in the same way. Do not ask one person, "Under what circumstances would you consider enlisting in the army?" and another, "If the United States were attacked by a foreign nation, would you consider joining the army?" Both of these questions relate to enlisting in the military, but the first one is an open question while the second is a closed question. The answers you receive to the first question have much more information value than the second, which could be answered "yes" or "no." If you do not ask people the same questions, your results may be inaccurate.

Be aware of time constraints. Although the results can help you determine interest, attitudes, and knowledge level, you do not want it to take too much time or be too complex. If your instructor allows you to pass out a questionnaire in class, make sure it takes only a few minutes to complete. Ask only what is necessary. Make sure the format fits your purpose.

FIGURE 4.5　When thinking about how to adjust to your audience, remember that part of adjusting your style is adjusting your dress. Suit your clothing to the situation.

Simply knowing about your audience is not enough; you have to use this information to adapt your speech. Adaptation is about tailoring what you say and how you say it to your audience. The next section provides you some guidelines for how to adapt your speech and style to your audience and situation.

4.4　Adapting to Different Audiences

Throughout this chapter and this textbook, you will read the words, "it may" or "it might," or "perhaps." We are provisional, or conditional, because audiences behave differently and have different expectations depending on their characteristics *and* the context or situation. Effective speakers adapt their messages based on audience characteristics, both demographic and psychographic, and the situation that brings the audience together. A politician may give a speech in New York City, then "tweak" it before appearing at a gathering in America's heartland. Adapting a speech may be easy or difficult. In public speaking class, it is important to keep in mind that your teacher is part of the audience. In other words, you have at least two audiences—the other students and the person who is grading you.

In addition, if your audience is informed about your topic and favorable to you and what you are suggesting, you would want to focus on actions and acknowledge and refute criticism. If you have audience members who have mobility limitations, you will want to ensure that there is wheelchair access throughout the room and not just in the front or in the back. Adapting to an audience is also about establishing a link with the people you are speaking to—those in the room and the other people who may hear your speech. The next section in this chapter provides some general guidelines for creating a link to most audiences; don't forget, audience members are frequently egocentric and need to know you are thinking about them.

The online lesson identifies some specific strategies for adapting to audiences with different attitudes toward your topic as well as accommodating audience members who may have some constraints. See Topics 1 and 2.

Delivering a Eulogy

At a funeral, we know the mood is somber, but depending on the person being remembered and the individuals gathered for the funeral, there might also be smiles, laughter, and storytelling. The circumstances may call for fond memory of a person's idiosyncrasies, or, in case of a tragic death, laughter may be totally inappropriate. If you're delivering a eulogy—a speech remembering the deceased—you need to adapt to the situation and the audience's mood.

It takes only seconds for your listeners to tune out your message. Convince your audience your message has value by centering your message on your listeners and adapting your message to that specific audience and situation. The following suggestions will help you build the type of audience connection that leads to the message being understood and well received.

4.4.1   Get to the Point Quickly

First impressions count. You may have heard that in a job interview, the interviewer makes a decision whether you are a good job candidate or not in the first few minutes. If you only have a few minutes to impress an interviewer—who is motivated to fill a position—think about how short of a period of time you have to capture the attention of an audience who may not be as focused on your presentation as you would hope. What you say in the first few minutes is critical. Tell your listeners how you can help them first, not last. Experienced speakers try to make connections with their listeners as they open their speeches—share what you know about your audience so that they know you have thought about them. If you don't get them focused on you and your topic right away, you may never get them to focus on you.

4.4.2   Be of the People, Not Above the People

No one wants to listen to speakers who consider themselves more accomplished, smarter, or more sophisticated than their audience. If you convey even a hint of superiority, your listeners will tune you out. As a speaker, you will learn that modesty inspires confidence. Presidents Bill Clinton, George W. Bush, and Barack Obama have all connected with their audiences by being humble and self-deprecating. At various annual dinners of the White House Correspondents' Association and the Radio and Television Correspondents' Association, each president demonstrated a sense of humor that showed he was easy to relate to:

> *This is a special night to me for a lot of reasons, Jay Leno's here. Now, no matter how mean he is to me, I just love this guy, because together, together, we give hope to gray-haired, chunky baby boomers everywhere.*
> —Bill Clinton (April 29, 2000)

In my recent press conference, John Dickerson of Time *magazine asked the question about what I considered my biggest mistake. It's an excellent question that totally stumped me. I guess looking at it practically, my biggest mistake was calling on John.*
—George W. Bush, (May 4, 2004)

A year ago, my approval rating was in the 30s, my nominee for the Supreme Court had just withdrawn, and my Vice President had shot someone. Ah, those were the good ol' days.
—George W. Bush, (May 4, 2004)

FIGURE 4.6 Humor can help an audience connect with the speaker and relate to the topic. Just be certain that your humor is appropriate to the situation and audience.

FIGURE 4.7 When Will Ferrell was the commencement speaker at Harvard University, he was clearly using humor to create a connection with his audience.

Yes, I think it is fair to say that when it comes to my presidency, the honeymoon is over. For example, some people now suggest that I'm too professorial. And I'd like to address that head-on by assigning all of you some reading that will help you draw your own conclusions. Others say that I'm arrogant. But I've found a really great self-help tool for this: my poll numbers.
—Barack Obama, (April 30, 2011)

Each of these presidents used his ability to be of the people to enhance his speech. By being part of the joke, each president endeared himself to the audience. This was especially impressive because each president was occasionally accused of being out of touch.

4.4.3 Use Humor

Humor can help you connect with your audience. Opening your speech with something that makes people smile or laugh can put both you and your listeners at ease. Humor encourages people to think of you as approachable rather than remote. Consider the opening of Will Ferrell's 2003 speech at Harvard on Class Day (the day before graduation).

This is not the Worcester, Mass., Boat Show, is it? I am sorry. I have made a terrible mistake. Ever since I left "Saturday Night Live," I mostly do public speaking now. And I must have made an error in the little Palm Pilot. Boy. Don't worry. I got it on me. I got the speech on me. Let's see. Ah, yes. Here we go.

You know, when Bill Gates first called me to speak to you today, I was honored. But when he wanted me to be one of the Roxbury guys, I —Sorry, that's Microsoft. I'm sorry about that. Star Trek Convention. No. NRA. NAACP. Dow Chemical. No. But that is a good one. That is a good speech. The University of Michigan Law. Johns Hopkins Medical School. I'm sorry. Are you sure this is not the boat show? No, I have it. I do have it on me. I do. It's here. Thank you.

His opening got their attention and made them laugh. Effective humor should be related in some way to the subject of your speech, your audience, or the occasion. Starting with a joke that is wholly unrelated to your topic is not appropriate. Also, remember that some people have difficulty using humor, and some do not gauge their listeners well and end up falling flat or offending.

Speaker Hint

Have a repertoire of three to five clean jokes—the type you can tell to any group of people. Sometimes a speaker needs to get the audience warmed up—a clean joke may help you.

4.4.4 Get Personal

Before leadership speaker and author Nido Qubein gives a speech, he learns the names of several members of his audience and their roles in the company. During his speech, he refers to these people and the conversations he had with them, creating a personal bond with his audience. Connections can be made by linking yourself directly to the group you are addressing and by referring to your audience with the pronoun "you" rather than the third person "they." The word "you" makes it clear that you are focusing attention on them. Here is an example in a speech delivered by Jeffrey R. Holland, as president of Brigham Young University, to a group of early childhood educators:

You are offering more than technical expertise or professional advice when you meet with parents. You are demonstrating that you are an ally in their task of rearing the next generation. In all that you do ... however good your work, and whatever the quality of life parents provide, there is no comparable substitute for families. Your best opportunity to act in children's best interests is to strengthen parents, rather than think you can or will replace them (1988, p. 559).

4.4.5   Encourage Participation

When a speaker invites the listeners to participate in the speech, they become part-ners in an event. One of the authors of this textbook has a friend, a first-degree black belt in karate, who gave a motivational speech to a group of college women at a state university in Michigan. At the beginning of her speech, and to the excite-ment of the crowd, she broke several boards successfully. She talked about her childhood, her lack of self-esteem, and her struggle to become a well-adjusted busi-nesswoman. She used the phrase, "I can succeed" several times during her speech, and encouraged her audience to join in with her. By the end of her speech, the group, standing, invigorated and excited, shouted with her, "I can succeed!"

Another way to involve your listeners is to choose a member of your audience to take part in your talk—have the volunteer help you with a demonstration, do some role playing—and the rest of the group will feel like one of its own is up there at the podium. Involve the entire audience and they will hang on your every word.

4.4.6   Examine Other Situational Characteristics

When planning your speech, other situational characteristics need to be consid-ered, including time of day, size of audience, and size of room. When speechwriter Robert B. Rackleff addressed his colleagues about the "art of speech writing," he offered this advice:

> *The time of day affects the speech. In the morning, people are relatively fresh and can listen attentively. You can explain things more carefully. But in the late afternoon, after lunch …, the audience needs something more stimulating. And after dinner, you had better keep it short and have some fireworks handy* (1987, pp. 311–312).

Rackleff was reminding his listeners about the connection between time of day and audience response. The relationship between physical surroundings and audience response is so strong that you should plan every speech with your surroundings in mind.

Motivational speaker Nido Qubein says there is a vast difference in how he approaches preparing for a speech to an audience of six people versus an audi-ence of six thousand people: In the first case, says Qubein, "I'm working with the audience and responding to them individually," but in the second, "I'm speaking to a more generalized audience and not really able to respond to facial expressions and other forms of feedback." The intimacy of a small group allows for a speaker-audience interchange not possible in larger groups. Small groups provide almost instantaneous feedback; large groups are more difficult to read.

Room size is important because it influences how loudly you must speak and deter-mines whether you need a microphone. As a student, you will probably be speak-ing in a classroom. But in other speaking situations, you may find yourself in a convention hall, a small office, or an outdoor setting where only the lineup of chairs determines the size of the speaking space.

If you are delivering an after-dinner speech in your own dining room to ten mem-bers of your reading group, you do not have to worry about projecting your voice to the back row of a large room. If, on the other hand, you are delivering a commencement address in your college auditorium to a thousand graduates, you will need to use a microphone. And keep in mind, proper microphone technique takes practice, preferably in the auditorium in which you will speak.

4.4.7   Learn As You Go

As you know from your classroom experience, hearing what your audience thought of your speech can help you give a better speech the next time around. Realizing the importance of feedback, some professional speakers hand out post-speech questionnaires designed to find out where they succeeded and where they failed to meet audience needs. At workshops, a feedback sheet is often provided that can be turned in at the end of the specific workshop or at any time during the day. Valuable information often emerges from these responses, which can help you adjust your presentation for the next occasion.

Finding out what your audience thought may be simple. In your public speaking class, your fellow classmates may give you immediate, written feedback. Your instructor will provide you feedback, so be sure to read it and use it for developing your next speech. In other situations, especially if you are running a workshop or seminar, you may want to hand out a written questionnaire at the end of your speech and ask listeners to return it at a later time. (A self-addressed stamped envelope will encourage a large response; an online survey development tool would also be a good choice.) Here are some questions you can ask:

1. Did the speech answer your questions about the topic? If not, what questions remain?
2. How can you apply the information you learned in the presentation to your own situation?
3. What part of the presentation was most helpful? Least helpful?
4. How could the presentation have better met your needs?

To encourage an honest and complete response, indicate that people do not have to sign their names to the questionnaire.

Another way to learn as you go is to pay attention to your audience during your speech.

The online lesson identifies some nonverbal cues your audience may give you and how to interpret what those cues mean. See Topic 2.

Adapting your speech and style to your audience and situation is an important part of the public speaking process. One part of adapting to your audience is to create a connection with them. You can enhance your connection by quickly letting the audience know why they should listen, staying on the same level as your audience, using humor, getting personal, and encouraging audience participation. Adapting to your audience also requires that you examine the situation and environment. After your speech, you can ask your audience to give you some feedback. It won't help you adapt to that audience, but it might help you prepare for your next speech.

FIGURE 4.9 According to a *Time* magazine poll, Jon Stewart is "America's Most Trusted News Anchor." As of April of 2011, there were more than 9,400 votes, and 44 percent of the voters selected Jon Stewart. While acknowledging his role as an entertainer who mocks the absurdity and hypocrisy of political pretenses, Stewart has earned a reputation for integrity and straight talking as a result of his criticism of television commentators and prominent news media outlets for failing in their responsibility to inform viewers by illuminating the political issues of the day.

FIGURE 4.8 It's not hard to read how this audience member is reacting. But what do you do if your audience is starting to look bored?

© 2012 wavebreakmedia ltd., Shutterstock, Inc.

Courtesy of Chad J. McNeeley/U.S. Navy.

4.5 Ethical Considerations

4.5.1 Our Freedom of Speech

Congress shall make no law respecting an establishment of religion, or prohibiting the free exercise thereof; or abridging the freedom of speech, or of the press; or the right of the people peaceably to assemble, and to petition the Government for a redress of grievances. (Establishment Clause of the First Amendment)

Since the First Amendment to the U.S. Constitution was passed in 1791, American citizens have had a constitutional guarantee of freedom of speech. As a student, you are allowed to interact with your teachers, and you have opportunities to speak before your class about issues of concern. You have the right to support publicly the political party of your choice, and you can engage in activities that reflect your social values. As a community resident, you have the right to speak before city council or the local school board to express agreement or disagreement with their policies. You can write a letter to an editor that supports or opposes the President of our nation. With the Internet, you have numerous and highly varied means of communication.

Freedom of expression comes with responsibility. In class, each speaker has the ethical responsibility to communicate accurately with sound reasoning and to decide what is said and best not said. This responsibility requires a speaker to be truthful without hesitation. As listeners, we are also given a responsibility: to respect the opinions of others, even those different from ours.

Freedom of expression is balanced by freedom of choice. In most situations, listeners have the ultimate power to listen or to focus elsewhere. It is the freedom to pursue our individual interests that keeps the freedom of speech of others in check. Yet, this is not always a perfect check. There are times when the audience is captive and has no real choice. Your classroom may be one of these cases, especially if there is an attendance policy that requires students to be there. It becomes the ethical responsibility of the speaker and host (your instructor) to more carefully monitor and, on occasion, censure inappropriate material on behalf of the captive audience.

Imagine This Scenario

Your son is in sixth grade and he, along with all his classmates, is required to give a 45-minute presentation on a topic of choice; your son chooses artificial intelligence in robots. The presentation requires visual aids and an activity that involves the audience. The teacher sends home a list of all the students' speech topics, one of which is abortion. Parents are allowed to identify topics they feel are inappropriate for their child, and you consider the ramifications of your 11-year-old son hearing about abortion. You are especially concerned because the speaker is also 11 years old, and you wonder what she will say for 45 minutes and what visual aid and activity she will use. Given the audience and topic, what ethical considerations does the speaker need to consider?

What about the ethical responsibility of the teacher? In this situation, what would you do? What are the implications of your choice for promoting free speech and inquiry?

© 2012 netbritish, Shutterstock, Inc.

We want to emphasize the importance of meeting your ethical responsibilities in any speech you give, whether it is informative, persuasive, or a speech to entertain. We begin by discussing the connection between ethics and public speaking and then turn to guidelines for incorporating ethical standards in your speeches.

4.5.2   Ethics and Public Speaking

ethics
The rules we use to determine good and evil, right and wrong. These rules may be grounded in religious principles, democratic values, codes of conduct, and bases of values derived from a variety of sources.

Ethics involve the rules we use to determine good and evil, right and wrong. These rules may be grounded in religious principles, democratic values, codes of conduct, and a variety of other sources. Without an ethical roadmap based on socially accepted values to guide you, you could disregard your audience's need for truth, and engage in self-serving deceit, ambiguity, intellectual sloppiness, and emotional manipulation. If you do, your credibility as a speaker is lost as your listeners turn elsewhere for a message—and a speaker—they can trust. Public speaking is a reciprocal process, and audience mistrust can stand in the way of communication. Therefore, an important aspect of being audience-centered is being ethical.

As citizens and consumers, we are bombarded by messages each day through various print and electronic media. Intense competition exists among these outlets as they strive to be the most-watched, most-read, tweeted, blogged, and so on. As media outlets look for bottom-line profits, ethical standards are occasionally bent. Such was the case in 1993, when *Dateline NBC* alleged that some General Motors pickup trucks had a tendency to explode during collisions. It was later revealed that those trucks had been rigged with incendiary devices to assure footage of an explosion. General Motors Corporation threatened litigation, which resulted in the on-air admission by journalist Stone Phillips that NBC used the devices without informing the viewers.

Power, status, and money have led to unethical behavior and deceptive speeches throughout our history, and public speaking is often a preferred instrument when this sort of abuse occurs. The media can play an important role in investigating unethical behavior and limiting future breaches. For example, during local, state, and national campaigns, the media provides the public with details of sexual misconduct, bribery, poor parenting, and unimpressive military service. No political candidate is immune, which leaves the public faced with the dilemma over who is really telling the truth. Ethical violations seem commonplace in media reports, but this suggests that ethics are more important now than ever.

Credits (left to right): Portrait of George Washington by Gilbert Stuart; Photo of Abraham Lincoln by Alexander Gardner; both courtesy of the Library of Congress. Photo of Richard Nixon courtesy of the White House Photo Office; Photo of Bill Clinton courtesy of Bob McNeeley, The White House.

FIGURE 4.10 Some politicians are regarded as honest and some are not viewed so favorably.

Every time you speak, you are risking your reputation. Listeners will forgive many things—stumbling over words, awkward gestures, lack of examples—but if you lie or mislead them, they may never trust you again. For some, maintaining strong ethical standards is second nature. For others, more deliberation is needed. Some speakers rationalize their unethical behaviors so they can continue to misguide their audiences.

4.5.3 The Link between Ethics and Values

Inherent to a discussion about ethics in public speaking is the concept of values and how they ground us. Values, as noted earlier in this chapter, are socially shared ideas about what is good, right, and desirable. They propel us to speak and act. They determine what we consider important and what we ignore, how we regard our listeners, and how we research and develop a speech. Values are communicated through what speakers say—and fail to say—through delivery, and through responsiveness to audience feedback.

You can speak out against anti-Semitism or remain silent. You can support, through public discourse, the university's right to displace poor families from their university-owned apartments to build another office tower or you can plead for a more humane solution. In a public speaking class, you have a forum to talk about those things you feel are right or wrong, desirable or undesirable. Though you may be hesitant to speak out, you may be surprised by how many others agree with you.

4.5.4   Ethos and Speaker Credibility

Although ethics seems to be a "hot button" topic in academic courses and governmental and organizational activities, it has been an important topic in speechmaking for more than 2,000 years. In references to rhetoric, Aristotle discussed the term **ethos**, meaning ethical appeal. In a translation by Lane Cooper (1960), we find that Aristotle defined ethos in terms of the intelligence, character, and goodwill a speaker communicates during a speech:

> *Speakers are untrustworthy in what they say or advise from one or more of the following causes. Either through want of intelligence they form wrong opinions; or, while they form correct opinions, their rascality leads them to say what they do not think; or, while intelligent and honest enough, they are not well disposed [to the hearer, audience], and so perchance will fail to advise the best course, though they see it.*

ethos
The characteristic spirit of a culture, era, or community as seen in its beliefs and aspirations.

© 2012 Panos Karapanagiotis, Shutterstock, Inc.

FIGURE 4.11 The Greek philosopher Aristotle (384 to 322 BCE) wrote extensively about ethics as the study of human character.

Aristotle believed speakers could abuse their ethical relationship with their listeners when they misinterpret information or fail to collect all the information needed to give a complete and fair presentation, and when self-interest leads them to dishonesty and lack of goodwill. For example, a developer comes into a community in the hopes of building a large superstore and, in a public forum, explains how many jobs and how much revenue will be brought to the community. The developer's self-interest in this project may result in his leaving out information, such as the negative impact the superstore will have on employees and owners of the community's smaller businesses. As ethical speakers, we need to make sure that we do not deceive out audience through omitting relevant information, distorting facts, or deliberately confusing the listeners.

Since Aristotle, scholars have made the distinction between intrinsic ethos and extrinsic ethos. Whereas **intrinsic ethos** is the ethical appeal found in the actual speech, including such aspects as supporting material, argument flow, and source citation, **extrinsic ethos** is a speaker's image in the mind of the audience. Extrinsic aspects include perceived knowledge and expertise, perceived trustworthiness, and speaker confidence and enthusiasm. Both intrinsic and extrinsic ethos contribute to a speaker's credibility. Communication theorists James C. McCroskey and Thomas J. Young (1981) tie speaker credibility to the audience's perception of the speaker as an expert, as a person to trust, and as a person with positive and honest intent. If you are too casual, unprepared, and have ignored the necessity to provide support for your claims, your credibility will be limited and you will have a negative reputation to overcome. An ethical speaker takes credit for his or her own ideas and, through oral source citation, credits others for their ideas. An ethical speaker will not mislead others through omission or confusion.

Engage in Dialogue with the Audience

According to Richard L. Johannesen, a scholar in rhetorical and communication studies, monologic and dialogic communication tendencies are clear signs that indicate speaker sensitivity to ethical responsibility. The least sensitive speakers, says Johannesen, engage in what he describes as **monologic communication**. From this perspective, the audience is viewed as an object to be manipulated and, in the process, the speaker displays such qualities as deception, superiority, exploitation, dogmatism, domination, insincerity, pretense, coercion, distrust, and defensiveness—qualities Johannesen considers unethical. About such communication, he has written (1974):

> *Focus is on the speaker's message, not on the audience's real needs…Audience feedback is used only to further the speaker's purpose; an honest response from receiver is not wanted or is precluded…*

In contrast, **dialogic communication** entails an honest concern for a listener's interests. This kind of speech, Johannesen asserts, "communicates trust, mutual respect and acceptance, open-mindedness, equality, empathy, directness, lack of pretense, and non-manipulative intent. Although the speaker in dialogue may offer advice or express disagreement, he does not aim to psychologically coerce an audience into accepting his view. The speaker's aim is one of assisting the audience in making independent, self-determined decisions" (p. 99).

intrinsic ethos
Ethical appeal found in the actual speech, including such aspects as supporting material, argument flow, and source citation.

extrinsic ethos
A speaker's image in the mind of the audience. Extrinsic aspects include perceived knowledge and expertise, perceived trustworthiness, and speaker confidence and enthusiasm.

monologic communication
A form of communication in which the audience is viewed as an object to be manipulated and, in the process, the speaker displays such qualities as deception, superiority, exploitation, dogmatism, domination, insincerity, pretense, coercion, distrust, and defensiveness.

dialogic communication
Communication that demonstrates an honest concern for a listener's interests.

Public speaking is an audience-centered activity, so all decisions made in the development process should take the audience into consideration. As you recognize the importance of speaker credibility and project firm ethical standards, we encourage you to reflect on the following habits and guidelines.

4.5.5 Promoting Ethical Speaking Habits

Ethical speakers respect their own integrity and the audience. Respecting your own integrity includes being fully prepared and knowledgeable, researching all sides of your topic and presenting balanced information, being honest with the information and careful with communication techniques. Part of showing respect for yourself is avoiding plagiarism and properly citing your sources. Ethical speakers show respect for their audience when they are sensitive to differences and concerned about the audiences' reactions and perspectives.

The online lesson identifies a key element of ethical speaking: respect. See Topic 3.

You can enhance your integrity and promote ethical communication by developing some habits. Rhetorical theorist Karl Wallace (1955) identified four habits that promote ethical communication. The following descriptions of these habits are specific guidelines to help you address them.

Habit of Search

The habit of search refers to putting forth effort to learn enough about your topic so you are able to speak knowledgeably and confidently. As you speak before your class, try to realize that, at that moment, you are the primary source of information about your chosen topic. You are responsible for presenting a message that reflects thorough knowledge of the subject, sensitivity to relevant issues and implications, and awareness that many issues are multifaceted.

Habit of Justice

This habit reminds us to select and present facts and opinions openly and fairly. We should not distort or conceal evidence. Instead, we offer the audience the opportunity to make fair judgments. To illustrate this point, the Food and Drug Administration requires the pharmaceutical industry to disclose side effects of medications in advertising. As a result, the consumer has the opportunity to make a judgment based on known information.

Habit of Public Motivation

As a speaker, you need to determine whether your motives for speaking are purely personal or whether they go beyond your own concerns. Ethical speakers reveal the sources of their information and opinion, which assists the audience in weighing any special bias, prejudices, and self-centered motivations in source materials. Avoid concealing information about your source materials or your own motives because, if revealed, the effectiveness of your message will be weakened.

A person may be motivated to give an informative speech on the warning signs of methamphetamine (meth) abuse because of the rise in the number of meth users and meth-related deaths in her community. Clearly, her specific purpose meets the habit of preferring public to private motivation, assuming she has reliable information on meth use and meth-related deaths. In contrast to public motivation is private motivation. If a teacher tries to convince students to sign up for internships in his department, not because it is a beneficial academic experience, but because as internship coordinator, he gets paid per student, his motivation is private. Keeping such hidden agendas is unethical behavior.

Habit of Respect for Dissent

This habit addresses the necessity for accepting views that differ from our own. Respect for dissent allows for and encourages diversity of argument and opinion. It involves seeing a different point of view as a challenge rather than as a threat. It does not mean we have to give in. We can still advocate our convictions while acknowledging that others may be as firm in their opposition to us. Ideally, in a free marketplace of ideas, healthy debate would ensure truth and wisdom be served.

Guidelines for Meeting Ethical Habits

In order to ensure these four habits are incorporated into your speech development, consider the following guidelines and pitfalls.

1. **Recognize the Power of the Podium**

   Have you ever watched a commercial and decided you *had* to have that product? Have you been in church when a minister tells about a needy homeless shelter, and you were compelled to donate at that moment? Have you heard a message about environmental hazards created by plastic bottles and tossed your next bottle of water in the recycle bin? These examples indicate that speaking is a powerful activity.

   Speakers may have national forums through the media or through their positions, such as members of Congress, and some abuse the power. An historical example is the "witch hunt" that occurred in the 1950s when U.S. Senator Joseph R. McCarthy used the podium to attack government employees, educators, individuals in the entertainment industry, and union activists, claiming they were directly contributing to the rise in communism in the United States and were being disloyal and un-American. McCarthy took advantage of the power of the podium by playing up to people's fears, using dramatic oratory, manipulating facts, and accusing critics of disloyalty. Examples of abuses by other speakers are easy to find. As speakers, we need to be aware that we may have the power to persuade and the power to pass on information to others—powers that must be used for the common good.

2. **Speak Truthfully**

   Whenever you speak before an audience, it is your ethical responsibility to be certain of your facts. If you present material as being true when it is not, you mislead your listeners and diminish your credibility. When your listeners realize your facts are wrong, they will trust you less. If, for example, during a speech on campus thefts you blame students for the majority of crimes, when, in fact, most thefts are committed by city residents, you will lose credibility with listeners who know the facts.

3. **Become Information Literate**

   When collecting supporting material for a speech, it is your ethical responsibility to determine whether you are quoting a professional who has conducted research or someone who is simply writing a story. Often you can answer this question by digging a little deeper in the library or by checking key websites.

© CORBIS.

FIGURE 4.12 Joseph McCarthy used his position and power to make claims about how communism was infiltrating the United States. He targeted individuals who were subsequently blacklisted and marginalized.

Certain sources have more credibility than others. If you are researching the need for college students to update vaccinations with booster shots, an article in *The New England Journal of Medicine* or *Science* would be preferable to an article in *Newsweek* or *Time*. Although the latter publications are generally reliable, scientific journals are the better choice for this specific type of information. Wikipedia may be very informative but is generally not considered a reliable source on its own, and your instructor may not approve using it as a source.

Information literacy refers to the ability to consume information wisely and appropriately. A handy way to remember to do this is found in the acronym, *PART.* See chart on the facing page.

Our world is changing rapidly. Old facts are often wrong facts, especially in such volatile areas as public safety and civil liberties. As you prepare your speech, take into consideration the need for currency in matters and issues that are relevant now. If you find credible evidence that appears to undermine your position, be honest enough to evaluate it fairly and change your position if you must. Throughout this process, keep in mind your ethical obligation to present accurate information to your listeners. Here are a few more common pitfalls to keep in mind:

1. **Avoid Purposeful Ambiguity**

   When we leave out specific detail, we can paint a misleading picture. Choose words carefully to communicate your point. Realize, for example, that references to "hazing abuses" may conjure images of death and bodily injury to some, while others may think of harmless fraternity pranks. Similarly, choose your supporting materials carefully. Ambiguities often stem from inadequate or sloppy research.

2. **Avoid Rumors and Innuendo**

   It is unethical to base your speeches on rumors, which, of course, are everywhere. We may be guilty of listening to them, and perhaps passing them along. Rumors are unproven charges, usually about an individual, that are often untrue. By using them as facts, you can tarnish—or ruin—a reputation and convey misleading information to your audience.

   It is also ethically unacceptable to use innuendo to support a point. **Innuendo** includes hints or remarks that something is what it is not. Essentially, they are veiled lies. Innuendo frequently surfaces in the heat of a strongly contested political race. The exaggerated rhetoric of opponents results in observations ranging from misstatements about events to hints about improprieties in the alleged behavior of the political opponent. Just before Barack Obama announced his bid for the presidency, stories surfaced about his early childhood education. As a young child, he spent several years in Indonesia, where he attended school. In an attempt to discredit him, some claimed that he was taught a radical form of Islam during this time. These remarks were proved to be untrue. An ethical speaker avoids any use of rumor or innuendo when preparing a speech. (See **FIGURE 4.13**.)

information literacy
The ability to articulate one's information needs; refers to the ability to consume information wisely and appropriately.

innuendo
Made up of hints or remarks that something is what it is not. Essentially, they are veiled lies.

PARTS

Point of View

Recognize whether there is a point of view or bias. Is the information making every attempt at being objective or is it likely biased to serve a special interest? Even if a source claims to be "fair and balanced," you may not be getting an unbiased view from any one reporter of that organization. Complicating matters more, oftentimes personalities play at different times the role of reporter in one instance and commentator in another. Discerning point of view is critical to consuming information intelligently.

Authority

Consider the credentials of both the author and publisher. Are they recognized as experts and/or leaders in the field? Does the author hold a terminal degree such as Ph.D. or M.D.? Is the publisher a scholarly or reputable news source? The issue of authority is challenging online. It is not always clear who is responsible for content on some web pages and blogs. In these cases, it is best to look for independent confirmation in other locations to ensure accuracy.

Reliability

Even if the point of view seems unbiased and the source checks out, consider whether you can believe in the accuracy and treatment of the information. Reliability is related to the credibility, or believability, of the source. Outdated information will not be as reliable as current information. Also, the speaker needs to determine whether or not the information makes sense, especially in light of where it was found. For example, recent research has shown that there are health benefits to eating chocolate and drinking a glass of red wine each day. Now, if the wine or cocoa industries commissioned those studies, one might question the reliability of the findings. If the science community came to these conclusions after independent tests, the information has greater credibility. An ethical speaker will look for the most recent, authentic, and unbiased information.

Timeliness

Timeliness refers to how current or up-to-date your information is. In some cases, information as recent as last year may be outdated. Depending on the topic, some information is still timely hundreds of years later. Evaluate how important recent information is to your topic as you gather information.

Consider this: If your specific purpose is to inform your class on the latest technology for diabetes management, a simple search may lead you to the insulin pump. However, by probing a little further and finding more recent information, you should find articles about the insulin inhaler, which has just recently hit the market.

Scope

Scope refers to the extent of your research. Check to see that your research has both depth and breadth. Does the information create an overview or develop a narrow portion of your topic? Determine who the information is intended for, and whether information is too technical and clinical, or too basic. Is it appropriate for a college audience?

© 2012 Entertainment Press/Shutterstock.com, Shutterstock, Inc.

FIGURE 4.13 Tom Cruise and Katie Holmes are the subject of constant rumors. Ethical speakers do not use rumors to make a point.

3. Uphold Unpopular Ideas

Speaking in support of the public good implies a willingness to air a diversity of opinions, even when these opinions are unpopular. According to Roderick Hart (1985), professor of communication, we must "accept boat rocking, protests, and free speech as a necessary and desirable part of [our] tradition" (p. 162). Your goal as a speaker can be to encourage the "ideal of the best ideas rising to the surface of debate" (p. 46).

Despite the statute of free speech in Western society, taking an unpopular stand at the podium is not easy, especially when the speaker faces the threat of repercussions. In the United States, a debate continues over intelligent design theory as a challenge to Darwin's theory of evolution. Dr. Richard Sternberg, editor of a highly respected scientific journal, was harassed and treated punitively after he published a paper on intelligent design by Stephen C. Meyer of Cambridge University. Meyer argued that intelligent design should be taken seriously. Having allowed the article to be published, Sternberg was the recipient of harsh criticism by officials of the Smithsonian Institution and the National Center for Science Education (NCSE). Sternberg indicated false charges were made against him. Some charged that he had not sought peer reviews of Meyer's essay. Some charged him with taking money under the table, and others called for his resignation as editor. Sternberg believes these accusations were all attempts to prevent scientific dissent. The message to him, in other words, was to be a gatekeeper of *acceptable* scientific ideas or "Don't rock the boat," which can be viewed as an unethical proposition.

4. **Avoid Hidden Agendas**

Suppose you are a real estate agent with a home for sale in a suburban community that is suffering from the real estate recession. There are many homes for sale but few buyers. You are among dozens of agents who will find it difficult to make a satisfactory living unless conditions improve. In order to attract potential homebuyers to your community, you give a series of speeches in a nearby city, extolling the virtues of suburban life. Although much of what you say is true, you bend some facts to make your community seem the most attractive and affordable. For example, you tell your listeners there are jobs available, when, in fact, the job market is slight (the rosy employment figures you use are a decade old). You mention that the community schools are among the top in the state, when, in fact, only one in five is ranked above the state average. With your goal of restoring your community to its former economic health, you feel justified in this manipulation.

Do the ends justify the means? While your intentions were good, your ethics were faulty. As a speaker, you have only one ethical choice: to present the strongest possible legitimate argument and let each listener decide whether or not to support your position.

5. **Avoid Excessive and Inappropriate Emotional Appeals**

As listeners, we expect speakers to make assertions that are supported by sound reasoning. We expect the speech to flow logically, and to include relevant supporting material. However, some speakers prey on our fears or ignorance and rely heavily on the use of excessive and inappropriate appeals to emotion. To be ethical, emotional appeals must be built on a firm foundation of good reasoning and should never be used to take advantage of susceptible listeners. In Chapter 11 on persuasive speaking, we examine further the nature of emotional appeals. However, following are four circumstances that create particularly troublesome ethical concerns.

Deception

Your speech creates a need in your audience through deception and requires an action that will primarily benefit you. It is manipulative and unethical to try to convince a group of parents that the *only way* their children will succeed in school is to purchase an educational program that is comprehensive in detail, according to the company *you* represent.

Manipulation

The emotional appeal is aimed at taking advantage of those particularly susceptible to manipulation. A bit of channel surfing late at night will bring the viewer to quite a number of infomercials full of emotional appeals to persuade the viewer to purchase expensive programs that are supposed to lead them to considerable wealth, health, or both.

Confusion

Emotional appeals are part of a sustained plan to confuse an audience and make them feel insecure and helpless. If, as a community leader, you oppose the effort to establish group homes for the developmentally handicapped by referring repeatedly to the threat these residents pose to the neighborhood children, you leave your listeners feeling vulnerable and frightened. Fear can become so intense that homeowners may dismiss facts and expert opinions that demonstrate developmentally disabled persons are neither violent nor emotionally disadvantaged.

Fallacies

You realize your logic will not hold up under scrutiny, so you appeal to audience emotions to disguise the deficit. Instead of relying on facts to convince your listeners, you appeal to their emotional needs. There are many ways unethical speakers disguise and deceive in order to achieve their specific purpose. Among them are the following: name calling, glittering generalities, testimonials, plain folks, and bandwagon. We will cover more about logical fallacies in Chapter 11 on persuasive speaking.

Fallacies

Bandwagoning is trying to convince listeners to support a point of view by telling them that "everyone else" is already involved. Example: "You need to come with us—everyone will be there."

© 2012 mtkang/Shutterstock.com, Shutterstock, Inc.

McDonald's uses a bandwagon appeal to encourage people to purchase their products.

Glittering generalities rely on audience's emotional responses to values such as home, country, and freedom. Example: *"Real Americans and patriots will support me"*

Name calling involves linking a person or group with a negative symbol. Example: *"Don't believe her; she's a liar and she's jealous of me."*

Plain folks is an effort to identify with the audience. Be cautious when a speaker tells an audience. Example: Politicians who are photographed with shirtsleeves rolled up—as if they are working in an office like "regular" people.

Testimonials involve using someone else's statement to endorse your point. Example: *"I go to see Dr. Bill (chiropractor) when I get bent out of shape on Sundays. Playing in a football game is like being in 30-40 car accidents."* Emmitt Smith (NFL All-time leading rusher)

4.5.6 Avoiding Unethical Practices

In *Ethics in Communication* (1990, p. 254), Richard L. Johannesen provides a number of ways speakers can avoid engaging in unethical speaking practices. The following questions relate to developing and presenting your ideas.

When Developing Your Speech, Ask Yourself:

- Have I used false, fabricated, misrepresented, distorted, or irrelevant evidence to support my arguments or claims?
- Have I intentionally used unsupported, misleading, or illogical reasoning?
- Have I oversimplified complex situations into simplistic either-or, polar views or choices?

When Giving Your Speech, Ask Yourself:

- Will I represent myself as informed or as being an "expert" on a subject when I am not?
- Will I deceive my audience by concealing my real purpose, self-interest, the group I represent, or my position as an advocate of a viewpoint?
- Will I distort, hide, or misrepresent the number, scope, intensity, or undesirable aspects of consequences or effects?
- Will I use "emotional appeals" that lack a supporting basis of evidence or reasoning, or that would not be accepted if the audience had time and opportunity to examine the subject themselves?
- Will I pretend certainty where tentativeness and degrees of probability would be more accurate?
- Will I advocate something in which I do not believe myself?

Chapter Summary

The most important relationship in public speaking is the relationship between speaker and audience. Being audience-centered means learning everything you can about your audience so you can meet its needs in your topic and your approach. Start by analyzing your audience based on demographics and psychographics. If you can learn what motivates your audience, how they spend their time, and what amuses them, you will be more likely to make a connection with them.

Successful speakers define the expectations that surround the speaking occasion. They learn how much interest their audience has in their topic and how much their audience knows about it before they get up to speak. Audience analysis is accomplished through the use of questionnaires based on fixed-alternative questions, scale questions, and open-ended questions. Audience analysis can also be conducted through observation and interviews.

To ensure a speaker-audience connection, show your listeners at the start of your speech how you will help them; have confidence your audience wants to hear you, even if they are more knowledgeable than you are. Present yourself as fitting into the group, rather than as being superior to the group. Refer to people in your audience and involve your listeners in your speech. When your speech is over, try to determine your audience's response through a post-speech evaluation-questionnaire.

Because of the many ethical abuses that have taken place in recent years, audiences have become skeptical about the ethics of public speakers. Ethical public speaking is anchored in the values of the speaker, his or her audience, and the larger society. Ethical speakers engage in a "dialogue" with their audience, communicating qualities such as trust and directness, while unethical speakers engage in a "monologue" as they manipulate their audience to their own end.

Once you have chosen your speech topic, recognize that ethics are part of every step of speech development and remember these guidelines: understand the power of the podium, speak truthfully and know your facts, use credible sources, use current and reliable information, avoid purposeful ambiguity, avoid rumors and innuendo, be willing to rock the boat, be clear in your motives, and avoid excessive and inappropriate emotional appeals and logical fallacies.

Key Terms

attitudes, 101

beliefs, 101

demographics, 91

dialogic communication, 115

ethics, 112

ethnicity, 95

ethnocentrism, 95

ethos, 114

extrinsic ethos, 115

fixed-alternative questions, 102

heterogeneous, 92

homogeneous, 92

information literacy, 118

innuendo, 118

intrinsic ethos, 115

monologic communication, 115

open-ended questions, 103

psychographic analysis, 92

psychographics, 92

questionnaire, 101

race, 95

sampling, 102

scale questions, 102

survey, 101

values, 101

Questions for Reflection

1. Why will a speech fail in the absence of audience analysis?
2. Why are some demographic characteristics important to the success of your speech in one situation but not so important in other situation?
3. How are behaviors, attitudes, beliefs, and values related?
4. Can speakers be ethical and adapt to their audiences at the same time?
5. Does adaptation imply audience manipulation or meeting the audience's needs?
6. What underlying principles should you use to conduct an effective audience analysis?
7. What steps can you take to ensure a positive speaker-audience connection?
8. How would you define the ethical responsibilities for a public speaker?
9. Who are public speakers you can think of who are not mentioned in this chapter but who you believe have spoken ethically and/or unethically?
10. What do you believe is an appropriate ethical relationship between self-interest and the needs of the audience?

Activities

1. Focusing on the specific purpose of your next speech, analyze the students in your public speaking class who will be your audience. Conduct several in-depth interviews with your classmates. Circulate a questionnaire. Based on the information you gather, develop an audience profile. Write a three- to four-page paper describing the attitudes, values, interests, and knowledge of your listeners as they relate to your topic and you. Finally, outline a strategy of audience adaptation that will serve your interests and the interests of your listeners.

2. Before delivering another speech, give every member of your class, including your instructor, an index card on which a seven-point scale is drawn, with 1 being the most negative point on the scale and 7 being the most positive. Ask your classmates to register the degree to which your speech was relevant to them. If most of the responses fall below the scale midpoint, analyze how you could have prepared a more successful speech.

3. Select a recent speech you have attended or a famous speech about which you have read that exemplifies a successful audience adaptation. In a written paper, analyze the factors that contributed to the audience's positive response and present your findings to the class. Conduct the same analysis for a speech that failed to meet the audience's needs.

4. Locate and select a speech—either in print or recorded—and critically analyze it in terms of the ethics of responsible speech.

5. Select a speaker and one of his/her speeches that you believe possesses considerable ethical appeal and write a brief paper on what you believe to be the speaker's intrinsic and extrinsic ethos.

6. Write a short paper or prepare a speech for delivery on the proposition that "through public speaking we wield enormous power for good and for evil." Then meet in small groups in class to discuss and explore each other's points of view.

References

Canary, D. J., and Hause, K. S. (1993). "Is there any reason to research sex differences in communication?" *Communication Quarterly, 41*, 129–144.

Churchill, G. A., Jr. (1983). *Marketing research: Methodological foundations* (3rd ed.). Chicago: The Dryden Press.

Cooper, L. (1960). *The rhetoric of Aristotle.* New York: Appleton-Century-Crofts.

Ferrell, W. (2003, June 4). Speech delivered on Harvard Class Day. Transcribed from video uploaded to www.youtube.com.

Hart, R. (1985). The politics of communication studies: An address to undergraduates. *Communication Education, 34*, 162.

Holland, J. "Whose children are these? The family connection," speech delivered at the 1988 Conference for the Association of Childhood Education International, April 23, 1988. Reprinted in *Vital Speeches of the Day*, July 1, 1988, 559.

Johannesen, R. L. (1974). Attitude of speaker toward audience: A significant concept for contemporary rhetorical theory and criticism. *Central States Speech Journal, 25*(2), 95–104.

——— (1990). *Ethics in communication.* Prospect Heights, IL: Waveland Press.

Kiechel, W. (1987, June 8). How to give a speech. *Fortune, 115*(12), 179.

Kushner, H. S. (2002). *When all you've ever wanted isn't enough: The search for a life that matters.* New York: Random House.

McCroskey, J. C., & Young, T. J. (1981). Ethos and credibility: The construct and its measurement after three decades. *Central States Speech Journal, 32*, 24–34.

Newsweek/Beliefnet Poll (2005, September 5). "Where we stand on faith." *Newsweek*, pp. 48–49.

Rackleff, R. B. "The art of speechwriting: A dramatic event," delivered to the National Association of Bar Executives Section on Communications and Public Relations, September 26, 1987. Reprinted in *Vital Speeches of the Day*, March 1, 1988.

Time magazine poll. Retrrieved from http://www.timepolls.com/hppolls/archive/poll_results_417.html

Wallace, K. (1987). An ethical basis of communication. *The Speech Teacher, 4*, 1–9.

Wolffe, R. (2008, January 6). "In his candidate's voice." *Newsweek*. Retrieved from http://www.thedailybeast.com/newsweek12008/01/05/in-his-candidate-s-voice.html

Woodward, G. C., & Denton, R. E., Jr. (2004). *Persuasion and influence in American life* (5th ed.). Long Grove, Ill.: Waveland Press.

Creating:

Speechwriting Tactics for Powerful Presentations

Unit 2

Chapter

5

© 2012, Ilya Ziatyev, Shutterstock, Inc.

Learning Objectives

After reading this chapter and completing the online activities for this lesson, you will be able to:

1. Select an audience-centered topic that fits the constraints of the assignment or situation.

2. Continue to develop your speech once a more appropriate topic is chosen.

3. Critique your speech.

Speech Preparation and Critiquing Speeches

INTRODUCTION

I remember the first time I prepared and delivered a speech. I was in sixth grade and had to give a 5-7 minute speech. The topic seemed easy—"introduce yourself." Well, I was new to the school, so no one really knew me, which made it both easier and harder. I wanted my new classmates to like me, so I knew my speech had to be good. The prior summer, during a vacation in Florida, my family had gone to a wax museum that featured a lot of different movie and TV stars, including replicas of Fonzie, Christopher Reeve as Superman, and Dolly Parton. We had lots of pictures, so I decided to use those pictures to tell the audience about my family—my dad Superman, my older brother Fonzie, and my mom Dolly. My thesis was, "To know about me, you have to know about my family." I organized my speech around different family members and the funny things they've done. I used the photos (enlarged so the whole audience could see them) to "introduce" my family. I spent hours organizing my speech and practicing so that I would feel confident in front of the class. However, I was so nervous that I was afraid I would forget everything or drop all my pictures.

On speech day, all the other kids gave pretty serious speeches—no one had created a family of celebrities, which made me even more nervous. When my turn came, I got up in front of all these kids I did not know and opened with a picture of Superman. At first the class was really quiet. Then one kid, Brad, started to laugh, and then others started to laugh, and I knew it was going to be okay. The audience critiqued me and thought I was funny; the teacher critiqued me and told me I received the second highest score! (He gave me a lot of feedback on how I could improve.) I was so relieved. I look back now and wonder what might be different in my life if that first speech had not gone so well—if I had not prepared so thoroughly and if the critiques I received had not been so helpful. Today, I am a college professor who teaches communication. I speak to audiences almost every day, but I still remember that feeling of connecting with the audience.

—**Virginia "Ginny" McDermott**

FIGURE 5.1 The inspiration for your speech can come from many places. Dolly Parton can inspire a speech about family, so be willing to be creative when selecting speech topics.

© 2012 stocklight/Shutterstock.com, Shutterstock, Inc.

© 2012 Petro Feketa, Shutterstock, Inc.

FIGURE 5.2 The more you know about your audience and the better you prepare, the more likely you are to achieve your intended effect.

Whether you embrace the opportunity for public speaking or feel the urge to run away, there are many things you can do to enhance your potential for success. What follows is an overview of key steps you should follow when preparing and presenting a speech. This overview is particularly important for your first major speech, although by now you have probably spoken in front of your classmates at least once.

Keep in mind that movement among these steps is normal. Also, more information about research, organization, and delivery will be found in the following chapters. Our goal throughout this textbook is to increase your knowledge about public speaking and your skill as a speaker and as a listener.

5.1 Selecting an Audience-Centered Topic

What Are You Going to Talk About?

This may be the most challenging part of preparing your speech. You talk to people every day, so you know you have plenty to say. However, in conversation, we can rely on the other person to also say things, which we use to figure out what to say next. In a speech, we do all the talking, which is intimidating. So, pick a topic you feel comfortable talking about. As you read in the opening story, Ginny talked about her family. She was more comfortable talking about them than she was talking about herself—and, with a large family, she had plenty of material.

It is never too early to think about possible topics for all your speeches during this term. Some students find a topic within five minutes of hearing about the assignment; for others, it may take weeks of reflection. This section is designed to make topic selection a productive experience for you.

Know the Constraints of the Speaking Assignment

- Is your general purpose to inform, persuade, or entertain?
- How long is the speech supposed to be?
- How much time do you have to prepare?
- What type of supporting material do you need?
- Do you have to incorporate sources?

Knowing the guidelines for the assignment will get you started in the right direction. Whether it is a speech for class, a speech at a fund-raiser, or a briefing at work, it is important to understand what is expected of you.

5.1.1 Use Different Methods to Generate Topics

Some instructors will give you a topic and others will provide strict limits. If you can choose, however, often the best place to begin your search for a speech topic is yourself. When the topic springs from your own interests, personal experience, or work experience, you bring to it motivation and information necessary for a good speech.

If no ideas come to you when thinking about a speech topic, develop an **interest chart** (see FIGURE 5.3). Write down two or three broad categories representing subjects of interest to you and divide the categories into parts.

interest chart
A visual display of possible topics.

As you can see in the chart below, the broad topic of politics can quickly become nine different topics. You can do this with any topic: sports, music, history, organizations, culture, travel. If you are having trouble thinking of a topic, select three broad topics and diagram the subtopics.

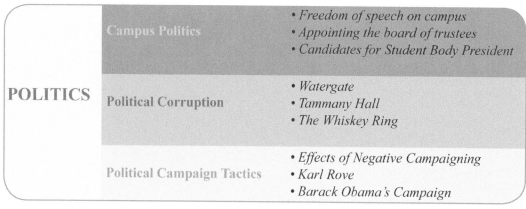

FIGURE 5.3 Using an interest chart, like the one shown above, will help you identify interesting components of broader topics. Start with a general interest, identify interesting subparts, and generate specific speech ideas.

5.1.2 Focus on Audience Factors and Length of Speech

Choosing a topic you know is the best place to begin, but you should also approach topic selection by determining *what your listeners might want to hear*. There may be some topics that you are really interested in, but it is important to think about your audience. For example, you may know a lot about the artificial insemination of cattle (including how to get the necessary material from the bulls), but perhaps your audience is not as fascinated with this topic. Although your authors think that almost any topic can be made interesting to an audience, some topics are more challenging and need to be carefully considered. Also, you should remember that not all topics are appropriate for classroom presentations.

Your online lesson provides resources that can help you coherently "map out" your ideas. See Topic 1.

brainstorming
A group activity intended to generate a large quantity of topics. Contributions are not judged while being generated.

If interest charts do not help you, you can ask your friends to **brainstorm** with you for topics. Brainstorming is a technique that will help you generate a large and varied list of topics. For topic identification, this is a two-step process: in step one, you should focus on quantity not quality. Ask your friends to take three to five minutes and just say all the topics they can think of; no one should criticize any topics offered. In fact, encourage unusual ideas. In step two, you and your friends should go through the list and discuss which topics might be most interesting.

In addition to selecting topics that you have interest in or your listeners want to hear, you can work to find a topic through current events and media prompts. For example, you could do an Internet search on "current events" or "top headlines" or "sports" or "politics." Broad topics will lead you to other topics. TABLE 5.1 below offers several possible topics:

Brainstorming is a technique to generate a large number of topics. Group members all generate topic ideas—in step one, everyone focuses on quantity not quality. No one should criticize any topics offered. In fact, unusual ideas should be welcomed.

In step two, the group should discuss which topics might be most interesting.

© 2012 winui, Shutterstock, Inc.

Through brainstorming, many topic ideas are gathered together.

TABLE 5.1 Broad Topics		
Acupuncture	Immigration legislation	Queen Noor
Biodiesel fuel	Job search skills	Reincarnation
Cameras in the courtroom	Killer bees	Salaries for athletes
Dream analysis	Learning disabilities	Teacher competency tests
Education cuts	Minimum wage	Unions
Food pyramid change	Noise pollution	Volunteering
Ghosts	Organ donation	World religions
Home schooling	Prison reform	Zero tolerance policies

Do not assume, however, that *any* topic is relevant. Some topics have been used so often, there isn't much left to say. If you are interested in a topic such as "smoking," think about your approach. Ask yourself, "Is this something they've heard 100 times before, or is there a new or creative approach I can take?" If you can't think of a new approach, then you might want to delete smoking as a topic. If you have a wealth of information, you need to determine what must be left out. If you do not have much knowledge about the topic, recognize where you need to do research, or choose another topic. If you know about the background of your audience, you can decide what information is most relevant and how much time should be spent on each point.

Linking Your Topic to Your Audience

Chapter 4 provided guidelines for analyzing and adapting to your audience. Knowing your audience will also help you select a topic and supporting material. In a college public speaking class, you may share similar background factors such as age, level of education, and geographical location. It is likely that you know *something* about your audience, but it is unlikely that you know all you need to know for an effective speech. We cannot stress how important it is to be audience-centered as you think about a topic. As stated throughout this textbook, public speaking is an audience-centered activity. Your reason for presenting a speech is to communicate your message to others in the clearest and most convincing way. One of the most important messages we have to impart is the following: ***An effective speaker analyzes and adapts to the audience***. In Chapter 4, we identified strategies for learning about your audience. After you've identified your topic, you should ask yourself a few more questions:

- What does the audience know about my potential topic(s)?
- Do they lean toward my point of view, or away from it?
- How does the setting and occasion influence my audience?
- What other factors might affect how my audience responds to me and/or my topic?

You have many decisions to make when selecting a topic that relate to the above questions. Audience demographics and knowledge of your potential topics may lead you to the conclusion that certain topics have been heard enough, or that there is little new to impart to an already knowledgeable audience. It is possible that your audience expects you to select a particular topic, or they believe you will present arguments that they "knew" you would cover. What should you do? Capitalize on how you're known or move out of your comfort zone.

5.1.3 Determine the General Purpose and Specific Purpose

What is your main purpose? Are you trying to entertain your audience, persuade them to change an attitude or behavior, or are you planning to provide them with information? The time you spend preparing your speech may be of little value if you do not determine what you want your speech to accomplish. At the beginning, you should clarify the general purpose and the specific purpose of your speech. Once accomplished, determine your thesis statement, which is the expression of your main idea.

General Purpose

general purpose
To inform, persuade, or entertain.

There are three **general purposes** for speeches:

1. to inform
2. to persuade
3. to entertain or inspire

If you want to explain the differences between a scooter and a motorcycle, the general purpose of your speech would be "to inform." If you think having a scooter on campus is more beneficial to students than driving a car, your general purpose would be "to persuade." If you hope to make people laugh after eating a good meal, your general purpose is "to entertain." Your instructor may tell you what the general purpose is, but it is important that you understand your purpose. If you are supposed to give an informative speech, make sure you are not selecting a persuasive topic.

Keep in mind, however, that it is difficult to deliver a speech that is *just* informative, *just* persuasive, or *just* entertaining. Often, in the perception of listeners, the purposes may converge or overlap. For example, as a speaker informs her audience about various options for eating a healthy breakfast each day, some audience members may interpret her speech as an attempt to persuade them to change their daily behavior.

To split or not split the infinitive? That is the question for English teachers

An infinitive is the basic form of a verb. An infinitive phrase expresses an action in its simplest form. It is usually preceded by the word "to": to inform; to persuade; to go; to buy. To write an effective purpose statement, be sure to start with a clear statement of what you want to achieve: to inform, to persuade, or to entertain. A clear infinitive statement will help you narrow your topic and select the appropriate supporting material.

Infinitive ———— Space   the Final Frontier. These are the voyages of the starship *Enterprise*.
Split Infinitive ———— Its five-year mission: to explore strange new worlds, to seek out new life and new civilizations, to boldly go where no man has gone before.

Specific Purpose

Once the general purpose is set for your speech, determine the **specific purpose**—the precise response you want from your audience. The specific purpose is important because it helps you focus your research and narrow down your support material. Specific purpose statements should be expressed as an **infinitive phrase** that includes the general purpose as well as the main thrust of your speech (this will usually be at the top of your speech outline). The specific purpose also identifies who the intended audience is. Here are two examples of specific purposes:

specific purpose
The precise response you want from your audience.

infinitive phrase
Expresses an action in its simplest form.

1. To inform the class of differences between the operations of an on-campus political club and an off-campus political party.
2. To persuade the Student Senate that requiring all college students to participate in service-learning projects benefits the student, college, and community.

Because the specific purpose identifies the audience who will hear your speech, it guides you in speech preparation. A speech on health care reform given before a group of college students should be constructed differently than a speech on the same topic given before an audience of retirees.

Below are two specific purpose statements written differently. See if you can pick out which is correct.

- **Topic 1A:** To persuade my audience that the Federal Drug Administration (FDA) should mandate regulation of dietary supplements.
- **Topic 1B:** To persuade my audience that the FDA should regulate dietary supplements and print more warning labels on prescriptions.
- **Topic 2A:** To inform my audience on the negative aspects of the Barbie doll.
- **Topic 2B:** To inform my audience on the positive and negative aspects of the Barbie doll.

A specific purpose statement should be written with one goal in mind. With the first topic, "A" is correct. "B" is incorrect because there are two different topics: dietary supplements and warning labels on prescriptions. Also, a specific purpose statement must be clear to all readers. Did you know what "FDA" was? Since it's likely that some people don't know, it makes sense to spell out the name first, and put the initials in parentheses. With the second topic, statement "A" is a persuasive speech that has been falsely identified as an informative speech. With little exception, without presenting both negative and positive aspects, your speech is inherently persuasive.

thesis statement
A one-sentence summary.

Although the general and specific purpose statements set the goals for your speech, the thesis statement, or your core idea, focuses on what you want to say. The **thesis statement** is the central message you want listeners to take with them; it's a one-sentence summary. (The thesis statement is frequently written or rewritten after the speech is fully outlined). The following examples show how one moves from a topic to the thesis statement.

> **Topic:** Study abroad
>
> **General purpose:** To inform
>
> **Specific purpose:** To explain to my class what is involved in the study abroad options available to them at our university.
>
> **Thesis statement:** Students interested in earning college credit while studying abroad have several options that differ in terms of academic content, location, length of stay, potential number of credit hours, and cost.
>
> **Topic: Study abroad**
>
> **General purpose:** To persuade
>
> **Specific purpose:** To convince my class that studying abroad will be a life-changing experience.
>
> **Thesis statement:** Studying abroad can be a life-changing experience because students gain knowledge in an academic area, face the unfamiliar, and interact with individuals from a different culture.

As you can see, although the topic is "study abroad," there are different aspects of studying abroad that one could address. The above example shows choices for an informative speech and persuasive speech. A speech with the general purpose to entertain could include humorous examples and illustrations of the trials and tribulations of studying abroad.

Remember that your speech has one of three general purposes, which, on the outline, should be stated in the infinitive. The specific purpose is an infinitive phrase, not a sentence. It should express one goal, not multiple goals. The thesis statement is one idea and should be stated as one cohesive thought.

A *thesis sentence* is a one-sentence summary of your speech. A thesis sentence provides you the answer to the question: "What is your speech about?"

Getting started on your speech is often difficult, so it is important to know how to generate topics that your audience will be interested in learning more about. Brainstorming, interest charts, and media prompts are a few of the ways to generate topics. When finalizing the decision, you need to consider your audience and the situations—not all topics are appropriate for all audience or all situations. Part of selecting a topic is identifying your general purpose: to inform, persuade, or entertain. After you've identified a topic that suits the general purpose, write your specific purpose, which identifies your audience and the response you want from them. Finally, write your thesis statement, which is a one-sentence summary of your speech.

5.2 Continue to Develop Your Speech

Once you've narrowed down your topic and developed your general and specific purpose statements, you need to start developing your speech. The next few chapters will help you research your topic, organize the material, create an outline, and make your presentation more interesting with language and presentational aids. To help you get started, we will preview some of the key parts of developing your speech.

5.2.1 Identify the Main Points

The body of your speech contains your key ideas and relevant supporting material. Main points help you organize your information. For example, you're interested in politics and think that political corruption would get the audience's attention. Since most of your classmates weren't born until 20 years after President Nixon's Watergate scandal, you thought they would want to know more about this important event. You conduct an audience analysis, and most of your class has heard of Watergate but do not really know what it was about. This is a perfect topic for your informative speech—now all you need to do is select your main points. You list the twelve topics you think the audience would want to know more about (see TABLE 5.2):

TABLE 5.2 Watergate Topics		
Woodward & Bernstein	"Deep Throat"—the anonymous source	Nixon's speeches
G. Gordon Liddy	Haldeman & Ehrlichman	The aftermath of the resignation
The Watergate Hotel	Nixon's resignation	Movies about Nixon and the scandal
The break-in	President Ford's pardon of Nixon	Walter Cronkite

You know right away that twelve points are too many. As you keep looking at your list, you notice that some of the points are related (Woodward & Bernstein, "Deep Throat," and Walter Cronkite) and some points aren't as central (Movies & Nixon's speeches). You decide to think about which points are the really important ones you want your audience to remember, and you decide:

a. The investigation
b. The hearings
c. The pardon

These main points will help you organize your information. Perhaps more important, organizing your speech around main points will help your audience remember the information you shared.

5.2.2   Develop Content through Research and Sound Support

Each main point made should be backed up by research and sound support. For example, if you want to persuade your audience that sales tax instead of real estate tax should be used to fund education, concrete evidence will be necessary to support your specific purpose. You can look for evidence at your library, on the Internet, through your local Board of Education, or your state or congressional representatives. Chapter 7 focuses on research and supporting materials, so for now, just realize that appropriate research is critical to your speech, and if you are having difficulties, speak with your instructor and/or ask a librarian.

5.2.3   Determine Where to Incorporate Technology

Before leaving this section about speech preparation, a brief discussion about technology is important. You will note that Chapter 13 is devoted to speaking in an electronic world, but for each speech, you need to decide whether or not technology should be incorporated and where it might be placed most effectively. You have several decisions to make when it comes to the use of technology.

First, not all speeches will be enhanced by technology. Although audiences may expect technology as part of presentation, you should make the decision about technology based on your topic, your situation, and your audience. For example, some speeches may be too short to warrant its use. Second, presentational software such as PowerPoint should not be the default use of technology, since using such presentational software to outline the major points of your speech may not be necessary or effective. Third, if you don't have time to practice your speech using the technology, you may be facing a train wreck. Your flash drive may not work, the set-up may not be easy to figure out, and the technology you hope to use may not be available.

© 2012 Dmitriy Shironosov, Shutterstock, Inc.

FIGURE 5.4 A library is a great place to start your research. Although online materials can be very helpful, your supporting material should come from a variety of sources.

© 2012 Alpha Spirit, Shutterstock, Inc.

FIGURE 5.5 There are many technology options for your speech. First, be certain that technology would enhance your speech. Second, pick the right technology. Third, know how to use the technology during your speech.

There are a lot of technology options for your speech. First, be certain that technology would enhance your speech. Second, pick the right technology. Third, know how to use the technology during your speech.

Once you know your speech topic and have identified your main points, you should consider whether or not to use technology, and if you choose to use it, determine where it will be most effective. Using technology could involve something as simple as a clicking on a relevant web site, using PowerPoint slides, or showing a YouTube clip. You might use multiple forms of media, and have music, video, and slides. No matter what you choose, it should enhance your message in some way and not substitute for content.

5.2.4 Draft the Introduction and Conclusion

If you spend days researching your first speech but only a few hours organizing your ideas, the result is likely to be a speech that fails to present your message in a focused way. To be effective, speeches require an easy-to-follow organizational plan that makes it possible for others to receive and understand your message. As you will see in Chapters 7 and 8, the logical way to organize your speech is to divide it into three parts: the introduction, body, and conclusion.

Introduction

Your first task as a speaker is to capture your audience's attention. You have a short period of time to get the audience to focus on you and your topic. This is why the introduction of your speech is so important. Although it is usually only 10 to 15 percent of the speech, the introduction is crucial. The **introduction** should capture the attention and interest of your audience, establish your credibility as a speaker, and preview your speech. You can accomplish these aims in many ways, such as humorous anecdotes or a dramatic or startling statement. For his informative speech, Jesse started with the following:

> *You walk into a bar, sit down, and notice something oddly unfamiliar. Where are the beer taps? Where are the liquor bottles? All you see are fish, tentacles, and an assortment of brightly colored items that are not familiar. You've walked into a sushi bar, my friend. I fell in love with sushi years ago, and so have millions of other Americans. Sushi has become increasingly popular over the past several years, and it has become a major force in the restaurant industry and culinary arts. My passion with sushi began when I started managing a sushi lounge in downtown Memphis called Bluefin. Throughout my three years at Bluefin, I learned quite a bit about the art form of making sushi. In order to appreciate sushi it helps to understand its history, the different styles, and common terms and ingredients associated with sushi.*

In his introduction, Jesse captures our attention through his vivid description of the bar. He establishes credibility by noting his work experience. Finally, in his last sentence, he presents a preview statement, which lets his audience know what he intends to cover in the body of his speech. He accomplishes the three goals of an effective introduction.

introduction
The first part of the speech, which includes the attention getter, preview, and frequently allows the speaker to establish credibility. Generally, the introduction comprises 10 to 15 percent of the entire speech.

conclusion
The final part of the speech, which includes a summary of main points, the final take-away message, and provides closure for the audience. Usually, the conclusion comprises 5 to 10 percent of the entire speech.

Conclusion

Your concluding remarks have three purposes: (1) to reinforce the message, (2) to summarize the main points, and (3) to provide closure in some way that relates your message to your listeners' lives. **Conclusions** are frequently the shortest part of the speech—perhaps 5 to 10 percent. Your final thought may take the form of a quotation, a statement, or a question that reinforces or even broadens the purpose of your speech. The conclusion of a persuasive speech may also describe the specific actions you want your listeners to take. A common technique in conclusions is to bring the speech "full circle" and tie the conclusion back to the introduction. Jesse accomplished the goals of a conclusion this way:

> *Now when you walk into a bar and see all the brightly colored fish and seafood, you have a better idea of what you just walked into. With knowledge on the history of sushi, its different styles, and common terms and ingredients, you can steer your palate in the right direction. I urge even the timid to try sushi, and try it more than once to experience the different flavors, textures, and styles. Sushi is not a fad, and sushi will make its way to your neck of the woods soon enough if it hasn't already. Impress your date with a bit of knowledge when you go to the new trendy sushi spot.*
>
> *I bet you'll look like quite the gourmet.*

5.2.5   Develop the Language of the Speech with Care

An enthusiastic young woman looked out into the audience of almost 1,500 people on her graduation day and was overwhelmed with the spirit that marked this important occasion. A hush fell over the crowd as she began her address as president of the senior class: *"You guys are all terrific! Awesome! This has been an awesome four years for us, right? Like, we have really made it! Wow!"* As she proceeded, reflecting on the events of the past four years, her comments were laced with slang that may have been suitable for the coffee shop or gatherings with friends but not for such a special occasion.

The words you choose to convey your message reflect your personality, your attitude toward your subject, occasion, and audience, and your concern for communicating effectively. Words are your primary vehicle for creating meaning. They set forth ideas, spark visions, arouse concerns, elicit emotions, but if not used carefully, produce confusion. Chapter 9 will help you consider how your language choices can enhance your speech, but here are some quick guidelines will help you choose your words with care.

Use Plain English

Let simple, direct language convey your message. Your audience should not need an interpreter. You could say "contusion" or "ecchymosis," but most audiences would find the word "bruise" easier to understand. Also, it is generally best to avoid the use of slang.

Remember That Writing and Speaking Are Different Activities

In a written report, the terms "edifice" and "regulations" and the phrase "in the eventuality of" may be acceptable; in public speaking, the words "building," "rules," and "if" are far more effective. Writing, in general, is a more formal process than speaking. Although your speech should sound conversational, you should take care to pronounce words correctly and articulately (avoid "I'ma go now" for "I'm going to go now").

Relate Your Language to Your Audience's Level of Knowledge

If you are describing drug testing in professional sports, do not assume your audience understands terms and phrases such as "false positives," "chain of custody," and "legal and individual safeguards." If you use these terms in your speech, you should define them in order to keep the message clear.

Use Language for Specific Effect

Assume you are giving a speech on the plight of America's working poor. Here are two possible introductions:

> Introduction #1: *"Although millions of Americans work a full day, they cannot pay their bills or provide for their families."*

> Introduction #2: *Millions of Americans come home each day, exhausted and covered with a layer of factory filth or kitchen grease. Their backbreaking labor has given them few rewards: They cannot pay their rent, buy shoes for their children, or eat meat more than once a week."*

The first example is not incorrect, but it may be ineffective: The second introduction is more powerful. It paints memorable word pictures. Keep your audience in mind as you choose effective language for communicating your ideas.

Be Culturally Sensitive

It *should* go without saying that inappropriate cultural references should be eliminated from your speech. There is always a chance that negative remarks will upset or anger the audience. At the very least, you will lose credibility. Being culturally sensitive in a global sense includes nationality and race. "Arabs" and "Middle Easterners" are nowhere near synonymous terms. Culture also relates to regions and groups of people. All Democrats are not liberal; all Republicans are not conservative. People on welfare are not inherently "lazy," just as people from New York City are not all "brusque." Avoid stereotyping and avoid making comments about the audience or audience members that may be offensive.

Practice!

Without practicing your speech, it's difficult to know whether or not the speech "flows" and the material "works" for you. Sometimes, the outline looks good, and you've developed appropriate transitions, main points, and supporting material, but when you speak aloud, you find that the speech is choppy and your word choice needs some tweaking. You may have particularly long words, names of authors, web sites, or organizations that you stumble over the first time you try. Practicing helps reduce such surprises during your speech, and, of course, demonstrates to your audience that you are prepared.

FIGURE 5.6 Comedian Michael Richards, best known for his role as Kramer on the popular television series *Seinfeld*, was booed off the stage after using derogatory terms to describe African Americans in his stand-up routine at a Hollywood comedy club in 2006.

Much of what you need to know about practicing is found in Chapter 3, "Verbal and Nonverbal Delivery." Keep in mind, however, that practicing allows you to work with your speaker's notes, to think about where it is appropriate to look at your audience, to determine where to pause, and decide when to emphasize certain words.

FIGURE 5.7 Practicing in front of a mirror will let you assess your nonverbal style. Practice, practice, practice is the best advice to ensure your success.

After you've identified your general and specific purpose, you need to develop the speech. Speeches, especially those in public speaking, are content driven, meaning you have to make and support your points. How many points you make is determined by your topic and the length of the speech, but generally, you will have two to five main points. More than five is often difficult to manage and difficult for the audience to remember. Each of these points requires that you research your topic and indicate your supporting material. Demonstrating your research enhances your credibility. You may be tempted to use technology because it's available, but you need to be sure that technology enhances your speech rather than distracts the audience or substitutes for important content. The final step in writing your speech is to develop the introduction and conclusion. These sections are not usually very long, but they are very important. The introduction focuses the audience on you and previews your topic and the conclusion reminds them about the important points and provides closure to the speech. When writing your speech, it is important to think about your language choices and how the audience will respond to your style. One way to ensure that your language is appropriate is the practice—practice out loud, practice in front of people, and practice with your technology.

5.3   Critiquing Speeches and Speakers

As an audience member in a public speaking situation, you listen to be informed on some topic, to be persuaded to change an attitude or engage in some specific behavior, or to be entertained. Your overall impression may be "I learned something" or "I am going to donate some money to that organization," or "That wasn't very funny." Your response is not random; you have some reason for your reaction.

Your feedback to the speaker, during and after the speech, is important. As an audience member, you have several options. Clapping, laughing, asking questions at the end of the speech, giving a standing ovation, walking out on the speech, and talking to the speaker afterward are all forms of feedback. At a workshop or seminar, you may be asked to provide written feedback for a speaker, and in a public speaking class, you may be asked to give written and/or oral feedback. As you think about your role as an audience member, you need to think about how you will evaluate the speakers and speeches (and, of course, how they will evaluate you when it's your turn to give a speech).

5.3.1   Key Criteria for Evaluating Speeches

Criticism may hurt our feelings, but we need to learn to accept others' feedback. When providing a critique, make sure you are constructive and focus on how to improve. All speakers need this feedback to improve the quality of their performance. You may feel reluctant to critique your classmates. Perhaps you think you don't have enough experience; perhaps you're worried about how they will critique you. But you should keep in mind that your comments would help your classmates develop as speakers by focusing their attention on areas that work effectively as well as areas that need improvement.

Feedback, in general, should be: (1) specific, (2) descriptive, and (3) appropriate.

Critique versus Criticize

To **critique** is to provide a detailed analysis and evaluation of the strengths and weakness of something. To criticize is to focus on the faults. Criticism is a necessary part of a critique, but a good critique also identifies the strengths a speaker can build on.

critique
To provide a detailed analysis and evaluation of the strengths and weakness of something.

Your online lesson includes examples of critiques and an activity to help you identify which statements are critiques and which are criticism. See Topic 3.

© 2012 Yuri Arcurs, Shutterstock, Inc.

FIGURE 5.8 Criticism may hurt our feelings, but we need to learn to accept others' feedback. When providing a critique, make sure you are constructive and focus on how to improve.

Feedback should be specific. It takes little time or effort to say, "Great speech!" or "Funny stories!" or "Huh?" General feedback is less likely to be helpful than more focused, directed, feedback. Instead of saying, "She was great," or "I certainly did not like his topic," say, "I liked the way she linked her own experiences as a lifeguard to the need for greater water safety," or "His discussion of the way accounting students are trained was irrelevant for an audience of non-accounting majors."

Feedback should be descriptive rather than evaluative. Years ago, sociologist Jack P. Gibbs developed a set of behavioral characteristics that he defined as either supportive or defensive behaviors (Tubbs, 2008). While listeners *evaluate* speeches, they do not have to be evaluative, which is synonymous with being judgmental. When a listener responds with evaluative comments, it is likely the speaker will become defensive. Instead, listeners can help create a more supportive environment by providing descriptive comments. So instead of saying, "Your reasoning was stupid," you can present something more descriptive, such as, "I didn't hear supporting material for your first point" or "The statistics you presented for your first point were 10 years old." With this specific feedback, the speaker could adapt his/her speech the next time.

Feedback given to a speaker should be appropriate. If someone has a facial tic, mentioning that it distracted you is not appropriate. If however, the speaker's hair hung over his eyes to the extent that one could not determine whether or not the speaker established eye contact, a comment to that effect would be appropriate. Appropriate also means that a reasonable amount of feedback has been provided—identifying two strengths and two elements to improve is usually sufficient. It is not reasonable to think that a person new to public speaking can change 15 things from one speech to another.

Because your classmates are likely to feel vulnerable and defensive about critiques, it is important to put them at ease by pointing out first what was right with their speech. Then you can offer suggestions for improving their presentation. Instead of saying, "Your views on the link between electromagnetic fields and cancer were completely unsupported," you might say: "Your examples were clear and crisp when you talked about how common electric appliances, including coffeemakers, emit potentially dangerous fields." Then you can add, "I don't think you were as clear when you started talking about how these fields can produce changes in body cells. More concrete examples would be helpful." Rather than saying, "Delivery needs work," you could write something more concrete, such as, "You had so much written on your note cards, you didn't look up. Perhaps having less on your note cards would make it easier to look at the class."

*Your online lesson provides some general guidelines for providing feedback to others. For some specific speech critique topics, review the **Criteria for Speech Critiques** sidebar on the facing page. See Topic 3.*

To encourage this type of criticism, many instructors ask students to use a speech evaluation form, similar to those found in your online lesson. This evaluation gives feedback to the speaker on a sliding scale and also gives listeners the opportunity to provide constructive comments. Try to provide as much written commentary as possible, for your explanations help speakers improve.

Your online lesson includes several examples of critique sheets. Are you including all these elements in your speech? Look over these and use them to evaluate your own speech. See Topic 3.

5.3.2   A Final Note about Self-Evaluation

Evaluating your own speech is difficult—we tend to be either hypercritical or somewhat oblivious to our errors. Although your first reaction after giving a speech might be to look at the comments others' wrote, we encourage you to first reflect on how *you* think you did. What were your strengths and weaknesses? Did you think you had appropriate organization, adequate research, and effective delivery? Were

Criteria for Speech Critiques

We present these with guiding questions that allow the critic to examine both content and delivery. These are *not* presented in order of importance.

Organization

1. Was the speech effectively organized?
2. Were the general and specific purposes clear and relevant to the assignment?
3. Were the functions of the introduction and conclusion clear (such as gaining attention and previewing)?
4. Were the main points clear?
5. Did the speaker use appropriate transitions and internal summaries?
6. Was an organizational pattern clear?

Research/Supporting Material

1. Did the speaker use effective and relevant material to support the thesis statement?
2. Was there evidence of sufficient research?
3. Was the supporting material current?
4. Did the speaker include a variety of supporting material?
5. Was the supporting material relevant, helpful, and credible?
6. Were sources integrated into the speech appropriately and cited correctly?

Analysis

1. Was the topic appropriate for the assignment/audience?
2. Was the structure of the speech consistent with the specific purpose?
3. Did the speaker make an effort to analyze the audience and adapt the speech to its needs?
4. Was the evidence that was presented relevant and concrete?
5. If used, did presentational aids contribute to the effectiveness of the speech?

Language

1. Did the speaker use clear and accurate language?
2. Did the speaker use various language techniques to engage the listener?
3. Were unfamiliar terms defined?
4. Was the language appropriate to the situation and the audience?

Verbal and Nonverbal Delivery

1. Did the speaker appear confident and self-controlled?
2. Did the speaker establish and maintain appropriate eye contact?
3. Were the speaker's movements and gestures meaningful?
4. Was the quality of the speaker's voice acceptable?
5. Did the speaker pronounce words correctly and articulate effectively?
6. Did the speaker look for and respond to feedback?
7. Did the speaker include relevant emphasis and pauses?
8. Was the speech relatively free of nonfluencies, such as "um," "er," "like," and so on?
9. Did the speaker use notes effectively?

you fluent? Enthusiastic? What positive aspects of your speech should you keep in mind for the next speech, and what should you try to avoid? Set a few goals for yourself, and view each speech as a learning experience.

Listening to the feedback from your classmates and instructor is an important first step; using that feedback for your next speech is the crucial second step. Your online lesson provides you with many ways to use the feedback you receive from your instructor and classmates. See Topic 3.

5.3.3   Receiving and Providing Relevant Feedback

How do you know if your speech was well done? How can you find out if your topic was appropriate? How can you tell if your audience thought you were credible? What should you do to improve your next speech? The speech critique will provide you the answers to the questions. Your instructor will give you a grade and feedback—be sure to read it and use those suggestions for your next speech. Your classmates may also provide you important feedback—pay attention during the speech and, if they complete critique sheets, review them. You also have an important role when you critique others—be sure to provide specific, descriptive, and appropriate feedback.

Chapter Summary

As public speaking instructors, we would prefer to cover everything in this textbook *before* you have to be graded. However, we know that is not possible. That said, this chapter was designed to help you with your first speech and to get you thinking about how speeches are evaluated. We have outlined steps for preparing to speak; each step involves reflection and decision making. Remember to select an audience-centered topic, develop content through research and sound support, draft the introduction, body, and conclusion, develop the language of the speech with care, and *practice!*

Constructive criticism is helpful to all speakers. When you evaluate a speech, consider addressing specific criteria, including organization, research and supporting material, analysis, language, and verbal and nonverbal delivery. In addition to critiquing others' speeches, spend some time on a self-evaluation so you can reflect on your own strengths and weaknesses, and set goals for future speeches.

Key Terms

brainstorming, 132

conclusion, 140

critique, 143

general purpose, 134

infinitive phrase, 135

interest chart, 131

introduction, 139

specific purpose, 135

thesis statement, 136

Questions for Reflection

1. What factors should you keep in mind when choosing a topic and framing a purpose for speaking?
2. Discuss with member of your class what is understood to be the relationships between a speaker's link to a topic, choice of a purpose, amount of information available, and the needs of the audience.
3. How does a speaker know when he or she has conducted adequate research for a topic and found sufficient supporting material?
4. Why is it important to look at aspects of speech content rather than focusing solely on delivery?
5. After looking at the list of criteria for evaluating speeches, how would you order them by perceived importance?

Activities

1. Take an inventory of what you believe to be your own strengths and weaknesses as a public speaker and establish goals as well as expectations you intend to pursue as you participate in this course.
2. Make a list of the basic steps in preparing your first speech for class. Study your list to see how it relates to the steps featured in this chapter.
3. Generate a list of topics, finding five topics for each of the following categories: self-generated, audience-generated, and research-generated.

Reference

Tubbs, S. (2008). *A systems approach to small group communication.* New York: McGraw-Hill.

Chapter

6

Learning Objectives

After reading this chapter and completing the online activities for this lesson, you will be able to:

1. Demonstrate competency in research principles.

2. Determine appropriate materials to support claims.

3. Accurately document sources of information used in the speech.

Research and Supporting Material

At a Glance

INTRODUCTION

With all of the decisions facing you at the beginning of the speech process, you may feel relief when your instructor approves the topic you have chosen, but your work has just begun. After choosing a topic and developing the general and specific purposes of your speech, it is time for research and to develop appropriate supporting material. Credibility is crucial. To a large extent, your listeners will evaluate your speech on the amount and relevance of research conducted and the types of supporting material used. The extent to which a speaker is perceived as competent is considered **speaker credibility**. A person's background, set of ethics, and delivery are all part of speaker credibility. **Message credibility**, on the other hand, is the extent to which the speech is considered to be factual and well supported through documentation (Roberts, 2010). It is this second type of credibility that is the focus of this chapter. Through research, one can find sufficient, relevant, and timely supporting material that will enhance a speaker's message credibility.

speaker credibility
The extent to which a speaker is perceived as competent is considered.

message credibility
The extent to which the speech is considered to be factual and well supported through documentation.

We live in an information society that produces far more information than we can use. Books are added to library collections on a regular basis, new information is found quarterly in journals, weekly in magazines, daily in newspapers, and moment to moment online. As a result of this information, one of your most important jobs will be to decide what is relevant and what is not, what you should incorporate into your speech and what you should discard. Setting goals on your own research requires that you stay focused on your specific purpose. Do the research you need to enhance your speaker and message credibility.

© 2012 Robert Kneschke, Shutterstock, Inc.

FIGURE 6.1 There are many places to find supporting material—do not limit yourself to just looking online.

6.1 Demonstrate Competency in Research Principles

In 2009, as President Obama declared October "Information Literacy Awareness" month, he declared:

> *Every day, we are inundated with vast amounts of information. A 24-hour news cycle and thousands of global television and radio networks, coupled with an*

immense array of online resources, have challenged our long-held perceptions of information management. Rather than merely processing data, we must also learn the skills necessary to acquire, collate, and evaluate information for any situation. (whitehouse.gov)

Information literacy is your ability to "recognize when information is needed and have the ability to locate, evaluate, and use effectively the needed information." (American Library Association, 1989).

© 2012 Aleksandar Mijatovic, Shutterstock, Inc.

© 2012 amasterphotographer, Shutterstock, Inc.

information literacy
The ability to "recognize when information is needed and have the ability to locate, evaluate, and use effectively the needed information."

Information Literacy Standards for Higher Education
(from the Association of College and Research Libraries)

The information literate student:

Standard 1: Determines the nature and extent of the information needed.

Standard 2: Accesses needed information effectively and efficiently.

Standard 3: Evaluates information and its sources critically and incorporates selected information into his or her knowledge base and a value system.

Standard 4: Individually or as a member of a group, uses information effectively to accomplish a specific purpose.

Standard 5: Understands many of the economic, legal, and social issues surrounding the use of information and accesses and uses information ethically and legally.

President Obama's comments relate directly to the purpose of this chapter. In order to develop a credible, effective speech, you must find and collect relevant information, and determine its effectiveness as it relates to the main or sub-points. Please take a moment to look at the information literacy competency standards for higher education in the shaded box above. While we frame this chapter within the context of research and supporting material, achieving these tasks successfully demonstrates standards of information literacy.

Researching and selecting supporting material are the building blocks that form the foundation of your speech. It gives you the tools you need to develop your specific purpose into a full-length presentation. The building blocks may include conducting your own **primary research**, which is collecting information that does not already exist. For example, interviewing experts on your topic will provide you direct answers to your questions. **Secondary research** is information that someone else collected, analyzed, and presented. If you review print and web-based information, you may be viewing secondary research. The result of this process increases your knowledge of the topic and enhances your credibility.

primary research
Collecting original data for the purpose of answering a question or questions.

secondary research
Reviewing information someone else collected, analyzed, and presented.

supporting material
Sources used to substantiate a claim or support a thesis.

The research process alone is not sufficient. You must determine how to use it most effectively. **Supporting material** is the information used in a particular way to make your case. For example, if you were preparing a speech to inform your class on services available in your community for individuals who are categorized as low income, your *research process* may lead you to an organization that specializes in debt consolidation, another that offers free or low-cost medical care, an agency that gives out food for low-income individuals, and an organization that supplies children with free school supplies. As you develop your speech, one of your points might be, "a variety of services are available in our community." For *supporting material*, a list of agencies provides examples of available services. As the types of supporting material can be varied, you must determine what is most suited to the topic and to your listeners.

Your online lesson reviews why supporting material is important and identifies the five functions of supporting material. See Topic 1.

6.1.1   Develop a Research Strategy

Every speech has some guidelines that will help you decide on your research strategy. In Chapter 4, we discussed the importance of knowing about your audience. Audience analysis requires that you research what your audience thinks about your topic and identify strategies to best reach them. You need to use the same techniques (plus some additional ones) to analyze and understand your topic.

The person asking you (or requiring you) to give a speech will likely provide you parameters regarding appropriate topics, length of speech, and perhaps even audience characteristics and expectations. To meet your audience expectations (and don't forget that if you're in a public speaking class, your instructor is part of your audience), you have to know the requirements of the speech. If you don't pay attention to the constraints of your presentation, you will not be successful—no matter how great your delivery. Once you know the answers to the following questions, you are ready to start the research process.

Throughout this textbook, we stress the importance of connecting with your audience. As explained in Chapter 4, a careful audience analysis gives you information about who they are and what they value and helps you to determine the depth and breadth of information needed for your speech. For example, if you were doing a how-to speech about editing digital photographs, you would want to know what software, if any, your audience uses. If your audience knows a lot about digital photography, you would want to consider researching the latest techniques and trends and demonstrating them. If your audience barely knows how to use a camera, you would need to research information aimed at beginners. Reflect again on your audience *after* you have gathered information to determine whether or not you have collected enough material and if it is the right type of material to meet your audience's needs and interests.

Knowing the Answers Checklist

Before you begin to research your topic for your public speaking course, it is important that you can answer the following questions. Put a check mark in the box if you already know the answer.

☐ What are the time constraints of the speech?

☐ What is the minimum number of sources required?

☐ How many different sources do you need? (If you use three different issues of *Newsweek*, do they count as one source or as three?)

☐ What style should guide your source citations? (e.g., APA, MLA)

☐ How recent do your sources need to be? (Can you use information that is thirty years old, twenty years old, ten years old?)

☐ Do you need both print and online sources?

☐ Does online access to a magazine count as a print source? Can you use all types of print sources? Do you need different types of print sources?

☐ Does your instructor allow you to count an interview as a source?

☐ Can you use a family member or yourself as a source?

☐ Do you have to use a presentational aid?

Your search may result in more questions, including the following:

What information is most essential to this topic?

What will have the greatest impact?

How much background do I need to give?

A *how-to speech* is a form of informative speaking, which is discussed in more detail in Chapter 10. In these speeches, you demonstrate to the audience how to do something.

Research Strategy Hint

When planning your research strategy, a good rule of thumb is to plan to spend one hour collecting supporting material for each minute of speech you will deliver. If your speech is seven minutes long, you will likely need devote seven hours of research to find and select the appropriate information.

© 2012 Borys Shevchuk, Shutterstock, Inc.

Use your favorite Internet video search engine to watch Microsoft Bing Commercials.

© 2012 amasterphotographer, Shutterstock, Inc.

To maximize your online search, consider clearinghouse web sites. For example, GPO Access is a comprehensive list of official Federal resources available at http://www.gpoaccess. gov/

© 2012 amasterphotographer, Shutterstock, Inc.

Where Should You Look for Information?

Have you seen any of the commercials for Microsoft's Bing search engine?

> Woman 1: We really need to find a new place for breakfast.

> Woman 2: *The Breakfast Club* in 1986, a cult classic starring members of the Brat Pack.

> Parent: So, do you want an LCD or a plasma?

> Child: Plasma is an ionized gas.

TABLE 6.1 Where to Start Looking for Information	
1. Assess your knowledge/skill	What knowledge or skill do you have in relation to this topic?
2. Visit the library	The library will provide you quick and easy access to databases, general reference works, and biographical indexes.
3. Review newspapers and magazines	Newspapers and magazines can provide you current information and great examples. You can also access information about your community.
4. Review government documents	The U.S. government funds research on almost every topic. Government sponsored research results are free and frequently available online. Look for government sponsored web sites (.gov) for everything from census information to health topics.
5. Interview experts, if appropriate	Will this speech be improved by interviewing someone with personal knowledge or expertise about this topic?
6. Search online	Although online sources are convenient, do you know how to maximize your search?

Assess Your Own Knowledge and Skills

Start your research process by assessing your own knowledge and skills. Most likely, you have direct knowledge or experience related to several topics. Having personal knowledge or experience can make an impact on your audience. A student with Type I diabetes can speak credibly on what it is like to take daily injections and deal with the consequences of both low and high blood sugar. A student who works as a barista at the local coffee shop can demonstrate how to make a good shot of espresso.

However, relying on your personal knowledge and experience is insufficient—you must do additional research. Experts in their fields are continually reading and updating their knowledge, and as a speaker, you have to demonstrate that you have fully researched your topic. Your personal knowledge will help you in your research process because you will be able to more critically evaluate the sources. You may have access to specialty periodicals or experts in the field. Your experience is only one form of supporting material—make sure you have other sources.

FIGURE 6.2 Libraries are great places to research your topic and work on group projects. Visit your library and talk with your librarians. You'll be surprised how they can help you with your research process.

© 2012 Robert Kneschke, Shutterstock, Inc.

Selecting a topic you are familiar with can help you feel more comfortable delivering your speech and will enhance your personal credibility.

© 2012 Borys Shevchuk, Shutterstock, Inc.

Visit the Library

Go to the library. Visit your library's web site. Talk to a librarian. Libraries have most of the resources you need to develop your speech, so you can get a lot of work done quickly. When gathering research for your speech, you should use a variety of sources, most of which you can access in the library. In addition to books, libraries offer other helpful sources of supporting material.

General reference materials. Seldom should your research start and end with the encyclopedia. The *World Book Encyclopedia* is helpful if you are unfamiliar with a topic or concept. It can provide facts that are concise as well as easy to read and understand. Encyclopedias are either general or specialized. General encyclopedias (e.g., *The Encyclopedia Americana* and *Encyclopedia Britannica*) cover a wide range of topics in a broad manner. Specialized encyclopedias, such as the *International Encyclopedia of the Social Sciences*, provide more detail on particular areas. Although encyclopedias are helpful as a basic resource, they generally are not accepted as main sources for class speeches. Use them to lead you to other information.

CAUTION I

Do not fall into Wikipedia's web of easy access and understanding. Its legitimacy is questionable. Several years ago, Stephen Colbert, host of the cable television show *The Colbert Report*, asked his viewers to log on to the entry "elephants" on Wikipedia.org to report that the elephant population in Africa "has tripled in the last six months." This online encyclopedia noted a spike in inaccurate entries shortly after the show aired. Most instructors discourage, if not ban, use of this online resource. Although teachers don't want students quoting the encyclopedia, librarians will point out that Wikipedia, like *World Book*, is sometimes useful for getting an overview of the topic, especially if you know nothing about the topic, but information should be verified by a different source.

© 2012 amasterphotographer, Shutterstock, Inc.

CAUTION II

Most instructors will not consider a dictionary a source. Check with your instructor before beginning your speech with, "According to Webster's dictionary, the word _____ means..." As Harris (2002) notes in his book on the effective use of sources, "Generally speaking, starting with a dictionary definition not only lacks creativity but it may not be helpful if the definition is too general or vague" (p. 35).

Biographical sources. Biographical sources provide information on an individual's education, accomplishments, and professional activities, which is useful when evaluating someone's credibility and reliability. A biographical index indicates sources of biographical information in books and journals whereas a biographical dictionary lists and describes the accomplishments of notable people. If you are looking for a brief background of a well-known person, consult the biographical dictionary first. If you need an in-depth profile of a lesser-known person, the biographical index is the better source. Some examples of these sources are *Author Biographies Master Index*, *Biography Index*, *The New York Times Index*, *Dictionary of American Biography*, *European Authors*, *World Authors*, and *Dictionary of American Scholars*. *Biography.com* is an excellent online source for individuals currently famous or infamous.

If you need direction, *ask a librarian*. Whether they are employed as reference librarians, information services librarians, or information technology or library media specialists, librarians are experts in finding information, and they can show you how to use the library's search engines and databases. With online and print resources being added daily, using the expertise of a librarian can make your job as a researcher much easier. Your library's home page may be helpful. Most college libraries belong to a "live chat" consortium on the web, where students may contact a librarian twenty-four hours a day. Also, you can try the Library of Congress online Ask-a-Librarian Service (www.loc.gov) and click on "Ask a librarian."

FIGURE 6.3 Many libraries' web sites have an option for you to message the librarian.

Review Magazines, Newspapers, and Journals

Magazines and newspapers provide the most recent print information. Once you identify ideas that connect with the needs of your audience, you can look for specific information in magazines and newspapers. Magazines and newspapers can be useful by providing (a) current, easily understood information, (b) other sources, (c) stories and anecdotes, and, in the case of newspaper and regional magazines, (d) information tailored to your community.

A **general index** is a comprehensive and cross-referenced collection of sources. You can search by topic, author, or other key information. General indexes cover such popular magazines and newspapers as *Time, Newsweek, U.S. News & World Report, The New York Times*, the *Chicago Tribune*, the *Wall Street Journal*, the *Christian Science Monitor*, the *Los Angeles Times*. Other popular indexes include *The New York Times Index, The Education Index, Humanities Index, Public Affairs Information Service Bulletin, Social Sciences and Humanities Index*, and *Social Sciences Index*.

© 2012 Aleksandar Mijatovic, Shutterstock, Inc.

You may also want to (or be required to) consult an academic journal. **Academic journals** are published collections of research articles and essays written by scholarly experts. Journal articles typically go through a peer-review process in which other experts read and critique the submission. Journal articles frequently feature primary research and differ from other periodicals in a number of ways.

general index
A comprehensive and cross-referenced collection of sources.

academic journal
Published collections of research articles and essays written by scholarly experts.

TABLE 6.2 Differences Between Periodicals and Journals

	Newspaper and Magazines	Academic Journals
Frequency of Distribution	Daily, Weekly, or Monthly	Monthly, Bimonthly, Quarterly, Yearly
Role of Author	Usually professional writers and subject generalists	Generally experts in their particular fields and affiliated with a university
Submission process	Author is generally an employee of the periodical or contracted to write a piece	Authors are not employed by the journal and the article is subject to a competitive selection process
Compensation	Paid by publisher	Usually not paid
Verification	Fact-checked	Peer-reviewed by other experts
Audience	General audience	Specialty audience, usually aimed at other researchers

Review Government Documents

Through the U.S. Government Printing Office (GPO) one can find unique, authoritative, and timely materials, including detailed census data, vital statistics, congressional papers and reports, presidential documents, military reports, and impact statements on energy, the environment, and pollution. However, it is now archive only and has been replaced, for the most part, by the Federal Digital System (FDsys) (http://www.gpo.gov/fdsys/).

6.1.2   Identify Different Sources for Research

Interviews are useful if you want information too new to be found in published sources or if you want to give your listeners the views of an expert. By talking to an expert, you can clarify questions and fill in knowledge gaps, and you may learn more about a subject than you expected. In the process, you also gather opinions based on years of experience.

Your online lesson will help you prepare to interview someone by explaining what to do before, during, and after the interview. We've also included four quick suggestions below.

1. **Contact the person well in advance.** Remember, you are the one who needs the information. Do not think that leaving one voice message is enough. You may have to try several times to contact the person. Schedule a date and time to interview that leaves you with plenty of time to prepare your speech.
2. **Prepare questions in advance.** Even though the person is an expert, you are the one who asks the questions, so have approximately five to seven questions prepared. Know the purpose, and make sure you know what topics need to be covered and what information needs to be clarified. You may also want to send the questions to the person before you meet.
3. **Develop questions in a logical order.** One question should lead naturally to another. Place the most important questions at the top to guarantee that they will be answered before your time is up.
4. **Stay within the agreed time frame.** If you promise the interview will take no longer than a half hour, keep your word, if at all possible. Do not say, "It'll just take a minute," when you need at least fifteen minutes. Build in a little time to ask unplanned questions, questions based on the interviewee's answers or for clarification.

Online Searches

A googol is a one with a hundred zeros, and yet, this does not begin to capture the amount of information available online. Starting your research by typing your topic into an online search engine like Google or Bing is like upending an entire library in a football field in the dark and using the light on your cell phone to search for a specific book.

Your online lesson includes a link that provides tips on maximizing your Internet searches. See Topic 1.

Consider using online databases such as ProQuest, InfoTrac, EBSCO, and Google Scholar. Google Scholar provides a simple way to broadly search for scholarly literature. From one place, you can search across many disciplines and sources: articles, theses, books, abstracts and court opinions, from academic publishers, professional societies, online repositories, universities and other web sites. Google Scholar helps you find relevant work across the world of scholarly research. EBSCO offers a similar service, and claims to be the most widely used online scholarly resource, with access to more than 100 databases and thousands of e-journals.

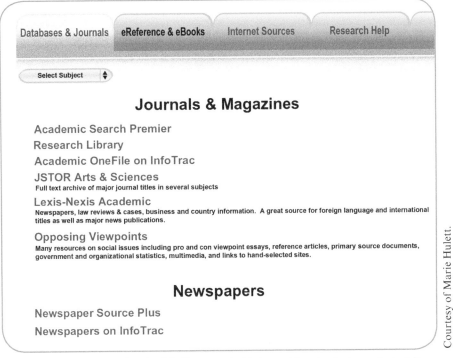

Courtesy of Marie Hulett.

FIGURE 6.4 Your college or local public library probably has guides, shortcuts, and tutorials for how to start a database search, but if not, your online lesson includes links to some demonstration videos.

Your online lesson will provide a demonstration of how to conduct "deep web research," which will provide you access to millions of sources of information that a general search engine, such as Google or Bing, won't show you. Deep research allows you to access information in journals. See Topic 1.

After reading this section on research, hopefully you are aware that it involves a significant time commitment. It is never too early to start thinking about your next speech topic and where you might find sources. Explore a variety of resources. Ask for help from your instructor or a librarian. Make sure you know the constraints of the assignment.

6.2 Evaluating Supporting Material

Your credibility as a speaker is linked to the credibility of the information you use. Your audience (especially your speech instructor) will evaluate if you have enough sources, a variety of sources, recent sources, and reliable sources. When selecting supporting material, you need to evaluate not only its usefulness but also its value. Evaluation of the source is especially important for online sources. Because of the cost and time involved in producing print materials, many of the sources have been reviewed and verified. Online sources, however, frequently do not undergo a thorough review and will require you to thoroughly analyze them. Ultimately, you are held accountable for the quality and credibility of the sources you use. The following criteria should guide your evaluation of all secondary sources (a source that presents information originally presented elsewhere).

Your online lesson will review the advantages and disadvantages of primary and secondary sources. See Topic 2.

6.2.1 Evaluation Criteria

As you access each source, especially web sites, it is important to evaluate its legitimacy as a source for your speech. Radford, Barnes, and Barr (2006), in their book *Web Research: Selecting, Evaluating, and Citing*, identify five evaluation criteria that serve as useful standards for evaluating online information.

Authority. Authority relates to the concept of credibility. As we know, virtually anyone can become a web publisher. A source that passes this first test contains information provided by an individual, group, or organization known to have expertise in the area. For online sources, the domain type (.gov, .edu, .org., and .com) will provide you some insight into who is responsible for the information. For print material, the publisher will help determine authority.

The three-letter extension of a web address (e.g., .gov or .com) was originally an indication of the type of the organization. A .com was a commercial business, a .org was a nonprofit, and .net was a network-related organization. Currently, however, these domain types are unrestricted and registrants can simply select .com, .org, and .net. A domain extension of .gov is limited to official government organizations, and the .edu extension is limited to accredited, degree-granting institutions of higher education. Domain extensions also include geographic indicators (e.g., .uk for United Kingdom and .jpn for Japan.) Organizations in the United States do not have a geographic identifier. Why do you think the United States does not use a geographic identifier?

Questions to guide evaluation include the following:

- What type of group published the information? (Educational institution? Government agency? Individual? Commercial business? Organization?)
- Can you identify the author(s)? (What is the organization or who is the person responsible for the information?)
- What are the credentials and possible biases of those responsible?

Accuracy. An accurate source is reliable and error-free. This can be difficult to assess, but you want to be sure that the content be verified and that evidence is provided and substantiated for each claim. Information may be taken out of context or deliberately misleading, so you need to be sure to assess the context of the information. You can assess context by verifying the information with another source and by examining the original full passage of an answer rather than just a single quote. The accuracy of online sources is clearly related to authority, since the sites with greater authority are most likely to have mechanisms for determining how something becomes "cite-worthy."

Questions to guide evaluation include the following:

- Is the information reliable and error free?
- Does the information confirm or contradict what is found in printed or other online sources?
- Are references given to the sources of information?

Objectivity. The extent to which web site material is presented without bias or distortion relates to objectivity. As you examine the material, you want to determine if it is presented as opinion or fact.

Questions to guide evaluation include the following:

- What is the age level of the intended audience? (Adults? Teenagers? Children?)
- Is the information on the site factual or an expression of opinion?
- Is the author controversial? A known conservative? A known liberal?
- What are the author's credentials?

Coverage. Coverage refers to the depth and breadth of the material. It may be difficult to determine the audience for the site. As a result, material may be too general or too specific. Determine if it meets your needs or if critical information is missing.

Questions to guide evaluation include the following:

- What is the intended purpose of the site? (Educational? Informational? Commercial? Recreational?)
- Who is the intended audience (General public? Scholars? Students? Professionals?)
- Is information common knowledge? Too basic? Too technical?
- Does information include multiple aspects of the issue or concern?

Currency. Currency refers to the timeliness of the material. Some web sites exist that have never been updated. Information may be no longer valid or useful. If you look

In writing, an ellipse (…) is the standard way to indicate that something from a quote was removed. (But be careful—just because there's not an ellipse doesn't mean it wasn't edited). Video material, however, has no common way to indicate that it has been edited and potentially presented out of context.

If the writing and style are problematic, you should be wary of the material. Mistakes with grammar and punctuation may indicate lack of careful review of the material.

© 2012 Borys Shevchuk, Shutterstock, Inc.

for "Most popular books of the year," and find a site from 2003, that information is no longer current or relevant. Looking at birth rates or literacy rates from the past would not produce relevant information if you are looking for the most recent information.

Questions to guide evaluation include the following:

- When was the site created?
- Is the material from the last few years?
- Is the web site updated?

When using these five criteria to evaluate your online information, remember that *all* criteria should be met, not just one or two of the above. Accurate and current information must also be objective. If critical information is missing (coverage), no matter how accurate and current the information is, it should be eliminated as a source.

6.2.2   Supporting Your Speech

Imagine a chef with a piece of steak, some cauliflower, and rice; the main ingredients for a dinner special. What the chef does with these raw materials will influence the response of the consumers. The chef decides whether to grill, broil, bake, steam, or fry. Different spices are used for different results. Numerous possibilities exist.

Research you gathered for your speech can be viewed as the raw material. Now you need to determine how to organize and present your information in the most effective way for your audience. It is important to spend sufficient time making choices about how much and what type of supporting material to include in your speech.

Supporting material gives substance to your assertions. If you say that *Casablanca* is the best motion picture ever produced in Hollywood, you are stating your opinion. If you cite a film critic's essay that notes it is the best movie ever, then your statement has more weight. You may find data that indicates how well the movie did, and a public opinion poll that ranked as the top movie. These different resources provide support. Just about anything that affirms a speaker's idea in some way can be considered supporting material.

When developing your speech, you also have many decisions to make. Consider the following example. Your public speaking professor asks your class to develop an informative speech addressing the problem of shoplifting. Which of the following two versions do you like better?

Version 1:

Shoplifting is an enormous problem for American retailers, who lose billions of dollars each year to customer theft. Not unexpectedly, retailers pass the cost of shoplifting on to consumers, which means that people like you and me pay dearly for the crimes of others.

Shoplifting is increasingly becoming a middle-class crime. Experts tell us that many people shoplift just for kicks—for the thrill of defying authority and for the excitement of getting away with something that is against the law. Whatever the reason, one in fifteen Americans is guilty of this crime.

Version 2:

> *Imagine walking up to a store owner once a year and giving that person $300 without getting anything in return. Could you afford that? Would you want to do that? Yet, that's what happens. Every year, the average American family of four forks over $300 to make amends for the crimes of shoplifters.*
>
> *Shoplifting is a big cost to big business. According to recent statistics from the National Association for the Prevention of Shoplifting, people who walk out of stores without first stopping at the cash register take with them more than $13 billion annually. That's more than $25 million per day. Their web site claims that one out of eleven of us is guilty of this crime. To bring this figure uncomfortably close to home—that's at least two students in each of your classes.*
>
> *Interestingly, shoplifting is no longer a poor person's crime. Hard as it is to imagine, many shoplifters can well afford to buy what they steal. Actress Lindsay Lohan received even more media attention in February of 2011, when she was charged with felony grand theft of a necklace from a jewelry store in Venice, California.*
>
> *Why do middle- and upper-income people steal? According to psychiatrist James Spikes, quoted in last month's* Ms. *magazine, shoplifters are "defying authority. They're saying, 'The hell with them. I'll do it anyway … . I can get away with it … .'" Psychologist Stanton Samenow, quoted in this past July issue of* Life *magazine, agrees: "Shoplifters will not accept life as it is; they want to take shortcuts. They do it for kicks."*

Although both versions say essentially the same thing, they are not equally effective. The difference is in the supporting materials. Notice that providing supporting material adds depth and breadth to the speech. Listeners are more likely to pay attention when they hear something that relates to their world in some way.

Forms of Support

Effective speeches generally rely on multiple forms of support. To give your speech greater weight and authority, at least five forms of support can be used. These include facts and statistics, narratives, explanations, testimony, and analogies. Each of these forms of support will be discussed, and guidelines for using them will be presented.

Your online lesson will provide more information about the purpose for each form of support and some additional guidelines. See Topic 2. The section below provides some specific guidelines.

Facts and Statistics

Nothing undermines a presentation faster than too few facts. **Facts** are pieces of information that are verifiable and irrefutable. **Opinions** are points of view that may or may not be supported in fact. Too often, speakers confuse fact and opinion when adding supporting material to a speech. For example, while it is a fact that Colin Firth won the 2011 Academy Award for Best Actor, it is opinion to state that he is the best actor in Hollywood.

facts
Pieces of information that are verifiable and irrefutable.

opinions
Points of view that may or may not be supported in fact.

As shown in TABLE 6.3, Facts serve at least three different purposes:

TABLE 6.3 What Facts Do	
Facts clarify your main point.	Facts remove ambiguity, making it more likely that the message you send is the message your audience will receive.
Facts indicate your knowledge of the subject.	Rather than say, "The League of Women Voters has been around for a long time," report, "The League of Women Voters was founded in 1919." Your audience wants to know that you have researched the topic and can discuss specifics about your topic.
Facts define.	Facts provide needed definitions that may explain new concepts.

In Megan's informative speech on "functional illiteracy," she defined the term in the following way:

> *While an illiterate adult has no ability to read, write, or compute, relatively few Americans fall into this category. However, some 30 million Americans can't read, write, compute, speak, or listen effectively enough to function in society. They cannot read street signs, write out a check, apply for a job, or ask a government bureaucrat about a Social Security check they never received. Although they may have minimal communications skills, for all intents and purposes, they are isolated from the rest of society. These people are considered functionally illiterate.*

Megan anticipated the potential confusion between the terms "illiteracy" and "functional illiteracy," and differentiated between these terms. While defining this term for your public speaking class is necessary, if the audience was comprised of literacy coaches, this would not be necessary.

Guidelines for Using Facts

Carefully determine how many facts to use. Too few facts will reveal that you spent little time researching, while too many may overwhelm your listeners. Sometimes, students want to impress their audience, or at least their instructor, with the amount of research completed for a particular speech. The desire to include all information may result in a "data dump," where facts are given in a steady stream with little or no connection to the speech or to each other. This results in an overload of information that is difficult to process.

Define terms when they are first introduced. The first time you use a term that requires an explanation, define it so that your meaning is clear. If you are talking about the advantages of belonging to a health maintenance organization, define the term the first time it is used.

Make sure your meanings are clear. Misunderstandings occur when your audience attributes meanings to terms you did not intend. Think about the following words: success, liberal, conservative, patriot, happiness, good, bad, and smart. Collectively, we do not agree on the meanings of these words. One person may define success in terms of material wealth, while another may think of it in terms of family relationships, job satisfaction, and good health. When it is essential that your audience understand the meaning you intend, take the time to make sure you take the time to define the term in the context you intend.

Statistics are the collection, analysis, interpretation, and presentation of information in numerical form. Statistics give us the information necessary to understand the magnitude of issues and to compare and contrast different points.

Basic Statistics Measures

The **mean** is calculated by adding all the numbers in a group and dividing by the number of items. It is the most widely used statistical measure and is commonly referred to as the *average*.

The **median** measures the middle score in the group. That is, half the values fall above it and half fall below.

The **mode** is the value that occurs most frequently.

© 2012 Qiun, Shutterstock, Inc.

FIGURE 6.5 Statistics can be misleading if they are used improperly or stated incorrectly.

statistics
The collection, analysis, interpretation, and presentation of information in numerical form.

mean
Calculated by adding all the numbers in a group and dividing by the number of items. It is the most widely used statistical measure and is commonly referred to as the *average*.

median
The middle score in the group.

mode
The value that occurs most frequently.

However, statistics can be misleading. For example, if one were to examine the Major League Baseball (MLB) salaries for 2011, one would note that the highest salary went to Alex Rodriguez of the New York Yankees. He earned $32,000,000. The average salary for the New York Yankees, however, was much lower—$6,756,300 (even so, it would take the average American household more than 135 years to make this much money). The median (score in the middle) salary was $2,100,000. As a comparison, the average salary of a player on the Kansas City Royals was $1,338,000 and the median was $850,000 (content.usatoday.com/sportsdata/baseball/mlb/salaries/team). In this case, simply discussing these salaries is not helpful, unless you want to make the point that salaries are not consistent. It might make

According to the U.S. Census Bureau (2010), median household income in 2009 was $50,221.

more sense to discuss the range of salaries or look at a particular group of players' salaries. When using statistics in your speech, it is important to understand what they mean.

Guidelines for Using Statistics

- **Be precise.** Make sure you understand the statistics before including them in your speech. Consider the difference between the following statements.

There was a 2 percent decrease in the rate of economic growth, as measured by the gross national product, compared to the same period last year.	The gross national product dropped by 2 percent compared to the same period last year.

In the first case, the statistic refers to a drop in the rate of growth—it tells us that the economy is growing at a slower pace but that it is still ahead of last year—while in the second, it refers to an actual drop in the gross national product in comparison to the previous year. These statements say two very different things.

- **Avoid using too many statistics.** Too many statistics will confuse and bore your audience and blunt the impact of your most important statistical points. Save your statistics for the places in your speech where they will make the most impact.

- **Round off your numbers.** Is it important for your audience to know that, according to the Census Bureau's daily population projection (www.census.gov/population/www.popclockus.html) on August 10, 2011, the U.S. population reached exactly 311,966,124? The figure will have greater impact—and your audience will be more likely to remember it— if you round it off to "almost 312,000,000."

- **Cite your sources.** As an ethical speaker, you need to make sure your statistics are correct. As a credible speaker, you need to cite your sources. For example, if you were talking about the popularity of Girl Scout cookies, you could mention that during peak production of Girl Scout cookies, according to the Little Brownie Bakery web site (www.littlebrowniebakers.com), 4,500,000 Thin Mints are produced each day, and 310,000 pounds of peanut butter are used each week to create Do-si-dos and Tagalongs.

- **Use visual aids to express statistics.** Statistics become especially meaningful to listeners when they are presented in visual form. Visual presentations of statistics free you from the need to repeat a litany of numbers that listeners will probably never remember. Instead, by transforming these numbers into visual presentations, you can highlight only the most important points.

Your online lesson will show you different ways to display statistical information. See Topic 2.

narrative
A retelling of events.

Narratives

Narratives are retellings of events and can enliven speeches in a way that no other form of supporting material can. Grounding material in the specifics of everyday life has the power to create a bond between speaker and audience, one that may last even after the speech.

Stories, personal experiences, and hypothetical scenarios are all forms of narratives. Although they differ in length, factual base, and source, their effectiveness lies in the extent to which they support the speaker's core idea.

Do you need a brief or extended narrative? Brief narratives can be used effectively throughout a speech to create interest or clarify events. Your decision to use them will depend on many factors, including the needs of your audience, the nature of your material, and your approach. Extended narratives are longer and richer in detail. They are used most effectively to build images and to create a lasting impression on the audience. Because of their impact, extended narratives should not be overused or used at inappropriate points. As with other forms of support, they should be reserved for the points at which they will have the greatest effect: in clarifying the message, persuading listeners to your point of view, or establishing a speaker-audience relationship.

Should your narrative be real or hypothetical? Sometimes the best stories are real, and come from your personal experience. By revealing parts of your life that relate to your speech topic, you provide convincing evidence and, at the same time, potentially create a powerful bond between you and your audience. Consider the student who has watched her mother die from lung cancer. The experience of hearing about the diagnosis, discussing treatment possibilities, and making final arrangements while her mother was alive can have a powerful effect on the audience. The words and emotion have great impact because the situation is real, not hypothetical, and the speaker provides a sense of reality to the topic.

Hypothetical stories, which are not based on actual events, are useful when you want to exaggerate a point or when you cannot find a factual illustration for your speech. To be effective, they must be tied in some way to the point you are trying to illustrate. A hypothetical format allows us to distance ourselves somewhat from a terrible situation since we aren't personally connected, but at the same time, we feel the emotional impact because the situation reflects reality.

It is important that your listeners know when you are using a hypothetical scenario and when you are not. Avoid confusion by introducing these stories in a direct way. You might start out by saying, "Imagine that you live next door to a college professor we'll call Dr. Supple," or "Let's talk about a hypothetical mother on welfare named Alice."

By their nature, narratives demand that listeners take an active part in linking the story to the speaker's main point. The story moves from beginning to middle, to end. Even if the speaker supplies the link after the narrative, audience members still make the connections themselves as they listen.

Explanations

An explanation makes something clearer and easier to understand. Throughout your speech, you will likely need various types of explanations, including definitions, examples, and descriptions of processes. If you were going to give an informative speech on equestrian competitions, you would likely need to define the term equestrian ("of or relating to horseback riding"), provide some examples of the different types of competitions or horses, and describe the scoring process. A variety of explanations will help the audience better understand your topic.

Definitions are important for clarity, but a definition is not usually considered a source. If you use a specific dictionary, you should cite it, but your instructor probably will not count it as one of your sources.

© 2012 Borys Shevchuk, Shutterstock, Inc.

example
A representation of a category.

A definition is a statement of the exact meaning of something. You should be sure to define a new term the first time you use it. Defining unfamiliar terms ensures that the audience understands what you are talking about, rather than leaving them confused or guessing. Sometimes, however, a definition does not really help the audience understand a concept. The definition of dog found on freedictionary.com is "a domesticated carnivorous mammal (*Canine familiaris*) related to foxes and wolves and raised in a wide variety of breeds." In situations like this, an example may help the audience understand the concept.

An **example** is a representation of something. If you were giving a speech about dogs, a definition may not be the most appropriate type of supporting material. However, you would likely want to include some examples (Labrador Retriever, Chihuahua, and Saint Bernard) to discuss characteristics of dogs. Examples add interest and impact. They should be representative because examples support your core idea only when they accurately represent the situation. No matter the type of example you use as supporting material, the following three guidelines will help you choose examples for your speeches:

Guidelines for Using Examples

- **Use examples frequently.** Examples are often the lifeblood of a speech. Use them to make your points—but only in appropriate places. When using examples to prove a point, more than one example generally is needed.

- **Use only the amount of detail necessary.** To make your examples work, you want to use only the amount of detail necessary for your audience and no more. The detail you provide in examples should be based on the needs of your audience. If your listeners are familiar with a topic, you can simply mention what the audience already knows. Interspersing long examples with short ones varies the pace and detail of your discussion.

- **Use examples to explain new concepts.** Difficult concepts become easier to handle when you clarify them with examples. Keep in mind that although you may be comfortable with the complexities of a topic, your listeners might be hearing these complexities for the first time. Appropriate examples can mean the difference between communicating with or losing your audience.

Description of Processes

Explaining how to do something can be challenging. When we are experts on a process, we frequently forget the small steps. One of the authors of this textbook recently was visited by some out-of-town relatives. Her directions included this phrase: "Turn left onto Farris, go three blocks, and make a right." About half an hour later, her aunt called and said they were lost. Well, Ginny had overlooked the circle (or rotary or roundabout) on Farris (see **FIGURE 6.6**). She thought it was obvious that they should continue on Farris and go halfway around the circle. Her aunt, instead, went all the way around the circle, crossed back over Hillcrest and Main, and was looking for Ginny's house on Johnson. An important type of supporting material is the description of a process—make sure you include all the relevant information in the correct order. Numbering the steps and including visuals are helpful.

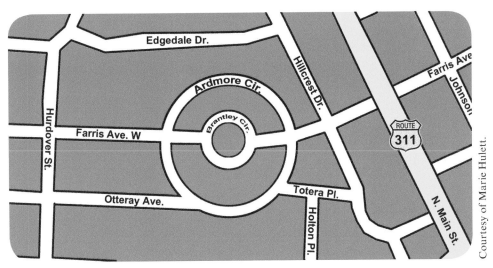

Courtesy of Marie Hulett.

FIGURE 6.6 Describing a process is like giving directions. The speaker has to be clear and thorough or someone will get lost.

Testimony

When you reference other people or use their words, either directly or through paraphrasing, you are attempting, in effect, to strengthen your position by telling your audience that people with special knowledge support your position or take your side. **Testimony** is a form of declaration, and you can use others' experience or opinions to support your claims. For example, short quotations from someone experienced in a topic may be an effective way to provide testimony.

testimony
Statements by someone who has experienced an event.

In order to be effective, however, testimony needs to be used in its proper context. Purposefully distorting the testimony of an expert to suit the needs of your speech is misleading and unethical. Common ways that testimony can be misleading is by quoting someone out of context or editing quotes to imply something different than what was intended. *Gelf Magazine*, a webzine, has called attention to some misleading testimony for movies. For example, promotional materials for the 2006 animated movie *Monster House* included this quote from A. O. Scott, film critic with *The New York Times*:

> "Monster House" is the best child-friendly movie of the summer so far … smartly written and a lot of fun."

However, the full quotation was, "If I say that 'Monster House' is the best child-friendly movie of the summer so far ('Ant Bully' and 'Barnyard' will expand the competition in the next few weeks), it may sound like extravagant praise—or maybe like faint praise." Credible speakers do not manipulate testimony.

Experience as testimony. Experience may be the most credible choice in some cases because someone was "on the scene." For example, if someone were to discuss the Egyptian revolution that culminated in February 2011 with President Hosni Mubarak's resignation, testimony of Egyptian nationals would provide great impact. Wael Ghonim, whose "tweets" offered both a narrative and a nudge to protesters, would be an excellent source because of his connection to the revolution

Quotations can also function as testimony. When quoting, or using any form of testimony, be sure to cite the source and note when it was said. Remember that the audience will assess the credibility of the person you are quoting, so select your quotes carefully.

© 2012 Borys Shevchuk, Shutterstock, Inc.

(CBSnews.com/stories/2011/02/12). Angered by the killing of a 28-year-old Internet activist, who was beaten to death after trying to expose police corruption, Ghonim created a Facebook page with the picture of the dead activist called, "We are all Khaled Said." Posted on January 25, it was instrumental in starting the antiregime protests, and also resulted in his arrest:

> *I was blindfolded for 12 days. I couldn't hear anything. I didn't know what was happening," he said. "I'm not a hero—I slept for 12 days. The heroes, they're the ones who were in the street, who took part in the demonstrations, sacrificed their lives, were beaten, arrested and exposed to danger* (adelaidenow.com, February 8, 2011).

His personal feelings and experiences provide greater impact than a simple description of the situation.

It is possible to use your own testimony when you are an expert. "Experts generally know more about their domain … [and] are better than novices at applying and using that knowledge effectively (Kolodner, 1983, p. 497). When you do not have the background necessary to convince your audience, use the testimony of those who do.

Opinion as testimony. In some circumstances, the opinion of a recognized authority may provide the credibility needed to strengthen your argument or prove a point. Jimmy Carter, former president and winner of the Nobel Peace Prize in 2002, is an outspoken critic of the Iraq War. At a news conference in July of 2005, CBS News quoted Carter as saying, "I thought then, and I think now, that the invasion of Iraq was unnecessary and unjust. And I think the premises on which it was launched were false" (www.cbsnews.com). Although he is clearly stating an opinion, Carter carries a certain amount of credibility because of his previous position as president of the United States and as a Nobel Peace Prize winner.

Courtesy of The Carter Center/Arne Knudsen.

FIGURE 6.7 Shown here receiving the Nobel Peace Prize in 2002, Jimmy Carter possesses credibility when he expresses his opinions because people are aware of his past accomplishments.

Your online lesson provides more information about how to paraphrase carefully and correctly. See Topic 3.

Guidelines for Using Testimony

- **Use only recognizable or credible testimony and quotations.** Before citing a person as an authoritative source, be sure that he or she is an expert and that you state your experts' credentials during your speech. As you review expert testimony, keep in mind that the more research you do, the more opinions you will find. Ultimately, your choice should be guided by relevance and credibility of the source. The fact that you quote Supreme Court Justice Elena Kagan in a speech on affirmative action is as important as the quote itself.

- **Choose unbiased experts.** How effective is the following testimony if its source is the owner of the Oakland Athletics?

  There is no team in baseball as complete as the Athletics. The team has better pitching, fielding, hitting, and base running than any of its competitors in the National or American League.

  If the same quote came from a baseball writer for *Sports Illustrated*, you would probably believe it more. Thus, when choosing expert testimony, bear in mind that opinions shaped by self-interest are less valuable, from the point of view of your audience, than those motivated by the merits of the issues.

- **Identify the source.** Testimony is based in using someone else's credibility to enhance your speech, so you must identify and credential your source. If it is reasonable to assume that your audience would also recognize your sources as an expert, simply stating their name may be sufficient. However, not all of your experts will be recognizable, so it is important to tell your audience why they are qualified to give testimony. If your expert is not well known, you should state his credentials first. For example, "According to Rick Steves, host and producer of the popular public television series *Rick Steves' Europe* and best-selling author of thirty European travel books, travelers should be wary of... ."

- **Develop techniques to signal the beginning and ending of each quotation.** Your audience may not know when a quote begins or ends. Some speakers prefer to preface quotations with the words, such as "to quote," "in the words of," and the more formal, "And I quote" followed by "end quote." Nonverbal ways (which are preferable to some) to indicate you are quoting are through pauses immediately before and immediately after the quotation or through a slight change of pace or inflection. It may be a good idea to use both techniques in your speech to satisfy your listeners' need for variety. Just do not make quotation signs with your fingers!

FIGURE 6.8 Indicating a direct quotation is best achieved either by verbally stating that it is a quote or by varying your vocal intonation. Air quotes—making the quote signals with your fingers—is the one method you should avoid.

analogy
A comparison made to show similarity.

Analogies

At times, the most effective form of supporting material is the **analogy**, which points out similarities between what we know and understand and what we do not know or cannot accept. Analogies fall into two separate categories: figurative and literal. Figurative analogies draw comparisons between things that are distinctly different in an attempt to clarify a concept or persuade. Biology professor and world-renowned environmentalist Paul Ehrlich uses an analogy of a globe holding and draining water to explain the problem of the world population explosion. The following is an excerpt from a speech delivered to the First National Congress on Optimum Population and Environment, June 9, 1970:

> *As a model of the world demographic situation, think of the world as a globe, and think of a faucet being turned on into that globe as being the equivalent of the birth rate, the input into the population. Think of that drain at the base of that globe—water pouring out—as being the equivalent to the output, the death rate of the population. At the time of the Agricultural Revolution, the faucet was turned on full blast; there was a very high birth rate. The drain was wide open; there was a high death rate. There was very little water in the globe, very few people in the population—only above five million. When the Agricultural Revolution took place, we began to plug the drain, cut down the death rate, and the globe began to fill up.*

This analogy is effective because it helps the audience understand the population explosion. It explains the nature of the problem in a clear, graphic way. Listener understanding comes not from the presentation of new facts (these facts were presented elsewhere in the speech) but from a simple comparison. When dealing with difficult or emotionally charged concepts, listeners benefit from this type of comparative supporting material.

Keep in mind that although figurative analogies may be helpful, they usually do not serve as sufficient proof in a persuasive argument. Ehrlich, for example, backed his analogy with facts, statistics, examples, and quotations to persuade his listeners that his analogy is accurate—that we were indeed in the midst of a population crisis.

A literal analogy compares like things from similar classes, such as a game of professional football with a game of college football. If, for example, you are delivering a speech to inform your classmates about Russia's involvement in the war in Afghanistan, the following literal analogy might be helpful:

> *The war in Afghanistan was the former Soviet Union's Vietnam. Both wars were unwinnable from the start. Neither the Vietnamese nor the Afghans would tolerate foreign domination. Acting with the determination of the Biblical David, they waged a struggle against the Goliaths of Russia and the United States. In large part, the winning weapon in both wars was the collective might of village peasants who were determined to rid their countries of the Superpowers—no matter the odds.*

Literal analogies serve as proof when the aspects or concepts compared are similar. When similarities are weak, the proof fails. The analogy, "As Rome fell because of moral decay, so will the United States," is valid only if the United States and Rome have similar economic and social systems, types of governments, and so on. The fewer the similarities between the United States and Rome, the weaker the proof.

Guidelines for Using Analogies

- **Use analogies to build the power of your argument.** Analogies convince through comparison to something the audience already knows. It is psychologically comforting to your listeners to hear new ideas expressed in a familiar context. The result is greater understanding and possible acceptance of your point of view.

- **Be certain the analogy is clear.** Even when the concept of your analogy is solid, if the points of comparison are not effectively carried through from beginning to end, the analogy will fail. Your analogy must be as consistent and complete as in the following example:

  In political campaigns, opponents square off against one another in an attempt to land the winning blow. Although after a close and grueling campaign that resembles a ten-round bout, one candidate may succeed by finding a soft spot in his opponent's record, the fight is hardly over. Even while the downed opponent is flat against the mat, the victor turns to the public and tells yet another distortion of the truth. "My opponent," he says, "never had a chance." Clearly, politicians and prize fighters share one goal in common: to knock their opponents senseless and to make the public believe that they did it with ease.

- **Avoid using too many analogies.** A single effective analogy can communicate your point. Do not diminish its force by including several in a short presentation.

Your online lesson will also discuss how illustrations (pictures, cartoons, graphs, and charts) can be used as supporting material. See Topic 2.

To enhance your credibility as a speaker, you need to enhance the credibility of your message. Once you have researched your topic and evaluated its value and trustworthiness, you need to select how you will present this supporting information. Whether you use facts and statistics, narratives, explanations, testimony, or analogies, you need to be sure that you follow the guidelines.

6.3 Documenting Information Accurately in Your Speech

citation
Evidence of the source used to support a claim. May be provided verbally and in a reference sheet.

Any research included in your speech needs to be cited appropriately in order to give due credit. A **citation**, whether mentioned verbally in the speech or included on the written reference page, indicates the source of a claim, quotation, or supporting material. If you interviewed someone, your audience should know the person's name, credentials, and when and where you spoke with him or her. If you use information from a web site, the audience should know the name of the web site and when you accessed it. For print information, the audience generally needs to know the author, date, and type of publication. Your credibility is connected to your source citation. Expert sources and timely information add to your credibility. Essentially, all research used in your speech needs to be cited. Otherwise, you have committed an act of plagiarism. Following are ways to cite sources in your speech. *Consult your instructor*, however, as he or she may have specific guidelines.

6.3.1 How to Cite Sources Accurately During Your Speech

Example 1

Correct source citation. In their 1998 book on family communication, researchers Yerby, Buerkel-Rothfuss, and Bochner argue that it is difficult to understand family behavior "without an adequate description of the historical, physical, emotional, and relational context in which it occurs."

Incorrect source citation. Researchers on family communication argue that it is difficult to understand family behavior without an adequate description of the historical, physical, emotional, and relational context in which it occurs.

Explanation. We need the date to evaluate the timeliness of the material. We need to know this information was found in a book, as opposed to a television show, a newspaper, magazine, or other source. We need the authors' names so we know who wrote the information, and so we can find the book.

Example 2

Correct source citation. According to a personal interview last week with Diane Ruyle, principal of Danube High School, fewer students are choosing vocational classes than they were ten years ago.

Incorrect source citation. According to Diane Ruyle, fewer students are choosing vocational classes.

Explanation. We need to know why the person cited Diane Ruyle. As a principal, she ought to be able to provide accurate information regarding course selection. Adding "than they were ten years ago" gives the listener a comparison basis. Also, we need to know that this interview was timely; it occurred "last week."

Example 3

Correct source citation. According to an Associated Press article published in *The New York Times* on August 9, 2010, "unlike in South Carolina, state laws in Iowa and New Hampshire require officials there to hold the first caucus and primary in the nation, respectively."

Incorrect source citation. "Unlike in South Carolina, state laws in Iowa and New Hampshire require officials there to hold the first caucus and primary in the nation, respectively."

Explanation. First, if this is published information, it should be cited. Second, since most of us do not know these facts, a citation is necessary. Otherwise, the listener may believe the speaker is making this up. The date provided allows us to check the source and shows us that the information is timely. No author was identified, and since Associated Press articles can be found in many newspapers, it is important to note this was found in *The New York Times*.

Common knowledge: Lincoln was the sixteenth President of the United States. (no citation needed)

Not common knowledge: Doris Kearns Goodwin, in her 2005 biography of Lincoln, entitled *Team of Rivals*, argues that part of Lincoln's success as a president is the result of his unorthodox willingness to appoint former political adversaries to his cabinet. (citation needed)

Example 4

Correct source citation. According to the American Diabetes Association web site accessed last week, "Cholesterol is carried through the body in two kinds of bundles called lipoproteins—low-density lipoproteins and high-density lipoproteins. It's important to have healthy levels of both."

Incorrect source citation. Cholesterol is carried through the body in two kinds of bundles called lipoproteins—low-density lipoproteins and high-density lipoproteins. It's important to have healthy levels of both.

Explanation. This information is not common knowledge, so it should be cited. Many different organizations might include such information on their web site, so it is important to note that it came from the American Diabetes Association (ADA). An audience would infer that the ADA is a credible organization regarding this topic. Using the words "last week" suggests current information on the ADA web site, which reinforces the timeliness of the material.

If you have questions about what counts as common knowledge, go to your online lesson. We will review some guidelines for determining whether you need to cite your information.

Your online lesson will show you how to create a reference page (bibliography). See Topic 3.

Information that is common knowledge does not usually need to be cited. However, any factual information or claim that is not commonly known requires that you provide a citation.

© 2012 Borys Shevchuk, Shutterstock, Inc.

Remember that although you *do not* need to cite sources when you are reporting your own original ideas or discussing ideas that are commonly held, you *must* cite sources when you are quoting directly or paraphrasing (restating or summarizing a source's ideas in your own words). You must also cite or indicate on the visual aid the source of an illustration, diagram, or graph. Providing the date of publication, date of web site access, credentials of the source, and/or type of publication where applicable will allow the listener to evaluate the credibility of the information. Failing to do so is plagiarism, which is a form of academic dishonesty. Not only may your speech grade suffer but your audience will question your credibility. Additionally, your instructor is encouraged to report incidents of academic dishonesty to the office on campus that deals with student misconduct.

Your online lesson will explain why it is important to cite sources in your speech and to properly document your sources in a reference page. You will be able to link to tutorials on two of the most common styles for citation and style guides: American Psychological Association (APA) and Modern Languages Association (MLA). See Topic 3.

Chapter Summary

Research gives you the tools you need to support your thesis statement. A solid research base increases your credibility. To begin your research strategy, assess your personal knowledge and skills. Then look for print and online resources. The librarian can lead you to valuable sources within the physical library as well as online. Regardless of the sources you use, it is important to question the accuracy, authority, objectivity, coverage, and currency of the source.

Supporting materials strengthen the main points of your speech and make you a more credible speaker. Among the most important forms of support are facts— verifiable information. Facts clarify your main points, indicate knowledge of your subject, and serve as definitions. Opinions differ from facts in that they cannot be verified. Statistical support involves the presentation of information in numerical form. Because statistics are easily manipulated, it is important to analyze carefully the data you present.

Narratives are stories within a speech that are linked to the speaker's main idea. Narratives engage the audience and personalize the topic. Hypothetical stories are fictional examples used to make a point. Personal narratives are anecdotes related to your topic that come from your own life. Explanations, including definitions, examples, and process descriptions, will help simplify complex topics and clarify processes.

When you use quotations, you cite the words of others to increase the credibility of your message. Your sources gain expertise through experience and authority. Analogies focus on the similarities between the familiar and unfamiliar. Figurative analogies compare things that are different, while liberal analogies compare things from similar classes. Literal analogies can often be used as proof.

Key Terms

academic journal, 157

analogy, 172

citation, 174

example, 168

facts, 163

general index, 157

information literacy, 151

mean, 165

median, 165

message credibility, 150

mode, 165

narrative, 166

opinions, 163

primary research, 152

secondary research, 152

speaker credibility, 150

statistics, 165

supporting material, 152

testimony, 169

Questions for Reflection

1. How important is research in the preparation of most speeches? How can an audience tell whether a speech lacks a sound research base?
2. Why is it important that you conduct both an audience analysis and reflect on your own knowledge and skills when it comes to developing your topic?
3. When you are considering information you found on a web site, how do you evaluate whether or not the information you found is appropriate to include as supporting material?
4. How can you best use the services of a librarian?
5. With the idea of a research strategy in mind, how will you determine the types and amount of support you will need to meet the specific purpose of your next speech?
6. Which supporting materials are most effective for clarifying a point and which are most appropriate for proof? Can some forms of support serve both aims? How?
7. In the hands of an unethical speaker, how can statistics and analogies mislead an audience? What is your ethical responsibility in choosing supporting materials?

Activities

1. Tour the libraries at school and in your community. In a written report, compare the facilities and use your findings as a guide when you research your next speech.
2. For your next speech assignment, develop and follow a search strategy that includes both interviews and library research.
3. Analyze the connection between your choice of topic and your choice of support.
4. Select three different forms of support and assess the strengths and weaknesses of each as evidence in public speeches.
5. Include in your next persuasive speech as many different forms of support as possible. After your speech, hand out a questionnaire to determine which form of support had the most effect.

References

American Library Association. (1989). Presidential committee on information literacy. Final report. Retrieved from http://www.ala.org/ala/mgrps/divs/acrl/publications/whitepapers/presidential.cfm

Dowling, C. G. (1988, August 1). Shoplifting. *Life*, p. 33.

Ehrlich, P. (1970, June 9). Speech delivered to First National Congress on Optimum Population and Environment.

Goldenberg, D. (2006, July 29). "The funniest movie you'll see this fiscal quarter." *Gelf Magazine*. Retrieved from http://www.gelfmagazine.com/archives/the_funniest_movie_youll_see_this_fiscal_quarter.php

Goodwin, D. K. (2005). *Team of rivals*. New York: Simon & Schuster.

Harris, R. (2002). *Using sources effectively: Strengthening your writing and avoiding plagiarism*. Glendale, CA: Pyrczak Publishing.

Kolodner, J. K. (1983). Towards an understanding of the role of experience in the evolution from novice to expert. *International Journal of Man-Machine Studies, 19*, 497–518.

Obama, B. (2009, October). Presidential proclamation for Information Literacy Awareness month. Retrieved from http://www.whitehouse.gov/the_press_office/Presidential-Proclamation-National-Information-Literacy-Awareness-Month/

Radford, M. L., Barnes, S. B., & Barr, L. (2006). *Web research: Selecting, evaluating, and citing*. Boston: Allyn & Bacon.

Roberts, C. (2010). Correlations among variables in message and messenger credibility scales. *American Behavioral Scientist 54*(1), 43–56.

Sawyer, S. (1988, September). Psychology of a middle-aged shoplifter. *Ms., 17*, p. 46.

U.S. Census Bureau (2010, September). Household incomes for states: 2008 and 2009. Retrieved from http://www.census.gov/hhes/www/income/income.html

Yerby, J., Buerkel-Rothfuss, N. L., and Bochner, A. P. (1998). *Understanding family communication* (2d ed.). Needham Heights, MA: Allyn & Bacon.

Chapter 7

© 2012, Laralova, Shutterstock, Inc.

Learning Objectives

After reading this chapter and completing the online activities for this lesson, you will be able to:

1. Explain and apply the appropriate patterns and strategies for a given speech topic.

2. Explain the benefit of connections within a speech.

3. List the steps in organizing and outlining the speech.

Organizing and Outlining Your Ideas

INTRODUCTION

We live in a rambling, technologically distracted culture; people rarely get to the point quickly as they attempt to balance casual conversation with the constant attention directed to their cell phones—an ill-timed text, tweet, or status update can completely disrupt the flow of successful face-to-face communication. Additionally, the inescapable presence of reality television has forced us to be subjected to a stream of consciousness from everyday people who have absolutely no plan when they speak. Watching a rerun episode of *The Hills* can further this point; the speaking that takes place while two of the show's "actresses" discuss a story from their clubbing experience the night before is often dangerously mind numbing. Usually the content is all over the place—no central idea, a variety of verbal fillers, some awkward moments of silence (which are generally filled with furtive glances to their cell phones), and a major lack of "getting to the point." Reality television serves as a reminder for what NOT to do as a public speaker. In order to capture your audience and successfully convey your information, you must have a plan for where you would like to end up and how you would like to get there. This plan represents the *organization* of your speech or the reasonable connection of your ideas. You *and* your audience will greatly benefit from your use of organization to "get to the point" in an interesting and sophisticated manner.

© 2012 Monkey Business Images, Shutterstock, Inc.

FIGURE 7.1 Technical distractions like text messaging can challenge organized and coherent speaking.

7.1 The Importance of Organizing a Speech

A good speech flows smoothly and consists of a clearly defined beginning, middle, and end, otherwise known as the introduction, body, and conclusion. Your introduction should hook the audience (through use of an attention getter), establish your credibility, and orient the audience to the direction and main points of the speech. The body of the speech ties directly to the introduction and expands on your main ideas, using details and support to fully develop your content and intent. The conclusion, simply stated, summarizes the body and provides a sense of closure. You and your listeners should be able to easily identify these parts of your speech. Also, listeners expect your speech to sound logical. A speech that is missing a clear introduction, or a presentation that has main points unrelated to the introduction, is a lot like reading a book or watching a film without a clear plot; it is tolerable for a while, but eventually we grow tired of waiting for a tangible point to be made. Consequently, a disorganized speech will probably cause your audience to lose interest, perceive you poorly, and begin to tune you out. It doesn't matter if you have gathered astounding facts or have incredible quotes to support your main ideas; if your speech isn't structured logically, it simply isn't going to be effective. Instead of just writing a speech without any clear sense of direction, you want to think about how to best organize it first. This chapter presents several different organizational patterns as well as a template for outlining. You have many decisions to make when organizing, such as the pattern of organization, the number of main points needed, what relevant sub-points to include, and where to put transitions and internal previews. These choices, however, are exciting ones because each brings you a step closer to your ultimate destination: a logical, well-organized, and successful speech.

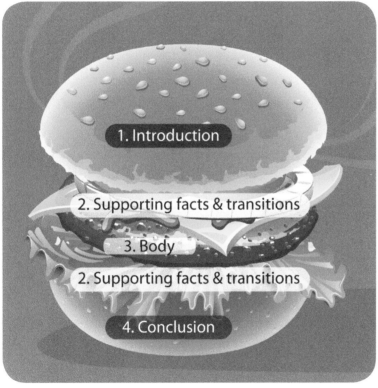

Courtesy of Don Vierstra.

FIGURE 7.2 Think of a well-organized speech like a hamburger, with the top and bottom buns representing the introduction and conclusion and the meat and condiments as the speech's body sections—all of the elements work together to create a unified entity.

7.2 Organizing the Body of Your Speech

When embarking on the journey to organize your speech, it is essential to first determine the *general purpose*. As mentioned earlier in this textbook, the general purpose of most every speech is to inform, persuade, or entertain. Once your

organization of ideas
The placement of lines of reasoning and supporting materials in a pattern that helps to achieve your specific purpose.

general purpose is solidified, you can begin to engage in an **organization of ideas**, which, in public speaking, refers to the placement of lines of reasoning and supporting materials in a pattern that helps to achieve your specific purpose. Following a consistent pattern of organization with interconnected main points enables your listeners to pay better attention to your message. An organized speech flows smoothly and clearly, starting with the introduction, moving through the body, and ending with the conclusion. The *introduction* should capture your audience's attention and indicate your intent. The *body* includes each of your main points and all supporting material as reflected in your specific purpose and thesis statement. The *conclusion* reinforces your message and brings your speech to a close. The introduction and conclusion definitely are important, but audiences expect you to spend the greatest deal of time and effort expanding on your main points. In order for the body of your speech to flow from the introduction, it is important to reflect first on your specific purpose and thesis statement.

Since your *specific purpose* is a statement of intent and your *thesis statement* identifies the main ideas of your speech, referring to them as you determine your main points will help you to achieve clarity. For example, consider a speech discussing how family pets help children with psychological problems. You might develop the following:

General Purpose: *To inform my audience about the benefit of therapy dogs*

Specific Purpose: *To explain to my audience how therapy dogs can provide psychological benefits for children with emotional problems.*

Thesis Statement: *Regular interactions with a therapy dog can help children with emotional problems to feel better about themselves, encourage the development of important social skills, and aid therapists in building rapport with difficult-to-reach patients.*

Your thesis statement indicates that your speech will address self-esteem, the development of social skills, and therapist rapport building. This suggests that there are many peripheral topics you will *exclude*, such as the type of dog, dog grooming tips, medical advancements in the treatment of canine leukemia, how to choose a kennel when you go on vacation, and so on.

Courtesy of Rachel A. Wegter.

FIGURE 7.3 As the speech example demonstrates, therapy dogs can bring joy and comfort to patients of all ages.

7.2.1   Select Your Main Points

After deciding on your general and specific purposes, organizing the body of your speech involves a **four-step process**:

1. Select the main points,
2. Support the main points,
3. Choose the best organizational pattern, and
4. Create unity throughout the speech.

Before you think about organizing your speech, you need to determine your main points. *Main points are the key ideas*, or the most important issues that you want to discuss with your audience; your main points will be reflected within your thesis statement. One way to establish your main points is through brainstorming, which involves generating a list of ideas consistent with the goals of your speech without critical evaluation.

Brainstorming, by nature, must initially be a judgment-free process. For example, if you are doing a speech on the benefits of water, during the brainstorming process you would write down every benefit you can think of without deeming some better than others. Ideas like "water is a hydrator," "water is fun to swim in, "water flushes out toxins," "water transports boats," "water can help you lose weight," "water puts out fires," and "water has no calories" may come to mind, but be mindful to list as much as you can before you begin selecting the most reasonable points. When choosing key ideas from a brainstormed list, you should look for logical connections between your ideas so that the points you settle on are easy to organize into a coherent and focused speech. In the water example, you may decide to select the reasons that support water consumption as a *health* benefit (which would naturally exclude "water is fun to swim in" and "water puts out fires"). Make sure to choose related points that are also distinct from each other—this way, you will avoid redundancy. In turn, you may select "water is a hydrator," "water flushes out toxins" and "water helps you lose weight" but NOT choose "water has no calories" because it is too closely related to "water helps you lose weight" and can be mentioned internally when you expand on that point. A good rule of thumb is to settle on no fewer than two and no more than five main points. If you have too few, your speech can feel underdeveloped; if you have too many, you may not have time to provide adequate support and ultimately confuse your listeners. An audience analysis should help direct you in terms of what points you need to make and the extent to which you need to support them.

> **four-step process**
> The way in which to organize a speech, which involves selecting the main points, supporting the main points, choosing the best organizational pattern, and creating unity throughout the speech.

© 2012 ra2 studio, Shutterstock, Inc.

FIGURE 7.4 Brainstorming can help you to effectively determine the main points you should include in your speech.

7.2.2 Support Your Main Points

After selecting your main points, use the supporting material (discussed in detail in Chapter 6) you have gathered to strengthen each main point. Many people bristle when they think about researching—the process can feel so overwhelming. The key to successfully finding supporting material is to think about the process systematically. As a small child, you may remember having a simple toy involving a collection of blocks in the form of shapes and box with shapes cut out of it; the goal was to put the correct block into its corresponding shape in the box. Circle blocks would be put the circle-shaped cutout and triangles in the triangle-shaped slot, however, if you tried to put the square block in the rectangle-shaped slot, it would not fit. Although the toy was basic by today's standards, it taught children a valuable lesson: put things where they fit.

© 2012 Christopher Hall, Shutterstock, Inc.

FIGURE 7.5 Much like this classic toy from childhood, your supporting material should fit within the overarching frames of your main points.

Locating supporting points is quite the same way—if you find material that "fits" with your main points, then you are simply sorting ideas and putting them where they belong. Patterns must be matched, rational links must be formed, and common sense must prevail. When you finish, each point underneath the main point is called a sub-point (and sub-sub-point, and so on). Each sub-point is an extension of the point it supports. If the connection seems forced (or, the "block" doesn't fit), reconsider the match. Here, for example, is one way to develop the three main points of the speech on water.

> **Main Point 1:** *Water is the single most effective hydrator in existence, thereby protecting us from dehydration.*
>
> > **Sub-Point 1:** Many people do not even know that they are dehydrated. Signs of dehydration include: fatigue, headache and muscle weakness.
> >
> > **Sub-Point 2:** Even mild dehydration, or 1 to 2 percent loss of your body weight, can sap your energy and make you feel tired.
> >
> > **Sub-Point 3:** Drinking eight 8-ounce glasses of water a day can effectively combat dehydration.

Main Point 2: *Drinking water helps to flush out the toxins that gather in the human body.*

    Sub-Point 1: Chemicals and preservatives found in everyday foods can build up in the body and harm organ function.

    Sub-Point 2: According to the Mayo Clinic, drinking water flushes toxins out of vital organs, which helps the body to function properly.

    Sub-Point 3: Those who drink water for detoxification purposes report better digestion, increased energy, and clearer skin.

Main Point 3: *Water consumption can aid in the weight loss process.*

    Sub-Point 1: Since water contains no calories, replacing soda, coffee, and alcohol with water will help the body shed excess weight.

    Sub-Point 2: Health experts agree that drinking at least 8 ounces of water before eating a meal can give off the feeling of fullness, thereby allowing an individual to eat less overall.

    Sub-Point 3: Frequently drinking water can also help the body to release stored water that collects in times when water consumption is low—this aids in losing unnecessary water weight.

As you weave your main points and support together, your speech should grow in substance and strength. It will be clear to your listeners that you have something significant to say and that you are saying it in an organized way.

The online lesson provides you with more examples of how to develop main and supporting points. See Topic 1.

7.2.3 Choose the Best Pattern for Organizing Your Main Points

The way you organize your main points depends on your specific purpose and thesis statement, the type of material you are presenting, and the needs of your audience. As you develop your main points, you need to consider what you want to emphasize.

Assuming you have established three main points, you need to choose how to weight your main points. That is, are you going to spend approximately the same amount of time on each point because they are all of equal importance, or are some points more compelling than others, requiring you to distribute your attention to the points differently? To help you decide, three options are possible. First, you may choose the **equality pattern**, which involves giving equal time to each point. This means that you will spend approximately the same time on each point as you deliver your speech. For example, if the body of your speech was six minutes long, each point would take about two minutes to develop.

Using the **strongest point pattern** is a second option. In this situation, you would spend the most time on your first (and strongest) point, a bit less time on your next point and the least amount of time on your final point. The goal is to get the audience to process, retain, and recall your strongest and most effective points. When testing memory, psychologists discovered that, when presented with a list of items,

equality pattern
An organizational pattern that involves giving approximately the same amount of time to each point.

strongest point pattern
You spend the most time in your speech on the first point, less time on the second point, and even less time on the last point of your speech.

primacy effect
The belief that it is the first point in your speech that listeners will most likely remember.

progressive pattern
Using your least important point first and your most important point last.

recency effect
The belief that it is the last point in your speech that listeners will most likely remember.

chronological organization
Information in a speech organized chronologically is focused on relationships in time; events are presented in the order in which they occur.

topical organization
The most frequently used organizational system tied to the unique needs of your topic; the nature and scope of your topic dictate the pattern of your approach.

spatial organization
An organization pattern in which the sequence of ideas moves from one physical point to another.

cause-and-effect organization
Focuses on arranging main points into causes and effects.

problem-solution organization
Especially common in persuasive speeches, the goal is to present an audience with a problem and then examine one or more likely solutions.

individuals remembered information that was presented either at the beginning of the list *or* at the end. The strongest point pattern, which weighs the first point heavier than the other points, reflects the phenomenon known as the **primacy effect**.

A third option is to follow a **progressive pattern**. This involves presenting your least important point first and your most important point last. If you choose to stress one point over another, you will spend the least amount of time speaking about your first, a bit more time on your next point, and the most amount of time on your last point. This pattern takes into consideration the **recency effect**, which suggests that people will remember most what they have just processed. Anyone who has heard the phrase, "What have you done for me lately?" understands the significance of the recency effect.

The pattern you choose depends on your topic and audience. Based on these three options, keep in mind that your strongest argument does *not go* in the middle of your main points.

In addition to organizing your main points by emphasis, your information should fit within an overall organizational framework. Many choices exist for any given speech but based on the specific purpose statement, one pattern of organization is generally more appropriate than the others. The five effective patterns of organization we will cover are **chronological**, **topical**, **spatial**, **cause-and-effect**, and **problem-solution**.

Chronological Organization

In a chronological speech, information is focused on relationships in time. Events are presented in the order in which they occur. When developing your speech chronologically, you can choose to organize your ideas by starting at the beginning and moving to the present, then looking to the future, or following a step-by-step process.

To show how different chronological organizational patterns affect the content and emphasis of a speech, we will choose a topic, establish different purposes for speaking, and show how the presentation differs when the organizational pattern is changed. The first example is representative of a typical chronological pattern (note how the dates in the main points move sequentially from 1951 to 1979):

Topic: The development of the European Union

Specific purpose: To inform the class about crucial events that occurred over a 40-year span that influenced the development of the European Union (EU).

Thesis statement: Although the European Union was created in 1993, with the signing of the Maastricht Treaty, the creation of a coal and steel community, establishment of a common market, and direct elections to the European Parliament were critical events that influenced its development.

Main points:

- West Germany, together with France, Italy, and Benelux, signed the Treaty of Paris in 1951, which created the European Coal and Steel community.

- In 1957, the Treaty of Rome established the European Economic Community, known as the common market to English-speaking countries.
- In 1979, the first direct elections to the European Parliament are held.

Chronological order can also be used to construct a **past-present-future** organizational pattern. For example, in a speech addressing the development of the European Union, one could present the same topic with a slightly different specific purpose statement that would lead to a different thesis statement and different focus for the main points. Consider the following past-present-future example:

Topic: The development of the European Union

Specific purpose: To inform the class how the European Union became a 27-member community that is poised to grow significantly.

Thesis statement: Developed after three important treaties, the 27-member European Union is poised to add another nine countries to its community

Main points:

- Treaties of Paris, Rome, and Maastricht were crucial to the development of the European Union.
- Currently, the European Union is a community of 27 member states that are connected both politically and economically.
- As an indicator of future growth, at least nine countries are potential candidates for inclusion in the European Union.

Using a past-present-future order allows you to provide perspective for a topic or issue that has relevant history and future direction or potential. Notice that in the regular chronological pattern, the three treaties are the main focus of the speech. In the past-present-future pattern, the three treaties would receive much less coverage.

Finally, chronological patterns can be used to describe the **step-by-step** order of a specific and clearly defined process. Here is a step-by-step description of how Academy Award (Oscar) winners are determined. Like the other patterns, the process shows a movement in time:

Step 1: *In December, the close to 6,000 members of the Academy of Motion Picture Arts and Sciences (comprised of actors, directors, producers, editors, screenwriters, and composers) receive a ballot to nominate the top five best in their occupational category, ranked by order of preference.*

Step 2: *Over the course of seven days, the nomination ballots are counted by hand using a complicated preferential voting system.*

Step 3: *The top five nominees in each category are determined when their first place rankings reach the "magic number," which reflects the total number of ballots for that category divided by number of nominees (five) plus one.*

Step 4: *The nominees are then placed on a new ballot and the entire Academy can vote for each category (one vote per category) with the most votes in each category determining the Oscar winners.*

past-present-future
A form of the chronological pattern that allows a speaker to provide perspective for a topic or issue that has relevant history and future direction or potential.

step-by-step
A form of the chronological pattern that is used to describe the steps, in order, of a process.

Spatial Organization

In speeches organized according to a spatial pattern, the sequence of ideas moves from one physical point to another—from London to Istanbul, from basement to attic, from end zone to end zone. To be effective, your speech must follow a consistent directional path. If you are presenting a new marketing strategy to the company sales force, you can arrange your presentation by geographic regions—first the East, then the South, then the Midwest, and finally, the West. If, after completing the pattern, you begin talking about your plans for Boston, your listeners will be confused.

So, in a speech on the European Union (EU), one could use a spatial organization pattern to discuss the growth of the EU over time.

- Six Western European countries joined to establish the European Union.
- Countries bordering the Eastern Mediterranean are candidates for inclusion in the European Union.
- As Central and Eastern European countries emerged from dictatorship, they wanted to join the European Union in order to avoid falling back into the Russian sphere of influence.

Notice the differences between the main points for this speech organized spatially, and the earlier examples of speeches organized chronologically. A speech with the above three points would focus more on the countries involved with the European Union than how the EU came about.

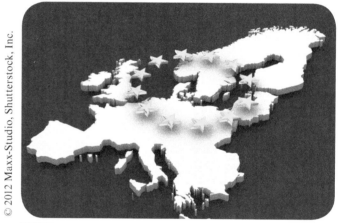

© 2012 Maxx-Studio, Shutterstock, Inc.

FIGURE 7.6 Spatial organization allows a speaker to map out his or her main points from place to place in an orderly and rational manner.

Cause and Effect

With the cause-and-effect organizational pattern, you can focus specifically on *why* something happened and *what* the consequences of the event or action were. The following topical statements could be developed into speeches that use a cause-and-effect pattern:

- Alcoholism damages American family life.
- Too much positive feedback in primary school results in young adults being unable to cope with life's problems.

- Fast food is a significant contributor to obesity in the United States.
- Traveling abroad reduces prejudice.
- Smoking hurts relationships.

Note that in each case, you would be trying to establish that something caused something to happen. For example, the effect alcoholism has on family life is that it causes harm. The effect traveling has on people is reducing prejudice. Therefore, traveling is seen as a cause. Some topics have direct links that can be made with facts and/or statistics ("Smoking causes cancer") and others have indirect connections that must be proved with facts and other forms of support, such as testimony, examples, or illustrations ("Smoking hurts relationships").

Problem-Solution Organization

A common strategy, especially in persuasive speeches, is to present an audience with a problem and then examine one or more likely solutions. For example, in a classroom speech, one student described a serious safety problem for female students walking alone on campus after dark. He cited incidents in which women were attacked and described unlit areas along campus walkways where the attacks had taken place. Next, he turned to a series of proposals to eliminate, or at least minimize, the problem. His solutions included a new campus escort service, sponsored and maintained by various campus organizations, the installation of halogen lights along dark campus walks, and the trimming of bushes where assailants could hide.

Occasionally, speakers choose to present the solution before the problem. Had this student done so, he would have identified how to provide effective security before he explained why these solutions were necessary. Many audiences have trouble with this type of reversal of ideas because they find it hard to accept solutions when they are not familiar with the problems that brought them about. Consider the topic below, which is developed using a problem-solution pattern.

> **Problem:** Children who participate in beauty pageants are forced to grow up too soon; they are subjected to harsh beautification processes like tanning and waxing and are expected to act like adults when on stage.

> **Solution:** Beauty pageants for children should have strict rules about how children prepare for and compete in such competitions. All children should be "natural" and allowed to behave like young people when competing.

If the speech opened with the solution, there likely would be audience members who would be confused about the need for new pageant regulations without understanding the current climate of child beauty pageants. In turn, beginning with the problem is a wise strategy to hook the audience and cause them to care about the issue.

Topical Organization

The most frequently used organizational system is not tied to time or space, problem or solution, or cause or effect, but, instead, to the unique needs of your topic. The nature and scope of your topic dictate the pattern of your approach.

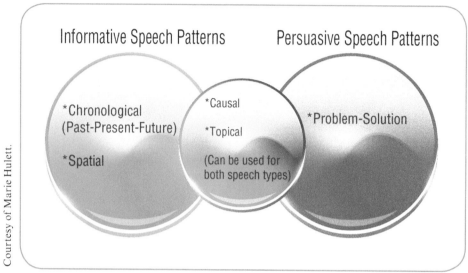

Courtesy of Marie Hulett.

FIGURE 7.7 The figure above shows which organizational patterns are best for informative and persuasive speeches and which patterns work well for both.

Working within the confines of your topic, you determine a workable pattern. If you are delivering a humorous speech on society's addiction to Facebook and other social networking sites, you can arrange your topics according to their level of humor. For example:

The *"friends"* that people have on Facebook who are not really friends at all.

The *constant checking of friends' status updates* when people are bored or faced with a difficult task that they would like to procrastinate.

The amount of time that people *spend playing Farmville or Mafia Wars.*

The fact that people take pictures of themselves, not just to immortalize the moment, but with instant uploading to Facebook in mind.

These topics relate to society's reliance on and relationship with Facebook, but there is no identifiable chronological pattern, so topical order makes sense. When organizing topically, think about how to link and order topics. Transitions can help the audience understand the connections and will be discussed in the following section.

FIGURE 7.7 above shows which organizational patterns are best for informative and persuasive speeches and which patterns work well for either speech type.

The online lesson gives you an opportunity to practice matching organizational patterns to different speech topics. See Topic 1.

7.2.4   Create Unity through Connections

Without connections, your main points may be difficult to follow. Consider a linked chain; if one or more of the links are faulty, the chain is compromised and isn't safe to wear. In turn, you will want to incorporate reasonable links between information in your speeches so that the audience can effectively follow along. To establish the necessary connections, use transitions, internal previews, and internal summaries.

© 2012 kavram, Shutterstock, Inc .

FIGURE 7.8 Transitions in your speech should logically lead the audience from one idea to the next.

Transitions

Transitions are the verbal bridges between ideas. They are words, phrases, or sentences that tell your audience how ideas relate. Transitions are critical because they clarify the direction of your speech by giving your audience a means to follow your organization. With only one opportunity to hear your remarks, listeners depend on transitions to make sense of your ideas.

It helps to think of transitions as verbal signposts that signal the organization and structure of your speech. **TABLE 7.1** offers several examples:

transitions
Verbal bridges between ideas, words, phrases, or sentences that tell your audience how ideas relate.

TABLE 7.1 Verbal Signposts		
"The first proposal I would like to discuss…"	→	This tells listeners that several more ideas will follow.
"Now that we've finished looking at the past, let's move to the future."	→	These words indicate a movement in time.
"Next, I'll turn from a discussion of the problems to a discussion of the solutions."	→	This tells your listeners that you are following a problem-solution approach.
"On the other hand, many people believe…"	→	Here you signal an opposing viewpoint.

TABLE 7.2 is a list of common transitional words that reflect the speaker's purpose in using them (Makay & Fetzger, 1984, p. 68):

TABLE 7.2 Suggested Transitional Words	
Speaker's Purpose	**Suggested Transitional Words**
To define:	*that is to say; according to; in other words*
To explain:	*for example; specifically*
To add:	*furthermore; also; in addition; likewise*
To change direction:	*although; on the other hand; conversely*
To show both sides:	*nevertheless; equally*
To contrast:	*but; still; on the contrary*
To indicate cause:	*because; for this reason; since; on account of*
To summarize	*recapping; finally; in retrospect; summing up*
To conclude:	*in conclusion; therefore; and so; finally*

Internal Previews and Summaries

internal previews
Extended transitions that tell the audience, in general terms, what you will say next.

Internal previews are extended transitions that tell the audience, in general terms, what you will say next. These are frequently used in the body of the speech to outline in advance the details of a main point. Here are two examples:

- I am going to discuss the orientation you can expect to receive during your first few days on the job, including a tour of the plant, a one-on-one meeting with your supervisor, and a second meeting with the personnel director, who will explain the benefits and responsibilities of working for our corporation.

- Now that I've explained to you that "vegan" means a "nondairy vegetarian," I will now share a sample vegan grocery store list and then discuss a few vegan dishes with easy-to-prepare recipes.

Although the first example would be found at the end of the introduction, notice that in the second example, the speaker combines a transition linking the material previously examined with the material to come. Previews are especially helpful when your main point is long and complex. They provide audience members with a "road map" of sorts that makes the speech journey much easier to follow.

Internal summaries follow a main point and act as reminders. Summaries are especially useful if you are trying to clarify or emphasize what you have just said, as is shown in the following two examples:

internal summaries
Follow a main point and act as reminders; useful to clarify or emphasize what you have just said.

- *In short, the American family today is not what it was forty years ago. As we have seen, with the majority of women working outside the home and with divorce and remarriage bringing stepchildren into the family picture, the traditional family—made up of a working father, a nonworking mother, and 2.3 kids—may be a thing of the past.*

- *By and large, the job market seems to be in flux for health care professionals, including nurses, aides, medical technicians, physical therapists, and hospital administrators.*

When summaries are combined with previews, they emphasize your previous point and make connections to the point to follow:

- *Overall, it is my view that television shows portraying pregnant minors should not be targeted specifically at the teenage demographic. As we have seen in recent studies, teenage pregnancies have increased with the rise in popularity of such "reality"-based programs as "Teen Mom" and "Sixteen and Pregnant." How far should reality television go to connect with its young MTV generation audience? We will discuss that next."*

- *Organization plays an important role in effective communication. The principles rhetoricians developed five centuries ago about the internal arrangement of ideas in public speaking have been tested by time and continue to be valid. Internal previews and summaries help you to create meaning with the audience by reinforcing the message and identifying what is coming next. Keep in mind that, unlike the DVR pause or skip back button on the remote control, audience members do not have the opportunity to replay or to stop for clarification. Using transitions, previews, and internal summaries are tools that you should use to facilitate understanding and reduce the potential for misunderstanding (Clarke, 1963; Daniels & Whitman 1981).*

		Main Points Checklist	
YES	**NO**		
		1. Does the body of my speech contain two to five main points?	
		2. Do the sub-points support the main points well?	
		3. Are the main points organized according in one of the following organizational methods? (Check all that apply)	
		Chronological Organization	
		Spatial Organization	
		Cause and Effect	
		Problem-Solution Organization	
		Topical Organization	
		4. Are my main points clearly separate from one another?	
		5. Reviewing the wording for my main points, have I used the same pattern of wording in each?	
		6. Have I balanced the time devoted to each main point?	
		7. Have I included transitions to make clear to my audience when I am moving from one point to another?	

Courtesy of Rachel Wegter and Marie Hulett.

FIGURE 7.9 Use the checklist above to confirm that the main points of your speech are sufficient, distinct, and well organized.

7.3 Constructing an Outline and Speaker's Notes

Presenting your ideas in an organized way requires a carefully constructed planning outline and a key-word outline to be used as speaker's notes. Both forms are critical to your success as an extemporaneous speaker—one who relies on notes rather than a written word-for-word manuscript to help you to deliver your content. Your outline is your diagram connecting the information you want to communicate in a rational, consistent way. It enables you to assemble the pieces of the information so that the puzzle makes sense to you and communicates your intended meaning to your audience. Think of outlining as a process of layering ideas on paper so that every statement supports your thesis. It is a time-consuming process, but one that will pay off in a skillful, confident presentation (Sprague & Stuart, 1992).

Be familiar with the criteria for each speech assignment. Each instructor has his or her own requirements. Some may want to see your planning outline and speaker's notes while others may not. Instead of a planning outline, your instructor may ask you to turn in a full-sentence outline that includes points, sub-points, source citation, and reference page, but excludes statements about transitions or speech flow. The following discussion is designed to help you develop and, by extension, deliver, an effective speech. Your instructor will have specific ideas about the outline and note cards.

© 2012 Helder Almeida, Shutterstock, Inc.

FIGURE 7.10 For a speech to be fully developed, it is essential to create subordinate points to support your coordinate points.

planning outline
Also known as the *full-content outline*, it includes most of the information you will present in your speech without including every word you plan to say.

7.3.1   The Planning Outline

The **planning outline**, also known as the *full-content outline*, includes most of the information you will present in your speech. It does not include every word you plan to say but gives you the flexibility required in extemporaneous speaking.

An outline consists of both coordinate and subordinate points, organized by a series of Roman numerals (e.g., I, II, III, IV, V, etc.), capital letters (e.g., A, B, C, D, E, etc.), numbers (e.g., 1, 2, 3, etc.), lowercase letters (e.g., a, b, c, d, e, etc.) and, in rare instances, lowercase Roman numerals (e.g., i, ii, iii, etc.). This rotation moves from number to letter alternately, with each letter or number getting smaller in stature.

Coordinate points are your main points and will require supporting material. **Subordinate points** support your main or coordinate points. These points provide relevant supporting material, such as facts, statistics, examples, or testimony. Every speech will have both coordinate and subordinate points. Consider the following arrangement to get a sense of how the coordinate and subordinate points are organized—note how each level is tabbed in so everything lines up reasonably and how each subordinate point supports the point above it. This arrangement will also help you to visualize the points as you read on:

I. **Main/coordinate point:** Wearing cosmetics can improve the way you look and feel about life.
  A. **Subordinate point:** A 2009 Harvard research study found that individuals who wear cosmetics are perceived as more attractive
    1. **Sub-Sub-point:** Cosmetics can allow the wearer to play up the features that she likes while concealing those she finds less satisfactory.
      a. **Sub-Sub-Sub-point:** Having control over which features you showcase allows you to present your "best self" to others.
      b. **Sub-Sub-Sub-point:** Those who are perceived as more attractive by others, often *believe* that they are more attractive.
    2. **Sub-Sub-point:** Cosmetics, then, are an easy and accessible way to have others see you in your best light.
  B. **Subordinate point:** Studies (Biola, 2011; Pepperdine, 2008) also reveal that individuals who wear cosmetics report a higher personal satisfaction with their appearance.
    1. **Sub-Sub-point:** When you look good, it is likely that you will feel good as well.
      a. **Sub-Sub-Sub-point:** Feeling good can give off an air of confidence.
      b. **Sub-Sub-Sub-point:** Having confidence is something for which everyone strives.
    2. **Sub-Sub-point:** Possessing a confident outlook can make the individual feel positive about life in general.

The online lesson includes a basic outline template for you to use when constructing brief speeches. See Topic 3.

Every outline should follow principles of outlining: **consistency**, **singularity**, **adequacy**, and **parallelism**.

Consistency. To help structure your speech logically, your outline should follow a similar or consistent pattern as reflected in the example above. Subordinate points are labeled with letters and numbers and the proper positioning of the main and subordinate points with reference to the left margin is critical, for it provides a visual picture of the way your speech is organized. Be consistent with your indentation. The main points are along the left margin, and each sub-point is indented.

coordinate points
Main points on an outline, often supported by subordinate points.

subordinate points
Supporting facts, examples, or evidence that fortify the coordinate points.

consistency
The continuity and well-organized pattern of coordinate and subordinate points within your outline.

singularity
The need for each main point to reflect a distinct area of the chosen topic.

adequacy
Reflects the need to have a sufficient amount of distinct main points in your speech, typically no fewer than two and no more than five.

parallelism
An organizational tool that relates your introduction to your conclusion.

Each sub-sub-point is indented under the sub-point. This visual image presents a hierarchy that expresses the internal logic of your ideas.

Singularity. Phrases and incomplete sentences will not state your points fluently, nor will they help you think in terms of the subtle interrelationships among ideas, transitions, and word choice. *Singularity* refers to the notion that each point and sub-point is comprised of one, separate, but logically connected, idea. A main point should not be, "We should all volunteer, and we should require that each person engage in six months of community service before age 21." These are two separate points. A well-constructed planning outline ensures a coherent, well-thought-out speech. Using full sentences defines your ideas and guides your choice of language.

Adequacy. The principle of adequacy helps you determine if you have included too little or too much information for each main point. Each level has at least two points. So, if you have a Roman numeral "I," minimally, you will see a "II." If you have a capital "A," minimally, you will see a "B." You should never have just one point or sub-point. As you develop your outline, check to see how many sub-points you have under each main point. Perhaps you are providing an information overload in one section but you lack support in another area. If you believe that there isn't more than one sub-point under a main point, then perhaps you do not have an adequate main point, and you need to rethink the general structure of your argument.

Parallelism. On the face of it, parallelism and consistency may sound like the same thing. However, consistency refers to the numbering of sections and points of your outline, whereas parallelism refers to how you construct your sentences. For example, if one point is, "Having a pet helps give children responsibility," another main point *should not* be stated, "When should you NOT have a pet?" Instead, that main point would be phrased something like, "Knowing when to not to have a pet is important. Below are a few brief examples:

>   Point 1: Destroyed are the great Redwoods that have survived over the centuries.

>   Point 2: Vanished are the small animals that used to flourish in the great forests of our nation.

>   Point 1: Joining the military will provide specific job skills.

>   Point 2: Staying in the military will provide stable income.

Parallelism goes beyond phrasing sentences, however. True parallel structure means that your introduction and your conclusion are related. For example, let's say that in your introduction to a speech on world harmony, you paint a picture of how life would be if all people on Earth lived together without war or international conflict. With parallel structure, you bring back this picture after the body of your speech, so that you can show your audience that if they did what you're asking them to do (travel, communicate with people from other countries, accept differences, or whatever you proposed) this is what life would be like. Using parallel structure is an effective organizational tool, and provides listeners with a solid sense of closure.

In summary, as you construct your outline, check to see that you are following the principles of outlining. Doing so will help identify strengths and weaknesses in support and logic, and overall, help you create an effective speech. The following template should provide you with sound speech organization:

Name:

Specific purpose:

Thesis statement:

Title of Speech

I. Introduction
   A. Attention Getter: (capture attention)
   B. Thesis Statement: (set tone, focus on topic, mention main points collectively)
   C. Credibility Statement: (establish credibility)
   D. Preview: (highlight main points to come)
   E. Transition Statement: (moves to first point)

II. Body Main Point #1:
   A. Sub-Point—Reason/Explanation:
      1. Sub-Sub-Point—Support:
      2. Sub-Sub-Point—Support:
         Sub-Sub-Sub-point support (if necessary)
         Sub-Sub-Sub-point support (if necessary)
   B. Sub Point—Reason/Explanation:
      1. Sub-Sub-Point—Support:
      2. Sub-Sub-Point—Support:
   C. Transition Statement:

III. Body Main Point #2:
   A. Sub-Point—Reason/Explanation:
      1. Sub-Sub-Point—Support:
      2. Sub-Sub-Point—Support:
   B. Sub-Point—Reason/Explanation:
      1. Sub-Sub-Point—Support:
      2. Sub-Sub-Point—Support:
   C. Transition Statement:

IV. Body Main Point #3:
   A. Sub-Point—Reason/Explanation:
      1. Sub-Sub-Point—Support:
      2. Sub-Sub-Point—Support:
   B. Sub-Point—Reason/Explanation:
      1. Sub-Sub-Point—Support:
      2. Sub-Sub-Point—Support:
   C. Transition Statement:

V. Conclusion
   A. Summarize:
   B. Restate Thesis:
   C. Creative/Memorable Close:

Notice the particulars:

- Your name, the specific purpose, thesis statement, and title of your speech are all found at the top of the page.
- Each section (introduction, body, and conclusion) is labeled.
- Each section begins with the Roman numeral "I." For the purpose of an outline, Roman numerals are created with a capital "I," or "V"—most speeches do not contain more sections than can be accommodated with a combination of "I"s and "V"s.
- As the outline moves from first- to second- to third-level headings, the specificity of details increases.
- Each point does not have to be developed identically. In some cases, there are sub-points. Sub-sub-points and sub-sub-sub-points (like the "a" and "b" in the example above). One point may need more development than another point.
- **Transitional sentences** are valuable additions to your planning outline. They are needed when you move from the introduction to the body to the conclusion of the speech. They also link various main points within the body and serve as internal previews and summaries.

transitional sentences
Phrases and sentences that help the speaker move from one major part of the speech to the next.

speaker's notes
An abbreviated key-word outline, lacking much of the detail of the planning outline. Although in a condensed format, these notes function as a reminder of what you plan to say and the order in which you plan to say it.

Check with your instructor to see if you should have a regular planning outline or a full-sentence outline. A full-sentence outline requires that each point be written as a complete sentence. This means no sentence fragments, and no more than one sentence per point.

Include at the end of your planning outline a reference page listing all the sources used to prepare your speech, including books, magazines, journals, newspaper articles, videos, speeches, and interviews. If you are unfamiliar with documentation requirements, check the style guide preferred by your instructor, such as the *American Psychological Association (APA) Publication Manual* (online access at www.apastyle.apa.org), and the *Modern Literature Association (MLA) Handbook for Writers of Research Papers* (online access at www.mla.org). For additional help with the style sheets, peruse the home page of the online writing lab at owl.english.purdue.edu. Also, there are some great cell phone apps, such as QuickCite, which can make your citation process a portable experience. Make sure to ask your instructor how detailed your source citation should be in the outline. Information for you to identify typically includes last name, credentials, type of book (or magazine, journal, web page, or other source), year/date of publication.

The online lesson includes an expanded outline template with every element necessary for you to construct a longer and more detailed speech. See Topic 4.

7.3.2   A Brief Overview of Speaker's Notes

Speaker's notes are an abbreviated key-word outline, lacking much of the detail of the planning outline. They function as a reminder of what you plan to say and the order in which you plan to say it. Speaker's notes follow exactly the pattern of your planning outline but in a condensed format.

Follow the same indentation pattern you used in your planning outline to indicate your points and sub-points. Include notations for the introduction, body, and conclusion and indicate transitions. It can be helpful to include suggestions for an effective delivery. You might remind yourself to slow down, gesture, pause, or transition in your presentational aids. This information will be helpful during your speech, especially if you experience public speaking apprehension. Consider the following speaker's notes for the outline on cosmetics usage mentioned earlier in this chapter:

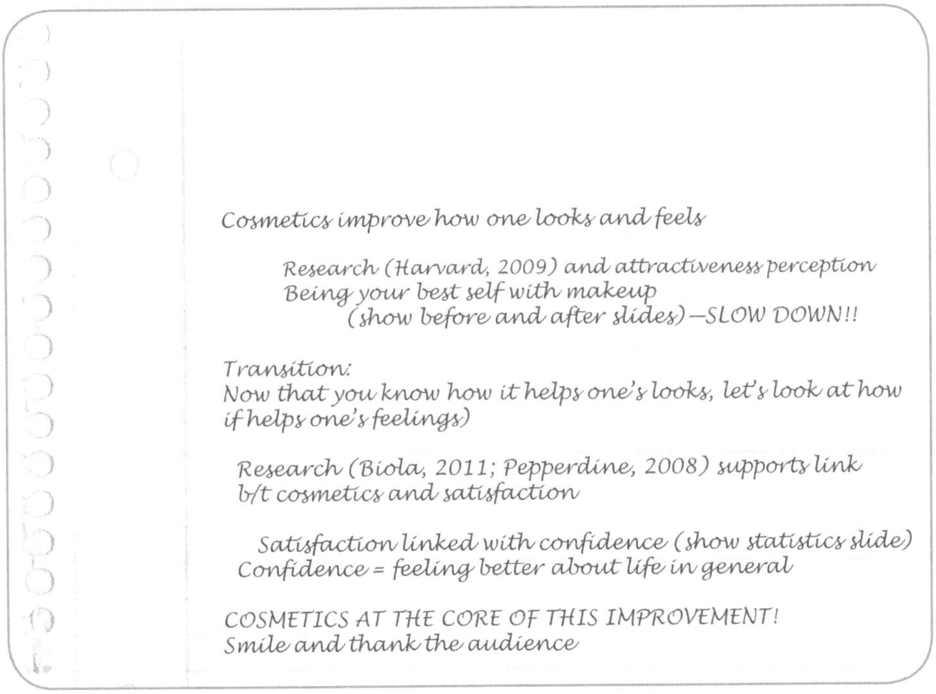

Courtesy of Rachel Wegter and Marie Hulett.

FIGURE 7.11 Speaker's notes consist of a small collection of only the most necessary ideas, key words, and delivery notes.

7.3.3 Guidelines for Constructing Speaker's Notes

- **Avoid overloading your outline.** Some speakers believe that having substantial information with them at the podium will give them confidence and make them more prepared. The opposite is usually true. Speakers who bombard themselves with too many details are torn between focusing on their audience and focusing on their notes. Too often, as they frantically move their heads up and down, they lose their place.

- **Include only necessary information.** You need just enough information to remind you of your planned points. At times, of course, you must be certain of your facts and your words, such as when you quote an authority or present complex statistical data. In these cases, include all the information you need in your speaker's notes.

- **Reduce your sentences to key phrases.** Instead of writing "The American Medical Association, an interest group for doctors, has lobbied against socialized medicine," write "The AMA and socialized medicine." Your notes should serve as a stimulus for what you are going to say. If you only need a few words to remind you, then use them. For example, Laura, who had directed several high school musicals, planned to discuss the various aspects of directing a high school musical. Her speaker's notes could include the following key words:

casting

blocking

choreography

singing

acting

Little else would be needed, since she can easily define and/or describe these aspects of directing. However, under the key word "casting," she might include "when to cast," and "how to cast." Relevant quotes or perhaps a reference to a dramatic story would be included in the notes as well.

- **Include transitions in an abbreviated form.** If you included each transition, your notes would be too long, and you would have too much written on them. Look at one of the transitions from the previous speech on child beauty pageants:

(Transition): *Because most of us believe that children should be able to pursue whatever interests them, I see a lot of confused faces in the audience. However, child beauty pageants actually squelch the childhood experience and cause children to grow up too fast.*

In this speech, we will identify the most significant problems with child beauty pageants, such as the use of harsh beatification processes. Next we will explore why children in pageants are being expected to act like adults and, finally, we'll examine how to correct and balance the competitive environment that is currently too intense for young children.

Instead of these two paragraphs, your speaker's notes might look like this:

Confused faces

Beauty pageants squelch childhood

Will discuss problems, causes, solutions

If you practice your speech, these words should suffice as notes. Abbreviate in a way that makes sense to you. Each person will have his or her own version of shorthand.

- **Notes must be legible.** Your notes are useless if you cannot read them. Because you will be looking up and down at your notes as you speak, you must be able to find your place with ease at any point. Do not reduce your planning outline to 8-point type and paste it to note cards. If you can type your notes, make sure they are formatted as 14-point type or larger. If you write your notes, take the time to write legibly. As mentioned previously in Chapter 3, notes should be on one side of the paper or note card only; also, make sure to number each note should they become shuffled or accidentally dropped. Consider this: You may have spent several hours researching, preparing, and organizing your speech. Why take the chance of reducing the impact of your speech by writing your notes at the last minute? In turn, prepare them with care and they will be an excellent asset to you speech delivery.

Chapter Summary

The first step in organizing your speech is to determine your main points. Organize your efforts around your specific purpose and thesis statement, and then brainstorm to generate specific ideas, and finally, group similar ideas. Your second step is to use supporting material to develop each main point. In step three, choose an organizational pattern. Arrange your ideas in chronological order, use a spatial organizational pattern, follow a pattern of cause and effect, look at a problem and its solutions, or choose a topical pattern. Your final step is to connect your main ideas through transitions, internal previews, and internal summaries.

As you develop your speech, your primary organizational tool is the planning outline, which includes most of the information you will present. The outline uses a traditional outline format, which establishes a hierarchy of ideas. The number of main points developed in your speech should be between two and five. The planning outline also uses complete sentences, labels transitions, and includes a reference list.

Speakers' notes, the notes you use during your presentation in an extemporaneous speech, are less detailed than the planning outline. They serve as brief reminders of what you want to say and the order in which you say it. They may include complete quotations and statistical data as well as important delivery suggestions. Speakers' notes are organized around phrases, not sentences, and they use the same format as the planning outline.

Key Terms

adequacy 197

cause-and-effect organization 188

chronological organization 188

consistency 197

coordinate points 197

equality pattern 187

four-step process 185

internal previews 194

internal summaries 195

organization of ideas 184

parallelism 197

past-present-future 189

planning outline 196

primacy effect 188

problem-solution organization 188

progressive pattern 188

recency effect 188

singularity 197

spatial organization 188

speaker's notes 200

step-by-step 189

strongest point pattern 187

subordinate points 197

topical organization 188

transitional sentences 200

transitions 193

Questions for Reflection

1. Take the topics of gun control, marriage, and Disneyland and apply the brainstorming process to determine main points for each speech topic. Which organizational patterns would work best for each topic and why?

2. In public speaking, what functions are served by transitions and summaries?

3. Why is it important to determine your thesis and main points before organizing the rest of the speech?

4. Review the essential requirements for the planning outline and speaker's notes. Why is it necessary to develop both outline forms, and why are both equally important in extemporaneous speaking? Explain the role each plays in different phases of a speech.

Activities

1. Read a speech from an online speech database or from another collection. Outline the speech, identifying the specific organizational pattern or patterns the speaker has chosen. Write a paragraph examining whether the pattern chosen effectively communicates the core idea.

2. Write a specific purpose statement for a speech then use three different organizational patterns to organize the speech.

3. Watch a speech online then listen to the speech to identify the organizational pattern. List the previews, transition, and summaries. Identify the core idea and its placement in the speech.

References

Clarke, M. L. (1963). *Rhetoric at Rome: Historical survey.* New York: Barnes & Noble.

Daniels, T. D., & Whitman, R. F. (1981). The effects of message introduction, message structure, and verbal organizing ability upon learning information. *Human communication research*, Winter, 147–160.

Makay, J., & Fetzger, R. C. (1984). *Business communication skills: Principles and practice* (2nd ed.). Englewood Cliffs, NJ: Prentice-Hall.

Sprague, J., & Stuart, D. (1992). *The speaker's handbook* (3rd ed.). San Diego, CA: Harcourt Brace Jovanovich.

Chapter

8

Learning Objectives

After reading this chapter and completing the online activities for this lesson, you will be able to:

1. Define the function and development of effective introductions.

2. Explain the purpose and process of creating memorable conclusions.

3. Identify common pitfalls associated with poorly crafted introductions and conclusions.

Introducing and Concluding Your Speech

At a Glance

INTRODUCTION

You never get a second chance to make a first impression. This maxim is true both in public speaking and life in general. When we meet an individual for the first time, the way that person carries him or herself is often emblazoned in our memory forever. That is, regardless of future interactions, that initial presence is what we naturally remember first. For example, Rachel, one of the authors of this textbook, remembers meeting her university president during her freshman year of college. He wore a suit and a warm smile and made a point of using her first name in conversation. These elements caused Rachel to perceive him as professional, positive, and passionate about the students and his job. It also was the lens through which she viewed their future interactions. He set a tone of mutual respect at their first meeting that extended throughout her entire college career. Additionally, his supportive words on the day Rachel graduated brought this cycle of respect full circle. First impressions matter and final impressions are lasting. Our knowledge of this phenomenon encourages us to adjust our own personalities and self-presentation to be appropriate when meeting others. For example, saying "hey" while wearing a swimsuit when meeting a friend of a friend at the beach and "high-fiving" them goodbye is a completely acceptable in light of the casual context. However, using the same salutation, wearing the identical attire, and closing with that high five when at a job interview would be employment suicide! Much like meeting others for the first time, introductions in a speech have a primacy effect mentioned previously in Chapter 7. Conclusions, like our goodbyes, employ the recency factor. To review, the *primacy/recency effect* suggests that we tend to recall more vividly the beginning and ending, and less of the middle of an event. When a series of candidates are interviewing for a job, the first and last candidates have an advantage because the interviewer is most likely to remember more about these two than the others. This theory also holds true for speeches; your audience will recall more of the beginning and ending of your speech than anything else.

© 2012 Yuri Arcurs, Shutterstock, Inc.

FIGURE 8.1 Much like a handshake, your speech introduction can leave a lasting impression on your audience and therefore should be competent and confident.

Consequently, the way in which you begin and end your speech is critical to your overall success. This chapter approaches introductions and conclusions in relation to how your speech can make a lasting impression. Two topics will be considered: (1) how to engage your audience at the beginning of your speech so they will be motivated to listen to the rest of it, and (2) how to remind your audience at the end of your speech what you said and why it was relevant.

The familiar speaker adage: "Tell them what you are going to say, say it, and then tell them what you said" addresses this truth. Beginning and ending a speech well helps your audience to remember and later, to use, the ideas you present. Let us begin with a closer look at introductions.

8.1 Functions and Development of Introductions

If well executed, your introduction can help your audience make a smooth transition to the main points of your speech, create a positive first impression, and set an appropriate tone and mood for your talk. If shoddily constructed, your audience may prejudge your topic as unimportant or dull and stop listening.

Consider the following example. One of authors of this textbook regularly teaches a communication class on small group dynamics. Over the course of the semester, students are assigned to work in a team of five or six to complete projects that result in presentations of varying lengths. The final project, which involves service learning, requires the groups to use their efforts to help in an area of need in their community. Their final presentation is comprised of a discussion on how they selected their project, why their social issue fits into the greater context of the world, and a step-by-step account of their collective experience.

These presentations are usually straightforward, involving a set of statistics about the area of need and a description of the service completed. While audience members are supportive, they are rarely taken aback by the innovation of the speeches, especially since they are all delivering something similar. One group, however, aimed to incorporate some creative measures into their presentation's introduction that grabbed the audience's attention early and encouraged them to attentively listen.

To start, the group asked the audience members to sit in their work teams. They then gave four of the six group members in each group a cookie and invited them to partake. While some group members were hesitant to eat, especially knowing that not everyone in their group had a cookie, they complied anyway. The presenters followed this experience by asking the two members in each group how it felt to watch others eat while they did not. They also asked those who had cookies what it felt like to eat in front of others who weren't given the snack. The responses were telling. Those without cookies felt disenfranchised, frustrated, and forgotten, while those who received cookies expressed feelings of guilt and reluctance.

The presenters then shared that more than 33 percent of all children in Orange County, California (where the some of the students in the class live), are at risk of hunger. Suddenly, the lightbulb went off for audience members; they realized that the cookie experiment was a way for them to visualize one-third of their group members facing food deprivation. The presenters followed up this startling statistic by informing the audience of their intended focus:

> *Hunger is all around us; it can be a slow and silent killer, even in America. It is likely that you have met a hungry person and perhaps didn't even know the severity of their problem. The reality is, hungry children abound. Sadly, their hunger affects their immediate and future well-being. If you could do something to help a hungry child, would you?*

> *This evening, we will be discussing both the childhood hunger problem in Orange County as well what we as a small group decided to do to help in this area. We will close with some ways for you to help those who are hungry in your own neighborhood.*

This active introduction with a personal application paved the way for audience members to be engaged in the rest of the presentation on childhood hunger in the community with a level of interest that would not have existed had the presenters simply opened with the statistic itself.

© 2012 Flashon Studio, Shutterstock, Inc.

FIGURE 8.2 Effective introductions should be energetic and memorable.

8.1.1   Functions of Introductions

The emphasis on strong opening comments has long been held as important. In the first century, Roman philosopher Quintilian posited that in order for a speech to be effective, an introduction must do four things. It should:

1. Focus attention on the topic and speaker
2. Provide a motive for your audience to care about your speech

3. Enhance your credibility as a speaker
4. Preview your message and organization

My aim, then, is the education of the perfect orator (Quintilianus, 1.Preface.9).

Illustration: credit F. Bleyswyk from 1720 Book.

FIGURE 8.3 Quintilian believed that every introduction should orient the audience to the topic, their reason for listening, and the credibility of the speaker.

1. Focus Attention on Topic and Speaker

Your introduction should first offer a personal greeting, capture and focus attention on your topic, and set an appropriate tone and mood.

• Personal Greeting

Many introductions contain a personalized greeting, which can be considered a preamble to your introduction. A personal greeting at the start of your speech acknowledges the audience and tells listeners that you see the speech as an opportunity to communicate your point of view. When Martin Luther King, Jr., looked out over the sea of faces on the Washington Mall on August 28, 1963, he began by telling his audience, "I am happy to join with you today in what will go down in history as the greatest demonstration for freedom in the history of our nation." Then he delivered his "I Have a Dream" speech. Personal greetings make the audience feel welcome and set the stage for what is to come. However, in a public speaking classroom (especially on a day when many students are delivering speeches), personal greetings can often borderline on feeling like an attempt to "warm up" the audience, which may feel repetitive after a few speakers have used this tactic; in turn, it may not be appropriate. Confirm with your instructor in advance to determine whether he or she prefers a greeting or that you simply start with the first intended word of your speech (generally your attention getter).

- ## Capture and Focus Attention

Every experienced speaker knows that the first few moments are critical to the success of a speech. In fact, we form favorable or negative impressions of an individual within one-tenth of a second of seeing them; it is, then, within these fleeting nanoseconds that your listeners decide whether they care enough to continue listening. You want your listeners to think, "This is interesting," or "I didn't know that," or "I never thought of it in quite that way," or "That was really amusing." The common denominator in each of these responses is heightened audience interest. Just like the presenters who had their audience experiencing the idea of food deprivation before actually discussing hunger in their community, the importance of capturing audience attention early in your speech is paramount.

- ## Set the Appropriate Tone and Mood

Imagine observing the following scenario: Krissy stood behind the podium beside the closed casket as she delivered the eulogy to tearful faces. Her sentimental message of grief was appropriate in every way except that she delivered the entire speech with a smile. This obvious disconnect between her words and facial expressions was a bit unsettling to say the least. When asked about it later, Krissy was surprised. She confessed that the smile was her attempt to communicate that she was glad to be there and honored to be performing such an important family duty. Unfortunately, Krissy did not create an appropriate tone and mood in her introduction.

mood
The overall feeling you hope to evoke in your audience.

tone
The emotional disposition of the speaker as the speech is being delivered.

The **mood** of a speech refers to the overall feeling you hope to evoke in your audience. **Tone** is the emotional disposition of the speaker as the speech is being delivered. Tone is created verbally by the words and ideas you select and nonverbally by the emotions you communicate. As it is during most funerals, the mood was of sadness and solidarity. Yet, Krissy's tone, as conveyed by her positive facial expressions, was upbeat and happy. Consider the desired mood and adjust your tone appropriately in the introduction. In this way, you ensure that your tone matches your reason for speaking and that your speech helps to create the desired mood in your audience.

Courtesy of Marie Hulett.

FIGURE 8.4 The mood and tone of the speech occasion should be reflected in your introduction and personal demeanor.

2. Provide a Motive to Listen

An effective speaker will quickly establish a reason for audience members to listen; you want to make sure that they understand what is in it for them. The small group presenters' introduction helped to build that critical relationship with their audience members. The presenters wanted their listeners to care about their message. They wanted them to decide from the outset that what they were sharing had meaning and importance. Although the introduction also helped make their point with its physical demonstration of food deprivation, its primary purpose was to build a psychological bridge that would last throughout the speech. Their well-designed demonstration led their audience to care about their topic because they had effectively related the topic of their presentation to something the audience cared about, their own group members' hunger.

The introduction should seek to establish common ground with the audience. By focusing on something you and your audience can share and announcing it early, you will help people identify with your topic. When people perceive that your message is meant for them and really is relevant to their lives, they will listen attentively.

© 2012 Daniel Korzeniewski, Shutterstock, Inc.

FIGURE 8.5 Very early in your speech, your audience will decide whether or not they will continue to listen to you. Delivering a strong and relevant introduction will influence them to decide in your favor.

3. Enhance Credibility

During your introduction, your listeners make important decisions about you. They decide whether they like you and whether you are credible. Your credibility as a speaker is judged largely on the basis of what you say during your introduction and the manner in which you say it.

The small group presenters reflected their credibility by demonstrating, in an interactive and participatory way, that they understood the problems of childhood hunger and that they cared enough about their audience—and topic—to come up with a creative way to present their ideas. Credibility also increases as you describe, fairly early, what qualifies you to speak about a topic. They could have said, "We want to talk to you about childhood hunger because it is more common than you think." In this case, they may not have established their credibility to the extent that their actual introduction accomplished.

FIGURE 8.6 Appropriate and well-crafted presentational aids can bring your message to life for your audience; since they reinforce your ideas, integrating presentational aids into your speech can also increase your credibility and help your audience to follow along more easily.

© 2012 auremar, Shutterstock, Inc.

Audiences may have an initial sense of your credibility even before you open your mouth to speak. Your introduction is an ideal place to positively enhance that impression. As we will discuss later in the textbook, you can think of your credibility in terms of your perceived competence, knowledge of the subject matter, concern for your audience, dynamism and personal ethics. In other words, if you know your subject, care about your audience, offer an enthusiastic delivery, and communicate a sense of ethical integrity, your audience's impression of your credibility will likely be positive. The content and delivery of your introduction must maximize these four aspects if you desire for your audience to focus and truly listen.

4. Preview Your Message and Organization

Finally, the small group presenters used their introduction to tell their audience what they would talk about during the speech. In a sentence, they previewed their focus:

> *This evening, we will be discussing both the childhood hunger problem in Orange County as well as what we as a small group decided to do to help in this area. We will close with some ways for you to help those who are hungry in your own neighborhood.*

This simple statement helped their audience members to make the intellectual connections necessary to follow their speech. Instead of wondering, "What will they talk about?" or "What is their point of view?" they were ready for the presentation to unfold.

As we said in the opening of this chapter, your audience will recall your message more fully if you tell them what you are going to say, proceed in saying it, and then remind them of what you said. Repeating key ideas helps us recall important information. But the first part of that, telling them what you are going to say, also serves to provide a preview of the organization you intend to use. If your audience knows the main points you intend to develop in your speech, they are less likely to be confused and distracted and will likely have an easier time of following along. So, an effective introduction might offer a preview statement similar to, "Today it is important that we better understand the nature of world hunger, explore creative solutions to this problem, and finally, see if some of these solutions might also be profitable to your business." In this example, the audience now knows that there will be three main points to the message.

Here is how Esther, a student at a Southern university, started her persuasive speech on junk food in the K-12 schools. The preview statement is bold and italicized:

> *According to a 2010 study from the University of Nebraska-Lincoln, schools that eliminated junk food from a la carte lines during school hours have seen an 18 percent reduction in overweight or obese students. This statement alone shows you that there is a direct correlation between junk food on campus and student health. While this is a good start, more needs to be done about junk food offered in schools. Changes have been made and are starting to be made across the country, but many states are not taking action. More people need to get involved in this movement because it will better the lives of many Americans.* ***I am going to discuss the present laws, health issues, and arguments having to do with the issues of junk food in schools.***

When Esther finished this statement, her audience had no doubt what her speech would cover. When you preview your message, your audience will listen and understand with increased clarity and will remember more of your message later.

8.1.2 Developing Introductions

There are many ways to accomplish Quintilian's four functions of an introduction. The following are ten different techniques often used in introductions. You might consider using one or combining several to provide the initial impact you want. This is one area where a little creativity can go a long way. Keep your audience in mind. A few of these techniques may be more appropriate or attention-getting for your specific audience and specific purpose than others so make sure to choose carefully when selecting your own attention getters.

1. Startling Facts/Intriguing Statements

Some introductions seem to force listeners to pay attention. They make it difficult to think of other things because of the impact of what is being said. The effectiveness of these introductions, in part, comes from the audience's feeling that the speaker's message is directed at them.

Here is how a student recently began a speech on the First Amendment and the trend toward politically correct speech in the United States:

> *Congress shall make no law respecting an establishment of religion, or prohibiting the free exercise thereof; or abridging the freedom of speech, or of the press; or the right of the people peaceably to assemble, and to petition the Government for a redress of grievances.*

> *Unless, what you have to say is politically incorrect.*

Starting with this oft-cited piece of the U.S. Constitution served as an intriguing statement, since it wasn't clear initially why he would include it in his speech. His last statement is startling, and very quickly gets to the heart of the issue. In this case, he took the familiar, and turned it on its side to arouse audience emotions.

Startling statements often challenge the listener. For example:

> *In a recent study, 75 percent of all American high school students reported not knowing how they feel about the First Amendment.*

> *They know how they feel about Snookie, iTunes, Taco Bell, YouTube, and the latest Droid cellular device, but they don't know how they feel about the First Amendment, the entity that enables their every moment of self-expression. Something is terribly wrong.*

2. Dramatic Story/Build Suspense

dramatic story
A narrative that incorporates elements of suspense, adventure, or perilous circumstances to gain the audience's attention at the start of a speech.

Closely related to the startling statement is the **dramatic story**, which involves listeners in a tale from beginning to end. Shortly after returning from a winter vacation break, Shannon delivered a speech to her classmates that began this way:

> *My friends and I were driving home from a party when suddenly, without warning, a pair of headlights appeared directly in front of our car. To avoid a collision, I swerved sharply to the right, forcing our car off the freeway into a ditch. It's funny what comes into your mind at moments like this. All I could think of was how Ryan Dunn, who was one of my favorite MTV stars, died while speeding and intoxicated a few weeks ago. After all those crazy stunts, living dangerously finally caught up with him … and he was only 34. I thought I was going to die too, just because of another driver's stupidity and carelessness. Obviously, I didn't die or even, thankfully, suffer any serious injuries. My friends are safe too, although my car was totaled. I'm convinced that we are all here today because we were sober, not speeding, and locked into place by our seat belts. Ryan Dunn might have been here too, had he thought twice before getting behind the wheel.*

quotation
A saying, presented verbatim, of an individual, usually placed at the beginning or end of a speech to establish emotional tone and get the audience thinking about an important concept.

Everyone in the audience knew what it was like to be driving home with friends—feeling safe and secure—only to be shocked into the realization that they were vulnerable to tragedy. Audience attention was riveted on the speaker as she launched into her speech on safe, sober driving and seat belt use.

3. Quotation and/or Literary Reference

You can capture audience attention by citing the words of others. If you use an appropriate poem, the words themselves may be compelling enough to engage your listeners. One of the best-known **quotations** from Shakespeare is what Jacques, a discontented, melancholy lord, says in *As You Like It*:

> *All the world's a stage, And all the men and women merely players; They have their exits and their entrances, And one man in his time plays many parts, His acts being seven ages.*

The first line and the first two lines are used most frequently when quoting this passage. It could be used in a speech that talks about people "acting" or "wearing masks" rather than being "real" with themselves. It can also be used to talk about the circle of life, how we want different things, or how we are "performing" roles in our lives.

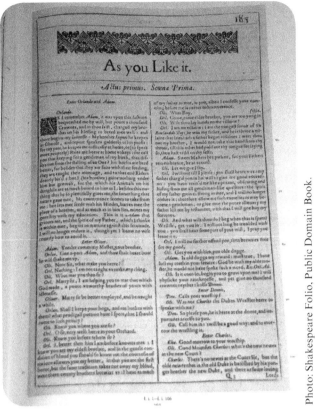

Photo: Shakespeare Folio, Public Domain Book.

FIGURE 8.7 Classic literature is a rich resource for quotations suitable for speech introductions.

The next piece of literature is also quoted frequently. For a longer speech, the entire poem could be read. For a shorter speech, only the last three lines are necessary. As Robert Frost, the well-known American poet, wrote in "The Road Not Taken":

> *Two roads diverged in a yellow wood, and sorry I could not travel both. And be one traveller, long I stood and looked down one as far as I could to where it bent in the undergrowth;*

> *Then took the other, as just as fair, and having perhaps the better claim, because it was grassy and wanted wear; though as for that, the passing there had worn them really about the same,*

> *And both that morning equally lay in leaves no feet had trodden black. Oh, I kept the first for another day! Yet knowing how way leads on to way, I doubted if I should ever come back.*

> *I shall be telling this with a sigh. Somewhere ages and ages hence: Two roads diverged in a wood, and I—I took the one less traveled by, and that has made all the difference.*

The last three lines can be the start of a speech about following your heart, not conforming, choosing your own path, making your own decisions, and resisting peer pressure.

The two examples above are passages written by famous people that have been used by others to start a speech or make some point. In addition to using the words of a well-known individual, you could also cite the words of a recognized authority

© 2012 Rafai Fabrykiewicz, Shutterstock, Inc.

FIGURE 8.8 Robert Frost's poem, "The Road Not Taken," provides inspiring thematic content that can be adapted for a speech introduction.

whose reputation enhances your topic. Here, for example, is how Keith, a college student in California, began his speech on cyberbullying to capture the attention of his audience. Quoting a knowledgeable expert, he began:

> *"Cyberbullying, as currently defined, is not a battle, but a plea for improved and increased attention to education, dialogue, bonding and engagement with our young people. In that regard, it is an opportunity with infinite potential to address ignorance, overcome orthodoxy and undertake the challenges of our shared knowledge society through ethical, educational, digital-bonding, and legally defensible policies and practices. Our children and society, as a whole, deserve no less." These are the compelling words of McGill University Associate Professor and expert in cyberbullying, Shaheen Shariff. By her definition of the issue, Shariff believes that cyberbullying is a psychological issue to address rather than a war to be won. In turn, clearly framing the issue, engaging in respectful dialogue and finding alternatives for those seeking attention in this manner will help to ameliorate this modern problem.*

In this case, the quotaion allows the speaker to skillfully lead into his thesis statement, which sets up the body of the speech to come.

4. Humor

At the beginning of a speech, humor helps break down the psychological barriers that exist between speaker and audience. Here is how Anne used humor at the start of a classroom speech on the problem of divorce in America:

Cheyenne and Katrina had been college roommates, but had not seen each other in the ten years since graduation. They were thrilled when they ran into each other at a college reunion and had a chance to talk.

"Tell me," asked Cheyenne, "has your husband lived up to the promises he made when he was dating you in college?"

"He certainly has!" said Katrina. "He told me then that he wasn't good enough for me and he's proven it ever since."

The class laughed, Anne waited, then:

I laughed too when I heard that story. But the fact remains that about half the marriages in our country end in divorce and one of the major reasons for these failures is that one partner can't live up to the expectations of the other.

Humor works in this introduction for two reasons. First, the story is genuinely funny; we chuckle when we hear the punch line. And, second, the humor is tied directly to the subject of the speech; it is appropriate for the topic and the occasion. It also provides an effective transition into the speech body.

Humor *can* work when it's self-deprecating. For example, one of the authors of this textbook was slated to do a presentation at a national conference and, because of a mix up in the start time, arrived fifteen minutes late to her eagerly awaiting audience. Clearly flustered and embarrassed about her tardiness, she became an exercise in self-deprecating humor at the start of her talk. She began by asking the audience of mostly communication professors a question:

How many of you would like your students to arrive to class on time, or even early? While I may not seem like the best representative for timeliness, and by the way, I apologize for being late…there was a mix up in the start time, I assure you that I have some tactics for making your students not want to miss any part of your class, even the beginning. I like to start class with an entertaining and interactive activity that students want to be present for and today I will tell you all about it.

© 2012 Anton Gvozdikov, Shutterstock, Inc.

FIGURE 8.9 Infusing appropriate humor into your introduction can encourage your audience to engage with enjoyment.

Again, humor makes the audience snicker, giggle, or feel at ease with an awkward situation and, when done properly, it can set the right tone for your speech. However, it is essential that you make sure you *can* do humor; the only thing worse than a joke falling flat at the start of the speech is the fact that this faux pas occurred at the beginning of the speech; that is, you have to deliver the rest of the speech with the effect of that unfunny joke "hanging" in the room. At the 2011 Academy Awards, the loudest laughter came when Billy Crystal took the stage away briefly from hosts Anne Hathaway and James Franco, who were *trying* to be funny but not very successfully achieving their goal. If your humor is planned, try testing it out on some friends or family members in advance to determine if it is indeed funny.

5. Rhetorical Question

rhetorical question
A question asked to spark audience contemplation of the speech topic; however, an answer is not desired nor expected.

When you ask your audience, "How many of you ate breakfast this morning?" you expect to see people raise their hands. When you ask a **rhetorical question**, however, you do not expect an answer. What you hope is that your question will cause your listeners to start thinking about the subject of your speech. The beauty of the rhetorical question is that it, when skillfully selected, can instantly get your audience in the right frame of mind for your speech content. Imagine a speech about the negative effects of snoring. It could start like this:

> *Have you ever been told you snore? Have you ever had to sleep in the same room with someone who is a loud snorer? Have you been told you have a "cute" little snore?*

These are all rhetorical questions. The speaker is not expecting someone to answer these questions aloud. The purpose is to get the audience to start collectively *thinking* about the topic. Hopefully, the speaker has their attention. Then the speaker continues:

> *If you don't snore, be grateful. If you do snore, you need to hear this. If you don't snore, but you marry "a snorer," well, good luck! Studies show that married couples argue about snoring as much as they do money; snoring couples have less sex than non-snoring couples, and over 20 percent of couples regularly sleep apart due to snoring. Ouch! Oh, and there's more. The non-snorer faces difficulties from sleep deprivation. In the next few minutes I'm going to describe the economic consequences of being sleep-deprived, including increased health care costs, automobile accidents, workplace accidents, and decreased job performance.*

The speaker linked the rhetorical questions and startling facts to audience, and previewed the main points in her speech. Out of respect for the audience, make sure that the rhetorical question indeed *sounds* rhetorical—the last thing you want to do is make the audience feel "tricked" by asking a rhetorical question that sounds more like a real question requiring an answer, get an answer from an audience member and then have to tell him or her that the question was actually rhetorical. Keep your eyes scanning the whole audience, rather than gazing at one or two individuals. The best rhetorical questions are probing in a personal way. They mean something to every listener and encourage active participation throughout your speech.

6. Illustrations, Examples, and Anecdotes

Speakers often begin with an interesting comment about the immediate surroundings or some recent or historical event. These openings are even more powerful when the speaker carefully plans these comments and incorporates a personal or human touch. Through the adept use of **illustrations** ("In the short time I will be talking with you, 150 violent crimes will have been committed in our nation…"), **examples** ("Lisa was a young woman from our community whose life was forever altered on January 18th…"), and **anecdotes** ("Once, while traveling on the subway, I noticed a shifty-looking man carefully watching each passenger enter and leave the car…"), speakers gather our attention to them and their message.

7. Physically Involve the Audience

Those audience members who are **kinesthetic learners** respond favorably to introduction tactics that allow them to move or interact with others in a physical manner. In a speech about the importance of sleep, a speaker could start by asking all students who got a good night's sleep to raise their hand. Then, the speaker could ask how many of them got 8 or more hours, 6 to 7 hours, or 5 hours or less. Depending on how the speaker defined a good night's sleep, the questions could lead the speaker to comment that, "Only a few of you actually got the sleep that you needed last night. Today, I hope to give you some reasons to go to bed earlier tonight."

Some speakers may ask the audience to yell, "Good morning," until they've been loud enough, thereby heightening everyone's senses and energizing the whole room. A speaker talking about the need for exercise may ask the audience to jump up and down for a few moments. During a graduation speech in 2003 at the University of Wisconsin, after thanking the administration, director and movie producer Jerry Zucker involved the audience physically when he started his speech with the following:

> Before I start my remarks, I'd like everyone just to do something for me. Very simply—so everyone can kind of just get to know everyone else—on the count of three, I'd like everyone to turn around and shake the hand of the person sitting right behind you. One, two, three—right now, everybody, please do that.

The physical contact that the audience might experience also has a scientific side; touch that lasts more than six seconds has been proven to release the "bonding chemical" oxytocin into the bloodstream which can create goodwill and positive feelings amongst the audience.

illustration
A story that engages the listeners on an emotional level and usually details a situation or instance; can be used during the introduction or conclusion of a speech.

example
Support that helps illustrate a point or claim.

anecdote
Usually a short narrative of interesting, amusing, or biographical incident.

kinesthetic learner
One who learns best through opportunities to engage in physical activity and interactive experience.

FIGURE 8.10 Getting your audience to physically interact can energize them and make them more receptive to your message.

8. Relate Personal Experience through Narratives

Sharing a **narrative** or several examples from your past with your listeners can be an effective start. Just like children love story-time, audience members tend to perk up when they begin to hear a story that feels personal and heartfelt, especially if it is about the speaker who is presenting. Be sure your personal experiences will not hurt your credibility and that they relate directly to your topic. Recently, a student giving a "speech of introduction" started this way:

> *I'll never forget my first week of boot camp. I was homesick, exhausted, and anxious about where my new career in the Marines would take me. One day, after a particularly difficult obstacle course, my drill sergeant came up to me and said, "Son, you may not feel like it now, but one day you are going to be a great Marine." After being shouted out and commanded so many times before, it was that quiet phrase that gave me hope and allowed me to persevere.*

The student's speech was to present a Marine Corps Drill Instructor Ribbon to his drill sergeant. He continued to describe what made his drill sergeant so exemplary and worthy of the recognition. It was a poignant and personal beginning with a story that related directly to the topic.

9. Use a Presentational Aid

Before the President of the United States speaks, the broadcast feed from the White House shows the presidential seal. This is no accident; it helps to draw attention to the upcoming speech and also helps reinforce the president's credibility. But you do not have to be the President to use this technique. Beginning your speech with an interesting sound recording, visual, or prop is guaranteed to draw attention to the beginning of your speech, too. Showing the U.S. debt clock or a clip on human trafficking grabs attention, as would a funny or startling YouTube video. One student brought a poster board covered with all the trash that she collected on a local beach in one hour to depict the grave problem of littering in public places. All in all, presentational aids appeal to **visual learners** who are captivated by what they see first, and hear second.

narrative
A short story, either truth-based or fictitious, presented to gain or hold attention and usually intended to convey deeper meaning.

visual learner
One who learns best thorough visual mediums including pictures, colors, film clips, and presentational slides.

Left: Courtesy of Coastline Community College; Right: © 2012 Benis Arapovic, Shutterstock, Inc.

FIGURE 8.11 Using presentational aids, like props, in your introduction can appeal to the visual learners in your audience.

10. Refer to the Situation

Skilled public speakers often begin with a positive comment related to the occasion, the person who spoke before them, the audience, the date, or even the physical location. Each of these may be more appropriate at one time than at another. For example, a commencement speaker at her alma mater might start with, "It's hard for me to believe that twenty-five years ago I sat exactly where you sit, listening to the commencement speaker with excited anticipation for my future." Or, if an audience was waiting outside in the rain to hear a Libertarian candidate who was late, the candidate might start with, "I bet there isn't a more committed group of voters than those of you here who have been standing in the rain waiting for me." When you are planning a speech, ask yourself if referencing the event, a prior speaker, the audience or the significance of this date in history would create interest and gather attention.

It should be noted that in a public speaking classroom, referring to the situation may feel repetitive since every audience member is likely present to deliver a speech on speech day. Also, keep in mind that your attention-gaining device must relate in some way to your topic or you run the risk of confusing your audience. Your choice should be guided by several other factors. First, consider the mood you are attempting to create. Second, consider your audience's expectations of you and the occasion. Third, consider how much time and resources each approach will require. Finally, consider your strengths and weaknesses—you may not be as strong at joke telling as recalling a powerful story.

The online course material provides you with resources to help you locate appropriate quotations, statistics, and jokes for your introductions. See Topic 1.

8.1.3 How to Introduce the Same Speech in Different Ways

Many topics lend themselves to different types of introductions. A startling statement, a dramatic anecdote, a quotation, or a humorous story may each serve as an effective introduction to the same speech. Here, for example, is the same speech introduced in three different ways. Note the specific attention getter being used, as well as the pronounced and well-balanced preview (that states the main points of the speech) in every case:

1. Startling Statement

Microwave cooking can be hazardous to your child's health. Children have been burned by opening bags of microwave-heated popcorn too close to their faces. Their throats have been scalded by grilled cheese sandwiches that feel cool to the touch, but are hot enough inside to burn the esophagus. These and other hazards can transform your microwave into an oven of destruction in the hands of a child.

> *What I would like to talk about today is how microwaves functions, how dangerous they can be to young children, and how you can safeguard your family from accidents involving microwaves.*

2. Dramatic Story

Nine-year-old Jenny was one of those kids who managed quite well on her own. Every day she got home from school at 3:30 P.M. while her parents were still at work and made herself a snack in the microwave. She had been using the microwave since she was five, and her parents never questioned its safety—that is, not until Jenny had her accident.

> *It began innocently enough. Jenny heated a bag of microwave popcorn in the oven and opened it inches from her face. The bag was cool to the touch, hiding the danger within. Hot vapors blasted Jenny's face, leaving her with second- and third-degree-burns.*

> *What I would like to talk about today is how microwaves functions, how dangerous they can be to young children, and how you can safeguard your family from accidents involving microwaves.*

3. Quotation

Three out of every four American homes have microwave ovens and with them a potential for danger. Louis Slesin, editor of "Microwave News," a health and safety newsletter, explains how this common kitchen appliance can present potential hazards for young children:

> *"On a rainy day," says Slesin, "a kid could climb up on a stool, put his face to the door and watch something cook for a long time. It's mesmerizing, like watching a fish tank, but his eye will be at the point of maximum microwave leakage. We don't know the threshold for cataract formation—the industry says you need tons of exposure, but some litigation and literature say you don't need much [for damage to occur]. Children younger than 10 or 12 shouldn't use the oven unsupervised. It's not a toy. It's a sophisticated, serious, adult appliance, and it shouldn't be marketed for kids"* (Shapiro, 1990, p. 56).*

> *I agree with Slesin, and what I would like to talk about today is how microwaves functions, how dangerous they can be to young children, and how you can safeguard your family from accidents involving microwaves.*

The point of providing these three examples is to demonstrate how differently an introduction can be constructed. Avoid "settling" for an introduction; carefully consider how you might create the most impact and select your tactics strategically.

8.1.4   Guidelines and Suggestions for Introductions

As you focus on crafting your introduction for your next speech, consider how you can create a strong and effective message. Remember, as in any recipe, no ingredient stands on its own, and often the whole is greater than the sum of its individual parts. Attention to each part of the process leads to an excellent final product. After choosing the most appropriate beginning, consider these general guidelines as you prepare and deliver your introduction.

An Introduction Can Be Prepared Before or After the Body of Speech

When you prepare an appropriate and captivating introduction is up to you. Some speakers report that writing the introduction first (following the determination of your main points and thesis) will help to "jump start" the creation of the rest of the speech. Others, however, maintain that the introduction will take form more easily

---

after you have created an outline of the body of your speech. The argument is that when some speakers attempt to create the introduction first, they invariably rewrite it several times as they continue to change the body of their message. At the end of the day, the choice is yours.

Make It Easy to Follow and Be Creative

Whether you are offering a startling statistic or asking a question, make sure to keep things simple. When you offer your thesis and even when you preview your main points for your audience, look for ways to be concise and straight-forward. However, keeping things simple does not mean that you need to compromise creativity. Recently, a student beginning his persuasive speech started with his arms open in a pleading gesture, zealously urging the class, "Please! Please I beg of you—stop washing your hands!" He then briefly noted the dangers of too much cleansing and stated his thesis. His enthusiastic approach and startling plea made for a creative introduction that was simple and easy to understand.

Consider your introduction as an invitation to creativity. The more creative your introduction, the more likely your audience will listen to the entire message.

Practice and Communicate High Energy

The most important part of your speech to practice thoroughly is the introduction, followed by the conclusion, and then the body. The first impression created by a well-practiced introduction lays the foundation for your ultimate success. It is difficult to communicate high energy if you are dependent on notes, so be sure to rehearse it many times. You should be able to speak to the audience for at least fifteen seconds without looking at your notes. One perk of thorough practice is that once you have established competence and fluidity with your content, you are freed up to deliver your introduction enthusiastically. Since introductions are relatively short, put your heart, mind, and energy into it. That means incorporating vocal variety, consistent eye contact, and natural gesturing to draw in your audience early. If you are truly engaged in the introduction, your audience is much more likely also to become involved in your message.

Engage Audience Nonverbally Before You Start

Poise counts! Recall that your speech actually begins as you rise to speak. Approach with confidence; once there, pause, catch and hold your audience's eye contact for a moment, and take a deep breath. Then, let the first intended word of your speech be the first word out of your mouth. Each of these measures is critical to beginning your speech effectively as they convey that you are in control and pleased for the opportunity to share.

Consider Time Constraints and Mood

When giving a five-minute speech, telling a long-winded, dramatic story would be inappropriate since you would end up using the bulk of your time on the introduction, leaving little time for the body and conclusion. The same is true of showing a one-minute video clip. Alternately, when delivering a 45-minute lecture, such a beginning would be wholly acceptable. The mood you are hoping to create in your audience is related to your tone, and vice versa. The introduction is your best chance to establish your tone and alter the mood of your audience while still honoring the established time constraints.

© 2012 Alexander Raths, Shutterstock, Inc.

FIGURE 8.12 Energy in your introduction can be conveyed through consistent eye contact, natural gesturing, and interaction with your audience.

8.1.5   Common Pitfalls of Introductions

Even when speakers have a pronounced understanding of the purpose and strategies related to introductions, they still possess the ability to make them less effective than they desire by unintentionally doing one of the actions on the list below.

1. Beginning with an apology

Do not use your introduction to apologize for mistakes you are likely to make, for inadequate visual aids, being ill-prepared, or even just plain ill. The audience will cringe when a speaker starts with, "Sorry, I was living it up in Las Vegas all weekend and now my voice is really hoarse…bear with me." Apologies set a negative tone that can make the audience unsympathetic, impatient, and jaded.

2. Being too brief or too long

Do not jump into the body of the speech or spend too much time setting up the speech. Your introduction should take between ten and twenty percent of your total allotted speaking time. Not adhering to this guideline means violating an audience expectation and potentially confusing or annoying them.

3. Giving too much away

While the introduction should provide a road map for your speech, you do not want to give the substance of your speech in your preview. Instead, use general terms to tell your audience what you intend to cover by using an attention getter and well-developed thesis statement only.

4. Reading

Do your best to memorize your introduction so that those first moments with the audience are as connected as possible. Do not *read* your introductory remarks to your audience; your script becomes a barrier between you and your audience. Worse yet, you will likely sound more like a reader than a public speaker.

5. Relying on shock tactics

Your victory will be short-lived if you capture audience attention by screaming at the top of your lungs, pounding the table, telling a crude, tasteless joke, or using material that has nothing to do with your speech. Just because it gets the audience's attention does not mean it is an authentic attention getter. In fact, your credibility will be challenged and the audience will trust you less because of the way you manipulated their attention. Using an innovative approach is effective as long as it is tasteful and inextricably linked to the topic of your speech.

6. Promising too much

Some speakers, who are fearful that their speech says too little, promise more than they can deliver in the hope that the promise alone will satisfy their listeners. It rarely does. Steer clear of rash or exaggerated assurances because once you set expectations in the introduction, the body of your speech has to deliver or you will lose credibility.

7. Using unnecessary prefatory remarks

Resist the urge to begin with "I can't believe I have to do this speech," or "I don't really feel ready for this," or "Okay, deep breath, here we go." Even if you feel these things, such verbal adaptors are likely to make you even more nervous and are also

Introduction QuickStarts

- **Startling Facts and Intriguing Statements**

  "Facebook can ruin your life."

- **Dramatic Story That Builds Suspense**

  "Kim will never forget the day she was kidnapped."

- **Quotation**

  In the words of James Dean, "Dream as if you'll live forever, live as if you'll die today."

- **Humor**

  "I wondered why the baseball was getting bigger, then it hit me."

- **Rhetorical Question**

  "Have you ever felt discriminated against?"

- **Illustrations, Examples, and Anecdotes**

  "Bobby thought that school felt a lot like prison."

- **Physically Involve the Audience**

  "I'd like for you to have a staring contest with the person sitting next to you. Ready, go!"

- **Personal Narrative**

  "Dinners with Grandpa always involved him telling me about his life during the Great Depression."

- **Use a Presentational Aid**

  "Kindly look at this image—do you see a beautiful girl or an old woman?"

- **Refer to the Occasion**

  "Today is a great moment in our nation's history."

likely to challenge the audience's perception of you as a competent and controlled speaker. Also, avoid using "uhs" and "ums" at the start, as many anxious speakers often do. Instead, as mentioned before, begin crisply and clearly with your planned opening statement.

8. Using long-winded poems, quotations, and prose

We understand that for full effect, an entire piece of prose or poetry should be read. We also know that editing a poem or piece of prose may be difficult. However, it is possible to find an appropriate nugget embedded within the piece that is perfect for your speech. Consider paraphrasing or moving the longer passage to the body of your speech. This will help you to maintain balance in your speech and also reflect a respect for the time constrains given.

9. Becoming someone else

Because your initial credibility is being established in the introduction, you will want to present a genuine and authentic view of yourself to your audience. Audience members respond to speakers who are "real," so be your best self when presenting. Avoid strange voices (either too high or too low), melodrama, and false personas if you hope to earn the respect of your listeners.

10. Overusing some techniques

Trite phrases, rhetorical questions, and dramatic, cataclysmic stories are often overused tactics that may not achieve the greatest response in a seasoned audience. Spend some time thinking about how to begin your speech in an original and creative fashion that compels the audience to want to hear more.

8.2   Functions and Development of Conclusions

Think of your conclusion as the pinnacle of your speech—the words you want to marinate in your listeners' heads as they exit the room. Too often, speakers waste the opportunity with endings like, "That's it," "I guess I'm finished now," or "I'm through. Any questions?" Or they simply stop talking, giving the audience no indication that they have finished their speech and causing an awkward tension as audience members ponder whether or not they should applaud. Then, they rush away from the front of room as if to escape impending doom. A strong conclusion, in contrast, comes full circle, providing the audience with a sense of "the end" in a manner that is summarizing and poignant. Just as an introduction establishes a first impression, a well-delivered conclusion leaves a lasting mark on your audience.

A conclusion should not be viewed as an afterthought. Understand that the conclusion is your last opportunity to have an impact. Just as the introduction should be clear and flow smoothly to the body of the speech, the body should flow smoothly to the conclusion. Following are three functions of conclusions to consider as you think about the transition from the body to the conclusion and determine how to create the greatest effect on your audience.

8.2.1   Functions of Conclusions

President George W. Bush addressed the nation in the evening following the tragic events in New York City on what has become known simply as 9/11. After talking about the terror that so many Americans experienced, he explained how the rescuers responded, and what the government is planning to do to prevent another attack. His conclusion is designed to touch the emotions of all Americans, and he provides closure at the end by stating the following:

> *Tonight, I ask for your prayers for all those who grieve, for the children whose worlds have been shattered, for all whose sense of safety and security has been threatened. And I pray they will be comforted by a Power greater than any of us, spoken through the ages in Psalm 23: Even though I walk through the valley of the shadow of death, I fear no evil for you are with me.*

> *This is a day when all Americans from every walk of life unite in our resolve for justice and peace. America has stood down enemies before, and we will do so this time. None of us will ever forget this day, yet we go forward to defend freedom and all that is good and just in our world.*

> *Thank you. Good night. And God bless America.*

© 2012 Anthony Correia, Shutterstock, Inc.

FIGURE 8.13 In the face of extreme human tragedy caused by terrorist attacks on New York City's World Trade Center, President George W. Bush addressed his grieving nation in a comforting, inclusive, and emotional manner that respected the both the victims and the heroes of 9/11.

President Bush's conclusion reflected the notion that strong endings to speeches reflect three key aims examined below:

1. *Summarize important information*
2. *Motivate listeners*
3. *Create a sense of closure.*

1. Summarizing Important Information

The transition from the body to the conclusion is pivotal in signaling the impending end of your speech. Your instructor and your own personal preference may help you decide how you want to tell your audience you are ending. Whether you use a formal "In conclusion…" or prefer something more casual, such as "Now, to wrap this up today…," you want your audience to clearly understand that you are about to finish. Audiences know that when you give them that signal, they are about to get an important recap of your key ideas.

According to speech communication professor John E. Baird, Jr. (1974), "Summaries may be effective when presented at the conclusion of a speech [because] they provide the audience with a general structure under which to subsume the more specific points of the speech" (pp. 119–127). Research indicates that in some instances summaries are not essential, but if your audience is unfamiliar with the content of your speech, or if the speech is long or complex, a summary will help reinforce your main points.

In the late 1980s, U.S. President Ronald Reagan spoke to the people of West Berlin about the Berlin Wall and its divisive effect on Germany and the Free World. In his closing, he reaffirmed the focal point of his speech, the need for the wall to be torn down, and ultimately signaled an end to the decades-old Cold War.

> *Perhaps this gets to the root of the matter, to the most fundamental distinction of all between East and West. The totalitarian world produces backwardness because it does such violence to the spirit, thwarting the human impulse to create, to enjoy, to worship. The totalitarian world finds even symbols of love and of worship an affront. Years ago, before the East Germans began rebuilding their churches, they erected a secular structure: the television tower at Alexanderplatz. Virtually ever since, the authorities have been working to correct what they view as the tower's one major flaw, treating the glass sphere at the top with paints and chemicals of every kind. Yet even today when the sun strikes that sphere—that sphere that towers over all Berlin—the light makes the sign of the cross. There in Berlin, like the city itself, symbols of love, symbols of worship, cannot be suppressed.*

> *As I looked out a moment ago from the Reichstag, that embodiment of German unity, I noticed words crudely spray-painted upon the wall, perhaps by a young Berliner: "This wall will fall. Beliefs become reality." Yes, across Europe, this wall will fall. For it cannot withstand faith; it cannot withstand truth. The wall cannot withstand freedom.*

> *And I would like, before I close, to say one word. I have read, and I have been questioned since I've been here about certain demonstrations against my coming. And I would like to say just one thing, and to those who demonstrate so. I wonder if they have ever asked themselves that if they should have the kind of government they apparently seek, no one would ever be able to do what they're doing again.*

> *Thank you and God bless you all.*

In the process of ending, an effective conclusion also strategically reiterates the main idea of the speech. Reagan's conclusion summarizes the main points of his speech, so the audience has more opportunity to process his main ideas. Two years later, in November of 1989, East Germans issued a decree for the wall to be opened, reuniting families, increasing freedom, and reflecting the aims of Reagan's speech.

2. Motivating Listeners

Great speakers do more than summarize in their conclusions; they motivate their audiences. In motivating your audience, you want to relate your topic to your listeners, communicate a feeling, and broaden the message.

- **Relate your topic to your listeners.** Your speech will achieve the greatest
  success if your listeners feel that you have helped them in some concrete
  way. Consider making this connection in your conclusion. At the Vermont
  Statewide Housing Conference in November of 2010, U.S. Secretary of
  Housing and Urban Development Shaun Donovan drew his speech to end
  with the following remarks:

  *For me, for President Obama, and for Senator Sanders, all this work comes
  down to a very simple belief: That no matter where you live, when you choose
  a home, you don't just choose a home. You also choose schools for your
  children and transportation to work. You choose a community—and the
  choices available in that community. A belief that our children's futures should
  never be determined—or their choices limited—by the zip code they grow up in.*

  *Like our President, I know change is never easy—that revitalizing our nation's
  communities, rural, urban, and suburban won't happen overnight. Nor will it
  happen because of any one policy or the work of any one agency or one party.
  But working together, in common purpose—in partnership—we can tackle our
  toughest challenges. We can push back on this crisis. We can build upon the
  remarkable change and sense of possibility you're catalyzing in communities
  across the state.*

  *And most important of all, we can create a geography of opportunity for every
  American—and every family. Ensuring we do is our goal today. Let us rise to
  meet it.*

In this brief passage, Donovan uses the word "community" four times. His use of
the inclusive "we" is yet another way to establish a group identity and a sense of
community. Donovan's conclusion clearly serves to motivate listeners to continue
to work to improve living conditions in the United States.

- **Communicate a feeling.** Perhaps more important, the conclusion sets the
  psychological mood listeners carry with them from the hall. A student
  speaking against aspartame noted at the beginning of her speech that she
  believed aspartame contributed to her previous depression and weight gain.
  She ended her speech by noting that eliminating aspartame from her diet
  lifted her depression and led to significant weight loss. Her passion about the
  topic and the relief she feels were clearly communicated.
- **Broaden your message.** Finally, the conclusion can be used to connect your
  topic to a broader context. If in your speech you talk about the responsibility
  of every adult to vote on Election Day, you can use your conclusion to tie the
  vote to the continuation of our democratic system. If your speech focuses on
  caring for aging parents, you can conclude with a plea to value rather than
  discard the wisdom of the elderly.

3. Create a Sense of Closure

By the time your audience hears the start of your conclusion, they should get the
feeling that the speech is coming to an end. Your tone and the words selected must
work together in harmony to express a sense of finality as the speech wraps up. The
next section explores some specific strategies for making your conclusion appropriate, compelling, and an adequate signal of the end.

8.2.2   Developing Conclusions

Strong conclusions can utilize a variety of tactics but always fulfill the same aim: to gracefully follow through and wrap things up. If you are having dinner with others the dessert often completes the dining experience. Consequently, when speaking, it is not enough to simply end with a comment: "Well, that's it, I think I've covered everything," leaving the audience hanging in the balance without a sense of closure. An effective conclusion tells your listeners your speech has ended in an intentional fashion. There are several techniques listed below that speakers use to create a sense of psychological closure.

1. Thanking as Transition

Although saying thank you at the end of the speech indicates that you are finished, it is no substitute for a statement that brings your discussion to a close. You can, however, use an initial thank you statement as a transition into your concluding remarks. For example, when Rachel, one of the authors of this textbook, received a teaching award, her acceptance speech ended with the following:

> *Everything I know about effective teaching I have learned by example from my own teachers. I would like to thank my first teacher, Laura, who also happens to be my mother. She homeschooled me at a time when this form of education was not common, trailblazing the way for others who desired to educate their children at home. Not only did she expose me to a myriad of subjects that rigorously challenged my mind, she also prepared me for a life of responsibility in my community, empowering me to connect, interact and ultimately help others learn and grow. As Albert Einstein once said, "Setting an example is not the main means of influencing another, it is the only means." I share this award with my Laura, my first teacher, whose intellect and care provided me with the invaluable example of what it means to truly teach others. This award inspires me to continue to strive to provide a positive example to my students, so that they may be empowered to help others learn and grow as well. Thank you.*

After saying thank you, Rachel explains why she was thanking people. Rather than ending by saying thank you to several individuals, she gives the speech more impact by quoting Albert Einstein, expressing what the award means to her, and leaving the audience with a final thought of gratitude.

2. Call to Action

As you wrap up your speech, you can make a direct appeal to your listeners, urging them to take a specific action or to change their attitudes. In a persuasive speech, the conclusion is where you make your most forcible and most memorable plea to persuade.

Living in an age of mass media, we are bombarded by calls to action every time we turn on the television. Advertisers plead with us to drop everything and buy their products. We see toll-free numbers flash across the screen, urging us to order knives or cleaning products or diet aids right away to secure the bonus gift. Televangelists urge us to contribute to their mission and celebrities encourage us to donate to their cause during a telethon. The fact that we are all accustomed to these messages makes them a natural conclusion to a speech.

In a speech designed to persuade her audience that vitamins supplements should be regularly taken by all Americans, Lynn, a public speaking student, ended her speech with a call to action:

> *It is easy to get excited about vitamins. In an age where people are taking prescription drugs for a variety of maladies, it is heartening to know that there are natural alternatives that do not require a prescription or inflict, in some cases, debilitating side effects to its consumers. We all want to be healthy, and, as stated before, our modern foods are simply not providing us with the nutrients we need to survive and thrive.*

> *Once reserved only for the wealthy, vitamins are more accessible and affordable than ever before. Who wouldn't want to take a pill that could help their immune system, digestive track, and energy levels, as well as fortifying hair and skin? While vitamins will not save the world, they can drastically improve our life experience. I challenge you to go to your local health retailer and purchase daily vitamin supplements. I am confident that you will like the difference that you see. Then, spread the word to your friends and family about the merits of vitamin supplements. Together, we can make American healthy again.*

You can see how Lynn makes her last persuasive appeal, and then asks the audience to do something specific and within their own realm of action and control.

FIGURE 8.14 Calling your audience to action can be a powerful way to conclude your speech. Speakers like Martin Luther King, Jr. (right), understood the potency of this action; he often integrated inspirational behavioral challenges into his oratory.

Photos: (left) Courtesy of NASA; (right) Dick DeMarsico, Library of Congress.

3. Use a Dramatic Illustration

Ending your speech with a dramatic story connected to your speech's main theme reinforces the theme in your listeners' minds. It is the last message of your speech the audience will hear and, as a story, it is the most likely to be remembered.

German Chancellor Angela Merkel spoke to the U.S. Congress on the twentieth anniversary of the fall of the Berlin Wall on November, 2009. In her speech, she thanked Americans for their support and for their role in helping to end the Cold

War. She also reminded U.S. politicians that the world will be looking to America and Europe for leadership in forging a global climate change agreement. She ended her speech with the following:

> *I am convinced that, just as we found the strength in the 20th century to tear down a wall made of barbed wire and concrete, today we have the strength to overcome the walls of the 21st century, walls in our minds, walls of short-sighted self-interest, walls between the present and the future.*
>
> *Ladies and gentlemen, my confidence is inspired by a very special sound— that of the Freedom Bell in the Schöneberg Town Hall in Berlin. Since 1950, a copy of the original American Liberty Bell has hung there. A gift from American citizens, it is a symbol of the promise of freedom, a promise that has been fulfilled. On October 3, 1990, the Freedom Bell rang to mark the reunification of Germany, the greatest moment of joy for the German people. On September 13, 2001, two days after 9/11, it tolled again, to mark America's darkest hour.*
>
> *The Freedom Bell in Berlin is, like the Liberty Bell in Philadelphia, a symbol which reminds us that freedom does not come about of itself. It must be struggled for and then defended anew every day of our lives. In this endeavor Germany and Europe will also in future remain strong and dependable partners for America. That I promise you.*

Courtesy of Voice of America.

FIGURE 8.15 Speech conclusions of all varieties benefit from a well-placed quotation. Norwegian Nobel Committee President Thorbjørn Jagland's speech used a befitting quote when congratulating Chinese human rights activist Liu Xiaobo on his Nobel Peace Prize in 2010.

4. Close with a Quotation

Closing a speech with the words of others is an effective and memorable way to end your presentation. The Nobel Peace Prize for 2010 was awarded to then-imprisoned Liu Xiaobo of China for his long and nonviolent struggle for human rights in his country. Thorbjørn Jagland, President of the Norwegian Nobel Committee, used a quotation in his concluding remarks.

Isaac Newton once said, "If I have seen further, it is by standing on the shoulders of giants."

When we are able to look ahead today, it is because we are standing on the shoulders of the many men and women who over the years—often at great risk—have stood up for what they believed in and thus made our freedom possible.

Therefore: while others at this time are counting their money, focusing exclusively on their short-term national interests, or remaining indifferent, the Norwegian Nobel Committee has once again chosen to support those who fight—for us all.

We congratulate Liu Xiaobo on the Nobel Peace Prize for 2010. His views will in the long run strengthen China. We extend to him and to China our very best wishes for the years ahead.*

The quote serves as a reference point for and transition to the comments that follow. Notice that the quote does not have to be the last words the speaker utters, but the conclusion either leads up to the quote or is contextually structured by the quote.

One of the most famous moments in oratory was the conclusion of President Ronald Reagan's address to the nation on the *Challenger* disaster from the Oval Office, January 28, 1986:

The crew of the Space Shuttle Challenger honored us by the manner in which they lived their lives. We will never forget them, nor the last time we saw them—this morning, as they prepared for their journey, and waved good-bye, and "slipped the surly bonds of earth" to "touch the face of God."

As in this example, quotations can be interwoven into the fabric of the speech without telling your listeners that you are speaking the words of others. If you use this technique, it is important that you use the quote exactly and attribute it to the writer.

5. Conclude with a Metaphor that Broadens the Meaning of Your Speech

You may want to broaden the meaning of your speech through the use of an appropriate metaphor—a form of figurative language that tells your listeners that you are saying more. At the onset of America's War on Terror, former Secretary of State Condoleezza Rice addressed the issue by using a medical metaphor to stress protective measures:

The United States is actively helping countries to improve their immune systems against terrorism. . . . It's like cutting out a cancer now in 60-plus countries

Without stating it directly, Rice clearly communicated an association between terrorists and a negative medical condition in need of surgical intervention. Her conclusion was that America's military forces would serve in the position of surgical team to help the world become healthy again. Her speech was not about actual illness, rather, it examined the motivation for U.S. military action in countries of the Middle East.

---

*© The Nobel Foundation 2010.

6. Conclude with Humor

If you leave your listeners with a humorous story, you will leave them laughing and with a reservoir of good feelings about you and your speech. To be effective, of course, the humor must be tied to your core idea.

A Hollywood screenwriter, invited to speak to students in a college writing course about the job of transforming a successful novel into a screenplay, concluded her speech with the following story:

> *Two goats who often visited the set of a movie company found some discarded film next to where a camera crew was working. One of the goats began munching on the film.*
>
> *"How's it taste?" asked the other goat, trying to decide whether to start chomping himself.*
>
> *"Not so great," said the first goat. "I liked the book better."*

The audience laughed in appreciation of the humor. When the room settled down, the speaker concluded her speech:

> *I hope in my case the goat isn't right and that you've enjoyed the films I've written even more than the books on which they were based.*
>
> *Thank you for inviting me to speak.*

Humor at the end of the speech is especially effective if it corresponds to the introduction and remains tasteful. In Colin Firth's acceptance speech when he received the Academy Award for Best Actor in 2011, he started his speech with humor, stating:

> *I have a feeling my career has just peaked. My deepest thanks to the Academy. I'm afraid I have to warn you that I'm experiencing stirrings. Somewhere in the upper abdominals which are threatening to form*

© 2012 Gemenacom, Shutterstock, Inc.

FIGURE 8.16 Witty remarks in the conclusion can leave a lasting positive impression on your audience.

themselves into dance moves. Joyous as they may be for me, it would be extremely problematic if they make it to my legs before I get off stage.

Firth's conclusion related directly to his introduction (which, as you will read momentarily, also satisfies Strategy #8—"Refer to Your Introduction"). The audience laughed when he finished with:

> *And to the Anglo-Italian-American-Canadian axis, which makes up my family and Livia for putting up with my fleeting delusions of royalty and who I hold responsible for this and for really everything that's good that's happened since I met her. Now if you'll all excuse me, I have some impulses I have to tend to backstage. Thank you very much."*

7. Encourage Thought with a Rhetorical Question

Rhetorical questions encourage collective thought amongst your audience. At the end of a speech, they leave listeners with a responsibility to think about the questions raised after your speech is over. Your question can be as simple as, "Can our community afford to take the step of hiring fifty new police officers? Perhaps a better question is, can we afford not to?" Rhetorical questions have the power to sway an audience with their emotional impact.

8. Refer to Your Introduction

In your conclusion, you can refer to an opening story or quotation or answer the rhetorical questions you raised. Here is how Shannon closed her speech on safety precautions when driving:

> *One thing I didn't tell you at the beginning of my speech about my accident was that for years I used to frequently drive above the speed limit and often resisted wearing my belt. I used to fight with my parents. I felt it was such a personal decision. How could they—or the state government, for that matter—dare tell me what to do?*

> *Thank goodness I had the sense to buckle up that day. And you can be sure that I will never get into a car without wrapping myself securely with my belt of life and driving within the speech limit. I hope that my experience will be enough to convince you to buckle up, too.*

Like matching bookends, closing your speech with a reference to your introduction provides balance as well as intellectual and emotional symmetry to your remarks.

9. Close with a "So the Next Time" Statement

Less direct than a challenge or a call to action, a "so the next time" statement helps listeners hypothetically apply new speech content to their future experiences in life. Consider Helen's conclusion to a speech of the importance of wearing sunscreen:

> *Today I have explored the dangers of the sun by highlighting the rise in skin cancer in America, examining the connection between sunbathers and those who develop cataracts and sharing some strategies that one can adopt to avoid sun damage. So the next time you feel like going outside and getting a "healthy tan," don't leave the house before putting on some sunscreen and wearing your shades. Your skin and eyes will thank you.*

The online lesson offers resources that will help you find appropriate creative closures for your conclusions. See Topic 2.

8.2.3   How to Conclude the Same Speech in Different Ways

Just as many topics lend themselves to different types of introductions, they also lend themselves to various methods of conclusion. Here, three different techniques are used to conclude a speech on learning to deal more compassionately with the elderly:

1. A Quotation That Personalizes Your Message

> *In 1878, in a poem entitled, "Somebody's Mother," poet Mary Dow Brine wrote these words: "She's somebody's mother, boys, you know, For all she's aged and poor and slow."*

> *Most of us are likely to be somebody's mother—or father—before we die. And further down the road, we're likely to be grandparents, sitting in a rocking chair, hoping that our children have figured out a more humane way to treat us than we have treated our elderly relatives.*

2. A Dramatic Story That Also Serves as a Metaphor

> *Not too long ago, I had a conversation with a doctor who had recently hospitalized an 82-year-old woman with pneumonia. A widow and the mother of three grown children, the woman had spent the last seven years of her life in a nursing home.*

> *The doctor was called three times a day by these children. At first their calls seemed appropriate. They wanted to be sure their mother was getting the best possible medical care. Then, their tone changed. Their requests became demands; they were pushy and intrusive.*

> *After several days of this, the doctor asked one of the children—a son— when he had last visited his mother before she was admitted to the hospital. He hesitated for a moment and then admitted that he had not seen her for two years.*

> *I'm telling you this story to demonstrate that we can't act like these grown children and throw our elderly away only to feel guilty about them when they are in crisis.*

> *Somehow we have to achieve a balance between our own needs and the needs of our frail and needy parents—one that places reasonable demands on ourselves and on the system that supports the elderly.*

3. Rhetorical Questions

> *Imagine yourself old and sick, worried that your money will run out and that your family will no longer want you. You feel a pain in your chest. What could it be? You ask yourself whether your daughter will be able to leave work to take you to the hospital—whether your grandchildren will visit you there—whether your medical insurance will cover your bills—whether anyone will care if you live or die.*

> *Imagine asking yourself these questions and then imagine the pain of not knowing the answers. We owe our elderly better than that.*

By providing these three examples, we hope that you recognize that it takes effort to create an effective conclusion, just as it takes time to create an introduction. Try to spend time thinking about how you can best reach your audience.

The online lesson explores conclusion pitfalls in greater depth so that you can avoid these mistakes. See Topic 3.

© 2012 R. Gino Santa Maria, Shutterstock, Inc.

FIGURE 8.17 Use your voice to confidently conclude your speech—it leaves a lasting impression on your audience.

8.2.4 Common Pitfalls of Conclusions

Knowing what *not* to do is almost as important as knowing what *to* do. Here is a list of approaches to avoid during your conclusion.

1. Don't use your conclusion to introduce a new topic.
Develop your main and subordinate points in the body of your speech, not in the conclusion. Bringing a new topic up after the conclusion can make the audience feel deceived, which most certainly can harm your credibility.

2. Don't apologize.
Even if you are unhappy with your performance, do not apologize for your short-comings when you reach the conclusion. Remarks like, "Well, I guess I didn't have that much to say," or "I'm sorry for taking so much of your time," are unnecessary and usually turn off the audience.

3. Don't end abruptly.
Just because you have made all your points does not mean that your speech is over. Your audience has no way of knowing you are finished unless you provide closure. A one-sentence conclusion is not sufficient closure. Instead, always include at least a summary and a creative closing statement.

4. Don't change the mood or tone.
If your speech was serious, do not shift moods at the end. A humorous conclusion would be inappropriate and lessen the impact of your speech.

5. Don't use the phrases, "in summary" or "in conclusion," except when you are actually at the end of your speech.

Some speakers use these phrases at various points in their speech, confusing listeners who expect an ending rather than a transition to another point.

6. Don't ask for questions.

Never risk asking, "Any questions?" Think about it, if there are no questions, you will be creating an awkward silence that is uncomfortable for both you *and* the audience—hardly the climactic conclusion you were hoping for. Also, most speech days in class are designed to have a number of speakers fill the class period. Answering questions or taking comments may interfere with the instructor's schedule.

If there is to be a question and answer session, consider it as a separate event from the speech. Complete your entire conclusion, receive your well-earned applause, and *then* field any questions.

Conclusion QuickStarts

- **Thanking as a Transition**

  "As I have relayed our collective need to recycle, I thank you for your attentiveness."

- **Call to Action**

  "In light of what we now know of identity theft, I challenge you to change your important passwords monthly."

- **Dramatic Illustration**

  "Imagine a world where everyone is colorblind."

- **Quote**

  To close, consider this, "A man with no enemies is a man with no character"—Paul Newman.

- **Metaphor**

  "Our ability to get along is like the notes of a symphony."

- **Humor**

  "To close, if you think nobody cares if you are alive, try missing a couple of payments."

- **Rhetorical Question**

  "And so I ask, what will YOU do to help the less fortunate?"

- **Refer to Introduction**

  "As I stated much earlier, the time for us to act is now."

- **Use a "So the Next Time" Statement**

  "So the next time you find yourself wanting dessert remember, once on the lips, forever on the hips."

7. Don't forget to thank your audience and host.

Part of your lasting positive impression will come from a sincere thanks offered to both your audience for their attention and your host (applicable in a non-classroom environment only) for allowing you the opportunity to speak. Saying "thank you" as the last words of your speech serves a two-fold purpose: (1) to be polite by expressing genuine gratitude for your audience and their support, and (2) to signal that your speech is over and it is an appropriate time for your audience to applaud.

8. Don't ignore applause.

Graciously accept the praise of your audience by looking around the room and saying thank you.

9. Don't run away.

Remember to keep your poise as you confidently make your retreat from the speaking platform. Being in too big a rush to sit down gives the appearance that you are glad it is over. You may be ready to leave, but stifle the urge to flee the podium and calmly take comfortable strides (while exhibiting good posture) as you head back to your seat.

10. Don't read it.

Just as with the introduction, the delivery of the conclusion is very important. Practice it enough that you are not dependent on your speaker's notes. Eye contact with your audience as you wrap up your message will reinforce your perceived credibility as well as your message's significance and lasting impression.

Chapter Summary

The primacy/recency effect underscores the importance of strong introductions and conclusions. Introductions serve several functions: they focus attention, provide a motive for the audience to listen, build speaker credibility, and preview the topic of your speech.

Several techniques can be used to capture audience attention in the introduction. Among these are startling statements, dramatic stories, quotations, humor, rhetorical questions, illustrations, examples, anecdotes, audience involvement, using personal experiences and visual aids, and making reference to your speaking situation. Your introduction will be successful if you follow established guidelines (such as making it clear and easy to follow), and practicing it as many times as needed, and by avoiding the common pitfalls.

The conclusion of your speech should summarize, motivate, and communicate closure. An effective conclusion reinforces your message, acts as a summary, relates your message to your listeners' lives, and connects your message to a broader context.

Among the techniques you can use to conclude your speech are a call to action, a dramatic story, a closing quotation, a metaphor that broadens meaning, humor, rhetorical questions, and a reference to the introduction.

Key Terms

anecdote, 221

dramatic story, 216

example, 221

illustration, 221

kinesthetic learner, 221

mood, 212

narrative, 222

quotation, 216

rhetorical question, 220

tone, 212

visual learner, 222

Questions for Reflection

1. What strategies are available for capturing audience attention in an introduction? What techniques are available for bringing closure to a speech?
2. How far is "too far" when attempting to gain your audience's attention?
3. What are the limitations and boundaries when it comes to humor?
4. What is the relationship between the effectiveness of a speech's introduction and conclusion and speaker credibility?
5. What mistakes do speakers commonly make in preparing the introduction and conclusion of a speech?
6. How do effective introductions and conclusions help meet the psychological needs of the audience?
7. Different cultures have diverse concepts of what is humorous. How should a sensitive speaker take these differences into account when crafting the introduction and conclusion to a speech?

Activities

1. Write a thesis statement for a speech, and then use different techniques to draft three distinct introductions and conclusions.
2. Examine the transcripts of two speeches in *Vital Speeches of the Day, Representative American Speeches,* or a similar collection. Analyze and assess the effectiveness of the speeches' introductions and conclusions. Consider the appropriateness of each for the topic, the audience, and the occasion.
3. Prepare a short persuasive speech with two different introductions and conclusions. Then deliver it in both forms to a small group. Ask the group which introduction and conclusion worked best. Find out how the choice influences your speech's specific purpose.

References

Baird, Jr., J. E. (1974, Summer). The effects of speech summaries upon audience comprehension of expository speeches of varying quality and complexity. *Central States Speech Journal,* 119–127.

Bush, G. W. (2001, September 11). *Address to the nation from the Oval Office.* Retrieved from http://edition.cnn.com/2001/US/09/11/bush.speech.text/index. html.

Donovan, S. (2010, November 18). Keynote address at the 2010 Vermont statewide housing conference. Retrieved from http://portal.hud.gov/hudportal/ HUD?src=/press/speeches_remarks_statements/2010/statement-111810.

Dority, B., McGarvey, M. G., & Kennedy, P. F. (2010). Marketing foods and beverages in the schools: The effect of school food policy on students' overweight measures. *Public Policy and Marketing, 2*(29), 204–218.

Firth, C. (2011, February 27). Acceptance speech delivered at the 83rd Academy Awards. Retrieved from http://www.indiewire.com/article/ in_their_own_words_the_complete_2011_oscar_acceptance_speeches#.

Jagland. T. (2010, December 10). The Nobel peac prize 2010—Presentation speech. Retrieved from http://www.nobelprize.org/nobel_prizes/peace/ laureates/2010/presentation-speech.html.

King, M. L., Jr. (1963). I have a dream, Speech delivered on August 28, 1963, in Washington, D.C. Reprinted (1988) in R. L. Johannesen, R. R. Allen, & W. A. Linkugel (Eds.), *Contemporary American speeches* (6th ed.). Dubuque, IA: Kendall Hunt Publishing Company.

Merkel, A. (2009, November 3). "We have no time to lose," speech to the United States Congress commemorating the twentieth anniversary of the fall of the Berlin Wall. Retrieved on March 2, 2011, from http://www.spiegel.de/ international/europe.

Princeton University (2006, August 23). Snap judgments decide a face's character, psychologist finds. *ScienceDaily*. Retrieved from http://www.sciencedaily. com- r/releases/2006/08/060822170919.htm.

Reagan, R. (1986, January 28). Address to the nation on the *Challenger* disaster from the Oval Office. Retrieved from http://history.nasa.gov/reagan12886. html.

———. (1987, June 12). Remarks at Brandenberg Gate, Berlin, Germany. Accessed at http://www.historyplace.com/speeches/reagan-tear-down.htm.

Rice, C. (2002, February 1). Remarks presented to the CPAC. Retrieved on June 30, 2011, from http://www.whitehouse.gov/news/releases/2002/02.

———. (2001, October 15). Press briefing on Asia-Pacific Economic Cooperation Meeting. Retrieved on June 30, 2011, from http://www.whitehouse.gov/news/ releases/2001/10/20011015-6.html.

Shariff, S. (2008). *Cyber-bullying: Issues and solutions for the school, the classroom, and the home.* New York: Routledge.

Shapiro, L. (1990, February 26). "The zap generation," *Newsweek 115*(9), 56.

Chapter

9

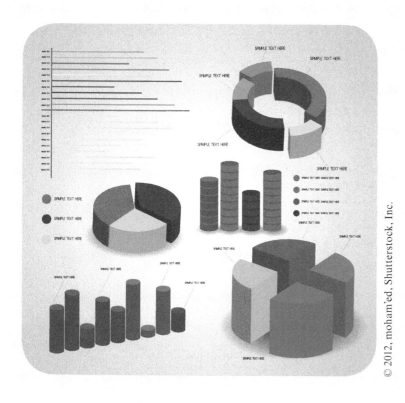

Learning Objectives

After reading this chapter and completing the online activities for this lesson, you will be able to:

1. Incorporate vivid and clear language in speech delivery.

2. Define common media/presentational aids and know when it is appropriate to use them.

3. Design and incorporate presentational aids into a speech.

Colorful Presentations: Vivid Language and Presentational Aids

At a Glance

INTRODUCTION

Language matters. It moves us to tears. It provokes us. It leaves us bewildered. It makes us laugh. Or, more accurately, the speakers *using* language influence our emotions and behavior. Your language will, in large part, determine the success of your speech. Through words, you create the vivid images that remain in the minds of your audience after your speech is over. Your choice of words and style of language influence your credibility as a speaker. By choosing language that appeals to your audience—by moving your audience intellectually and emotionally through the images of speech—you create a bond that encourages continued listening.

As students, you already know how the use of language in a novel can separate a mediocre story from a classic. Many novels have the same premise, but the novel written with elegance and imagery will have more power than pedantic prose. In fact, you may be asking yourself, "What is pedantic prose?" When something is pedantic, it is fussy, overworked, and perhaps pretentious (and frequently written by professors). The power of language is not linked to the number of characters in a word; it is linked to selecting words to convey emotions, ordering words for the way they sounds, and selecting the right word to convey a thought. The following are first sentences in famous novels:

Out of the blackness of sleep a dream formed.

—*The Heart Is a Lonely Hunter* by Carson McCullers (1940)

It is a truth universally acknowledged that a single man in possession of a good fortune must be in want of a wife.

—*Pride and Prejudice* by Jane Austen (1813)

It was the best of times, it was the worst of times, it was the age of wisdom, it was the age of foolishness, it was the epoch of belief, it was the epoch of incredulity, it was the season of Light, it was the season of Darkness, it was the spring of hope, it was the winter of despair, we had everything before us, we had nothing before us, we were all going direct to Heaven, we were all going direct the other way—in short, the period was so far like the present period, that some of its noisiest authorities insisted on its being received, for good or for evil, in the superlative degree of comparison only.

—*A Tale of Two Cities* by Charles Dickens (1859)

Call me Ishmael.

—*Moby Dick* by Herman Melville (1850)

Many years later, as he faced the firing squad, Colonel Aureliano Buendía was to remember that distant afternoon when his father took him to discover ice.

—*One Hundred Years of Solitude* by Gabriel García Márquez (1967)

Do you notice how simple the language is in each sentence? Does the sentence capture you enough that you want to know what happens next? Well, just like great novelists select their words carefully, great speakers do not focus simply on what they want to say—they focus on how it should be said.

Courtesy of Marie Hulett.

FIGURE 9.1 The language used in novels can paint a powerful picture of different times and places. Notice, however, that language used in the quoted passages from these classic novels is also simple and easily understood.

In this chapter, we identify characteristics of spoken language and provide guidelines for using words and sentences more effectively. We also address pitfalls—aspects of language that speakers should avoid. Finally, humor is discussed. Although we encourage you to use humor, you need to understand that humor has its risks. It should be appropriate to the audience and to the occasion.

Although language sets the tone in a speech, you may want to also use presentational aids to clarify your message and direct the audience's attentions. Presentational aids, whether they are pictures, videos, models, or music, draw attention to a specific point or help clarify a complex idea. The second section of this chapter focuses on the benefits of using presentational aids (frequently called visual aids). The different types of presentational aids are explored and criteria are given for their use and display. Rather than discuss the specifics of how to effectively develop and present information through technology (e.g., PowerPoint tips and on-camera hints), these presentational aids will be discussed in Chapter 13, "Public Speaking in an Electronic World."

9.1 Understanding Language

What does the word "successful" mean to you? How about "friend," "patriot," or "God"? These words have different meanings to different people. Understanding language requires recognizing that meanings are in people, not in words.

1. **Language Is Arbitrary and Ambiguous.**

   A word only means what we decide it means. There is nothing inherently profane in curse words—we've simply decided that some words are "bad" words. On television, writers can use the B-word to describe a female dog and the A-word to describe a donkey as often as they like. However, during certain programming times, they cannot use these words to describe people. If someone says, "I'm fine," it may mean that she's mad, sad, or fine.

2. **Language Is Abstract and Symbolic.**

   Symbols are important and language allows us to express thoughts and feelings and describe events that cannot be seen or touched.

3. **Language Is Evolving.**

   The way we communicate today is very different from the way we communicated hundreds of years ago. The words we use change and our styles change. Words like "cool," "hip," and "groovy" are used by different generations. We also change how we describe things in an effort to change how people react to it. The following are two examples of how descriptions of emotional states and corporate events have changed over time.

   Shell shock ➤ *Combat fatigue* ➤ *Post-traumatic stress disorder*

   Firing ➤ *Layoffs* ➤ *Downsizing* ➤ *Rightsizing*

FIGURE 9.2 The denotative meaning of successful is "having a favorable outcome." The connotative meaning of the word "successful" varies from person to person: money, love, winning, achieving, or simply living.

4. **Language Is Powerful.**

   "I now pronounce you man and wife." These words are powerful enough to change lives (when uttered by the appropriate person). Although words are arbitrary, if someone calls you a "bad" name, you likely have an emotional reaction.

   Understanding how to use language will help you organize your speech. It is important to recognize your words have power, but that the meaning of the words can change over time and vary from person to person. Select your words with care, and organize your words for speaking, not writing.

9.1.1 Language Choices in Writing and Speaking

Whether you are planning a speech or preparing a paper, you need to consider your word choice and sentence structure. Speech writing, however, requires a different style than manuscript writing. For example, read this passage:

> He splayed a hand out over the photographs, trembling fingers not quite touching the shiny surfaces, and then he turned and leaned toward me, slowly, with the improbable grace of a tall tree falling. He buried his face in my shoulder and went very quietly and thoroughly to pieces.

—Diana Gabaldon, *Voyager* (1994)

This is a well-written passage that conveys the emotion in the scene. The reader can picture the event and the characters' movements. Now, imagine that you were giving a speech about the emotional effect of trauma and you wanted to share your experience as a counselor. Would you phrase your story the same way? Unless the audience knew you were reading from a book, the above passage would be an odd way to express yourself in a speech.

There are four important differences between writing and speaking.

TABLE 9.1 Differences Between Writing and Speaking	
Writing	**Speaking**
Formal	Informal
Static	Dynamic
Irreversible	Revisable
Distant	Immediate

1. Writing is much more formal than speaking. We learn to speak by listening; we are taught to write through formal education. Although we follow grammatical rules during conversation, the rules are less rigid.
2. As a speaker, your language is dynamic—you express energy and your delivery can affect how people interpret your words. Writing is static—the meaning of the words is solely within the listener. Have you ever sent an email in which you expressed sarcasm or tried to be funny? Did the recipient misunderstand? The static nature of writing can hinder expression. When speaking, your delivery can convey irony or humorous intent.
3. Writing is also irreversible, which is why we take great care; if you've written it down, your mistakes and misstatements may be there forever. But, there are no typos in speaking and even a mispronunciation can be glossed over. In speaking, we can start a sentence again, correct a word, or clarify a point.
4. We can the tone or event the content of a speech in mid-sentence because our audience is immediate—they are hearing the words as we deliver them. In writing, your audience is distant and you may not see how they react. As a speaker, you need to consider these differences and consider how the sentence will be heard.

Although we write and speak differently, some of the differences are becoming less fixed. Technology allows us to record a speech that will be seen later and viewed by distant audiences. We can also write in real time—an audience can read what we write as it is typed. Chapter 13, "Public Speaking in an Electronic World," will provide you with some guidelines for how to adapt to a changing world.

Language and Culture

When you think about language and culture, what comes to mind? Is it the different languages people speak? When it comes to understanding language, however, we do not mean understanding different languages (although that is helpful). The intersection of language and culture is about the effect that culture has on language and how language choices reflect culture.

© 2012 Stuart Monk/Shutterstock.com, Shutterstock, Inc.

FIGURE 9.3 There are many different languages spoken in the world. If you've ever visited the United Nations, you will see multiple translators in every room. Public speaking in a multicultural world does not require knowing all of the languages, but it does require that speakers adapt to the norms and expectations of different regions.

linguistic relativity
A theory that proposes that language shapes the way we see the world; also known as the **Sapir-Whorf hypothesis**.

The theory of **linguistic relativity**, also known as the **Sapir-Whorf hypothesis**, proposes that language shapes the way we see the world. To describe a friend in Spanish, a speaker has to specify the sex of the friend and say either "amigo" or "amiga." In English, the word *friend* does not convey information about the person's sex. The traditional view of the Sapir-Whorf hypothesis is that language affects the way people think; consequently, Spanish-speaking people would think about friends differently than English-speaking people. Although this theory is contested (Stapel & Semin, 2007), it helped linguistics, psychology, and communication researchers to start to consider other links between culture and language. It may be debatable if language shapes thought, but language does reflect the priorities and perspectives of a culture. A famous example is that Eskimos have many more words for snow than most other cultures—snow is an important part of their lives, and so they developed fine distinctions for types of snow and developed words that expressed these distinctions. In TABLE 9.2 below, you will see all the Thai words for "smile." How many English words for can you think of for "smile"? You probably think of "grin" and "smirk," perhaps even "simper," but what other words come to mind? If there are many more Thai words for smile, what might that indicate about their culture?

Thai Word	English Translation
TABLE 9.2 Thai Words for Smile	
Yim cheun chom	I-admire-you smile
Yim thak thaan	I-disagree-with-you-but-go-ahead-and-propose-your-bad-idea smile
Yim sao	The sad smile
Yim mai awk	I'm-trying-to-smile-but-can't-smile
Yim thang nam taa	The "I'm-so happy-I'm-crying" smile
Yim thak thaai	The polite smile for someone you barely know
Fuen Yim	The stiff smile, also known as the "I-should-laugh-at-the-joke-though-it's-not-funny" smile
Yim mee lessanai	The smile that masks something wicked in your mind
Yim yaw	The teasing, or "I-told-you-so" smile
Yim yae-yae	The "I-know-things-look-pretty-bad-but-there's-no-point-in-crying over-spilt-milk" smile
Yim haeng	The dry smile, also known as the "I-know-I-owe-you-the-money-but-I-don't-have-it" smile
Yim cheua-cheuan	The "I-am-the-winner" smile; the smile given to a losing competitor
Yim soo	The "smile-in-the-face-of an-impossible-struggle" smile

SOURCE: Holmes, H. & Tangtongtavy, S. (1998). *Working with the Thais: A guide to managing in Thailand.*

The theory of linguistic relativity argues that language reflects a culture's priorities. When you see all these Thai words for smile, what does it tell you about the Thai culture?

Your online lesson will help you develop a fuller understanding of how language and culture intertwine. We will explore how language choices include and exclude people and provide guidelines for using inclusive language. Specifically, we will address how sexist and racist language can minimize people, how heteronormative language can exclude certain experiences, and how slang and jargon are used to speak only to certain groups of people. There will be exercises to identify these language barriers and showing you how to avoid these statements.

The online course material identifies language barriers that can exclude your listeners and provides guidelines for using inclusive language. See Topic 1.

9.1.2   Guidelines for Improving Language and Style

Words are the tools of a speaker's trade. A carpenter uses a saw, a hammer, and nails to construct a building. A speaker uses language to construct a speech. When used effectively, they can move an audience to action or to tears. They can change minds or cement opinions. Words can create a bond between you and your listeners or they can destroy a relationship. A speaker has numerous tools to choose from when building a speech. Here are some tools that will enhance the style of your speech.

Rhythm

rhythm
The systematic and regular arrangement of sounds.

Perhaps the most important characteristic of spoken language is rhythm. **Rhythm** is the systematic and regular arrangement of sounds. The rhythm of a piece of music creates different moods. It creates a sense of calm and serenity that allows us to listen and reflect or it may create the urge to dance like a maniac. Rhythm is important in spoken language, also. It is the speech flow or pattern that is created in many ways, including the use of parallel structure, repetition, and variations in sentence length.

Read aloud Patrick Henry's famous line, "Give me liberty or give me death," to illustrate the importance of rhythm:

> *I know not what course Others may take. But as for me, Give me liberty Or death.*

Now read the original, and notice the greater impact:

> *I know not what course Others may take. But as for me, Give me liberty Or give me death.*

Portrait by Peter F. Rothermel 1817–1895.

FIGURE 9.4 Patrick Henry's words are remembered as a key moment in history—they moved people to action. Consider how your phrases sound and whether they will resonate with your audience.

By taking out one of the repetitive "give me" phrases, the rhythm—and impact—of the sentence changes. As you develop your speech, consider the following ways you can use rhythm to reinforce your ideas and to maintain audience attention.

Use parallel structure. First, create rhythm by using parallel structure. Parallelism involves the arrangement of a series of words, phrases, or sentences in a similar form. In his inaugural speech, President John F. Kennedy stated, "If a free society cannot help the many who are poor, it cannot save the few who are rich." Also using parallel structure, in his first inaugural speech, President Richard M. Nixon stated, "Where peace is unknown, make it welcome; where peace is fragile, make it strong; where peace is temporary, make it permanent" (My Fellow Americans, 2009). Parallel structure emphasizes the rhythm of speech. When used effectively, it adds harmony and balance to a speech that can verge on the poetic.

A more recent example of parallel structure can be seen when Tina Fey accepted the Mark Twain Prize for American humor at the Kennedy Center in November, 2010. The structure of "I am proud" gives rhythm to her speech and allows her to make important points rather succinctly.

> "I'm so proud to represent American humor, I am proud to be an American, and I am proud to make my home in the 'not real' America. And I am most proud that during trying times, like an orange [terror] alert, a bad economy or a contentious election that we as a nation retain our sense of humor" (washingtonpost.com, November 14, 2010).

If you tap along while you read the first sentence, you will see how the structure of each phrase is similar. If there is rhythm to your structure, your speech simply sounds more pleasurable.

© 2012 Joe Seer/Shutterstock.com, Shutterstock, Inc.

FIGURE 9.5 Tina Fey, a comedian and Emmy Award-winning actress, is also a writer who has won multiple awards from the Writers Guild of America. As a writer, she understands the importance of using speech patterns to make an impact.

Repetition. If you want "the truth, the whole truth, and nothing but the truth" about creating rhythm in a speech, this tip is for you. Repeating ideas (especially in groups of three) can create rhythm. Winston Churchill once said, "If you have an important point to make, don't try to be subtle or clever. Use a pile driver. Hit the point once. Then come back and hit it again. Then hit it a third time—a tremendous whack." Experienced speakers know that saying things three times gets their point across in a way saying it once cannot—not simply because of repetition but because of the rhythmic effect of the repetition of three.

Many presidents have used this device during important speeches. You can hear the emotional impact of Abraham Lincoln's words in his Gettysburg Address when he said, "We can not dedicate, we can not consecrate, we can not hallow this ground." Franklin Roosevelt's words created an impact during his second inaugural address when he observed, "I see one-third of a nation, ill-housed, ill-clad, ill-nourished." (My Fellow Americans, 2009). The simple cadence and rhythm of this structure helps make these statements memorable.

Contemporary speakers also use the rule of three in their speeches. In the Tina Fey quote above, she used this device twice. She identified three things she is proud of, and in her next sentence, she identified three issues in the United States. Steve Jobs, then CEO of Apple Computer, in his 2005 commencement address to Stanford University, gave advice on living by explaining what it was like to learn he was dying. His doctor told him to get his affairs in order. In Jobs's words, "It means to try to tell your kids everything you thought you'd have the next 10 years to tell them in just a few months. It means to make sure everything is buttoned up so that it will be as easy as possible for your family. It means to say your goodbyes." If Jobs had instead provided a litany of things to do, the passage would not have been as powerful. As you can see, when you repeat phrases, it works best to employ parallel structure.

Try this device in your classroom speeches. For example, in a speech of tribute, you might say, "I am here to honor, to praise, and to congratulate the members of the campus volunteer fire department."

Here are some classic techniques for repetition and parallel structure:

Vary sentence length. The rhythm of speech is affected by how well you combine sentences of varying lengths. Long sentences can convey the variety in a scene, but they can also be confusing. Short sentences can be powerful. But too many short sentences in a row can be choppy or boring. A combination of long and short sentences adds rhythmic interest. On June 1, 1997, Mary Schmich, columnist for the *Chicago Tribune*, wrote an essay she described as a commencement speech, called, "Wear Sunscreen." In addition to imploring graduates to wear sunscreen, Schmich provides several words of advice, including the following excerpts:

> *Do one thing every day that scares you.*

> *Sing.*

> *Keep your old love letters. Throw away your old bank statements.*

> *Stretch.*

Techniques for Repetition and Parallel Structure

Anaphora is the repetition of the same word or phrase at the *beginning* of successive clauses or sentences. Martin Luther King, Jr., used this technique in his "I Have a Dream" speech. He started eight sentences in a row with that phrase.

Epistrophe is the repetition of a word or expression at the *end* of phrases, clauses, or sentences. Lincoln used this device in the phrase, "of the people, by the people, for the people." It is an effective technique for emphasis.

Alliteration is the repetition of the initial consonant or initial sounds in series of words. Alliteration can be used effectively in speeches, such as when the Wizard of Oz said: "Step forward, Tin Man. You dare to come to me for a heart, do you? You *clinking, clanking, clattering collection of caliginous* junk. … And you, Scarecrow, have the effrontery to ask for a brain! You *billowing bale of bovine* fodder!" (*The Wizard of Oz*, 1939).

Antithesis is the use of contrast, within a parallel grammatical structure, to make a rhetorical point. During a press conference in November of 2008, President Obama used antithesis when he said, "If we are going to make the *investments we need*, we also have to be willing to shed the *spending that we don't need*" (*New York Times*, November 25, 2008).

anaphora
The repetition of the same word or phrase at the *beginning* of successive clauses or sentences.

epistrophe
The repetition of a word or expression at the *end* of phrases, clauses, or sentences.

alliteration
The repetition of the initial consonant or initial sounds in series of words.

antithesis
The use of contrast, within a parallel grammatical structure, to make a rhetorical point.

Schmich's commencement speech is filled with humor and advice, but its impact is due, in part, to the variation in sentence structure. Rhythm is a critical element. The rhythm of this speech is so engaging; it captured the attention of musical artists who developed their own version of Schmich's advice, including Baz Luhrmann's "Everybody's Free (to Wear Sunscreen)" and John Safran's "Not the Sunscreen Song."

Word Order

The second technique to enhance the style of your speech concerns word order, which relates to the order in which ideas should be arranged in a sentence. In general, the last idea presented is the most powerful. Consider this famous line spoken by John F. Kennedy at his inauguration:

Ask not what your country can do for you, ask what you can do for your country.

Versus:

Ask what you can do for your country, ask not what your country can do for you.

The second way of ordering the phrase loses some power. Because speech is slower than silent reading, individual words take on more importance, especially those appearing at the end of the sentence. Be sure to order your words so that the audience has time to process the most important points.

Concreteness

On a continuum, words range from the most concrete to the most abstract. Concrete language is rooted in real-life experience—things we see, hear, taste, touch, and feel—while abstract language tells us little about what we experience, relying instead on more symbolic references. Compare the following:

TABLE 9.3 Abstract versus Concrete

Abstract	Concrete
Bad weather	Hail the size of golf balls
Nervousness	Trembling hands; knocking knees
An interesting professor	When she started throwing paper airplanes around the room to teach us how air currents affect lift, I knew she was a winner.

Concrete words and phrases create pictures in listeners' minds and can turn a "ho-hum" speech into one that captures listener attention. Winston Churchill understood this premise when he said, during World War II, "We shall fight them on the beaches," instead of "Hostilities will be engaged on the coastal perimeter" (Kleinfeld, 1990). Consider the differences between these two paragraphs:

Version 1

On-the-job accidents take thousands of lives a year. Particularly hard hit are agricultural workers who suffer approximately 1,500 deaths and 140,000 disabling injuries a year. One-fifth of all agricultural fatalities are children. These statistics make us wonder how safe farms are.

Version 2

Farmers who want to get their children interested in agriculture often take them on tractors for a ride. About 150 children are killed each year when they fall off tractors and are crushed underneath. These children represent about half the children killed in farm accidents each year—a statistic that tells us farms can be deadly. About 1,500 people die each year on farms, and an additional 140,000 are injured seriously enough so they can no longer work.

In Version 2, the images and language are more concrete. Instead of wondering, "how safe farms are," Version 2 declares that "farms can be deadly." Instead of talking about "disabling injuries," it tells us that workers "are injured seriously enough so they can no longer work." Concrete language paints a more vivid picture allowing the audience to understand the situation on a more emotional that is likely to stay with them long after a speech is over.

Complete Your Thoughts and Sentences

Focus on completing every sentence you start. This may seem like common sense, but many people do not follow this advice when speaking before groups. Although in casual conversation we accept that many sentences trail off in conversational speech, in a speech, if you do not complete your thoughts your audience may find you less credible. Imagine if a speaker delivered his point this way:

In many states, your signature on your driver's license makes you a potential organ donor. If you are killed . . . According to the laws in these states, if you are killed in an auto accident, the state has the right … Your organs can be used to help people in need of organ transplants. There are sick people out there who need the kidneys, corneas, and even the hearts of people killed. Think about it. When you are dead, you can still give the gift of life.

By not completing his thoughts, the speaker appears less confident and less prepared. It is also possible that the audience will get bored or frustrated and simply tune out.

On the other hand, we encourage you to *violate* this rule by incorporating sentence fragments, where relevant. Keep in mind that carefully chosen sentence fragments can contribute to clear communication. Here is an example:

Is Christmas too commercial? Well, maybe. It wasn't that long ago when the holiday season began after Thanksgiving. Now, the first Christmas catalogs reach shoppers in September. Before summer is over. Before the temperature has dropped below 90 degrees. Even before Labor Day.

Do not confuse sentence fragments with the incomplete thoughts and sentences discussed earlier. In the case above, the fragments are intentional and are used effectively to enhance meaning.

Use the Active Voice—Most of the Time

Rules of grammar and style operate for the spoken language as well as the written language. One rule to follow involves using the **active voice**. When speaking or writing in active voice, the subject of the sentence performs the action: "I did that" rather than "It was done by me." When speakers or writers make the object of an action into the subject of a sentence, they are using **passive voice**. A direct speaking style involves the use of the active rather than passive voice as often as possible. The following examples demonstrate the difference between the passive and active voice:

Version 1: Passive voice
Students in an English class at Long Beach City College were asked by their teacher to stand in line. After a few minutes, the line was broken by a student from Japan who walked a few yards away. The behavior demonstrated by the student shows how cultural differences can affect even the simple act of waiting in line. In this case, the need for greater personal space was felt by the student who considered it impolite to stand so close.

Version 2: Active voice
An English teacher at Long Beach City College asked the class to stand in line. After a few minutes, a Japanese student broke the line and walked a few yards away. The student's behavior demonstrated how cultural differences affect even the simple act of waiting in line. In this case, the student felt the need for more personal space because the Japanese culture considers it impolite to stand so close.

In Version 2, the same sentences rephrased in the active voice show the subject of the sentence in action. In addition to using fewer words, the active voice is more direct, easier to follow, and more vigorous. We encourage the use of the active voice.

active voice
When the subject of the sentence performs the action.

passive voice
When speakers or writers make the object of an action into the subject of a sentence.

When Is It Appropriate to Use Passive Voice?

- If the object is more important than the subject: *The Debt Ceiling Bill was passed by a narrow vote.*
- If the subject is unknown or unimportant: *Hundreds of dogs, cats, and other pets were abandoned after the hurricane.*
- To achieve an objective tone. *In step two, the surveys were administered to the students.*

Use Language to Create a Theme

A key word or phrase can reappear throughout your speech to reinforce your theme. Each time the image is repeated, it becomes more powerful and is likely to stay with your listeners after your speech is over. In Chapter 4, we mentioned that Jon Favreau, President Obama's speechwriter, is credited with developing the "Yes we can" slogan of the campaign. This slogan was used to create a theme that resonated with voters and tapped into people's desire for change and action. By using "yes we can" as a consistent theme during the campaign and in speeches, President Obama delivered a message that was effective and memorable.

Use Imagery

imagery
Creating a vivid description through the use of one or more of our five senses.

When constructing your speech, consider using a variety of language techniques to enhance imagery. **Imagery** involves creating a vivid description through the use of one or more of our five senses. Using imagery can grab and audience and create a great impact and lasting memory. Mental images can be created using many devices, including metaphors, analogies, and similes.

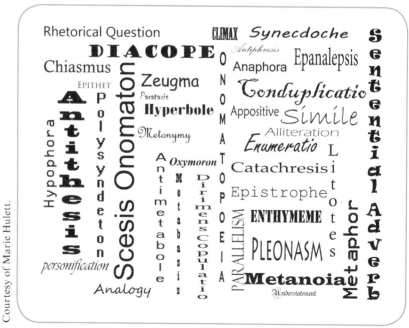

Courtesy of Marie Hulett.

FIGURE 9.6 There are many rhetorical devices you can use. These devices help make your speech more interesting by "mixing it up."

Metaphors. A **metaphor** is a "mental equation when something is compared to something else" (Miller, 2004, p. 13). Speakers use metaphors to help the audience connect a new idea to something they already known. Through metaphors we can understand and experience one idea in terms of another. For example, if you ask a friend how a test went, and the friend responded, "I scored a home run," you would know that your friend felt good about the test. In his "Sinews of Peace" speech to Westminster College in Fulton, Missouri, Prime Minister Winston Churchill used the following metaphor on March 5, 1946: "An iron curtain has descended across the continent." During his inaugural address, President Bill Clinton said, "Our democracy must not only be the envy of the world but also the engine of our own renewal."

metaphor
A mental equation when something is compared to something else.

analogy
An extended metaphor, but instead of a simple comparison, it's more like an argument.

Information + Metaphor = Understanding

Metaphors work the way visuals work—they help the audience see, understand, and remember your information; they are "a shortcut to instant understanding" (p. 13) and are especially useful when you think you will encounter resistance, indifference, or negativity to your speech (Miller, 2004).

Analogy. An **analogy** is an extended metaphor, but instead of a simple comparison, it's more like an argument. Analogies can help the audience understand the message in a way a simple statement cannot. Here's an example from Dyan, a teacher's aide in a kindergarten class. She was asked to develop a lesson on bullying. At the start of her lesson, she handed each child a piece of construction paper, a hole punch, and a roll of tape.

> *Okay everyone, I want you to think about some of the mean things you have said in the last few days. Maybe you were mad at your mom or dad, or grandma or grandpa, and you yelled something hurtful. Maybe your brother or sister took something of yours and you called them a bad name. Maybe your feelings were hurt by someone in this class and you said something mean to them.*

> *Now, for each mean thing you said, I want you to punch a hole in the piece of paper. Punch as many holes as you need.*

> *When we say mean things, it's important that we apologize. So, all together, let's say, "I'm sorry." On the count of three; one, two three: "I'm sorry."*

> *Apologies show other people that we care about them. So, now as a way to show that you apologized, please tape the paper back together again. Take the little holes and tape them back in the paper. (Students taped their papers for a few minutes).*

> *Everyone hold up your paper. What do you see? Yep, the paper is not the same. Even though you apologized and tried to put it back together again, the paper still looks like someone punched holes in it. This is what our mean words do to other people—even if you say you're sorry, the other person remembers them and it leaves little scars. So, be careful with your words.*

This analogy helped the kindergarteners quickly understand and relate to a topic that was abstract: bullying. By relating it to another, more concrete example, kids could see the relationship between the topics.

"A woman is like a tea bag. You never know how strong she is, until she gets into hot water."

—Eleanor Roosevelt

similes

Create images as they compare the characteristics of two things that are not alike using the words "like" or "as."

Analogies are especially helpful when you need to explain a new process or new procedure to a group who has little or no background with the topic. To create an analogy, use something familiar to your audience and look for characteristics in that object that you can compare to aspects of your process.

Similes. **Similes** also create images as they compare the characteristics of two things that are not alike using the words "like" or "as." Here are two examples Ann Beattie uses in her novel, *Picturing Will*: "Falling snow looked as solid as pearls. Tar could look like satin"; and "Wayne reacted like someone whose cat has proudly brought home a dead mouse" (Beattie, 1989). By relaying concrete images, a simile can accelerate a listener's comprehension—like the way properly inflated bike tires speed up your commute. Like metaphors and analogies, a simile can make your speech more vivid and help the audience understand your topic. Although these rhetorical devices can enliven your speech, guard against using images that are trite or too familiar.

Signals

A final guideline of spoken language involves using signals. You may reread an important passage in a book to appreciate its meaning, but your audience hears your message only once—a fact that may make it necessary to signal critical passages in your speech. The following signals tell your listeners to pay close attention:

- *This cannot be overemphasized…*
- *Let me get to the heart of the matter…*
- *I want to summarize…*
- *My three biggest concerns are…*

Although all speakers hope to capture and hold listeners' attention throughout their speech, you must draw people back to your message at critical points. Signals are more necessary in spoken language than in print.

9.1.3 Language Choices That Detract from a Speech

Although your speaking style—the distinctive manner in which you speak to produce the effect you desire—like your style of dress, is personal, it is important to realize that some aspects of styles enhance communication while others detract. You may have a great sense of humor, but some may be put off by your lack of seriousness. You may be very bright and reflective, but your quiet tone may tire your audience. You have read several language guidelines for creating an effective speech. Your online lesson will review the several language choices that detract from your speech and provide some hints on how to avoid these errors. Here's a brief overview of these pitfalls.

Long and Unnecessary Words

Using long and unnecessary words violates the first principle of language usage, which is to be simple and concrete. When you read on your own, you have the opportunity to reread something or to look up a word you do not understand. In a speech, you do not have the rewind option, and if the audience does not understand, they will lose interest.

Lack of Content, Masking Meaning, or Using Euphemisms

As a speaker, you want to be clear and to provide something meaningful for your audience. Avoid sentences that lack content, mask meaning, or include **euphemisms** (words or phrases that are substituted for other words or phrases to put what is being discussed in a more positive or negative light). Sentences that say nothing or, worse yet, mask meaning can damage a speaker's credibility. Listeners wonder what to believe, and begin to question the speaker's competence. By the time listeners start asking these questions, the speech has almost certainly failed.

euphemisms
Substituting a mild or vague term or phrase in place of a blunt or harsh word or phrase.

Words Used Incorrectly or Mispronounced

"There are no typos in speaking and even a mispronunciation can be glossed over." We wrote that sentence at the start of this chapter. Honest mistakes in pronunciation, brought on by nerves or compressed time, are easily overlooked. Repeated errors in pronunciation or word meaning, however, demonstrate a lack of knowledge or practice and can affect your credibility.

Jargon, Slang, and Profanity

Listeners almost always expect a degree of decorum in a formal speech, requiring that certain language be avoided. Profanity, of course, is the most obvious offender, but using jargon or slang can also be inappropriate. Terms like "ain't," and "you guys" should be used *only* for specific effect. In public discourse, they can violate an audience's sense of appropriateness—or propriety.

Exaggeration and Clichés

Exaggerations are statements made to impress, not aiming for accuracy. Clichés are statements that are so overused that they no longer have any real meaning. Exaggerations and clichés can bore your listeners because they suggest that both your vocabulary and imagination are limited.

Powerless Language

Language can communicate a sense of mastery of your subject, or it can communicate doubt and hesitancy. When speakers communicate with hesitancy, uncertainty, or tentativeness, audiences generally perceive them to have low impact and little power.

Humor

Nothing brings you closer to your audience than humor. Humor reveals your human side. It relaxes listeners and makes them respond positively. Through a properly placed anecdote, you let your audience know that you are not taking yourself—or your subject—too seriously. Even in a serious speech, humor can be an effective tool to emphasize an important point.

Humor can have a positive effect on an audience. When appropriate humor is used in informative speaking, the humor enhances the speaker's image by improving the audience's perception of the speaker's character (Gruner, 1985). Humor can also help audiences remember over a longer period of time (Carlson, 2011).

Humor works only if it is carefully used and only if it is connected to the theme of your speech. Here are five guidelines for the effective use of humor in a speech.

© 2012 Yuri Arcurs, Shutterstock, Inc.

FIGURE 9.7 Using humor effectively can relax you and help the audience remember your speech.

1. Use Humor Only If You Can Be Funny

Some speakers do not know how to be funny in front of an audience. On a one-on-one basis they may be funny, but in front of a group, their humor vanishes. They stumble over punch lines and their timing is bad. These people should limit themselves to serious speeches or "safe" humor.

2. Laugh at Yourself, Not at Others

In his humble acceptance speech after receiving the Academy Award for Best Actor in 2011, Colin Firth's humorous comments included a few jabs at himself. His first words were, "I have a feeling my career has just peaked" (NowPublic.com, February 28, 2011). After thanking the Academy, he then remarked:

> *I'm afraid I have to warn you that I'm experiencing stirrings. Somewhere in the upper abdominals, which are threatening to form themselves into dance moves. Joyous as they may be for me, it would be extremely problematic if they make it to my legs before I get off stage.*

Speakers who make themselves the object of their own humor often endear themselves to their listeners. Amy Bippus (2007), who explores the effect of humorous communication, examined how political candidates' use of humor affected audiences. In her study, half of the participants read part of a debate in which the candidate poked fun at himself:

> *I know I can go a bit overboard when I get going. My daughter even said that maybe the moderator should have music to drown me out when I go on too long, like they do at the Emmy awards.*

The other half of the study participants read the same debate but the candidate instead made fun of his opponent:

> *You must excuse me, but when I am right, I get angry. Mr. Patillo, on the other hand, gets angry when he is wrong. As a result, we are angry at each other much of the time.*

In this study, the political candidate's humor was seen as more effective when it was self-directed rather than other directed. In fact, the participants (all college students) who read the debate except in which the candidate made fun of his opponent attributed it more to hostility. Self-directed humor was attributed more to mood improvement and common ground.

It can be effective to tell a joke at your own expense, but it is in poor taste to tell a joke at the expense of others. Racial, ethnic, or sexist jokes are rarely acceptable, nor are jokes that poke fun at the personal characteristics of others. Although stand-up comics like Dane Cook, Jeff Foxworthy, and Chris Rock may get away with such humor, public speakers cannot.

3. Understated Anecdotes Can Be Effective
An economist speaking before a group of peers starts with the following anecdote:

> I am constantly reminded by those who use our services that we often turn out a ton of material on the subject but we do not always give our clients something of value. A balloonist high above the earth found his balloon leaking and managed to land on the edge of a green pasture. He saw a man in a business suit approaching, and very happily said: "How good it is to see you. Could you tell me where I am?"

> The well-dressed man replied: "You are standing in a wicker basket in the middle of a pasture." "Well," said the balloonist, "You must be an economist." The man was startled. "Yes, I am, but how did you know that?"

> "That's easy," said the balloonist, "because the information you gave me was very accurate—and absolutely useless" (Valenti, 1982, pp. 80–81).

This anecdote is funny in an understated way. It works because it is relevant to the audience. Its humor comes from the recognition that the speaker knows—and shares—the foibles of the audience.

4. Find Humor in Your Own Experiences
The best humor comes from your own experiences. In general, avoid books of jokes and stories from the Internet. Humor is all around you. You might want to start now to record humorous stories for your speeches so that you will have material when the need arises. If you decide to use someone else's material, you have the ethical responsibility to give the source credit. You might start with, "As Jerry Seinfeld would say…" This gives appropriate source citation and makes clear that line or story is meant as a joke. Usually you will get bigger laughs by citing their names than if you tried to convince your audience that the humor was original.

5. Avoid Being Not Funny
We use the double negative to make a point. When an audience responds with a spontaneous burst of applause or laughter, there is little that will make you feel better—or more relaxed—as a speaker. Its effect is almost magical. However, when the humor is distasteful to the audience or highly inappropriate, a speaker may find no one is laughing.

Ricky Gervais hosted the 2010 Golden Globe Awards, and his humor received very mixed reviews. Without making specific reference to Mel Gibson's 2006 arrest for drunk driving, Gervais quipped, "I like a drink as much as the next man … unless the next man is Mel Gibson" (www.dailymail.co.uk). Just before introducing

Colin Farrell, Gervais remarked, "One stereotype I hate is that all Irishmen are just drunk, swearing hell-raisers. Please welcome Colin Farrell" (www.dailymail. co.uk). He also made reference to Paul McCartney's expensive divorce, and Hugh Hefner's marriage to a woman 60 years younger than he. While some jokes were well received, some felt that Gervais stepped over the line, even for a comedian.

© 2012 Featureflash/Shutterstock.com, Shutterstock, Inc.

FIGURE 9.8 English comedian, actor, and writer Ricky Gervais received decidedly mixed reviews for his controversial quips and derisive jibes as host of the Golden Globe Awards in 2010 and 2011. His risky humor illustrates the danger of being not funny when addressing an audience.

It is important to keep in mind that humor is criticism. We laugh at things people do, what they say, how they react, and so on. In fulfilling our ethical responsibilities, however, we need to remember that while someone or some event is being mocked, the speaker needs to do so with taste and appropriateness.

So, to avoid being *not* funny, audience analysis is vital. As a beginning public speaker, we urge you to err on the side of caution. It is better to avoid humor than to fail at it. While most humor is risky, there are certain things you can be fairly sure your audience will find funny. Stick with those, and try riskier humor as you gain confidence and experience. You might also check with a friend or classmate if you have any question about the humor of a line or story.

9.2 Presentational Aids

A picture is worth a thousand words. We've all heard that statement. Now, we don't necessarily agree. A picture may be worth a thousand ill-chosen and boring words, but you can use words to create images and connect with your audience. However, why not have both?

FIGURE 9.9 Is a picture really worth a thousand words? When creating your presentation aids, be creative—you can also use words to create a picture.

9.2.1 Functions of Presentational Aids

Presentational aids function in a variety of ways. They are more than "add-ons" or "class requirements." Your instructor may require you to use presentational aids not only to enhance the effectiveness of your speech but also to learn how to work with them as you speak. Following are five functions of presentational aids.

1. Presentational Aids Engage Listeners

Have you ever seen a lotto billboard alongside an interstate? As you approach it, you can see the jackpot amount increasing as the digital numbers change constantly. When a presentational aid is well prepared, little can compete with it to capture—and hold—audience interest. We live in a visual age. Images that surround us in the mass media make us more receptive, on conscious and unconscious levels, to visual presentations of all kinds. We are attuned to these presentations simply because they are visual—a phenomenon you can use to your advantage during a speech.

One student wanted to emphasize how fast the world's population is growing. During her speech, she accessed a web site (worldometers.info) that keeps a digital tally of births, and kept the digital counter on the screen for about a minute. Then she made reference to the number of births that had occurred during that time frame. It kept the interest of the class.

A well-placed, professional-looking presentational aid will draw attention to the point you are trying to make or to the statistics you want the audience to process.

Our suggestions: In an effort to maintain interest and attention, try to limit each visual to one main point. Leave details out. Use as few words as possible. Be aware of spacing, and do not crowd the images. If there is too much information or the slide looks too "busy," you will lose attention and interest.

2. Presentational Aids Provide Clarity

The audience listening to a speech that includes explanations of where the oil spills took place needs to view a map with necessary detail included. In FIGURE 9.9, the words and the illustration work together to create meaning.

Visuals will help you show a process or explain a complex idea. Pictures would help someone learn to tie a tie. If a speaker gave everyone in the audience a tie and then presented a visual of each step, the audience could practice together.

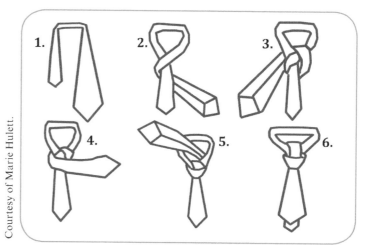

Courtesy of Marie Hulett.

FIGURE 9.10 A visual aid should only include the most important elements. This visual of a tie includes the pictures and relies on the speaker to explain the process.

Presentational aids have the power to clarify complex ideas but do not eliminate the need to explain verbally the complex details of a process. Presentational aids take the place of many words and, therefore, shorten the length of a speech. They do not replace words, and one or two statements are insufficient verbal support for a series of visual displays. But presentational aids and words *in combination* can reduce the amount of time you spend creating word pictures.

Our suggestion: Keep your visuals simple. You may want to demonstrate your expertise by including all the bells and whistles available to you, but you don't want to overwhelm the listener. Eliminate extraneous material. You may want to use a second visual rather than including more information than your listeners can process.

Your online lesson will provide specific guidelines for developing effective visual aids. We will also provide you some key resources for selecting visuals. See Topic 2.

3. Presentational Aids Make Abstract Ideas Concrete

Few of us enjoy abstractions. If you are delivering a speech on the effects of the 2010 BP oil spill in the Gulf of Mexico, it may not be enough to tell your audience that the spill released more oil than the *Exxon Valdez* spill in Alaska's Prince William Sound. It is far more effective to refer to a diagram that illustrates the extent of the difference. FIGURE 9.11 shows the enormity of the disaster and eliminates any confusion audience members may have about the extent of the disaster.

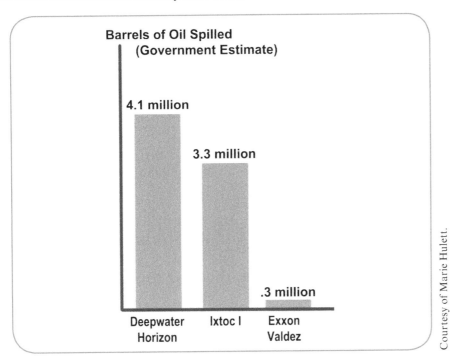

Courtesy of Marie Hulett.

FIGURE 9.11 A simple bar graph can display information clearly so it is easier to understand. A programmed display showing the course of impact can also provide powerful imagery. Visit this web site to see an interactive version of the spread of the oil spill: http://www.nytimes.com/interactive/2010/05/01/us/20100501-oil-spill-tracker.html.

Along with this visual, you explain:

- British Petroleum's Deepwater Horizon rig exploded on April 20, 2010. Over the course of the next three months, almost 5 million barrels of crude oil emptied into the Gulf of Mexico.

- This was the worst accidental oil spill in history. According to *The New York Times* Gulf oil spill tracking web site (2010), whose source is the National Oceanic and Atmospheric Administration, this disaster exceeded Ixtoc I. Until it was capped in March of 1980, Ixtoc I leaked an estimated 3.3 million barrels (140 million gallons) of crude oil into Mexico's Bay of Campeche. As you seen in the diagram, the BP oil spill leaked 13 times more oil than the *Exxon Valdez*.

- *Time* magazine reporter Bryan Walsh did a follow-up article one year after the spill, and reported that approximately 1,000 square miles of water over the original Deepwater Horizon site were still off-limits. We won't know the full effects of this oil spill for years to come.

Although photographs of the spill would be effective in showing its devastation, the simple bar chart comparing the BP spill to two other famous oil spills highlights the enormity of the disaster. The bar chart provides us with a visual picture that makes the situation much more easily understood. Sometimes we need to see something in order to process it effectively.

4. Presentational Aids Create Memorable Messages

Did you read the newspaper this morning? What do you remember from it? Chances are, if you read the paper, a photo comes to mind—the picture of a firefighter rescuing a child from a burning building or the president of your university getting a pie in the face at the end of a fund-raiser. You may have read the articles that accompanied these pictures, but the images are likely to have had the greatest impact.

The tendency for an audience to recall pictures longer than words gives speakers an important advantage. The Occupational Safety and Health Administration, stresses the importance of visual aids and indicates that three days after an event, people retain 10 percent of what they heard from an oral presentation, 35 percent from a visual presentation, and 65 percent from a visual and oral presentation (OSHA Office of Training and Education, 1996). Using a simple bar graph to display this information makes it easier to understand these significant differences (see FIGURE 9.12).

Presentational aids have persuasive power. Business speakers, especially those in sales, have long realized that they can close a deal faster if they use visual aids. A

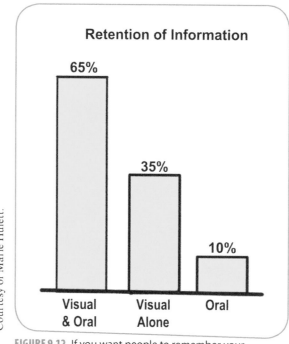

FIGURE 9.12 If you want people to remember your key points, reinforce them with a visual.

study by the University of Minnesota and the 3M Corporation found that speakers who integrate visuals into their talks are 43 percent more likely to persuade their audiences than speakers who rely solely on verbal images (Vogel, Dickson, & Lehman, 1986).

5. Presentational Aids Help to Organize Ideas

As with every other aspect of your speech, presentational aids should be audience-centered. They may be eye-catching and visually stimulating, but they serve a more practical purpose. The flow and connection of a speaker's ideas are not always apparent to an audience, especially if the topic is complicated or involves many steps. Flow charts, diagrams, graphs, and tables can help listeners follow a speaker's ideas.

TABLE 9.4 Communication Taxonomy

Decorative	Add aesthetic appeal or humor	Art on the cover of a book Visual of a general in a military lesson on ammunition
Representational	Depict an object in a realistic fashion	A screen capture A photograph of equipment
Mnemonic	Provide retrieval cues for factual information	A picture of ten forks stuck in a door to retrieve meaning of a Spanish word for fork: *tenador*
Organizational	Show qualitative relationships among two or more variables	A two-dimensional course map
Relational	Show quantitative relationships among two or more variables	A line graph A pie chart
Transformational	Show changes in objects over time or space	An animation of a weather cycle A video showing how to operate equipment
Interpretive	Illustrate a theory or principle	A schematic diagram of equipment An animation of molecular movement

SOURCE: Clark, R. C., & Lyons, C. (2010). *Graphics for learning* (2d ed.). San Francisco: Pfeiffer.

9.2.2 General Criteria for Using Presentational Aids

Your decision to include an aid should be based on the extent to which it enhances your audience's interest and understanding. The type of aid you choose should relate directly to the specific purpose of your speech and information you intend to convey. Training documents provided by the U.S. Department of Labor remind speakers that presentational aids "enable you to appeal to more than one sense at the same time, thereby increasing the audience's understanding and retention level" (OSHA Office of Training and Education, 1996).

The online lesson will provide specific guidelines for selecting presentational aids. Consider whether one is necessary for your speech, whether you have the skill to create it, whether you can transport it safely (without loss or breakage), whether you have the time and know how to use it effectively in the speech, whether everyone in the audience will be able to see and understand it easily, whether you are allowed to bring it into the venue, and whether it might be considered misleading, offensive, or ethically questionable. See Topic 2.

9.3 Types of Presentational Aids

Presentational aids fall into two general categories: traditional presentational aids (e.g., objects, images, models, and handouts) and technology-based presentational aids (e.g., audio, video, and presentation software).

Traditional presentation aids. Traditional presentation aids do not require any fancy equipment. Although these types of aids may not feel as fancy as showing a video, there are some important advantages. First, these aids are easy to develop and use. They don't require any special equipment—they likely don't even require electricity. Second, you have complete control over how they are integrated into your speech. When using technology based presentational aids, you are at the mercy of the technology. Every presenter has faced a glitch and had to improvise. If you have a poster, there are very few glitches.

Actual objects. Actual objects are real objects. Get any two or more speech teachers together, and quickly a list is generated of objects brought to class: guns (a long time ago), prosthetic breast, snakes, bikes, food, insulin pump, lasso, running shoes, paintings, granite, and so on. One student who had been stricken with bone cancer as a child, a condition that required the amputation of her leg, demonstrated to her classmates how her prosthetic leg functioned and how she wore it. Not one of her listeners lost interest in her demonstration.

Another student, concerned about the vast amount of disposable diapers that linger in our landfills, brought to class a (heavy) week's worth of dirty diapers from one infant. In addition to having some shock value (students being grossed out), it left a powerful image to accompany her statistics about the "shelf life" of a dirty diaper, and the average amount of space diapers consume in a community landfill.

As these examples demonstrate, actual objects can be effective visual aids. Because you are showing your audience exactly what you are talking about, they have the power to inform or convince unlike any other presentational aid.

In addition to the general criteria, when thinking about bringing an object to class, you need to be concerned with safety. Make sure the object you intend to use will not pose a safety risk to you or to your audience. Animals certainly fall into this category as well as chemicals and weapons. You may feel safe with your object(s), but that does not mean your classmates will feel safe. You think your little pet scorpion is adorable but it may terrify your classmates. Finally, ensure that any object you want to use is allowed on your campus.

Models. If you decide that an actual object is too risky, a three-dimensional model may be your best choice. Models are commonly used to show the structure of a complex object. For example, a student who watched his father almost die of a heart attack used a model of the heart to demonstrate what physically happened during the attack. Using a three-dimensional replica about five times the size of a human heart, he showed how the major blood vessels leading to his father's heart became clogged and how this blockage precipitated the attack.

Models are useful when explaining various steps in a sequence. A scale model of the space shuttle, the shuttle launch pad, and its booster rockets will help you describe what happens during the first few minutes after blast-off.

When considering using a three-dimensional model, you need to take into account the construction time and availability. It is possible you already have the model or you know where you can borrow one, so no construction time is needed. If, however, you need to create the three-dimensional model from a kit or your own imagination, you need to consider how much time it will take you to put it together. You do not want your construction time to take longer than your speech preparation.

Handouts. If you want your audience to follow along with your process or be able to redo the steps at home, you may want to provide a handout. Handouts have pros and cons. They show your preparation and help keep the audience focused on your topic. They will also cue the audience's memory, making your impact lasting. However, the handouts can be distracting because your audience will focus on what is in their hand rather than you. Be sure that your handouts are professional looking and only include the key information. Do not outline your speech—simply include the steps to the process you want them to master.

Images. Photographs are the most realistic image and can have the greatest impact. For a speech on animal rights, a photo of a fox struggling to free his leg from a trap will deliver your message more effectively than words. If you are speaking about forest fire prevention, a photo of a forest destroyed by fire is your most persuasive evidence.

To be effective, photos must be large enough for your audience to see and using magazine or newspaper photos will not be as clear as a photo. If a photo is important to your presentation, consider enlarging it so the entire audience can see.

When you cannot illustrate your point with a photograph—or would rather not use one—a drawing is an adequate alternative. A drawing is your own representation of what you are describing. If you are demonstrating the difference between a kettledrum and a snare drum, a simple drawing may be all you need. If you want to extend your explanation to show how musicians are able to control the pitch of the sound made by a drum, your drawing must include more detail. The location of the screws used to tighten the skin of the drum must be shown as well as the relation between the size of the drum and the pitch of the sound.

A detailed drawing showing the arrangement and relation of the parts to the whole is considered a diagram. **FIGURE 9.13** is a simple diagram of a kettledrum. Labels are often used to pinpoint critical parts.

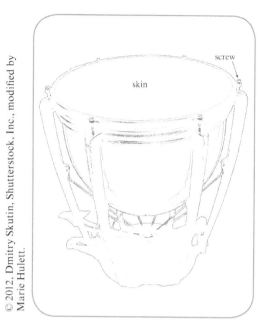

© 2012, Dmitry Skutin, Shutterstock, Inc., modified by Marie Hulett.

FIGURE 9.13 A simple diagram can show how the parts of objects such as this drum interact.

Avoid attempting a complex drawing or diagram if you have little or no artistic ability. Do not attempt to produce these drawings while your audience is watching. Prepare sketches in advance that are suitable for presentation. Keep your audience's needs—and limitations—in mind when choosing sketches. Too much detail will frustrate your audience as they strain to see the tiniest parts and labels. And when people are frustrated, they often stop listening. Imagine the glazed look in the audience's eyes in a basic speech course as they listen to someone using **FIGURE 9.14** to discuss every dimension of the UH-60 Black Hawk helicopter.

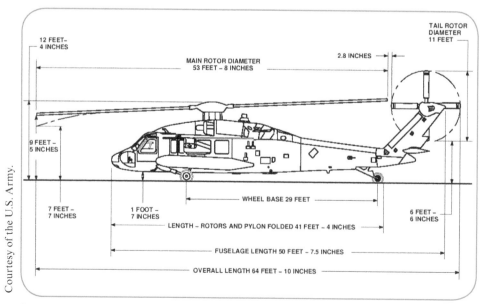

Courtesy of the U.S. Army.

FIGURE 9.14 An intricate line drawing will only serve to frustrate your audience as they strain to see the details. Keep illustrations simple.

There are many image types you can select. TABLE 9.5 describes some of the considerations you should be mindful of in making your selection.

TABLE 9.5 Image Types

Image Type	Ideas For Use
Maps	Geographical representations. Ensure that the map *only* includes the points you are talking about—modify if necessary.
Tables	Tables focus on words and numbers presented in columns and rows. Tables are used most frequently to display statistical data.
Charts	Charts help the speaker display detailed information quickly and effectively. Charts can summarize data in an easy-to-read format, they can illustrate a process, or they can show relationships among things. **Flow charts** are used to display the steps, or stages, in a process. **Organizational charts** reflect our highly structured world. You may want to refer to an organizational hierarchy in a speech if you are trying to show the positions of people involved in a project.
Graphs	When referring to statistics or when presenting complex statistical information, a visual representation can be extremely effective because it has the ability to simplify and clarify. **Bar graphs**: A simply side-by-side bar display of the frequencies of various entities. **Pictographs** are most commonly used as a variation of the bar graph. Instead of showing bars of various lengths comparing items on the graph, the bars are replaced by pictorial representations of the graph's subject. **Line graphs** allow you to show a trend over time. **Pie graphs**, also known as *circle graphs*, show your audience how the parts of an item relate to the whole. The pie chart is one of the most popular and effective ways to show how parts of a whole are divided.

Your online lesson will provide links to web sites that you can use to create colorful tables, charts, and graphs. See Topic 2.

No matter what type of two-dimensional aid you choose, clarity is essential. It may happen that you create a two-dimensional aid that makes your audience think, "What does it *mean*?" Any presentational aid you use must clarify rather than confuse. If the aid contains too much information, your audience will be unable to process easily, and you may lose their attention. If you use graphs, pie charts, maps or tables, information must be understandable. For example, if you have an *x*-axis and a *y*-axis, they should be clearly labeled so your audience knows what you are referring to quickly and easily.

Caution: Although photographs are effective aids, avoid the negative impact. If a photograph truly offends or disgusts your audience, you have reduced the impact of your message.

Displaying Images

When you decide to use a line graph to illustrate the volatility of the marketplace, your next decision involves how to display the graph. Speakers have numerous options for displaying two-dimensional presentational aids. The amount of time used and money does not necessarily indicate the effectiveness of a presentational aid. Sometimes emphasizing important points on a flip chart or using prepared overhead transparencies (if projectors are available) will be perfectly acceptable. TABLE 9.6 focuses on how to display the two-dimensional aid. In particular, we discuss the benefits and disadvantages of using blackboards, large post-its, posters, and flip charts.

TABLE 9.6 Ways to Display Two-Dimensional Aids

	Advantages	Disadvantages
Poster Board	Relatively inexpensive.	Not everyone has the time, talent, or patience to create a professional-looking poster.
	Useful in classrooms where computer-generated technology is not available.	Displaying the poster may be a problem if you do not have an easel or a chalkboard with a chalk tray.
	They can display any type of two-dimensional information.	They may get damaged during transportation. (Hint: select a bigger, thicker poster board.)
Flip Chart	Allow for spontaneity.	May not be seen by all.
	Can be prepared in advance *or* during your speech.	May be distracting.
	Can use fill-in-the-blanks to keep audience focused.	Requires very neat handwriting.
	Can show a sequence of visuals.	
	Do not require electricity.	
	Economical.	
Repositionable Note Pad (poster-sized post-it)	You do not have to worry about chalk, tape, push pins, or staples.	May not look as professional as some other display techniques.
	Tremendous flexibility—can be prepared ahead of time or developed during the speech.	May not be easily seen by everyone.

Hint: In general, display your poster, flip chart, and perhaps even repositionable note pad on an easel. It looks more professional than leaning it on a blackboard, pages can be turned with little difficulty, and it provides needed support. Be sure an easel or similar stand is available. Many speakers come prepared with elaborate poster-board-mounted visuals only to find that they have no place to display them. If you place the flip chart on the blackboard, make sure it is stabilized, and that pages can be turned without dropping the chart.

Suggestions for Using Traditional Presentational Aids

Do not let your presentational aid leave the lectern. When you pass things around the room, you compete with them as you speak. Your listeners read your handouts, play with foreign coins, eat cookies you baked, and analyze your models instead of listening to you. If handouts are necessary, distribute them at the end of the speech. When appropriate, invite people to take a close look at your displays after your speech.

Be aware of timing and pauses. Timing is important. Display each visual only as you talk about it. Do not force people to choose between paying attention to you and paying attention to your aid. If you prepare your flip chart in advance, leave a blank sheet between each page and turn the page when you are finished with the specific point. Cover your models with a sheet. Turn the projector off. Erase your diagram from the blackboard. Turn your poster board around. These actions tell your audience that you are ready to go on to another point.

Display your presentational aid, and then pause two or three seconds before talking. This moment of silence gives your audience time to look at the display. You do not want to compete with your own visual aid. Try to avoid long pauses as you demonstrate the steps in a process. To demonstrate to his class how to truss a turkey, a student brought in everything he needed, including a turkey, string, and poultry pins. He began by explaining the procedure but stopped talking for about five minutes while he worked. Although many members of the class paid attention to his technique, several lost interest. Without a verbal presentation to accompany the visual, their attention drifted to other things. Long periods of silence are not a good idea. Because most audiences need help in maintaining their focus, keep talking.

9.3.1 Technology-Based Presentational Aids

Virtually all classrooms have black or white boards and projection equipment. As funds become available and technology costs decrease, more and more classrooms will be technology-enhanced. Students will bring their jump drives to class and incorporate PowerPoint presentations into their speeches. This does not mean, however, that *all* previous technology is rendered useless. Instances still exist where a tape-recording or slide projector may make more sense than a computer-generated slide presentation. This next section discusses audio and projected images.

Audio Clips

Not all presentational aids are visual, and incorporating some audio into your speech is a simple task. If you are trying to describe the messages babies send through their different cries, using an audio clip may be appropriate, just as it would for a discussion of contemporary music. Of course, in a technology-enhanced room, students can access music and many sounds on the computer.

Take care when using an audio clip. Time is an issue, and the clip can overshadow the oral presentation if it consumes too much time. The inexperienced speaker may not have the audio clip set up at the right spot or the right volume, and recording quality may be an issue. Getting set up on the computer may take too much time. Students need to check the equipment to make sure it is working, the volume is set correctly, and that it is properly queued.

Video

In certain situations, the most effective way to communicate your message is with a video. In a speech on tornadoes, showing a video of the damage done by a tornado is likely to be quite impressive. Showing snippets of a press conference or showing a movie clip to illustrate or emphasize a particular point can also be interesting and effective.

The novice speaker giving a five-minute speech may not edit the video carefully enough, however. The result may be four minutes of video and one minute to speak. If you choose an audio or video clip, practice with them, plan how to use them, and know how to operate the equipment. Know what to do if the equipment fails. YouTube may be a great source for many videos, but be sure that it is edited or cued for your speech.

It is also possible to be upstaged by your video clip. Your visual presentation—rather than your speech—may hold center stage. To avoid this, carefully prepare an introduction to support the video clip. Point your listeners to specific parts so they focus on what you want rather than on what happens to catch their interest. After the visual, continue your speech, and build on its content with the impact of your own delivery.

Your online lesson will provide a variety of guidelines for using traditional presentational aids. See Topic 2.

When thinking about using video, do not forget to allow for sufficient set-up time. Check the equipment to make sure you can operate it and that it is in good working order. Remember also, a darkened room can disrupt your presentation if you need to refer to detailed notes, and if you want students to take notes, the room may be too dark.

9.3.2   Presentation Software

PowerPoint has been around for almost 25 years and has changed the way we deliver presentations. Before PowerPoint, creating presentation aids for a public speaking class was generally limited to the traditional aids or, if students wanted audio, they had to bring a "boom box" with them to class. We imagine that by now, most of you have used PowerPoint and that perhaps all of you have seen a PowerPoint presentation. This next section offers details about how to effectively use electronic presentation software. Your online lesson for this chapter also has hints on how to use electronic presentation software most effectively, and Chapter 13, "Public Speaking in an Electronic World," will also discuss how to use PowerPoint.

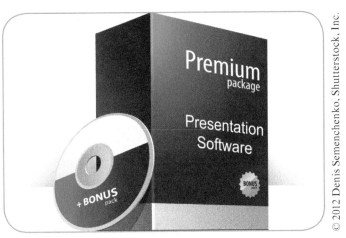

FIGURE 9.15 PowerPoint and other types of presentation software provide presenters with many options for how to visually engage the audience.

PowerPoint and other presentation software (e.g., Prezi; Keynote; Flair) have a number of advantages. First, slides can be made for each point, which provides visual repetition for the audience. Second, the software is relatively easy to use and is very flexible—speakers can include many different features. A third important advantage is that the information on the slide can be used to cue the speaker. If you lose your place, all you need to do is look at the slide.

Although PowerPoint is perhaps one of the most common presentational aids, there are some disadvantages. First, it is everywhere. A common complaint we hear among students and colleagues is, "It's another PowerPoint presentation." Second, if your audience is more technologically proficient than you are, your slide presentation may seem amateurish. When one of the authors of this textbook was conducting communication training seminars in the technology division of a company, she knew that everyone in the audience was more knowledgeable about technology than she was. So, she decided to skip PowerPoint and "surprise" the tech department with a low-tech seminar—handouts and writing on the white board. The tech people said they loved it because it was refreshing to not have to watch a PowerPoint presentation. Their reaction highlights one of the disadvantages of PowerPoint—it is very common. When something is expected, it loses it punch. People expect PowerPoint, so it does not necessarily grab the audience's attention. PowerPoint also increases the likelihood that speaker will let the slides do the work and that the audience will pay attention to the slides and not the speaker. When using PowerPoint, make sure you stay focused on the audience and that you keep them focused on you.

Your online lesson will provide a variety of guidelines for using technology-based presentational aids. See Topic 3.

TABLE 9.7 "Old School" Technology

	Advantages	Disadvantages
Traditional Slides	The slides already exist, and your library may have an extensive slide collection. Audience may be charmed by the technology.	Not knowing how to operate the slide projector. May be more difficult to find.
Overhead Projection Systems	Allows you to face your listeners and talk as you project images onto a surface. May be used in normal lighting. Images can be altered as you speak, such as underlining a phrase for emphasis or adding a key word. Audio and video clips can be embedded in the slides and activated by the speaker for emphasis.	The images may become disorganized. It is sometimes challenging to keep the visuals and speech content running smoothly.

When incorporating technology-based presentational aids, keep in mind the following important tips:

Make sure the equipment is working but be prepared for failure.
Set up in advance. Make sure equipment is working *before* class, and know how to operate the equipment. This includes CDs, DVDs, and the computer. Instructors are frustrated when time is wasted, and students will be bored if each speaker wastes valuable class time trying to figure out how the equipment works. If you intend to hook up your laptop to a projector, make sure that there is a connector and know how to make the connections. When things go wrong, *you* have to take responsibility for not being prepared.

Also, be prepared for equipment failure. What is Plan B? How much time are you willing to waste before you acknowledge that you cannot use the computer? Your audience may be sympathetic to your troubles, but we really do not want to hear you complain. Your presentation may be acceptable without the slide show. Perhaps you need to bring in a jump drive *and* email it to yourself. Maybe you want to use handouts or, as a back-up plan, write on the blackboard. The key here is the old Boy Scout motto, "Be prepared."

Use multimedia presentations only with careful planning and practice.
Multimedia presentations can be effective, but they can be challenging. Gracefully moving from a flip chart to the computer to an overhead projector while maintaining audience interest requires skill that comes from practice and experience. Mixing media increases your chance that something will go wrong. You can mix media successfully, but careful planning and preparation is essential.

Chapter Summary

Spoken language differs from written language in several important ways. In many cases, spoken language requires redundancy; it affects the order of ideas, and requires that the speaker pay attention to rhythm. Spoken language may also require that you signal your audience before you present important material.

The most effective language is simple, clear, and direct. Use short, common words instead of long, unusual ones; avoid euphemisms and jargon; eliminate unnecessary words that pad your speech; be direct and concrete and avoid exaggeration. To improve your speaking style, avoid clichés, complete your thoughts, and use sentence fragments for specific effect. Avoid profanity, slang, and jargon, as well as sentences that say nothing. Because certain phrases communicate uncertainty, avoid using them during your presentation.

Try to engage the imagination of your listeners through the use of rhetorical devices that paint memorable word pictures. Use language to create a theme. Regardless of the choices you make, be certain your language fits your personality, position, and the needs of your audience. The effective use of humor requires that you have confidence in your ability to make people laugh. Do not use humor if you have never been funny. Laugh at yourself, not others. Use understated anecdotes. And remember, humor is everywhere. Find humor in your own experiences. Seriously!

Presentational aids serve many different functions in a speech. They help to create interest in your subject; they make complex ideas clear and abstract ideas concrete. They help make your message memorable; they help to organize you.

Presentational aids include a variety of choices, such as actual objects, three-dimensional models, two-dimensional reproductions, and technology-based visual aids. Two-dimensional reproductions include photographs, diagrams and drawing, maps, tables, and charts. Two-dimensional visual aids can be mounted on poster board and displayed on an easel, displayed on a flip chart, or written on repositionable note pads. Technology-based visual aids include slides, film, videotape and audiotape, overhead projections, and computer-generated images.

Effective presentational aids are simple; they use bold, contrasting colors and they are large enough for everyone to read with ease. To present effective aids, choose the points in your speech that need visual support; set up your presentation in advance; never let your presentational aids upstage you. Use multimedia presentations only if they are well planned and rehearsed. Avoid repeating what your audience sees in the visual and learn to display each aid only when you are talking about it. Focus on your audience, not your visual. Display your visual, and then pause before talking, although you need to avoid long pauses during demonstrations. Do not circulate your presentational aids around the room. Choose visuals appropriate for the audience and occasion and rehearse your presentation.

Key Terms

active voice 257

alliteration 255

analogy 259

anaphora 255

antithesis 255

epistrophe 255

euphemisms 261

imagery 258

linguistic relativity 250

metaphor 259

passive voice 257

rhythm 252

Sapir-Whorf hypothesis 250

similes 260

Questions for Reflection

1. How is spoken language different from written language?

2. How can language contribute to or detract from the effectiveness of your speech?

3. Why must language fit the needs of the speaker, audience, occasion, and message?

4. What do you need to consider when choosing proper language in a speech?

5. What language techniques can you employ when you speak?

6. What are some of the language pitfalls that reduce the effectiveness of your speech?

7. How does humor affect the speaker-audience relationship?

8. What are the functions of presentational aids?

9. What are the different types of presentational aids?

10. What are the general criteria for using presentational aids?

11. What criteria must be met when thinking about particular presentational aids?

12. What should you know about displaying presentational aids?

13. What should you keep in mind as you design and develop a PowerPoint presentation?

Activities

1. Read aloud a written report you wrote for another class, and then analyze whether the report's language is appropriate as a speech. Analyze the changes necessary to transform the report into an effective oral presentation.

2. Select a speech from *Vital Speeches of the Day* or from another collection in your library. Study the language of the speech and write an assessment of its effectiveness, strengths, and weaknesses. Because the language was intended to be spoken, you might have to read the speech aloud during your evaluation.

3. Begin collecting humorous ideas, stories, and incidents for your next speech. As you develop your ideas, blend the humor into the speech, remembering to practice your delivery with a tape recorder.

4. Plan to use presentational aids in your next speech. Spend enough time designing and preparing the visuals so they will have the impact you want.

5. Contact several business or professional speakers in your campus community or hometown. Based on what you have learned in this chapter, interview them about using visual aids in their presentations. Report your findings to your class, paying special attention to the similarities and differences in their approaches.

6. Locate individuals on your campus or in your community who produce presentational aids for speeches. Interview these specialists to learn the information they need to design effective aids and how much they cost. Consider both two-dimensional and technology-based visual aids and write a report on your findings.

References

Austen, J. (1813/2003). *Pride and prejudice*. New York: Barnes & Noble Classics.

Beattie, A. (1989). *Picturing will*. New York: Bantam Books.

Bippus, A. (2007). Factors predicting the perceived effectiveness of politicians' use of humor during a debate. *Humor: International Journal of Humor Research, 20*(2), 105–121. DOI: 10.1515/HUMOR.2007.006

Carlson, K. A. (2011). The impact of humor on memory: Is the humor effect about humor? *Humor: International Journal of Humor Research, 24*(1), 21–41. DOI: 10.1515/HUMOR.2011.002

Dickens, C. (1859/2005). *A tale of two cities*. New York: Prestwick House.

Gabaldon, D. (1994). *Voyager*. New York: Random House.

Gruner, C. R. (1985). Advice to the beginning speaker on using humor—What the research tells us. *Communication Education 34*, 142–147.

Holmes, H., & Tangtongtavy, S. (1998). *Working with the Thais: A guide to managing in Thailand*. Bangkok, Thailand: White Lotus Co., Ltd.

Jobs, S. (2005, June 14). *"You've got to find what you love," says Jobs* (Commencement address). Stanford Report. Retrieved from http://news.stanford.edu/news/2005/june15/jobs-061505.html.

Kleinfeld, N. R. (1990, March 11). Teaching the 'Sir Winston' method. *New York Times*, 7.

Márquez, G. G. (1967/2003). *One hundred years of solitude*. New York: Harper & Row.

McCullers, C. (1940). *The heart is a lonely hunter*. New York: Houghton Mifflin.

Melville, H. (1951/2003). *Moby Dick*. New York: Bantam Classics.

My Fellow Americans: Presidential Inaugural Addresses. (2009). St. Petersburg, FL: Red and Black Publishers.

OSHA Office of Training and Education (1996). Presenting Effective Presentations with Visual Aids. U.S. Department of Labor. Retrieved from http://www.osha.gov/doc/outreachtraining/htmlfiles/traintec.html

Schmich, M. (1997, June 1). Advice, like youth, probably just wasted on the young. *Chicago Tribune*. Retrieved on June 10, 2007, from http://www.chicagotribune.com.

Stapel, D. A., & Semin, G. R. (2007). The magic spell of language: Linguistic categories and their perceptual consequences. *Journal of Personality and Social Psychology, 93*, 23–33. DOI: 10.1037/0022-3514.93.1.23.

The New York Times (2010, August 2). Tracking the oil spill in the Gulf. Retrieved from http://www.nytimes.com/interactive/2010/05/01/us/20100501-oil-spill-tracker.html.

Valenti, J. (1982). *Speak up with confidence*. New York: William Morrow.

Vogel, D. R., Dickson, G. W., & Lehman, J. A. (1986). Persuasion and the role of visual presentation support: the UM/3M study. Commissioned by Visual Systems Division of 3M.

Walsh, B. (2011, April 9). The BP oil spill, spill: One year later, how healthy is the Gulf now? *Time*. Retrieved from http://www.time.com/time/health/article/0,8599,2066031,00.html#ixzz1WetJNi4S.

Connecting:

Adapting Your Speech for Diverse Audiences and Situations

Unit

3

Chapter 10
Informative Speaking

Chapter 11
Persuasive Speaking

Chapter 12
Speaking for Special Occasions

Chapter 13
Public Speaking in an Electronic World

Chapter 14
Presenting to or Working with Small Groups or Teams

Chapter

10

© 2012, Marin Balcerzak, Shutterstock, Inc.

Learning Objectives

After reading this chapter and completing the online activities for this lesson, you will be able to:

1. Describe the importance of informative speaking and its relevance to your life.

2. Define criteria for a strong informative speech topic.

3. Identify different ways to organize the informative speech.

Informative Speaking

At a Glance

Chapter Summary

Key Terms

Questions for Reflection

Activities

References

INTRODUCTION

informative speech
Type of speech that communicates information and ideas in a way that an audience will understand and remember.

Whether you are a nurse conducting CPR training for new parents at the local community center, a museum curator delivering a speech on impressionist art, or an auto repair shop manager updating your workers on the implications of a recent manufacturer's recall notice, your **informative speech** goal is *to communicate information and ideas in a way that your audience will understand and remember.* You want your audience to gain understanding of your topic. In your job, community activities, and in this public speaking class, remember that the audience should hear *new* knowledge, not facts they already know.

In this chapter, we first distinguish informative speaking from persuasive speaking. Next, we identify different types of informative speeches. Finally, goals and strategies for informative speaking are presented.

The online lesson further identifies the chief differences between informative and persuasive speaking by examining informative and persuasive speech outlines on the same topic. See Topic 1.

10.1   Informative versus Persuasive Speaking

When she was younger, one of the authors of this textbook remembers her parents telling her a story about how they took a free tour of a resort while they were traveling. It was their intent to learn more about the resort so, if they were ever in that part of the country again, they could know if they would like to stay there. Instead of gaining valuable information, however, they were bombarded by a pushy salesperson that told them why they should buy a timeshare at the resort. Details, history, and highlights (otherwise known as information) were replaced with arguments, rhetorical tactics, and sales pitches (elements of persuasion). After that unsettling

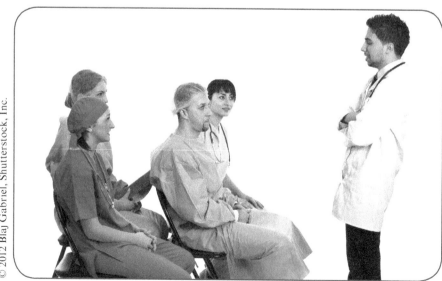

© 2012 Blaj Gabriel. Shutterstock, Inc.

FIGURE 10.1 Speaking informatively can take place in a variety of situations, including the workplace.

experience, her parents vowed to be mindful of "free tours." Informative and persuasive speaking clearly have different aims. As a speaker, it is important to know the profound differences between these types of speaking so that your responsibilities to both the topic and your audience are successfully fulfilled. To clarify this goal, the next few pages will differentiate between these speech types.

When you deliver an informative speech, your intent is to enlighten your audience—to increase understanding or awareness and, perhaps, to create an appreciation of the topic. In contrast, when you deliver a persuasive speech, your intent is to influence your audience to agree with your point of view, to change attitudes or beliefs, or to bring about a specific, desired action.

10.1.1 The Purpose of Informative Speaking

Maintaining the integrity of these different purposes can be a challenge. For example, if you developed an informative speech on the consequences of calling off a marriage at the last minute, your main points might include relationship damage (friends and family), emotional trauma, and financial difficulties. These are acceptable informative topic areas. If, however, in your speech you instead suggest that engaged couples in your audience implement safeguards to prevent emotional or financial damage, you are being persuasive implicitly. When you tell the men in your audience that they should obtain a written statement from their fiancées pledging the return of the engagement ring if the relationship ends, you are asking for explicit action, and you have blurred the line between information and persuasion.

The key to informative speaking is *intent*. If your goal is to expand understanding, your speech is informative. If, in the process, you also want your audience to change their minds or agree with your point of view, you may be crossing the line into persuasive territory.

To ensure that your speech is informative rather than persuasive, begin by crafting a clear, specific purpose that reflects your intent. Compare the following two specific purpose statements:

> **Specific purpose statement #1 (SPS#1)** To inform my listeners about cosmetic surgery, specifically the various cosmetic surgery procedures one can get, how much these procedures cost, and how such procedures have influenced society's perception of beauty.

> **Specific purpose statement #2 (SPS#2)** To inform my listeners about the rampant outbreak of cosmetic surgery procedures plaguing society, their exorbitant costs, and how they have tainted our culture's perception of beauty.

While the intent of the first statement is informational, the intent of the second is definitely persuasive. The speaker in SPS#1 is likely to discuss various cosmetic surgeries, such as rhinoplasties and tummy tucks, the fees that individuals pay for these surgeries, and how the surgeries are related to a new conceptualization of beauty. The speaker in SPS#2 uses subjective words such as "outbreak," "plaguing," and "tainted" to preview the information. Most likely, this speech would focus more on the negative impact that cosmetic surgery has had on society at large. In turn, writing your specific purpose statement first can be a great aid to guarantee that you are indeed engaging in informative speaking.

10.1.2 Types of Informative Speaking

Although all informative speeches seek to help audiences understand, there are three distinct types of informative speeches. A **speech of description** helps an audience understand *what* something is. When you want to help the audience understand *why* something is so, you are delivering a **speech of explanation**. Finally, when you want to focus is on *how* something is done, choose a **speech of demonstration**. Each of these types, as well as their most logical organizational patterns, will be discussed in more detail.

The online lesson provides additional examples of speeches of description, explanation, and demonstration. See Topic 1.

10.1.3 Benefits and Purposes of Informative Speeches

speech of description
Type of speech that helps an audience understand *what* something is.

speech of explanation
Type of speech that helps an audience understand *why* something is so.

speech of demonstration
Type of speech that focuses on *how* something is done.

Speeches of Description

Describing the circus to a group of youngsters, describing the effects of an earthquake, and describing the social media networking habits of young adults are all examples of informative speeches of description. These speeches paint a clear picture of an event, person, object, place, situation, or concept. The goal is to create images in the minds of listeners about your topic or to describe a concept in concrete detail. Here, for example, is a section of a speech describing a relatively new event—the poetry slam. We begin with the specific purpose and thesis statement:

> **Specific purpose:** To explain to my audience how poetry slams moved the performance of poetry to a competitive event.
>
> **Thesis statement:** In order to understand the poetry slam, one must understand its history, the performance, and the judging process.
>
> Imagine reading a piece of poetry in a quaint bookstore with bongo drums playing in the background as a mellow audience snaps their fingers in appreciation. This is how some perceive the traditional poetry reading. Imagine instead, a smoke-filled bar, filled with rowdy individuals, many inebriated, anticipating being entertained in three-minute intervals by young poets yearning for the adrenaline rush found in fierce competition. This is how a poetry reading becomes the poetry slam.
>
> Slam poetry is a competitive event founded by Chicago author Mark Smith in the mid-1990s. Individuals perform original poetry designed to elicit an emotional response, and then are judged by experts in the poetry community. Venues across the United States include the Bowery Street Poetry Club in New York, Green Mill in Chicago, and the national slam competition hosted in a different city each year.
>
> (Source: http://www.nuyorican.org/poetryslam.php)

In this excerpt, the speaker describes a competitive outlet for poets. Audience members learn that this event takes place in bars and clubs, and audience members respond fully. One gets a feeling for the setting through vivid language usage. Organizational patterns (discussed in greater detail in Chapter 7) that work best with speeches of description include the topical pattern, spatial pattern, chronological pattern, and narrative pattern.

Speeches of Explanation

Speeches of explanation deal with more **abstract topics** (ideas, theories, principles, and beliefs) than speeches of description or demonstration. They also involve attempts to simplify complex topics. The goal of these speeches is audience understanding. How substance abuse affects the mind, why gas prices continue to rise, or how volunteering can improve one's self-esteem are all examples of speeches of explanation.

abstract topics
Topics that are not grounded in tangible element, but instead are ideas, theories, principles, and beliefs.

To be effective, your speech of explanation must be designed specifically to achieve audience understanding of the theory or principle. Avoid complicated language, too much jargon, or technical terms by using verbal pictures that define and explain. Here, for example, a speaker uses vivid imagery to explain how color blindness can affect an individual's life.

> *I don't remember any mention of color blindness when I got my driver's license. I learned at an early age that the white traffic light was green, the light orange was yellow, and the darker orange was red. After high school I considered joining the army, hoping to go into computers or electronics. I soon learned that color blindness banned me from both of these. That may be the only limitation I ever found from this trait.* (Quote appears on martymodell.com/colorblindness/chogg.htm web site)

While the previous description suggests that color blind individuals have ways of coping, the following specifics provide much more concrete information on how this lesser-known condition functions:

> *Eyes with a deficiency of cones and pigment might be colorblind. That is, people "with normal cones and light sensitive pigment (trichromasy) are able to see all of the different colors and subtle mixtures of them by using cones sensitive to one of three wavelengths of light—red, green, and blue. A mild color deficiency is present when one or more of the three cones' light-sensitive pigments are not quite right and their peak sensitivity is shifted (anomalous trichromasy— includes protanomaly and deuteranomaly). A more severe color deficiency is present when one or more of the cones' light-sensitive pigments is really wrong (dichromasy—includes protanopia and deuteranopia)."* (Quote appears on TestingColorVision.com web site)

If the first is presented alone, listeners are limited in their ability to anchor the concept to something concrete. The second explanation, which provides definitions, is much more effective when combined with the first. Some organizational patterns that you might use for a speech of explanation include the topical pattern, cause-and-effect pattern, chronological pattern, and circular pattern.

Speeches of Demonstration

Speeches of demonstration focus on a process by describing the gradual changes that lead to a particular result. These speeches often involve two different approaches, one is *how*, and the other is a *how to* approach. Here are four examples of specific purposes for speeches of demonstration:

To inform my audience *how* college admissions committees choose the most qualified applicants.

To inform my audience *how* excessive tanning threatens health.

To inform my audience *how* to sell an item on eBay.

To inform my audience *how* to create a scrapbook.

Speeches using a "how" approach have audience understanding as their goal. They create understanding by explaining how a process functions without teaching the specific skills needed to complete a task. After listening to a speech on college admissions, for example, you may understand the process but may not be prepared to take a seat on an admissions committee. Consider the following sample speech segment on communication apprehension:

> Why does the prospect of public speaking make so many individuals extremely apprehensive? The fear associated with public speaking is it not just psychological; there are also *physiological* elements at play that interact with your mind, creating a vicious cycle of fear. How do these components work together? Consider this—when you mind registers feelings of nervousness, it can trigger a racing heartbeat, sweaty, shaky palms, and even a dry mouth. Once you notice that these physical conditions are present, you become more uncomfortable and uneasy (*"oh no, my hands are trembling … it feels like everyone is focusing on them!"*), creating even more physical reactions like rapid breath (to deal with the racing heartbeat) and blanking out (which can come with extreme stress). This relationship between physical and mental process is significant in *how* you process communication apprehension.

In contrast, *"how-to"* speeches try to communicate specific skills sets, such as selling an item on eBay or making a pineapple upside-down cake. Compare the previous "how" example discussing caffeine with the following "how-to" presentation on "how to" identify whether a Louis Vuitton handbag is authentic or counterfeit.

> *If the cost of a designer purse seems to good to be true, it might be a fake. With the increase of e-commerce and the deregulation of manufacturing in foreign countries, counterfeit handbags are a becoming a significant problem. One designing house that has found itself victim to counterfeit many times over is Louis Vuitton. Fortunately, there are steps that you can take to determine whether the bag you are interested in is indeed authentic. First, the only way that you can be entirely sure is to purchase your bag from an authorized Louis Vuitton dealer. If, however, you are dazzled by the deals found on a web site or online auction, then carefully check for the following earmarks of authenticity:*

> 1. *Correct stampings (on an authentic LV bag, they should be dark gray instead of black).*
> 2. *Perfect symmetry in the monogram pattern.*
> 3. *Even spiral stitching.*
> 4. *Clean and fused hardware.*
> 5. *Finally, an accompanying dust bag with sharp, rather than round, edges and an LV logo on the front.*

If your bag passes this inspection, you just might have the genuine article on your hands!

Notice that the "how-to" speech has several steps. These are generally in chronological order, and once learned, should result in "mastery" of a particular ability or skill.

FIGURE 10.2 Speeches of demonstration typically benefit from the use of presentational aids like charts, graphs, and props.

One clear difference between the speech of demonstration and speeches of explanation is that the speech of demonstration benefits from presentational aids. When your goal is to demonstrate a process, you may choose to complete the entire process—or a part of it—in front of your audience. The nature of your demonstration and the constraints of time affect your choice. If you are giving CPR training, a human form, otherwise known as "CPR Annie," will be necessary for audience members to truly grasp the concept. If you are demonstrating how to prepare California rolls, however, your audience does not need to watch you boil rice and dice avocados; prepare in advance to maintain audience interest and save time. When organizing your speech of demonstration, consider the chronological pattern, cause-and-effect pattern, and spatial pattern.

TABLE 10.1 is a tool to help you to determine the appropriate organizational pattern for each type of informative topic you might select:

TABLE 10.1 Organization Patterns and Specific Informative Speech Type Possibilities

Topic Type	Pattern Type	Examples
Issues	Topical, cause-effect, chronological, circular	Hunger, miracles
Processes	Chronological, narrative	Blood donation, asking someone out
Concepts	Topical, cause-effect, circular	Racism, gravity
Events	Chronological, narrative, cause-effect	The Olympics, a lunar eclipse
Objects	Topical, spatial	A cell phone, a Swiss army knife
People	Topical, narrative, chronological	James Dean, Harriet Tubman

10.2   Selecting an Informative Topic

To determine the type of informative speech you will deliver, you should chose a topic early in the planning process. Because an informative speech involves conveying relevant and interesting content to your audience, settling on just one topic can be challenging. At the end of the day, your topic should be interesting to you; if you don't care about it, neither will your audience. Here are some tips for choosing an engaging informative topic that is right for you and the audience.

1. **Choose a topic that reflects your personal interests.** Your hobbies and fascinations are natural options and will allow you to share something effortless and genuine with your audience.

2. **Explore current events.** Often audience members get snippets of news on popular topics but rarely do they receive all the details—your speech can illuminate an issue so the audience really understands its breadth and depth.

3. **Select a topic you'd like to know more about.** Informative speaking can be a wonderful opportunity for you to research on a topic about which you've always been curious—both the audience *and* you will benefit from your preparation and newly gained knowledge.

4. **Aim for relevance, appropriateness, and focus.** Strong informative speech topics must be relevant to the audience ("What is in it for me?"), appropriate for the speaking situation (consider time constraints and audience demographics), and focused enough to cover effectively (e.g., "famous battles of World War II, rather than World War II as a whole).

5. **Experiment with brainstorming.** Whether you try listing all topics that you find interesting and narrow it down from there, or create a graphic organizer like a **topic map** (or *interest map*), the important part of brainstorming is to avoid judging your ideas until you've exhausted all possibilities—you might be surprised with what you come up with!

topic map
A graphic organizer or diagram (also known as an *interest map*) that allows you to represent the connections between topics as ideas, images, or words. Such maps provide a visual framework for organizing information in terms of a line of argument or a train of thought.

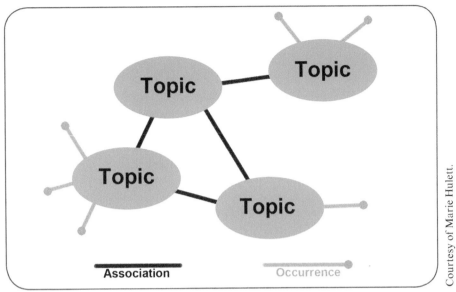

Courtesy of Marie Hulett.

FIGURE 10.3 When deciding on a topic, creating a topic or interest map allows you to hone in on subjects that you may find interesting.

10.3 Goals and Strategies of Informative Speaking

Although your overarching goal in an informative speech is to communicate information and ideas so that your audience will understand, there are also more specific goals of informative speaking. Whether you are giving a speech to explain, describe, or demonstrate, you should consider the following five goals: be accurate, objective, clear, meaningful, and memorable. After each goal, we present two specific strategies for achieving that goal.

Be Accurate

You should strive to present the truth and nothing but the truth. This is achieved by understanding the importance of careful research for verifying information that you present. When gathering information, follow the "**Three Cs**": facts must be **correct**, **current**, and **credible**. Research is crucial to attaining this goal. Do not rely solely on your own opinion; find support from other sources. For example, in a speech talking about financing college costs, you may want to discuss how much debt college students have. After talking with your friends, you may believe that students are in "a lot" of debt. After doing research, you find a source from the Huffington Post web site in February, 2010, that states recent college graduates are carrying an average of $23,200 of debt. This provides solid support.

However, if you looked at a publication from the National Center for Education Statistics in 2000, you would find that in 1997, 46 percent of undergraduates had no debt from college, and the average loan debt was $10,100. Information that is not current may be inaccurate or misleading. Offering an incorrect or outdated fact may hurt speaker credibility and cause people to stop listening. The following two strategies will help you present accurate information.

correctness
The accuracy of the material (Is it error free?); one of the three "Cs" of informative speaking.

currency
The timeliness of the material (Is the information up to date?); one of the three "Cs" of informative speaking.

credibility
The reliability of the material (Does the information come from a trustworthy source?); one of the three "Cs" of informative speaking.

1. **Question the source of information.** Is the source a nationally recognized magazine or reputable newspaper, or is it from someone's rant on a random blog? As you know, virtually anyone can post to the Internet so check to see if your source has appropriate credentials, which may include education, work experience, or verifiable personal experience.

2. **Consider the timeliness of the information.** As demonstrated above, information can become dated. There is no hard and fast rule about when something violates timeliness, but you can apply some common sense to avoid problems. Your instructor may take this decision making out of your hands by requiring sources from the last several years or so. If not, the issue of timeliness relates directly to the topic. If you wanted to inform the class about the health care system in America, relying on sources more than a few months old would be misleading because political developments occur continuously.

Be Objective

Present information fairly and in an unbiased manner. Purposely leaving out critical information or "stacking the facts" to create a misleading picture violates the rule of objectivity and compromises your ethics as a speaker. The following two strategies should help you maintain objectivity.

1. **Take into account all perspectives.** Combining perspectives creates a more complete picture. Avoiding other perspectives creates bias, and may turn an informative speech into a persuasive one. In a speech on "how to get a fair record deal," the record label executive may have an entirely different perspective on what the process looks like in contrast to the experience of the artist herself. They may be using the same facts and statistics, but interpreting them differently. An impartial third party (e.g., you, the speaker) trying to determine how the process is in actuality needs to examine both sides and attempt to remove obvious bias.

2. **Show trends.** Trends put individual facts in perspective as they clarify ideas within a larger context. The whole—the connection among ideas—gives each detail greater meaning. If a speaker tries to explain how to purchase a home, it makes sense to talk about the home buying in relation to what it was like a year ago, five years ago, ten years ago, or even longer, rather than focus on today or last week. Trends also suggest what the future will look like.

The online lesson explains ways to maintain objectivity during the planning and delivery of your informative speech. See Topic 3.

Be Clear

To be successful, your informative speech should not confuse your audience. When a message is not organized clearly, the audience can become frustrated and confused and, ultimately, they will miss your ideas. Conducting careful audience analysis helps you understand what your audience already knows about your topic and allows you to offer a clear, targeted message at their level of understanding. The following two strategies are designed to increase the clarity of your speech.

1. **Define unfamiliar words and concepts.** Unfamiliar words, especially technical jargon, may prevent your audience from learning. If your audience members

don't understand, your speech will fail to inform. When introducing a new word, define it in a way your listeners can understand. Because you are so close to your material, knowing what to define can be your hardest task. The best advice is to put yourself in the position of a listener who knows less about your topic than you do and prepare accordingly. In addition to explaining the dictionary definition of a concept or term, a speaker may rely on two common forms of definitions: operational and through example.

Operational definitions specify procedures for observing and measuring concepts. For example, in the United States an IQ test (Intelligence Quotient) is used to define how "smart" we are. According to Gregory (2004), someone who scores between 95 and 100 is of average intelligence, a score of 120 or higher is above average, and a score of 155 or higher is considered "genius." The government tells us who is "poor" based on a specified income level, and communication researchers can determine whether a person has high communication apprehension based on his or her score on McCroskey's Personal Report of Communication Apprehension.

operational definitions
Definitions that specify procedures for observing and measuring concepts.

exemplar definitions
Definitions that help explain a complex concept by providing familiar examples.

Exemplar definitions help the audience understand a complex concept by giving the audience a "for instance." In an effort to explain what is meant by the term "white-collar criminal," a speaker could provide several examples, such as Jeff Skilling, (former Enron executive convicted on federal felony charges relating to the company's financial collapse), Rod Blagojevich (former Illinois governor found guilty of making false statements to the FBI), and Wesley Snipes (actor convicted of tax evasion who started his three-year prison term in December, 2010).

2. **Carefully organize your message.** Find an organizational pattern that makes the most sense for your specific purpose. Descriptive speeches, speeches of demonstration, and speeches of explanation have different goals. Therefore, you must consider the most effective way to organize your message. As previously mentioned, *speeches of description* are often arranged in spatial, topical, and chronological patterns. *Speeches of explanation* are frequently arranged chronologically, or topically, or according to cause-and-effect or problem-solution. *Speeches of demonstration* often use spatial, chronological, and cause-and-effect or problem-solution patterns.

The online lesson provides you with outline templates to help you effectively organize your informative speech. See Topic 3.

Be Meaningful

A meaningful, informative message focuses on what matters to the audience as well as to the speaker. Relate your material to the interests, needs, and concerns of your audience. A speech to a parents group explaining the differences between public and private schools may not be meaningful in a small town with one school. Here are two strategies to help you develop a meaningful speech:

1. **Consider the setting.** The setting may tell you about audience goals. Informative speeches are given in many places, including classrooms, community seminars, and business forums. Audiences may attend these speeches because of an interest in the topic or because attendance is

required. Settings tell you the specific reasons your audience has gathered. A group of adults at public library listening to an expert discuss the tragedy of human trafficking may want to get involved with the cause, while a group of college students listening to the same lecture in a sociology class may be fulfilling a graduation requirement.

2. **Avoid information overload.** When you are excited about your subject and you want your audience to know about it, you can find yourself trying to say too much in too short a time. You throw fact after fact at your listeners until they can't listen to any more information. Saying too much is like touring London in a day—it cannot be done if you expect to remember anything. Information overload can be frustrating and annoying because the listener experiences difficulty in processing so much information. Your job as an informative speaker is to know how much to say and, just as importantly, what to say. Long lists of facts and statistics are impersonal and mind-numbing. Be conscious of the relationship among time, purpose, and your audience's ability to absorb information. Tie key points to anecdotes and humor. Your goal is not to "get it all in" but to communicate a tangible message as effectively as possible.

Be Memorable

Speakers who are enthusiastic, genuine, and creative and who can communicate their excitement to their listeners deliver memorable speeches. Engaging examples, dramatic stories, and tasteful humor applied to your key ideas in a genuine manner will make a long-lasting impact.

1. **Use examples and humor.** Nothing elicits interest more than a good example, and humorous stories are effective in helping the audience remember the material. For example, when giving a speech on how to break up with a significant other, talking about how you are a "bona fide expert" on the subject will garner some chuckles, but more important, pique the audience's interest.

2. **Physically involve your audience.** Ask for audience response to your speech: "Raise your hand if you have a question about. …" Seek help with your demonstration. Ask some audience members to take part in an experiment that you conduct to prove a point. For example, to illustrate a point on human memory, ask the audience to close their eyes and then try to visualize what clothing they are wearing.

10.3.1 Guidelines for Effective Informative Speeches

Regardless of the type of informative speech you plan to give, there are characteristics of effective informative speeches that extend across all categories. As you research, develop, and present your speech, keep the following nine characteristics in mind.

Consider Your Audience's Needs and Goals

The best informative speakers know what their listeners want to learn from their speech. A group of Weight Watchers members may be motivated to attend a lecture on dieting to learn how to lose weight, while nutritionists drawn to the same speech may need the information to help clients. Audience goals are also linked to knowledge. Those who lack knowledge about a topic may be more motivated to listen

Fielding Audience Questions and Unexpected Distractions

In an informative speech, you should be prepared to field questions from your audience. Additionally, you may be faced with an interruption from the audience or a disruption in the surrounding environment. Here are some tips to help you handle these high-pressure, unexpected moments with grace and finesse:

Knowing how to successfully answer the questions generated by your audience is a valuable speaking skill.

© 2012 Yuri Arcurs, Shutterstock, Inc.

- Decide whether you want questions during your presentation or at the end. If you prefer they wait, tell your audience early in your speech or at the first hand raised something like, "I look forward to answering any questions you may have at the end of the presentation, where I have built in some time for them. Thanks!"

- When fielding questions, develop the habit of doing four things in this order:

   1. Thank the questioner.

   2. Paraphrase the question in your own words (for the people who may not have heard the question and to clarify your understanding of the question).

   3. Answer the question briefly.

   4. Then ask the questioner if you answered their question.

- Note that the second step in answering questions is to paraphrase the question in your own words. This provides you with the opportunity to point questions in desirable directions or away from areas you are not willing to go. Paraphrasing allows the speaker to clarify the question and stay in control of the situation.

- For any question, you have five options:

   1. Answer it. (It's OK if the answer is, "I do not know."

   2. Bounce it back to the questioner, "Well, that is very interesting. How might you answer that question?"

   3. Bounce it to the audience, "I see, does anyone have any helpful thoughts about this?"

   4. Defer the question until later, "Now you and I would find this interesting, but it is outside the scope of my message today. I'd love to chat with you individually about this in a moment."

   5. Promise more answer later, "I would really like to look further into that. May I get back to you later?"

- When random interruptions occur, do not ignore them. As an option, you can call attention to the distraction; this allows your audience to get it out and then return their attention to you. For example, if the noisy air conditioner kicks on full blast in the midst of your speech, try saying, "Well, I am glad it is working" and continue on with your content.

Effective speakers know and use all five as strategies to keep their question-and-answer period positive, productive, and on track. All in all, the more prepared you can be for potential interaction with your audience and your environment, the more competent you will be in your approach!

and learn than those who feel they already know the topic. However, it is possible that technology has changed, new information has surfaced, or new ways to think about or do something have emerged. When speaking, you need to find a way to engage those who are less motivated.

Make connections between your subject and your audience's daily needs, desires, and interests. The more relevant you can make your topic, the more the audience will want to tune in. For example, some audience members might have no interest in a speech on the effectiveness of halfway houses until you tell them how much money is being spent on prisons locally, or better yet, how much each listener is spending per year. Now the topic is more relevant. People care about money, safety, prestige, family and friends, community, and their own growth and progress, among other things. Show how your topic influences one or more of these and you will have an audience motivated to listen.

Consider Your Audience's Knowledge Level

If you wanted to describe how to use eSnipe when participating in eBay auctions, you may be speaking to students who have never heard of it. To be safe, however, you might develop a brief pre-speech questionnaire to pass out to your class. Or you can select several individuals at random and ask what they know. You do not want to confuse them with information that is too advanced for their knowledge level but you do not want to bore the class with mundane minutiae, either. Consider this example:

> *As the golf champion of your district, you decide to give your informative speech on the game. You begin by holding up a golf club and saying, "This is a golf club. They come in many sizes and styles." Then you hold up a golf ball. "This is a golf ball. Golf balls are all the same size, but they come in many colors. Most golf balls are white. When you first start playing golf, you need a lot of golf balls. So, you need a golf club and a golf ball to play golf."*

Expect your listeners to yawn in this situation. They do not want to hear what they already know. Although your presentation may be effective for an audience of children who have never seen a golf club or ball, your oversimplified presentation will be insulting for most adult audiences. Instead, make sure that your topic possesses content that your audience will *want* to process; give them information that they may not have had before listening to you.

Capture Attention and Interest Immediately

As an informative speaker, your goal is to communicate information about a specific topic in a way that your listeners understand. In your introduction, you must first convince your audience that your topic is interesting and relevant. For example, if you are delivering a speech on hand washing, you might begin like this:

> *Imagine that every time you touch a doorknob or rail, your hands become infested with millions of tiny entities that are happy to make their home on your flesh. While some of these beings are harmless, others have the ability to make you very sick. These entities are microorganisms—in most cases, germs—that transfer to and dwell on your hands when you touch public fixtures. The good news is, you can combat these critters and their potential harm with a regular and thorough hand-washing regimen.*

This approach is more likely to capture audience attention than a basic statement on the otherwise obvious importance of washing one's hands.

Sustain Audience Attention and Interest by Being Creative, Vivid, and Enthusiastic

Try something different. Change your pace to bring attention or emphasis to a point. Say the following phrase at a regular rate: "We must work together!" Then say it again, more slowly and with different emphasis: "We must." "Work." "Together!" or "We must work." "Together!" or "We." "Must work." "Together!" Slowing down to emphasize each word gives the sentence much greater impact. Varying rate of speech can be an effective way to sustain audience attention.

Also, show some excitement! Talking about tai chi, the Marine Corps, or monetary inflation with spirit and energy will keep people listening. Delivery can make a difference. Enthusiasm is infectious, even to those who have no particular interest in your subject. It is no accident that advertising campaigns are built around catchy slogans, jingles, and other memorable language that people are likely to remember long after a commercial is over. We are more likely to remember vivid and committed language rather than dull language.

FIGURE 10.4 Committed delivery involving vocal and physical energy, strong eye contact, and creative language encourages your audience to focus on your message.

Cite Your Sources While Speaking

Anytime you offer facts, statistics, opinions, and ideas that you found in research, you should provide your audience with the source. In doing this, you enhance your own credibility. Your audience appreciates your depth of research on the topic, and you avoid accusations of plagiarism. However, your audience needs enough information in order to judge the credibility of your sources. If you are describing how the CBS television series *Blue Bloods* became the network's most popular show in recent years, it is not sufficient to say, "Rex Miro states..." because Rex Miro's qualification to comment on this show may be based on the fact that he watches television regularly. However, by adding, "Rex Miro, entertainment reporter for the *Los Angeles Times*, states...," we know that he has more credibility.

The online lesson encourages you to explore the Internet to find different ways to verbally cite your sources when speaking informatively. See Topic 3.

Signpost Main Ideas

Your audience may need help keeping track of the information in your speech. Separating one idea from another may be difficult for listeners when trying to learn all the information at once. You can help your audience understand the structure of your speech by creating oral lists. Simple "First, second, third, fourth..." or "one, two, three, four..." help the audience focus on your sequence of points. Here is an example of **signposting**:

> *Having a Vespa scooter in college instead of a car is preferred for two reasons. The first reason is a financial one. A Vespa gets at least 80 miles per gallon. Over a period of four years, significant savings could occur. The second reason a scooter is preferred in college is convenience. Parking problems are virtually eliminated. No longer do you have to worry about being late to class, because you can park in the motorcycle parking area. They're all around us.*

Signposting at the beginning of a speech tells the audience how many points you have or how many ideas you intend to support. Signposting during the speech keeps the audience informed as to where you are in the speech.

Relate the New with the Familiar

Informative speeches should introduce new information in terms of what the audience already knows. Analogies can be useful. Here is an example:

> *When your romantic relationship is filled with strife, taking a step back is a lot like imposing a "time-out" during an intense point in an athletic event. This cooling-off period can help you to gather your thoughts, reflect on your behaviors, and decide your next plan of action, just like it does when you are playing a sport. Getting to stop mid-play allows us the time to decide if what we are doing is helping or hurting our overall outcome. Similarly, in relationships, taking a "break," rather than a full-fledged breakup, gives us a chance to see what needs to be done to either salvage or terminate the relationship. The majority of couples who have long-standing relationships admit that taking a healthy time out can clarify feelings and improve relational satisfaction.*

Most of us can relate to the "time out" concept referred to in this example, so providing the analogy helps us understand the "step back" period for a struggling relationship. References to the familiar help listeners assimilate new information.

Use Repetition

Repetition is important when presenting new facts and ideas. You help your listeners by reinforcing your main points through summaries and paraphrasing. For example, if you were trying to persuade your classmates to purchase a scooter instead of a car, you might have three points: (1) A scooter is cheaper than a car; (2) A scooter gets better gas mileage than a car; and (3) You can always find a nearby parking spot for your scooter. For your first point, you mention purchase price, insurance, and maintenance cost. As you finish your first point, you could say, "So a scooter is cheaper than a car in at least three ways: purchase price, insurance,

signposting
Using oral lists, such as "first, second, third," to help your audience understand the structure of your speech.

and maintenance." You have already mentioned these three sub-points, but noting them as an internal summary before your second main point will help reinforce the idea that scooters are cheaper than cars.

FIGURE 10.5 The use of presentational aids can clarify and enliven your speech, especially for visual learners.

© 2012 iofoto, Shutterstock, Inc.

Offer Interesting Visuals

As Cyphert (2007) states, "There is no doubt that good visual design can make information clearer and more interesting" (p. 170). He elaborates:

> *"Audience expectations have changed, not merely in terms of technical bells and whistles available in the creation of visual aids, but with respect to the culture's understanding of what it means to deliver an eloquent public address."*

Your audience expects you to put effort into your presentation. This means more than practicing. Using pictures, charts, models, PowerPoint slides, and other presentational aids helps maintain audience interest. Use humorous visuals to display statistics, if appropriate. Demonstrate the physics of air travel by throwing paper airplanes across the room. With ever-increasing computer accessibility and Wi-Fi in the classroom, using computer-generated graphics to enhance and underscore your main points and illustrations is a convenient and valuable way to help you inform your audience effectively.

10.3.2 Ethics of Informative Speaking

Think about the advertising you see on television and the warning labels on certain products you purchase. Listening to a commercial about a new weight-loss tablet, you believe you have just found a solution to get rid of those extra twenty pounds you carry with you. Several happy people testify about how wonderful the drug is, and how it worked miracles for them. At the end of the commercial, you hear a speaker say, "This drug is not for children under 16. It may cause diarrhea, restlessness, sleeplessness, nausea, and stomach cramps. It can lead to heat strokes and heart attacks. Those with high blood pressure, epilepsy, diabetes, or heart disease should not take this medicine." After listening to the warnings, the drug may not sound so miraculous. We have government regulations to make sure consumers make informed choices.

As an individual speaker, *you need to regulate yourself.* A speaker has ethical responsibilities, no matter what type of speech he or she prepares and delivers. The informative speeches you deliver in class and those you listen to on campus are not nearly as likely to affect the course of history as those delivered by high-ranking public officials in a time of war or national political campaigns. Even so, *the principles of ethical responsibility are similar for every speaker.*

calculated ambiguity
A speaker's planned effort to be vague, sketchy, and considerably abstract.

The President of the United States, the president of your school, and the president of any organization to which you belong all have an obligation to inform their constituencies (audiences) in nonmanipulative ways and to provide them with information they need and have a right to know. Professors, doctors, police officers, and others engaged in informative speaking ought to tell the truth as they know it, and not withhold information to serve personal gain. You, like others, should always rely on credible sources and avoid what political scientists label as **calculated ambiguity**—a speaker's planned effort to be vague, sketchy, and considerably abstract. In everyday life, calculated ambiguity occurs when someone you do not want to spend time with asks you what you are doing on the weekend, and you reply, "This and that." If you offer this individual your exact plans, he or she may ask to join you; if you truthfully have no plans as of yet, you now have no excuse to turn the individual down. In turn, you opt for ambiguity to avoid awkwardness.

You have many choices to make as you prepare for an informative speech. Applying reasonable ethical standards will help with your decision making. An informative speech requires you to assemble accurate, sound, and pertinent information that will enable you to tell your audience what you believe to be the truth. Relying on outdated information, not giving the audience enough information about your sources, omitting relevant information, being intentionally vague, and taking information out of context are all violations of ethical principles.

Chapter Summary

Informative speeches fall into three categories. Speeches of description paint a picture of an event, person, object, place, situation, or concept; speeches of explanation deal with such abstractions as ideas, theories, principles, and beliefs; and speeches of demonstration focus on a process, describing the gradual changes that lead to a particular result.

A somewhat blurry line exists between informative and persuasive speaking. Remember that in an informative speech, your goal is to communicate information and ideas in a way that your audience will understand and remember. The key determinant in whether a speech is informative is speaker intent.

As an informative speaker, you should strive to be accurate, objective, clear, meaningful, and memorable. Preparing and delivering an effective informative speech involves applying the strategies identified in this chapter. In order to increase accuracy, make sure you question the source of information, consider the timeliness, and accurately cite your sources orally. Being objective includes taking into account all perspectives and showing trends. Crucial to any speech is clarity. To aid your audience, carefully organize your message, define unfamiliar words and concepts, signpost main ideas, relate the new with the familiar, and use repetition.

Audience members have gathered for different reasons. No matter what the reason, you want your speech to be meaningful to all listeners. In doing so, consider the setting, your audience's needs and goals and knowledge level, and try to avoid information overload. An informative speaker also wants people to remember his or her speech. In order to meet that goal, try to capture attention and interest immediately, sustain audience attention and interest by being creative, vivid, and enthusiastic, use examples and humor, offer interesting visuals, and physically involve your audience.

As you prepare your informative speech, make sure the choices you make are based on a reasonable ethical standard. You have an obligation to be truthful, and we presented many ways for you to accomplish this as you prepare your speech as well as when you deliver it.

Key Terms

abstract topics, 289

calculated ambiguity, 302

correctness, 293

credibility, 293

currency, 293

exemplar definitions, 295

informative speech, 286

operational definitions, 295

signposting, 300

speech of demonstration, 288

speech of description, 288

speech of explanation, 288

topic map, 292

Questions for Reflection

1. How does speaker intent differentiate informative from persuasive speaking?
2. How do the three types of informative speeches differ?
3. What are the characteristics of an effective informative speech?
4. What is the purpose of providing five goals for informative speeches?
5. How can effective visuals enhance an informative speech?
6. What role do ethics play in informative speaking?
7. List some examples of calculated ambiguity.

Activities

1. Attend an informative lecture on campus (not a class lecture). Assess whether the lecture was strictly informative or whether it was also persuasive. Describe and explain your findings in a written reflection.

2. Try to explain a difficult concept (e.g., gravity, how to play chess, how credit cards work) to a small child. How did your delivery of the content differ from how you would tell a peer? Record your results.

3. Attend another informative lecture in your community. Take notes on the effectiveness of the speaker's message. Describe the techniques the speaker used to improve communication. Evaluate the speech on the message and the presentation using the evaluation form available in the online lesson.

References

Cyphert, D. (2007). Presentation technology in the age of electronic eloquence: From visual aid to visual rhetoric. *Communication Education 56*(2), 168–192.

Gregory, R. J. (2004) *Psychological testing: History, principles, and application.* Needham, MA: Allyn & Bacon.

Waggoner, T. L., Jr. Color Deficiency excerpt retrieved from the web site: TestingColorVision.com.

Chapter

11

© 2012, mangostock, Shutterstock, Inc.

Learning Objectives

After reading this chapter and completing the online activities for this lesson, you will be able to:

1. Construct an effective persuasive argument.
2. Select and develop an appropriate persuasive speech topic/issue.
3. Develop an effective persuasive speech.

Persuasive Speaking

At a Glance

Chapter Summary

Key Terms

Questions for Reflection

Activities

References

INTRODUCTION

Shaun White:

> *I love teaming with the best. That's why I'm here at St. Jude Children's Research Hospital. Our research has changed the way the world treats brain tumors, leukemia, and sickle-cell. We help children all across America. Now these kids have hope.*

Kids:

> *And a sense of humor...*

Marlo Thomas:

> *Give thanks for the healthy kids in your life, and give to those who are not. Donate now at StJude.org or donate wherever you see our magnifying glass.*

(Source: http://www.tg.stjude.org/patients/#evan)

© 2012 CarlaVanWagoner/Shutterstock.com, Shutterstock, Inc.

FIGURE 11.1 Shaun White, two-time Olympic gold medalist in the halfpipe, is a spokesperson for St. Jude Children's Research Hospital.

11.1 Understanding Persuasion

persuasion
Any attempt to influence the thoughts, feelings, or behavior of another.

You don't have to be an Olympic Gold Medalist or a national spokesperson for a charitable organization to know how important it is to persuade an audience.

Persuasion is any attempt to influence the thoughts, feelings, or behavior of another, and we cannot escape attempts at persuasion. Either you are the one trying to convince someone of something, or you are the target of the persuasive act. Here are a few way that we can influence, and be influenced:

- You encourage your friend to go to dinner with you.
- A salesperson tries to convince you to buy an extended warranty.
- You try to get your employer to give you a raise.
- Your child asks you to let him or her stay out pass curfew.
- You appeal to your legislator to vote in favor of a universal health care bill.

Many times throughout the day, we try to convince people to share our opinions or attitudes about very small things ("Xbox is better than Wii") and very significant things ("We shouldn't have children until we are married."). The reverse is also true. Through emails, instant messages (IMs), advertisements, commercials, infomercials, and conversations, others attempt to influence you. In fact, the market research firm Yankelovich estimates that "a person living in a city 30 years ago saw up to 2,000 ad messages a day, compared with up to 5,000 today" (Story, 2007). Persuasion permeates your life, all day every day.

(upper left, bus) © 2012 Rafal Olechowski, Shutterstock, Inc.; (right, bus stop shelter) © 2012 Antony McAulay, Shutterstock, Inc.; (lower left, billboard) © 2012 Roman Sigaev, Shutterstock, Inc., all modified by Marie Hulett.

FIGURE 11.2 Persuasion is everywhere. It is estimated that we are exposed to thousands of advertisements each day.

Learning the tools of persuasion will help you become both a stronger advocate for what matters in your life and a more skilled analyst of attempts to persuade you. Everything from your daily interactions and friendships to your career advancements and raises is linked to your persuasive abilities. Those who study persuasion gain a competitive edge.

The online lesson will review the four stages of persuasion. See Topic 1. Knowing the stages will help you shape your message to a particular audience. Just like with any sequence, you do not attempt the second stage until you are sure the first stage is completed.

1. *Creating awareness*
2. *Generating understanding*
3. *Searching for agreement*
4. *Moving toward action*

11.1.1 Goals of Persuasion

"Persuasion is a form of attempted influence in the sense that it seeks to alter the way others think, feel or act, but it differs from other forms of influence" (Simons, 2001, p. 7). We are not talking about coercion or bribes or pressure to conform. Persuasion is accomplished through communication. Careful consideration of the goals of persuasion, the aims of your speech, and the type of proposition on you are making will help focus your persuasive message.

To better understand why some persuasive messages work more effectively than others, go to your online lesson and review the material on general principles of persuasion. You will learn about what motivate listeners, what helps predict an audience's response, how fear appeals work, how to sequence a message, and what you can realistically expect from an audience. See Topics 1 and 2.

Critical to the success of any persuasive effort is a clear sense of what you are trying to accomplish. As a speaker, you must define for yourself your overall persuasive goals and the narrower persuasive aims. Two important goals of persuasion are to address attitudes and to move an audience to action.

Speeches That Focus on Attitudes
In this type of speech, your goal is to convince an audience to share your views on a topic (e.g., "The tuition at this college is too high" or "too few Americans bother to vote"). The way you approach your goal depends on the nature of your audience.

When dealing with an audience opposed to your topic, you face the challenge of trying to change their opinions. The more change you hope to achieve, the harder your persuasive task. In other words, asking listeners to agree that U.S. automakers need the support of U.S. consumers to survive in global markets is easier than asking the same audience to agree that every American who buys a foreign car should be penalized through a special tax.

By contrast, when you address an agreeable audience, your job is to reinforce existing attitudes (e.g., "U.S. automakers deserve our support"). When your audience has not yet formed an opinion, your message must be geared to presenting persuasive evidence. You may want to explain to your audience, for example, the economic necessity of buying U.S. products.

Speeches That Require Action

Here, your goal is to bring about actual change. You ask your listeners to make a purchase, sign a petition, attend a rally, write to Congress, attend a lecture, and so on. The effectiveness of your message is defined by the actions your audience takes. Motivating an audience to action requires knowing your audience and understanding their perspective. The following is an example of a speech that could only have been effective at a very specific time, a very specific place, and with a very specific audience.

Courtesy of Suzan Cooke.

FIGURE 11.3 Harvey Milk was a political activist and the first openly gay man to be elected to public office in California. His 1978 speech, delivered at the San Francisco Gay Pride Day Parade, is commonly called "The Hope Speech."

In the 2008 film *Milk*, Sean Penn played Harvey Milk, a community organizer and San Francisco City Supervisor. Penn won an Academy Award for portraying Harvey Milk, who was the first openly gay person elected to public office in California. In the film, Sean Penn as Harvey Milk delivered a powerful persuasive speech at the Gay Freedom Parade in San Francisco.

> *My name is Harvey Milk and I'm here to recruit you. I want to recruit you for the fight to preserve your democracy. Brothers and sisters, you must come out! Come out to your parents, come out to your friends, if indeed they are your friends. Come out to your neighbors, come out to your fellow workers. Once*

> *and for all, let's break down the myths and destroy the lies and distortions. For your sake, for their sake. For the sake of all the youngsters who have been scared by the votes from Dade to Eugene.*
>
> *On the Statue of Liberty it says, "Give me your tired, your poor, your huddled masses yearning to be free." In the Declaration of Independence, it is written, "All men are created equal and endowed with certain inalienable rights."*
>
> *So for Mr. Briggs and Mrs. Bryant, and all the bigots out there, no matter how hard you try, you can never erase those words from the Declaration of Independence! No matter how hard you try, you can never chip those words from the base of the Statue of Liberty! That is where America is! Love it or leave it!*

Motivating your listeners to act is perhaps the hardest goal you face as a speaker since it requires attention to the connection between attitudes and behavior. Harvey Milk achieved his goal by knowing his audience. As you have likely already learned, what people feel is not necessarily what they do. Even if you convince your audience that you are the best candidate for student body president, they may not bother to vote. Similarly, even if you persuade them of the dangers of smoking, confirmed smokers will probably continue to smoke. Researchers have found several explanations for this behavior.

An attitude is likely to predict behavior when specific attitudes and behaviors are involved, the attitude is directly linked to the intention to behave a certain way, and when the listener's attitude is influenced by firsthand experience (Zimbardo, 1988, pp. 618–619). Firsthand experience is a powerful motivator. An experiment by D. T. Regan and R. Fazio (1977) proves the point:

> A field study on the Cornell University campus was conducted after a housing shortage had forced some of the incoming freshmen to sleep on cots in the dorm lounges. All freshmen were asked about their attitudes toward the housing crisis and were then given an opportunity to take some related actions (such as signing a petition or joining a committee of dorm residents). While all of the respondents expressed the same attitude about the crisis, those who had had more direct experience with it (were actually sleeping in a lounge) showed a greater consistency between their expressed attitudes and their subsequent behavioral attempts to alleviate the problem (pp. 28–45).

Therefore, if you were a leader on this campus trying to persuade freshmen to sign a petition or join a protest march, you would have had greater persuasive success with listeners who had been forced to sleep in the dorm lounges. Once you establish your overall persuasive goals, you must then decide on your persuasive aims.

11.1.2 Persuasive Aims

Determining your persuasive goal (attitude change or action) is a critical first step. Next, you must define the narrower persuasive aims or the type and direction of the change you seek. Four persuasive aims define the nature of your overall persuasive goal.

(GO sign) Courtesy of Judy Garvey; (merge sign) © 2012 John Rawsterne, Shutterstock, Inc.; (stop sign) © 2012 Booka, Shutterstock, Inc.; (detour sign) © 2012 Booka, Shutterstock, Inc.

FIGURE 11.4 Just like traffic signs direct traffic, persuasive speakers need to know how to direct the audience. To do so effectively, you need to know about your audience's current attitudes and behaviors.

Adoption. When you want your audience to start doing something, your persuasive goal is to urge the audience to adopt a particular idea or plan. As a spokesperson for the American Cancer Society, you may deliver the following message: "I urge every woman over the age of forty to get a regular mammogram."

Continuance. Sometimes your listeners are already doing the thing you want them to do. In this case, your goal is to urge continuance. For example, the same spokesperson might say:

> I am delighted to be speaking to this organization because of the commitment of every member to stop smoking. I urge all of you to maintain your commitment to be smoke free for the rest of your life.

Speeches that urge continuance are necessary when the group is under pressure to change. In this case, the spokesperson realized that many reformed smokers constantly fight the urge to begin smoking again.

Discontinuance. You attempt to persuade your listeners to stop doing something:

> I can tell by looking around that many people in this room spend hours sitting in the sun. I want to share with you a grim fact. The evidence is unmistakable that there is a direct connection between exposure to the sun and the deadliest of all skin cancers—malignant melanoma.

Deterrence. In this case, your goal is avoidance. You want to convince your listeners not to start something, as in the following example:

> We have found that exposure to asbestos can cause cancer twenty or thirty years later. If you have flaking asbestos insulation in your home, don't remove it yourself. Call in experts who have the knowledge and equipment to remove the insulation, protecting themselves as well as you and your family. Be sure you are not going to deal with an unscrupulous contractor who is likely to send in unqualified and unprotected workers likely to do a shoddy job.

Speeches that focus on deterrence are responses to problems that can be avoided. These messages are delivered when a persuasive speaker determines that an audience possesses something the speaker sees as highly threatening or likely to result in disaster. The speaker may try to bring about some sort of effective block or barrier to minimize, if not eliminate, the threat or danger. College students, for example, may find themselves listening to a persuasive presentation for the purchase of an extended warranty on a new laptop they just bought. The thrust of such a persuasive speech is to give peace of mind in the event of malfunction through use of an effective and convincing extended warranty presentation.

The Audience in Persuasive Speaking

Imagine the following situations:

- You will speak before your church's congregation to persuade them to vote to withdraw from your church's national organization because of the church's stance on gay clergy.

- You will talk to a student group on campus about the benefits of spending a semester with the Disney College Program in Orlando, Florida.

- You will speak before your City Council, urging them to implement a curbside recycling program.

- You will speak before a group of parents of a high school musical cast in order to get them to volunteer to help make flyers, sell tickets, sell concessions, monitor students during rehearsal, work on the set, work backstage, sell advertisements, work with costume rental, and design and sell T-shirts.

© 2012 Davi Sales Batista, Shutterstock, Inc.

FIGURE 11.5 Before trying to persuade an audience, you need to consider what they already think and feel about you and your topic.

Your success or failure to get your audience to act in the situations above is determined by a number of factors. Knowing who your listeners are is important. But, in a persuasive speech, knowing the attitude of your audience you have is rather crucial, and trying to determine the needs of the audience is also important to your success.

In the online lesson for Chapter 4, we categorize audience attitudes as active, favorable, neutral, apathetic, unfavorable, or hostile. These categories can be generalized as follows: (1) they agree with you, (2) they don't agree with you, or (3) they are undecided.

TABLE 11.1 Categories of Audience Attitudes

Active	Favorable	Neutral	Apathetic	Unfavorable	Hostile
Can be classified as...		Can be classified as...		Can be classified as...	
Agreeable		Undecided		Opposed	

The agreeable audience (i.e., active or favorable audiences) has a positive attitude toward you and your topic. Your main objective is to reinforce what they already accept. You want to strengthen their existing agreement and support or use it to encourage behavioral change. You also want to keep them enthused about your point of view or action plan.

Strategies to reach an agreeable audience:

- Do not rehash information already known and accepted.
- Strengthen the audience's resistance to the persuasive attempts of those who oppose your perspective.

The Inoculation Theory of Persuasion

The inoculation theory of persuasion uses a vaccine analogy to explain how to build up an audience's support. Introducing a small amount of a virus into a person's system, and allowing the body to build up immunity to the virus, is how inoculations for measles and chicken pox work. Similarly, if a speaker introduces the other side of a persuasive argument and provides the counterargument, the audience can systematically process the information and become inoculated against an opposing viewpoint.

Steps to the Inoculation Theory:

- Warn the audience of the other view and how your view may be attacked.
- Provide an overview of the other view with a weak attack ("you will hear others say … ").
- Get the audience to actively think about your view and why it is valid.

With the opposed audience, you have to reach those who do not agree with you, are not friendly or sympathetic, and who most likely will search for flaws in your argument. Your objective in this case is to get a fair hearing. Persuasive speakers facing a group that does not agree with them need to set reasonable goals. Also, developing arguments carefully by using fair and respected evidence may help persuade an audience that disagrees with you.

Strategies to reach an opposed audience:

- Seek common ground.
- Acknowledge differences—make sure you do not set your attitudes, beliefs, or values to be "right" and the audience's to be "wrong."

Speaking before an undecided audience can be difficult because you don't know whether they are uninformed, indifferent, or neutral. This audience is neither friendly nor hostile, but most likely, they are not automatically on your side.

Strategies to reach an undecided audience:

- If the audience is uninformed, provide them with the necessary information.
- If the audience is indifferent, get their attention and give them a reason to care.

Knowing the audience's disposition toward you and your topic will help you structure a more effective persuasive speech. Speakers should also consider the needs of the audience. The persuader can develop lines of reasoning that respond to pertinent needs. Human needs can be described in terms of logic or what makes sense to a listener but needs are immersed in emotions of the individual as well.

Psychologist Abraham Maslow classified human needs according to a hierarchy of needs. Maslow believed that our most basic needs—those at the bottom of the hierarchy—must be satisfied before we can consider those on the next levels. In effect, these higher level needs are put on "hold" and have little effect on our actions until the lower level needs are met. When writing a persuasive speech, it is important to understand your audience's needs. For example, a speech encouraging your classmates to purchase a Ferrari will not be persuasive if they are worried about paying rent.

The online lesson provides an in-depth review of Maslow's hierarchy of needs. See Topic 1.

Persuasive attempts are ubiquitous. On any given day, we are exposed to hundreds or thousands of persuasive appeals. Understanding the elements of persuasion will help us be more successful in our attempts and more knowledgeable about others' persuasive appeals. Persuasive speakers generally focus on changing an audience's attitudes or motivating the audience to action (which is quite difficult). When targeting behavior, speakers encourage audience to start, stop, continue, or avoid certain actions. Audiences may be agreeable, undecided, or opposed to a speaker or topic, so perhaps the most important part of understanding persuasion is understanding the audience.

11.2 Developing Persuasive Arguments

11.2.1 Types of Persuasive Propositions

Within the context of persuasive goals and aims, you must decide what type of persuasive message you want to deliver. Are you dealing with a question of fact, value, or policy? To decide, look at your thesis statement. In persuasive speeches, the thesis statement is phrased as a proposition that must be proved.

For example, if your thesis statement was, "All college students should be required to take a one-credit Physical Education course each year," you would be working with a proposition of policy. If instead, your thesis statement was, "Taking a Physical Education course each year will benefit all college students," this would be a proposition of value.

Propositions are necessary because persuasion always involves more than one point of view. If yours were the only way of thinking, persuasion would be unnecessary. Because your audience is faced with differing opinions, your goal is to present your opinion in the most effective way. The three major types of propositions are those of fact, value, and policy.

The online lesson includes an activity that tests your ability to distinguish among arguments of fact, value, and policy. See Topic 2.

Proposition of Fact. A **proposition of fact** suggests the existence of something. Using a proposition of fact, you try to prove or disprove some statement. Because facts, like beauty, are often in the eye of the beholder, you may have to persuade your listeners that your interpretation of a situation, event, or concept is accurate. Like a lawyer in a courtroom, you have to convince people to accept your version of the truth. Here are four examples of facts that would require proof:

proposition of fact
A proposition of fact suggests the existence of something.

proposition of value
Assertion rooted in judgments based on deep-seated ideals.

1. Water fluoridation can lead to health problems.
2. College is not the place for all students.
3. Hunting is a way to control the deer population.
4. American corporations are not paying enough in taxes.

When dealing with propositions of fact, you must convince your audience that your evaluation is based on widely accepted standards. For example, if you are trying to prove that water fluoridation can lead to health problems, you might point to a research article that cites the Environmental Protection Agency (EPA) warning that long-term exposure to excessive fluoridation can lead to joint stiffness, pain, and weak bones. You may also support your proposition by citing another research study that reports that children who are exposed to too much fluoridation may end up having teeth that are pitted and/or permanently stained.

Informative speakers become persuasive speakers when they cross the line from presenting facts to presenting facts within the context of a point of view. The informative speaker lets listeners decide on a position based on their own analysis of the facts. By contrast, the persuasive speaker draws the conclusion for them.

Proposition of Value. Values are deep-seated ideals that determine what we consider good or bad, moral or immoral, satisfying or unsatisfying, proper or improper, wise or foolish, valuable or invaluable, and so on. Persuasive speeches that deal with **propositions of value** are assertions rooted in judgments based on these ideals. The speaker's goal is to prove the worth of an evaluative statement, as in the following examples:

1. It is *wrong* to criminalize recreational or medicinal use of marijuana.
2. Violence in professional sports is *unjustified*.
3. Plagiarism is terribly *dishonest* for anyone who engages in it to complete an assignment.

When you use words that can be considered judgments or evaluations, such as those italicized above, you are making a proposition of value. When designing a persuasive speech based on a proposition of value, it is important to present facts, statistics, or examples to support your points. Also, using expert opinion and testimony will provide credible support.

proposition of policy
A proposition that proposes a course of action.

ethos
Ethical appeals or appeals based on moral character.

logos
Rational appeals or appeals based on facts and logic.

pathos
Emotional appeals or appeals designed to get the audience to feel a certain way.

Proposition of Policy. Propositions of policy propose a course of action. Usually, the speaker is arguing that something should or should not be done. Propositions of policy are easily recognizable by their use of "should" "ought to" "have to," or "must":

1. Campus safety should be reevaluated by the college administration.
2. The same general student academic standards ought to apply to student athletes, too.
3. Collegiate athletes should be paid.
4. Animals should not be used for product testing in scientific laboratories.

In a policy speech, speakers convince listeners of both the need for change and what that change should be. Policy speeches can also give people reasons to continue listening, agree with that position, and, sometimes, to take action.

Propositions of policy have both fact and value aspects to them. Facts need to support the need for the course of action, and values are inherently part of the policy statement. For example, in a speech about using animals for product testing, the person giving the speech against it most likely values animals, and believes in the humane and ethical treatment of animals.

A speaker's persuasive appeal, in summary, derives from the audience's sense of the speaker's credibility as well as from appeals to an audience's emotion and logic. At times, one persuasive element may be more important to one audience than others. Many speakers try to convince audiences based primarily on logical appeal, some use mainly emotional appeals, and others rely on their image and credibility as a speaker. The most effective speakers consider their audience expectations and intended outcomes. Now, we will turn our attention to a powerfully influential sequence of steps often used to organize persuasive messages.

11.2.2 Elements of Persuasion

Persuasion is attempting to influence others through communication. Critical building blocks of persuasion have been studied by generations of rhetorical scholars, starting with Aristotle. Persuasion is intended to influence choice through what Aristotle termed **ethos**, **pathos**, and **logos**. These three elements provide the underpinnings of our modern study of persuasion.

Ethos and the Power of the Speaker's Credibility

In a persuasive speech, you are asking listeners to think or act in ways needed to achieve your specific purpose, a desired response. As a speaker, you must decide not only what to tell your audience but also what you should avoid saying. Aristotle believed that *ethos*, which is based on moral character, makes speakers credible and worthy of belief. Audiences trust speakers they perceive as honest and well intentioned.

Dimensions of Speaker Credibility

What your audience knows about you before you speak and what they learn about your position during your speech may influence your ability to persuade them. Credibility can be measured according to two primary dimensions: competence and trustworthiness.

Character may almost be called the most effective means of persuasion.

— Aristotle

© 2012 Borys Shevchuk, Shutterstock, Inc.

Courtesy of Trip Gould, modified by Marie Hulett.

FIGURE 11.6 There are many ways to establish credibility, but silly, superficial comments can backfire.

Competence. In many cases, your audience will decide your message's value based on perceived speaker competence. Your listeners will first ask themselves whether you have the background to speak. If the topic is crime, an audience is more likely to be persuaded by the Atlanta chief of police than by a postal worker delivering his personal opinions. Second, your audience will consider whether the content of your speech has firm support. When it is clear that speakers have not researched their topic, their ability to persuade diminishes. Finally, audiences will determine whether you communicate confidence and control of your subject matter through your delivery.

Source credibility has many dimensions, including expertise, trustworthiness, goodwill, dynamism, extroversion, composure, likability, and sociability. Competence and trustworthiness are the two dimensions that appear on most research of credibility (Brodsky, Griffin, & Cramer, 2010).

Courtesy of Chad Christian, High Point University.

FIGURE 11.7 High Point University President Nido Qubein shares his experience with first-year students at the President's Seminar. As a business leader, author, and self-made millionaire who, at age 17, arrived from the Middle East with $50, President Qubein's ethos keeps the students focused on his speech about life skills.

Trustworthiness. When someone is trying to persuade us to think or act a certain way, trusting that person is important. And although competence is important, research has shown that the trustworthy communicator is more influential than the untrustworthy one, regardless of his or her level of expertise (Pornpitakpan, 2004).

Audience perceptions of your trustworthiness are based largely on your perceived respect for them, your ethical standards, and your ability to establish common ground. Audiences gauge a speaker's respect for them by analyzing the actions a speaker has taken before the speech. If a group is listening to a political candidate running for office in their community, they will have more respect for someone who has demonstrated concern for their community through past actions.

Trustworthiness is also influenced by the audience's perception of your *ethical standards*. Telling the truth is the paramount ethical standard for the persuasive speaker. If your message is biased and you make little attempt to be fair or to concede the strength of your opponent's point of view, your listeners may question your integrity.

Your credibility and your ability to persuade may increase if you convince your audience that you share "common ground." In the popular 2006 movie *300*, Queen Gorgo addresses a reluctant Spartan Council, pleading with them to send the Spartan army into battle. Rather than appealing to the council as queen, she is made to appeal to common ground in the opening:

> "Councilmen, I stand before you today not only as your Queen: I come to you as a mother; I come to you as a wife; I come to you as a Spartan woman; I come to you with great humility." (www.americanrhetoric.com)

Although few can identify with being a queen, most feel a sense of identification with a humble mother, wife, woman, or citizen. With this common ground appeal in place, the stage is set for the queen to persuade the council to side with her. In this instance, Queen Gorgo establishes a common ground through identifying with her audience and provoking them to identify with her.

Does credibility make a difference in your ability to persuade? Pornpitakpan (2004), who examined five decades of research on the persuasiveness of speaker credibility, found that "a high-credibility source is more persuasive than is a low-credibility source in both changing attitudes and gaining behavioral compliance" (p. 266). Lifelong learning in the art of persuasion involves building and enhancing your speaker competence and trustworthiness.

Pathos and the Power of Emotion

Aristotle argued that *pathos*, which is an appeal to the audience's emotions, is an integral part of persuasion. He explained:

> "The emotions are those things through which, by undergoing change, people come to differ in their judgments and which are accompanied by pain and pleasure, for example, anger, pity, fear, and other such things and their opposites." (Aristotle, 350 BCE/2007).

Emotional appeals have the power to elicit happiness, joy, pride, patriotism, fear, hate, anger, guilt, despair, hope, hopelessness, bitterness, and other feelings. Some subjects are more emotionally powerful than others and lend themselves to emotional appeals. Look at the following list of topics in **TABLE 11.2**:

TABLE 11.2 Topics That Trigger Emotional Responses	
The homeless	Sex education in school
Abused children	Teaching evolution in school
Cruelty to animals	Gun control
Death penalty	Terrorist attacks

Many of these topics can cause listeners to have emotional responses. Emotional appeals are often the most persuasive type of appeal because they provide the motivation listeners need to change their minds or take action. For example, instead of simply listing the reasons high fat foods are unhealthy, a more effective approach is to tie these foods to frightening consequences:

> Jim thought nothing could ever happen to him. He was healthy as an ox—or so he thought. His world fell apart one sunny May morning when he suffered a massive heart attack. He survived, but his doctors told him that his coronary arteries were blocked and that he needed bypass surgery. "Why me?" he asked. "I'm only 42 years old." The answer, he was told, had a lot to do with the high fat diet he had eaten since childhood.

We must not forget that emotional appeals are powerful, and as such, can be tools of manipulation in the hands of unscrupulous speakers who attempt to arouse audiences through emotion rather than logic. For example, in an effort to lose weight, individuals may be sold pills or exercise equipment that may be useless, or worse, a true health risk. Those selling the products prey on people's fear and other negative feelings about their bodies in order to convince them to accept the emotional message ("lose weight, look beautiful, gain friends, have a great life").

FIGURE 11.8 Created as part of a high school distracted driving campaign in North Carolina, this poster uses pathos to reach the intended audience. What effect would a broken cell phone have? Can an appeal to pathos go too far?

The speaker has an ethical responsibility when using emotional appeals. The ethically responsible speaker does not distort, delete, or exaggerate information for the sole purpose of emotionally charging an audience in order to manipulate their feelings for self-centered ends. For example, using a story about how your mother died of breast cancer as the attention getter in your persuasive speech arguing for the use of embryonic stem cells in research would be an unethical manipulation of emotions if your mother had not had breast cancer.

Logos and the Power of Logical Appeals and Arguments

Logos, or logical appeals and arguments, refer to the "rational, factual basis that supports the speaker's position" (Walker, 2005, p. 3). For example, if a friend tried to convince you *not* to buy a new car by pointing out that you are in college, have no savings account, and are currently unemployed, that friend would be making a logical argument.

FIGURE 11.9 As portrayed by Leonard Nimoy (shown left, attending a fan convention) on the television show *Star Trek*, Mr. Spock based all of his arguments on logic. Sherlock Holmes (shown right), from the Arthur Conan Doyle novels, used logic to solve his cases. These characters were both credible to others because of the power of their arguments.

Logical, critical thinking will increase your ability to assess, analyze, and advocate ideas. Decades ago, Stephen Toulmin (1958), a British philosopher, developed a model of practical reasoning that consists of three basic elements: claim, data, and warrant. To construct a sound, reasonable statement as a logical appeal for your audience, you need to distill the essential parts of an argument:

1. The claim is a statement or contention the audience is urged to accept. The claim answers the question, "So what is your point?

   Example: It's your turn to do the dishes; I did them last time.

   Example: You need to call your sister this week; she called you last week.

2. The data is evidence in support of an idea you advocate. Data provides the answer to, "So what is your proof?" or "Why?"

   Example: It looks like rain. Dark clouds are forming.

   Example: When I stop at McDonald's on the road, they seem to have clean bathrooms. We should stop there.

3. The warrant is an inference that links the evidence with the claim. It answers the question, "Why does that data mean your claim is true?"

   Example: Augie is running a fever. I bet he has an ear infection.

   Example: Sarah will be on time. There isn't any traffic right now.

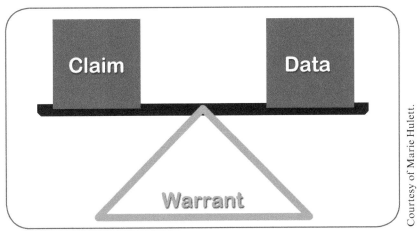

Courtesy of Marie Hulett.

FIGURE 11.10 Effective persuasive speeches use strong arguments to connect the claim and the evidence.

To put the three elements of an argument together, let's consider another example. At a restaurant, you take a bite of a steak sandwich and say, "This is the worst sandwich I have ever tried." With this announcement you are making a claim that you *infer* from tasting the meat.

The evidence (data) is the food before you. The warrant is the link between data and claim is the inference, which may be an *unstated belief* that the food is spoiled, old, or poorly prepared, and will taste bad.

When you reason with your audience, it is important to provide claims, warrants, and data your audience will understand and accept. Sound reasoning is especially important when your audience is skeptical. Faced with the task of trying to convince people to change their minds or do something they might not otherwise be inclined to do, your arguments must be impressive.

We persuade others that a claim or conclusion is highly probable by inductive and deductive reasoning. You must have strong evidence and show that you have carefully reasoned the support of your points. Only when strong probability is established can you ask your listeners to make the *inductive* leap from specific cases to a general conclusion, or to take the *deductive* move from statements as premises to a conclusion you want them to accept. We will look more closely now at inductive and deductive reasoning.

Inductive reasoning involves generalizing from specific examples and drawing conclusions from what we observe. Inductive reasoning moves us from the specific to the general in an orderly, logical fashion.

Deductive reasoning moves us from the general to the specific, drawing conclusions based on the connections between statements that serve as premises. Rather than introducing new facts, deductions enable us to rearrange the facts we already know, putting them in a form that will make our point.

© 2012 Borys Shevchuk, Shutterstock, Inc.

11.2.3 Argument Fallacies

fallacy

An argument that seems plausible but turns out on close examination to be misleading.

Sometimes speakers develop arguments either intentionally or unintentionally that contain faulty logic of some kind. A **fallacy** is traditionally regarded as an argument that seems plausible but turns out on close examination to be misleading (Hample et al., 2009). So, whether the speaker intended to misuse evidence or reasoning in order to complete his/her persuasive goal, the result is that the audience is led to believe something that is not true. There are many fallacy types, but most fallacies can be categorized as either a fallacy of claim, fallacy of evidence, fallacy of reasoning, or fallacy of response, as shown in TABLE 11.3 below.

TABLE 11.3 Categories of Fallacies			
Fallacies of claims	**Fallacies of evidence**	**Fallacies of reasoning**	**Fallacies of responding**
An illogical statement about how events relate to each other	The use of illogical or misleading information	An illogical statement about how events relate to outcomes	The use of illogical or misleading statements about or in response to another person
Slippery Slope	Red Herring	Hasty Generalization	Ad Hominem Attack
False Dilemma	Bandwagon Appeal	*Post hoc ergo propter hoc*	Straw Man Fallacy

We review one example from each fallacy category below. The online lesson reviews additional types of logical fallacies. Be sure to complete the activity in which you match statements to the logical fallacy they represent. See Topic 2.

Slippery Slope. A speaker using this fallacy claims that if we take even one step onto the "slippery slope," we will end up sliding all the way to the bottom—that we can't stop. In other words, there will be a sort of chain reaction that will end in some dire consequence. Slippery slope arguments are not fallacies if the speaker can show a causal connection between the claims.

Suppose, for example, a student was preparing a persuasive speech against embryonic stem cell research. The speaker argues that although scientists' stated intentions are to just use the donated embryos that had been created for artificial insemination, legalizing all embryonic stem cell research would soon lead to people creating embryos so they can sell them. Then, people would terminate pregnancies for research. Finally, scientists will start cloning embryos and perhaps people. Speakers use the slippery slope argument to play on the audience's fears, even though the arguments frequently lack specific evidence.

FIGURE 11.11 A slippery slope is a logical fallacy in which a speaker proposes that one event will inevitably lead to a sequence of events.

Hasty Generalization. A hasty generalization is a fallacy based on quantity of data. A faulty argument occurs because the sample chosen is too small or is in some way not representative. Therefore, any conclusion based on this information is flawed. Stereotypes about people are common examples of this fallacy—you meet one person from New York City who is rude and then stereotype all people from New York City as rude. Imagine getting a "B" on a test, and asking the students on your right and left what grade they received. Finding out they also received a "B" on the test, you tell your roommates, "Everybody received a 'B' on the test."

Suppose you're in a public speaking class that you think is easy. You talk to two friends who share your view. You conclude this class is easy. The problem is, many people find public speaking scary and difficult. Also, it is possible that various public speaking teachers differ in their expectations for students as well as in their grading standards.

Red Herring. A red herring occurs when a speaker attempts to divert the attention of the audience from the matter at hand. Going off on a tangent, changing the focus of the argument, engaging in personal attacks, or appealing to popular prejudice are all examples of the red herring fallacy.

The red herring fallacy appears regularly in interpersonal communication. If during an interview, Lindsay Lohan (or any other young, troubled celebrity) was asked about her pattern of substance abuse, and she responded, "I have been in the entertainment industry since I was a small child, and it's really hard growing up in this business," her response would be a red herring. Lindsay would be attempting to take the focus off her substance abuse issues and aim it toward the entertainment industry. As audience members, it is important that we examine a person's response to ensure they answered the question.

Ad Hominem Attack. This occurs when a speaker attacks the person rather than the substance of the person's argument. A personal attack is often a cover-up for lack of evidence or solid reasoning. Name calling and labeling are common with this fallacy, and the public is exposed to the ad hominem fallacy regularly through political shenanigans. While fallacies do not meet ethical standards, politicians have gotten elected based on attacks on their opponents rather than refuting stances on issues.

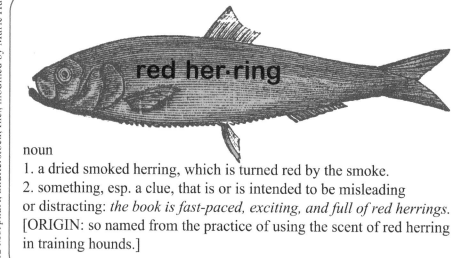

©2012 Morphart, Shutterstock, Inc., modified by Marie Hulett.

noun
1. a dried smoked herring, which is turned red by the smoke.
2. something, esp. a clue, that is or is intended to be misleading or distracting: *the book is fast-paced, exciting, and full of red herrings.*
[ORIGIN: so named from the practice of using the scent of red herring in training hounds.]

FIGURE 11.12 The red herring fallacy occurs when a speaker attempts to divert a listener's attention. The term is thought to derive from the manner in which scent hounds were trained. To confuse them, trainers would drag a red herring across the scent of a fox. The dogs would be trained until they stayed on the correct scent.

Tina Fey, who won an Emmy Award for her spoof of then-Vice Presidential candidate Sarah Palin, notes that those who dislike her NBC television show *30 Rock* do not identify evidence that it's not funny or original. Instead, she says, "Let's face it, between Alec Baldwin and me there is a certain fifty percent of the population who think we are pinko Commie monsters" (Hirsen, 2011).

FIGURE 11.13 When a person attacks another person rather than the argument that is being posed, they are making an ad hominem attack.

When developing your speech, what type of message do you want to deliver? If you are trying to prove or disprove something, you are making a proposition of fact. If your goal is to prove the worth or something, you are making a proposition of value. A proposition of policy proposed a course of action. Once you have decided on your message, you need to consider how to best reach your audience: ethos, pathos, or logos (although a combination of all three may work best). Messages that emphasize the personal qualities of a speaker rely on ethos. When a speaker uses emotional appeals, he is using pathos. A logical appeal, or logos, relies of evidence to persuade an audience. When making an appeal, be careful that your arguments are not fallacious. Fallacies of claims, evidence, reasoning, and responding rely on arguments that appear to be plausible but are actually misleading.

11.3 Organizing Persuasive Speeches

Earlier in this textbook, we presented different ways to organize your speech. Certain organizational patterns are unique to the persuasive speech pattern. In Chapter 7, we presented the problem-solution pattern, which involves presenting an audience with a problem and then examining one or more likely solutions. For a persuasive speech, the speaker would persuade the audience to accept one particular solution. We also noted the cause and effect pattern, which entails arranging main points into causes and effects. The persuasive speaker would construct a case for the audience that would persuade them to accept the cause-effect connection.

Below, we present three more possible organizational patterns: comparative advantage, criteria satisfaction, and Monroe's motivated sequence. Our primary focus is on the latter, since this pattern follows the normal process of human reasoning as it presents a clear way to move through the problem-solving process.

11.3.1 Comparative Advantages

comparative advantage organizational pattern
A speech organization pattern that compares the pros and cons of choices.

A **comparative advantage organizational pattern** is useful when the audience already agrees that there is a problem that needs to be solved. The problem may not be a grave problem, but it is one that may have several potentially acceptable solutions. As a speaker using this pattern, you try to convince the audience that your plan is the best plan. You can place alternative solutions or plans side by side and discuss the advantages and disadvantages of each. To some extent, this organizational pattern can be viewed as a structured process of elimination.

For example, Rosa, a sophomore at a new Florida university, is active in student government. She is developing a persuasive speech about her school's new mascot. In three weeks, the students will vote on which mascot they want to adopt: the alligator, the panther, or the hurricane.

Mascot 1: The Alligator

Advantages: Clear connection to the state; can have a live mascot; fearsome.

Disadvantages: Overused at Florida schools; ugly; keeping a live mascot is expensive; people associate gender with the alligator and it would need a name.

Mascot 2: The Panther

Advantages: Beautiful; the state animal; can have a live mascot; powerful.

Disadvantages: Used at many colleges and universities; keeping a live mascot is expensive; people associate gender with the panther and it would need a name.

Mascot 3: The Hurricane

Advantages: Unique; powerful and unstoppable; associated with Florida; crowd roaring sounds like a hurricane; famous drink that can be made at tailgate parties; no live mascot is involved, so is inexpensive; no gender associated with the mascot and it would not need a name.

Disadvantages: No ready-made costume; no live mascot.

Using a comparative-advantages pattern, Rosa can compare the three mascots possibilities and show how the hurricane is a superior choice as a mascot. Rosa cannot simply list the advantages and disadvantages—she must explain why the hurricane is better than the other choices. Since she did not present just one solution—"there's only one choice for mascot"—her audience should be persuaded by her balanced analysis.

TABLE 11.4 Criteria Satisfaction

The Snuggie®	Bumpits™	BarkOff™
The Ab Roller®	The Gyro Bowl™	Heeltastic™
magicJack™	Mister Steamy	PediPaws™

If you've ever watched an infomercial, you've seen a **criteria satisfaction organizational pattern**. When using the criteria-satisfaction pattern, you demonstrate how your idea has the features that your audience needs. It is a clear pattern that is useful when you have an audience opposed to your idea or unfamiliar with what you are proposing. You can help establish a "yes" response from your audience through the identification of criteria they find acceptable. You indicate the necessary criteria and then show how your solution meets or exceeds the criteria.

Consider a "Calendar committee" trying to convince the local school board to change the dates for beginning and ending the school year. The committee might argue that any solution should meet the following criteria.

- acceptable to teachers
- acceptable to parents
- cost effective (not having to turn on air conditioning too soon)
- enhances education or at least does not interfere with learning environment
- includes appropriate start and ending dates for each term
- balances mandatory and optional vacation and teacher institute dates

Based on these criteria, the committee could present the solution to the school board that meets all of these criteria. With the criteria-solution pattern, it is important that you find criteria your audience will accept. For example, if the committee had identified one of the criteria as "starts as late as possible and ends as early as possible," that might not have been viewed acceptable criteria by the school board. Similarly, the criteria may differ, depending on circumstances. In a small college town, having spring break and holiday breaks at the same time the college has them may be an appropriate criterion, but in a large city that has several colleges and universities, this may not be as important.

The online lesson demonstrates how to combine the criteria satisfaction and comparative analysis organizations in a sales presentation. See Topic 3.

11.3.2 Monroe's Motivated Sequence

As emphasized throughout this textbook, effective communication requires connecting with your audience. This audience awareness is particularly important in speeches to persuade, for without taking into account the mental stages your audience passes through, your persuasion may not succeed. The **motivated sequence**, a widely used method for organizing persuasive speeches developed by the late communication professor Alan Monroe, is rooted in traditional rhetoric and shaped by modern psychology.

The method focuses on five steps to motivate your audience to act, and as Monroe would tell his students, they follow the normal pattern of human thought from attention to action. The motivated sequence clearly serves the goal of action if all five steps are followed. When the goal is to move your audience to act, each of the following five steps, in order, would be needed.

criteria satisfaction organizational pattern
A speech organization pattern that uses established criteria to evaluate options or actions.

motivated sequence
A five-step speech organization pattern that leads to action.

If you want only to persuade the audience there is a problem, then only the first two steps are necessary. If the audience is keenly aware of a problem, then a speaker may focus only on the last three steps.

The online lesson presents the five steps to Monroe's motivated sequence and explains how to develop each step. See Topic 3.

Step One: Attention.

Persuasion is impossible without attention. Your first step is to capture the minds of your listeners and convince them that you have something to say that is important to them. Many possibilities were discussed in Chapter 8, "Introducing and Concluding Your Speech." For example, a student talking about baseball injuries began his speech by saying:

> *Imagine being 10 years old, playing baseball on a sunny Saturday, when you are called up to bat. The pitcher winds up—you're ready—the pitcher sends the ball towards you and you swing with all your might. You know you caught a piece of the ball, and you did. The problem is, you've caught the ball with your face, not your bat. At first, you don't even know that you're hurt, but then you look down and see blood. When you start to call for your mom, something comes out of your mouth. It's your front two teeth.*
>
> *You may think I am smiling at you because this is a hypothetical story. No. I am smiling at you so that you can see my two front teeth—they're fake because I caught a ball with my face when I was 10 years old.*

The student's personal story and imagery surely engaged all listening. His opening also establishes his credibility and introduces his topic. In your attention step, you must catch your audience's attention, introduce and make your topic relevant and establish your credibility, too.

Step Two: Need.

In the *need step*, you describe the problem you will address in your speech. You hint or suggest at a need in your introduction, then state it in a way that accurately reflects your specific purpose. Your aim in the need step is to motivate your listeners to care about the problem by making it clear the problem exists, is significant, and affects them. You can illustrate the need by using examples, intensifying it through the use of carefully selected additional supporting material, and *linking* it directly to the audience. Too often, the inexperienced speaker who uses the motivated sequence will pass through the need step too quickly in haste to get to the third step, the satisfaction step. Let us look at how a student could develop the need step about baseball injuries:

> *Although for most of us baseball is associated with summer days and good times, baseball is also associated with traumatic injuries. According to a 2001 article in the scientific journal* Physicians and Sports Medicine, *from 1987 to 1996, almost 30,000 children were injured playing Little League.*

Next, the speaker skillfully connects the problem to the audience's needs and points to its seriousness and relevance:

Many of you have played Little League baseball and softball, and you may be sitting there thinking that it's a safe game. After all, you have to wear a helmet when you're up to bat. However, consider this—more than 12,000 of the injuries were to the teeth and face. In other words, there are 30,000 adults just like me—injured while playing a game. And it's not just broken noses and busted teeth—the Little League Baseball's Insurance group estimates that 25 percent of Little League injuries are serious. In fact, during the 10 years of injuries reported in this study, 13 children died of the injuries they sustained while playing in the Little League.

And, just so you know how serious this is—the numbers that I've shared with you reflect only those injuries tracked by the Little League Association—the numbers don't reflect schoolyard games or neighborhood matches.

Step Three: Satisfaction.

The *satisfaction step* presents a solution to the problem you have just described. You offer a proposal in the form of a proposition you want your audience to adopt and act upon. A clear explanation as well as statistics, testimony, examples, and other types of support ensure that your audience understands what you propose. You also have to show your audience how your proposal meets the needs you presented earlier in your speech. To be sure everyone understands what you mean, you may wish to use several different forms of support accompanied by visuals or audiovisual aids. An audience is usually impressed if you can show where and how a similar proposal has worked elsewhere. Before you move to the fourth step, you need to meet objections that you predict some listeners may hold. We are all familiar with the persuader who attempts to sell us a product or service and wants us to believe it is well worth the price and within our budget. In fact, a considerable amount of sales appeal today aims at selling us a payment we can afford as a means to purchasing the product, whether it is an automobile, a vacation, or some other attractive item. If we can afford the monthly payment, a major objection has been met.

Here is how the student speaker suggested solving the problem of head injuries in Little League Baseball:

Well, "some sort" of protection has been developed. American Health reports that Home Safe, Inc. has found an all-star solution. Teams like the Atlee Little Leaguers in Mechanicsville, Virginia, have solved many of their safety problems by wearing face shields. The molded plastic shield snaps onto the earflaps of the standard batter's helmet. Most youth teams require the use of a batter's helmet, but with this shield they could add complete facial protection, including the eyes, for a cost of under $15 per shield. Some might say that is expensive, but former little leaguer Daniel Schwartz's head injuries have cost his family $23,000 so far.

Step Four: Visualization.

The *visualization step* encourages listeners to picture themselves benefiting from the adoption of your proposal. It focuses on a vision of the future if your proposal is adopted and, just as important, if it is rejected. It may also contrast these two visions, strengthening the attractiveness of your proposal by showing what will happen if no action is taken.

Positive visualization is specific and concrete. Your goal is to help listeners see themselves under the conditions you describe. You want them to experience enjoyment and satisfaction. In contrast, negative visualization focuses on what will happen without your plan. Here you encourage discomfort with conditions that would exist. Whichever method you choose, make your listeners feel part of the future. Returning to our Little League speech example, here would be an appropriate visualization step:

> *Imagine yourself on a quiet and lazy summer afternoon watching your own child, a niece, a nephew, a cousin, or a neighborhood friend up to bat in an exciting youth-league baseball game. Think about the comfort you will experience when you see that she or he has the proper safety equipment on so that there is no possibility that a speeding baseball will take his or her life, or result in any permanent disability. See for a moment the face and the form of a child enthusiastically awaiting the pitch and see as well this child effectively shielded from impact that could come from a missed pitch.*

Step Five: Action.

The *action step* acts as the conclusion of your speech. Here, you tell your listeners what you want them to do or, if action is not necessary, the point of view you want them to share. You may have to explain the specific actions you want and the timing for these actions. This step is most effective when immediate action is sought.

Many students find the call to action a difficult part of the persuasive speech. They are reluctant to make an explicit request for action. Can you imagine a politician failing to ask people for their vote? Such a candidate would surely lose an election. When sales representatives have difficulty in closing a deal because they are unable to ask consumers to buy their products, they do not last long in sales. Persuasion is more likely to result when direction is clear and action is the goal. Here is how we might conclude our Little League example:

> *We must realize, however, that it may be awhile before this equipment scores a home run, so now it is your turn up to bat. If you are personally interested in protecting these young ballplayers, spread the word about these injuries, especially to businesses that sponsor youth teams. Encourage them to purchase safety equipment for the teams and then to sponsor them only on the condition that the equipment be used. Additionally, I ask for your signature on the petition I am circulating. This will send a loud message to our representatives in Congress.*

In order to create closure and reinforce the need to act, our final comment might be:

> *Now that we have discovered how children are being seriously injured and even killed while playing baseball, I know that you agree that given the children's lack of skill, we need to mandate the use of face shields. So take them out to the ball game, but make it one that children can play safely, because children may be dying to play baseball, but they should never die because of it.*

Remember the five-step sequence if you want to lead your audience from attention to action. The motivated sequence is effective, and like all tools of persuasion, can be misused. The line between use and abuse of persuasive tools warrants further examination.

FIGURE 11.14 When using Monroe's motivated sequence, make sure that your action step is very clear. Ask the audience to do something specific, like sign a petition to require faceguards in Little League baseball and softball games.

Ethics and Persuasive Speaking

The importance of ethics is stressed both implicitly and explicitly throughout this textbook. Ethics provide standards of conduct that guide us. The ethics of persuasion call for honesty, care, thoroughness, openness, and a concern for the audience without manipulative intent. The end does *not* justify the means at all costs. In a society as complex as ours, one marked in part by unethical as well as ethical persuaders, the moral imperative is to speak ethically.

The authors of this textbook belong to a professional organization called the National Communication Association, which publishes a credo for ethical communication that includes the following:

> "Ethical communication is fundamental to responsible thinking, decision making, and the development of relationships and communities within and across contexts, cultures, channels, and media. Moreover, ethical communication enhances human worth and dignity by fostering truthfulness, fairness, responsibility, personal integrity, and respect for self and others. ..." (Pearson et al., 2006, p. 521).

The choice between right and wrong is not simple. Informing people on a particular topic assumes providing knowledge to an audience that, in turn, learns more about the topic. In a persuasive speech, however, you are asking listeners to think or act in ways called for to achieve your specific purpose.

As members of an audience, many of the choices we make are inconsequential, such as which soft drink to buy at a convenience store or which magazine to read in a doctor's waiting room. Far more important, however, is the decision to reject our religious beliefs in order to embrace new ones. Even the purchase of an expensive automobile is a considerable decision for us when weighed against the selection of soft drink.

As a speaker, you must decide not only what to tell your audience but what you should avoid saying. Speakers need to be mindful of their audience's needs and values, and weigh benefits of successful persuasion against possible risks or harms. If a doctor, for example, prescribes a medication for a patient that results in the patient having to fight addiction to the medication, was that an appropriate act on the part of the doctor?

As you prepare for any persuasive speech, you should respect your audience. Be informed, be truthful, be clear on your motives, use various appeals ethically, avoid misleading your audience through faulty argument, and work to create the most effective, honest persuasive message.

Chapter Summary

The two overall persuasive goals are to address audience attitudes and to move an audience to action. Four specific persuasive aims define the focus of your speech. These aims include adoption, continuance, discontinuance, and deterrence. Your point of view, or thesis statement, is expressed in the form of a proposition that must be proved. Propositions take three basic forms: fact, value, and policy.

Your credibility as a speaker is determined by the way the audience perceives you. Credibility is measured in terms of trustworthiness and competence. A persuasive speaker constructs arguments that have emotional, logical, and ethical, or mythic appeal. Emotional appeals (pathos) can be powerful because they provide the motivation for action and attitude change. As a persuasive speaker, you should be conscious of ethical standards (ethos) and what the implications are of the choice you are asking your audience to make. The audience needs to be treated to the truth, without manipulative intent.

Arguments that have faulty reasoning are considered fallacies. Fallacies can distract and mislead listeners as well as pose ethical problems. Fallacies discussed in this chapter are attack on the person, hasty generalization, slippery slope, and red herring.

The persuasive speaker needs to consider how to construct an effective persuasive appeal. Three organizational patterns were discussed: comparative-advantages, criteria-satisfaction, and Monroe's motivated sequence. Monroe's motivated sequence includes five steps designed to motivate the audience to action: attention, need, satisfaction, visualization, and action. The motivated sequence is a widely used method for organizing persuasive speeches that follows the normal pattern of human thought from attention to action.

Key Terms

comparative advantage
   organizational pattern, 328

criteria satisfaction
   organizational pattern, 329

ethos, 318

fallacy, 324

logos, 318

motivated sequence, 329

pathos, 318

persuasion, 308

proposition of fact, 317

proposition of policy, 318

proposition of value, 317

Questions for Reflection

1. What are the dimensions of credibility, and how important is credibility to the overall effectiveness of a persuasive speech?
2. How would you define persuasion, persuasive goals, and persuasive aims? Illustrate your definitions with specific examples.
3. Why is the motivated sequence audience-centered? How does the motivated sequence relate to Maslow's hierarchy of needs?
4. When would comparative-advantages or criteria-satisfaction be more appropriate organizational patterns than Monroe's motivated sequence?
5. What are ethical, logical, and emotional appeals? How are these appeals distinct, yet interrelated?
6. How important is evidence in a persuasive speech? How important are ethics in persuasive speaking? Does the importance depend on the audience and its shared needs and expectations? Is there a relationship among evidence, emotions, and credibility, or is evidence simply a matter a presenting the facts?

Activities

1. List three people you recognize as spokespersons on important public issues. In a written analysis, describe the *ethos* of each speaker.
2. Select a persuasive political speech and analyze the reasoning used in the speech. Present an oral analysis to the class.
3. Find transcripts, excerpts, or detailed news accounts of a well-known courtroom trial. Write a 500- to 750-word essay on the role of persuasive appeals in the attorneys' opening and closing arguments. Your focus should be on the strengths and weaknesses of the attorneys' persuasive appeals.
4. Prepare a five- to six-minute persuasive speech, organizing it according to the motivated sequence. Prepare a written analysis of why the speech fits the requirements of the sequence. Then deliver the speech to your class.
5. Look through an anthology of speeches, such as *Vital Speeches of the Day*, or a video collection, to find an effective persuasive speech. Evaluate the persuasion used in the speech according to what you learned in this chapter.
6. Look for pictures or visual aids that convey persuasion relevant to the discussion in this chapter.

References

Aristotle (2007). *On rhetoric: A theory of civic discourse (2d ed.).* (G.A. Kennedy, Trans.). New York: Oxford University Press.

Brodsky, S. L., Griffin, M. P., & Cramer, R. J. (2010). The witness credibility scale: An outcome measure for expert witness research. *Behavioral Sciences and the Law, 28*(6), 892–901. doi: 10.1002/bsl.917.

Ehninger, D., Monroe, A. H., & Gronbeck, B. E. (1978). *Principles and types of speech communication*, (8th ed.). Glenview, IL: Scott Foresman.

Hample, D., Sells, A., & Valazquez, A. L. I. (2009). The effects of topic type and personalization of conflict on assessments of fallacies. *Communication Reports, 22*(2), 74–88.

Hirsen, J. (2011, April 13). Tina Fey Voices Palin Parody Pangs; 'Idol' Voting Needs Reboot. Retrieved on July 8, 2011 from http://www.newsmax.com/Hirsen/Tina-Fay-Palin-Parody/2011/04/13/id/392760.

Pearson, J. C., Child, J. T., Mattern, J. L., & Kahl, D. H., Jr. (2006). What are students being taught about ethics in public speaking textbooks? *Commmunication Quarterly, 54* (4), 507–521.

Pornpitakpan, C. (2005). The persuasiveness of source credibility: A critical review of five decades' evidence. *Journal of Applied Social Psychology, 34*(2), 243–281.

Regan, D. T., & Fazio, R. (1977). On the consistency between attitudes and behavior: Look to the method of attitude formation. *Journal of Experimental Social Psychology, 13*(1), 28–45.

Script excerpt from *Milk* (2008). Courtesy of Universal Studios Licensing LLC.

Simons, H. (2001). *Persuasion in society.* Thousand Oaks, CA: Sage Publications.

Story, L. (2007, January 15). Anywhere the eye can see, it's likely to see an ad. *New York Times.* Retrieved from: http://www.nytimes.com/2007/01/15/business/media/15everywhere.html.

Toulmin, S. (1958). *The uses of argument.* Cambridge, England: University Press.

Transcript from *300* obtained from American Rhetoric Movie Speeches. Retrieved July 8, 2011 from http://www.americanrhetoric.com/MovieSpeeches/moviespeech300queengorgo.html.

Walker, F. R. (2005). The rhetoric of mock trial debate: Using logos, pathos and ethos in undergraduate competition. *College Student Journal, 39*(2), 277–286.

Zimbardo, P. G. (1988). *Psychology and life* (12th ed.). Glenview, IL: Scott, Foresman.

Chapter

© 2012, Larry St. Pierre, Shutterstock, Inc.

12

Learning Objectives

After reading this chapter and completing the online activities for this lesson, you will be able to:

1. Recognize which situation requires which type of special occasion speech.

2. Develop and deliver a special occasion speech.

Speaking for Special Occasions

At a Glance

Chapter Summary

Key Terms

Questions for Reflection

Activities

References

INTRODUCTION

As with other forms of public speaking, a speech delivered on a special occasion can rise to the level of the extraordinary. Certainly as a college student, few ceremonies are likely to be more important than your commencement ceremony. In the following excerpt from his 2010 commencement address at Syracuse University, Jamie Dimon, chief executive officer of JPMorgan Chase, acknowledged the mixed feelings individuals have about Wall Street executives by setting up the speech in the following manner:

Courtesy of Shannon DeCelle.

FIGURE 12.1 To protest Jamie Dimon's commencement address at Syracuse University in 2010, students removed their robes while he spoke.

> *Graduating today means you are through with final exams, through with submitting term papers, all that nervousness, the cold sweat of sleepless nights preparing to answer seemingly impossible questions. Well, that's a feeling we banking executives know pretty well these days—we call it "testifying before Congress."*
>
> *I am honored to be here today, but I also know that some of your fellow students have raised questions about me being your commencement speaker....Today I will talk about what it takes to be accountable, in the hope that it might be valuable to you in years to come.*

Like all good ceremonial speeches, Dimon expressed sincere feelings about the event and his audience. He addressed the banking controversy head-on, and his interest in accountability is relevant to an audience of college graduates. He even managed to use humor, which, in this case, was appropriate and enhanced his speech. Dimon understood what a ceremonial speech required and crafted his speech to the situation and his audience. Some students who were initially critical of Dimon admitted that his speech had a good message (Olshan, 2010).

Even though there are many types of special occasion speeches, and each speech type has specific guidelines, there are some general guidelines that are important for all special occasion speeches. In this chapter, we will review the general guidelines, and then we will explain some of the most common special occasion speeches, provide some advice on how to write and deliver different types of special occasion speeches, and offer some tips on assembling your speech and integrating humor. By the end of the chapter, you will understand the requirements of creating speeches to celebrate, honor, or mourn.

Do you want to hear some of the most famous special occasion speeches? The online lesson has a recording of Ronald Reagan's Challenger *disaster address. See Topic 1. We recommend that you use your favorite search engine to find other famous speeches, such as Lou Gehrig's farewell speech and Martin Luther King's "I Have a Dream" speech.*

12.1 General Guidelines for Special Occasion Speeches

Most likely, you will have to develop and deliver a special occasion speech at least once in your lifetime. A special occasion speech is "special" because of the occasion—when you give a wedding toast, if you have to deliver the eulogy at a funeral, if you're selected as the commencement speaker, or even when you introduce someone at a public event. Although "special," these speeches are given every day and follow the same format as all speeches—introduction, body, and conclusion. These speeches also require that you meet the audience's expectations, tailor your remarks to the event, and use appropriate structure and style.

12.1.1 Ensuring That Your Speech Meets Expectations

Ceremonies and the speeches that mark them are surrounded by sets of expectations. An expectation is a set of beliefs we have about what will or should happen. When someone violates our expectations, we tend to have strong reactions. If a speaker violates our expectations in a negative way, for example, by cursing at a serious, formal event or being obviously unprepared, we may devalue the person and message. If the speaker violates our expectation in a positive way, for example, by being a much better speaker than we expected, our impression of him or her may be enhanced. Mourners listening to a eulogy, graduates listening to a commencement address, and members of a wedding party toasting the new couple expect certain words, gestures, and acts. Do not disappoint them. The words you choose to mark the occasion should remind people of the event they are commemorating. Even if you are sure everyone realizes the reason for your speech, explain it anyway. For example, it is difficult to imagine an awards presentation speech that did not mention the background and purpose of the award and the reason the recipient was chosen. Similarly, a speech of acceptance that failed to say thank you would be less than appropriate.

What Do You Expect?

What do you expect from speakers at certain events? How should the person delivering a eulogy at a funeral behave? What do you expect from a wedding toast?

Have you ever seen someone deliver a speech that was inappropriate? How did you react? Expectancy violation theory contends that people have expectations about how others will behave (both verbal and nonverbal). This theory examines what happens when someone deviates from the expectations. For example, if an audience is expecting a formal presentation, and the speaker uses slang and profanity, the audience may negatively evaluate the speaker—regardless of the content of the presentation. If you are interested how deviations affect interactions, read more about this theory (Affifi & Metts, 1998).

Your online lesson will review some of the specific expectations you need to consider when delivering a speech for a special occasion, including the formality of the event, the situation requirements, the host's expectations, consideration for appropriate emotional displays, and the importance of accurate information. See Topic 1.

12.1.2 Tailoring Your Remarks to the Audience or Occasion

If you are selected (or required to) deliver a special occasion speech, you need to remember that it is not just your speech, it is someone else's event. Make sure you tailor your speech, style, and deliver to the audience and occasion. Saying what people expect is not the same as delivering a generic speech that could be given before any audience on a similar occasion. It is not enough to change a few facts here and there and give the same speech of introduction no matter who the audience is. For example, introducing a candidate at a fund-raiser attended by close friends and colleagues will sound different than introducing that same candidate before a group of citizens gathered for a candidates' forum. In the first situation, the audience knows the candidate and supports his or her positions on issues. In the second situation, the audience may not know the candidate, and may be unclear as to his or her stance on various social issues and community hot buttons as well.

The online lesson identifies other important parts of tailoring your message—who you should thank, who needs to be acknowledged, and providing context so the audience knows why you were selected to speak. See Topic 1.

12.1.3 Using Appropriate Structure, Content, Style, and Delivery

There are certain stylistic devices that are common to different special occasion speeches. If you know these devices, you can use them appropriately. The next section in this chapter overview the occasions, but some common techniques are to use humor and personal stories. The more you say about the people and the occasion, the more intimate and fitting your speech becomes. Personal anecdotes—especially humorous ones—help create the feeling that the speech was written for that event and no other.

Actress Lisa Kudrow gave the 2010 commencement address at Vassar College, her alma mater. She begins the speech by saying:

Thank you, President Hill, for inviting me to speak, and thank you to the Class of 2010 for not protesting ... seriously. I was wondering what I should say to you—there are so many possibilities you know? So I asked some of you—and by "some" I mean two—who I happened to see in passing (it was convenient for me). Well, I couldn't ask every one of you. It's not like there's some kind of social network wherein I could communicate with such a large number of people at once. ...

© 2012 Tina Gill/Shutterstock.com, Shutterstock, Inc.

FIGURE 12.2 Shown here attending a film premiere, Lisa Kudrow delivered a commencement address at Vassar in 2010. When people deliver a commencement address, they typically dress in academic regalia—even if they did not attend or graduate from college (although Lisa Kudrow did graduate from Vassar).

After including some humor in her introductory remarks, Kudrow connects with the audience further by describing her graduation from Vassar in 1985. She provides a personal anecdote, with humor, that shows the quick transformation from biology major to actress. Her first job after graduation was with her father, who was a headache specialist:

I immediately started to work with him on a study concerning hemispheric dominance and headache types. I won't go into the details, but I could! The important thing was that I was on my way to getting published, then on to a graduate program at whichever very impressive university accepted me. Six months after graduation, I dumped that plan and decided to become an actress. Then I was cast on the show Friends and now I'm here. Any questions?

Not every occasion is one in which humor is anticipated or expected, but as Lisa Kudrow illustrates, it can draw the audience in, and personal anecdotes keep them listening and interested. At the end of this chapter, we will discuss some guidelines for using humor.

The online lesson reviews some questions you should ask yourself before deciding what approach to take in your special occasion speech. This lesson will also overview two strategies to enhance the audience's response: identification and magnification. See Topic 1.

Special occasion speeches are a unique form of public speaking that most of us will be asked to deliver at some point. Although the needs of the specific situation will dictate the form and structure of the speech, there are some common guidelines. First, it is important that your speech meets the audience's expectations about the situation. Second, you need to make your speech specific to the event—be personal and ensure that the speech is not generic. Finally, pay attention to the stylistic devices of the speech type and use appropriate structure, content, style, and structure.

12.2 Types of Ceremonial Speeches

There are many occasions that call for a speech. Sometimes we want to pay tribute to someone. Occasionally, we need to accept an award. We may be asked to give a commencement or keynote address. Frequently, we have to introduce another presenter. If you have attended a banquet, you may have even heard an after-dinner speech. This chapter reviews some of the most common special occasion speeches and provides you with tips on what to do and how to outline your speech.

12.2.1 Speeches of Tribute

In our society, we frequently honor people's achievements. The achievement may range from a job well done to a life well lived, but in each situation, someone delivers a speech about the person. Three of the most common tribute speeches are award presentations, eulogies, and toasts.

Award Presentations

award presentation
A speech delivered as part of a ceremony to recognize an individual or group chosen for special honors.

The **award presentation** is delivered as part of a ceremony to recognize an individual or group chosen for special honors. Our personal and professional lives are marked, in part, by attendance at, or participation in, awards ceremonies to recognize personal achievement. In December of 2010, President Obama and First Lady Michelle Obama hosted an awards ceremony at the Kennedy Center that included talk show host Oprah Winfrey and singer-songwriter Paul McCartney among its honorees. Numerous stars and celebrities paid tribute to these honorees,

FIGURE 12.3 Special occasion speeches are determined by the situation, but almost all of us will have to deliver a special occasion speech at some point.

(toast, upper left) © 2012 AISPIX, Shutterstock, Inc.; (funeral eulogy, lower left) © 2012 JustASC/Shutterstock. com, Shutterstock. Inc.; (commencement speaker Tommy Lasorda) Courtesy of Marie Hulett.

including John Travolta, Alec Baldwin, and Willie Nelson. These tribute speeches each adhered to the guidelines for honoring someone.

Specific Guidelines for Award Presentations

Every award presentation should accomplish several goals. A speech marking the presentation of the "Reporter of the Year" award for a student newspaper is provided in excerpts below to illustrate four specific guidelines for speeches of presentation.

1. **State the Importance of the Award.** Many scholarships and awards are available to qualified students. A scholarship may be significant because the selection criteria include finding the individual with the most outstanding achievement, whether it be academic, athletic, service oriented, or in recognition of special circumstances. Regardless of the award's monetary value, the audience needs to know why the scholarship is important. You may need to describe the achievements of the individual or individuals for whom the award has been established.

   Here is the beginning of a speech of presentation, as Tom speaks about his fellow reporter, Kathryn Remm.

   I am pleased to have been asked by our editorial staff to present the "Reporter of the Year" award—the college's highest journalistic honor. This award was established six years ago by a group of alumni who place great value on maintaining our newspaper's high standard of journalism.

In this example, Tom clearly states the importance of the award when he mentions that it is the college's highest journalistic honor.

2. **Explain the Selection Process.** The selection process may involve peers, students, teachers, or a standard committee. The audience needs to know that the award was not given arbitrarily or based on random criteria. Explaining the criteria and selection process may help to further establish the significance of the award. If the award is competitive, you may wish to mention the nature of the competition, but do not overemphasize the struggle for victory at the expense of the other candidates.

The following passage illustrates how this guideline can be followed effectively. Tom continues:

The award selection process is long and arduous. It starts when the paper's editorial staff calls for nominations and then reviews and evaluates dozens of writing samples. The staff sends its recommendations to a selection committee made up of two alumni sponsors and two local journalists. It is this group of four who determines the winner.

3. **Note the Honoree's Qualifications.** Many organizations honor their members and employees. For example, Midas Auto Service recognizes various dealers at their annual conference, including the "South Central Regional Dealer of the Year." The awards are based on criteria such as regional retail sales, overall retail image, and customer satisfaction. Edward Jones chooses employees for the Partner's Award, which is based on sales and service efforts over the past year. The nature of the award will suggest what you should say about the honoree. The following example shows why the reporter is being recognized.

This year's honoree is Kathryn Remm, the community affairs reporter on the paper. Almost single-handedly, Kathryn reached out to non-college community residents and established channels of communication that have never been open. In a series of articles, she told students about the need for literacy volunteers at the community library and for "Big Brothers" at the local Boys Club.

4. **Be Brief.** The key to a successful award presentation is brevity. Choose your words with care so that the power of your message is not diminished by unnecessary detail. Within this limited context, try to humanize the award recipient through a personal—perhaps humorous—anecdote.

Helpful Outline for an Award Presentation

1. Greeting and reference to the occasion
2. History and importance of the award
3. Brief description of the qualifications for the award
4. Reasons for this person receiving the award
5. Announcement of the recipient's name
6. Presentation of the award

SOURCE: (Harrell, 1997)

As a final note about speeches of presentation, occasionally it is appropriate to ask past recipients of the award to stand up and receive applause. This decision should be based, in part, on your conviction that this acknowledgment will magnify the value of the award to the current recipient as well as to the audience.

Eulogies

Eulogies are perhaps the most difficult commemorative speeches to make, since they involve paying tribute to a family member, friend, colleague, or community member who died. It is a difficult time for the speaker as well as the audience. A eulogy generally focuses on universal themes such as the preciousness and fragility of life, the importance of family and friends at times of great loss, and the continuity of life.

eulogy
A speech that honors someone who has passed away.

While working on this textbook, one of the authors was asked to deliver the eulogy at her stepfather's funeral. Although this was a very difficult time, she wanted to honor her stepdad Mike, and help the rest of the family manage their grief. The eulogy was especially difficult because Mike died as the result of injuries from a car accident; he was only 61. As she stood at the gravesite, looking at her 91-year-old stepgrandmother and her mother, she felt herself choking up. The viewing and mass had been so emotional that she knew if she cried, everyone's sadness would be magnified.

After talking for a few minutes about Mike's approach to life—live in the moment, never hold a grudge, and always take time to fish—she reminded everyone how lucky they were to have known Mike. She ended the eulogy by asking everyone to remember Mike as he liked to spend every evening—sitting on the front porch, dog asleep at his feet, smoking a cigarette, drinking a beer, and rubbing a lottery scratch-off (Mike was an eternal optimist). As Mike's family and friends smiled at this image, she pulled out a large stack of lottery scratch-offs, which opened up like an accordion, and said, "And now, I ask everyone to take one of these lottery tickets, and, as a tribute to Mike, scratch it off. We all know Mike is hoping that we are each a winner." She invited Mike's four granddaughters, ages 5 through 11, up, handed each a stack of tickets, and told them to make sure everyone got one. As the little girls started handing out lottery tickets, you could feel the mood change. Switching from oppressive sadness, people started laughing and saying, "Now, this is a funeral Mike would like." Although not every funeral ends with more than 100 people scratching off lottery tickets, this one did.

Eulogies are difficult. If you ever have to honor a loved one by delivering a eulogy, there are five guidelines that will help you develop and present a eulogy.

1. Acknowledge the Loss and Refer to the Occasion.

Your first words should focus on the family and/or significant others of the deceased. Talk directly to them, taking care to acknowledge by name the spouse, children, parents, and special friends of the deceased. It is safe to assume that all members of the audience feel loss. People come together to mourn because they want to be part of a community; they want to share their grief with others. By using "we" statements of some kind, you acknowledge the community of mourners. For example, you might say, "We all know how much Andrew loved his family," or "I am sure we all agree that Andrew's determination and spirit left their mark."

2. Celebrate Life Rather than Focusing on Loss.

Some deaths are anticipated, such as dying from ailments related to old age or after a lengthy illness. Others are shocking and tragic, and those left behind may have unresolved issues. Although it is appropriate to acknowledge shared feelings of sadness and even anger, the eulogy should focus on the unique gift the person brought to the world. At Michael Jackson's memorial service, his daughter, Paris Katherine, spoke the final words in celebration of her father: *"Ever since I was born, Daddy has been the best father you could ever imagine. … I just wanted to say I love him so much"* (Thompson, 2009). Inviting the audience to remember and celebrate the deceased's contributions is an important way to honor the person.

3. Use Quotes, Anecdotes, and Even Humor.

Nothing is better than a good story to celebrate the spirit of the deceased. A well-chosen story can comfort as it helps people focus on the memory of the person's life. Fitting anecdotes need not be humorless. On the contrary, according to professor of journalism Melvin Helitzer, euphemisms such as "a loving husband," "a loving father," "a wonderful person" mean far less to people than a humorous account of an incident in the person's life. Helitzer explains: "To say the deceased had a wonderful sense of humor and I remember the time… ," helps mourners get through the experience of attending the memorial as they recall pleasant memories (Heller Anderson, 1990).

You may choose to quote others and turn to the remarks of noted public figures or you may choose to use words from the deceased, as Cate Edwards did in 2010 at her mother Elizabeth Edward's funeral. Cate, in mentioning her mother's wisdom, shared this insight from Elizabeth: *"You almost always regret prints, but you'll never regret wearing solids"* (Bellow, 2010). This quote also demonstrates how humor can be an appropriate part of a eulogy.

Appropriate Humor in Eulogies

Humor and anecdotes are often used in eulogies, but you want to make sure that it is appropriate. Talk your ideas over with a few people prior to actually delivering the eulogy. In the earlier example, one of the textbook authors was concerned that ending her eulogy with lottery tickets might seem disrespectful, so she asked a couple of relatives if they thought it was fitting. She was especially concerned about her grandmother's reaction, but she shouldn't have worried. After everyone had a lottery ticket, she walked over, gave her grannie a hug, and said, "I hope that you're the big winner." Her grannie replied, "Me, too. I am going to rub it off on the casket because he will bring me good luck."

You do not need to rely on quotes from writers, poets, famous actors, or politicians. You may choose to include the words of friends and family of the deceased. As part of her eulogy at her mother's funeral, a daughter said the following:

> *After reading the cards sent by her many friends, it made sense to include some of what others thought of her. I'd like to share a few of these: "She was so full of enthusiasm and curiosity about everything. Whatever project she took on, she did it with a flair that no one else could match." "A gentle person who really*

did make a difference in each life she touched." "A warm, vibrant personality, and so much courage." "I doubt that anyone has left more happy memories."

Eulogies

Eulogies, in addition to memorializing the deceased, can also connect the audience to each other. Below are some famous eulogies; we encourage you to search for these speeches on the Internet—many have YouTube videos. Each of these speeches did more than simply connect the audience present—they continue to connect audiences around the world.

Oprah Winfrey's eulogy for Rosa Parks (2005)

Bruce Springsteen's eulogy for Clarence Clemmons (2011)

Kevin Costner's eulogy for Whitney Houston (2012)

Chief Justice Earl Warren's eulogy for President John F. Kennedy (1963)

President Barack Obama's eulogy for Senator Ted Kennedy (2009)

Ossie Davis' eulogy for Malcolm X (1965)

Howard K. Stern's eulogy for Anna Nicole Smith (2007)

Margaret Thatcher's eulogy for Ronald Reagan (2004)

Robert Kennedy's eulogy for Dr. Martin Luther King, Jr. (1968)

Charles Spencer's eulogy for Diana Spencer, Princess of Wales (1997)

Jawaharlal Nehru's eulogy for Mahatma Gandhi (1948)

Shown here in 1955 (with Martin Luther King, Jr.) at the time of the Montgomery Bus Boycott, Rosa Parks became a notable figure in the U.S. Civil Rights Movement.

Courtesy of U.S. Information Agency.

And don't forget, there are many ways to memorialize someone. Although speeches are the standard approach, sometimes a song can be the best eulogy. To see how effective a simple song can be, search for Jim Henson's memorial service held on May 21, 1990, in New York City's Cathedral of St. John the Divine (similar performances occurred at the memorial service held on July 2, 1990, in London's St. Paul's Cathedral):

The Muppets (and Henson's fellow Muppeteers) singing "Just One Person" at Jim Henson's memorial service (1990)

Big Bird singing "Bein' Green," at Jim Henson's memorial service (1990)

Jim Henson, creator of The Muppets, attending the 41st Emmy Awards Ceremony in 1989.

Courtesy of Allen Light.

The person and occasion of the individual's death should provide guidance in terms of what qualities to highlight and stories to tell. Remember, also, a eulogy can include input from others; so, do not hesitate to seek advice from others close to the person being eulogized.

4. Work to Control Your Emotions.

Composure is crucial. If you have any questions about your ability to control your grief, suggest that someone else be chosen. As you offer comfort to others, try not to call undue attention to your own grief. Although an expression of loss is appropriate, uncontrolled grief is generally out of place. If you do not think you can make it through the eulogy without falling apart, have someone else deliver it or bring someone up to the podium with you who can take over, if necessary.

The appropriateness of expressions of grief is culturally determined. Although we advise you to control your emotions, in some cultures clear demonstrations of grief would be expected and appreciated. In your family, what is the appropriate way to publicly express grief and mourning?

5. Be Sincere and Be Brief.

Speak from the heart by shunning such clichés as "words cannot express our sorrow," "the family's loss is too much to bear," and "we were all privileged to know him." Rely instead on personal memories, stories, and feelings. Focus also on your delivery for it will affect the sincerity of your message. Eulogies need not be lengthy to be effective. The following is an excerpt from a eulogy a woman gave for her father that indicates how she felt about him.

> *Throughout the years, he has been there for my failures and successes, providing me with meaningful advice. His opinion has always been very important to me. My father was a warm and loving man, a man of integrity, a great teacher. I miss him and I love him.*

Depending on the wishes of the family, several individuals may be called upon to eulogize the deceased. A brief, sincere speech will be greatly appreciated by those attending the memorial service.

Helpful Outline for Eulogy
(Can Be Used for Speech of Tribute if Honoree Is Alive)

1. Expression of respect and love for the honoree
2. Reasons for paying tribute to this person
3. Review of the person's accomplishments and contributions
4. Clarification of how this person has touched the lives of others
5. Closing appeal to emulate the good qualities of this person
SOURCE: (Harrell, 1997)

Toasts

It is thought that the custom of toasting began when the Norsemen, Vikings, and Greeks lifted their glasses in honor of the gods. But the newer "toast" derives from the seventeenth century British custom of placing toasted bits of bread in glasses to improve the taste of the drink. As the concept of the **toast** evolved, so did the customs surrounding it. In England, those proposing the toast got down on "bended" knee. In France, elaborate bows were required. In Scotland, the toast maker stood with one foot on a chair, the other on a table. Today, Western tradition dictates the clinking of glasses (Bayless, 1988).

toast
A brief message of good will and congratulations.

You are more likely to be asked to deliver a toast than any other form of tribute. Toasts are given at engagements, weddings, graduations, confirmations, births, the sealing of business deals, at dinner parties, and so on. They are brief messages of good will and congratulations.

Here are three guidelines to help you deliver a memorable toast:

1. Prepare a Short, Inspirational Message and Memorize It.

If you are the best man at your brother's wedding, the mother of the new college graduate at her graduation dinner, or a close associate of an executive just promoted to company president, you may be asked in advance to prepare a toast to celebrate the occasion. Even though most toasts are generally no more than a few sentences long, do not assume that you will be able to think of something appropriate to say when the glasses are raised. To avoid drawing a blank, write—and memorize—the toast in advance.

2. Choose Words with Care That Address the Audience and Occasion.

There is a time to be frivolous and a time to be serious. The audience and the occasion will suggest whether it is appropriate to be humorous or serious, inspirational or practical. Here is an example of an appropriate toast to a new law partner:

> *Ken has been a tower of strength for all of us. When four partners were sick with the flu at the same time last year, Ken worked round the clock, seven days a week, to meet our deadlines. Here's to Ken—the best lawyer in town and the newest partner of our law firm.*

Helpful Outline for a Toast

1. Introduce yourself, explain your relationship to the honoree
2. Thank the people hosting the event (if it is a hosted event)
3. Tell a brief story about the person/people you are toasting (If you are toasting a couple, be sure to address both people in the toast)
4. Offer a few words of thanks, appreciation, acknowledgment, or advice
5. Raise your glass and invite the audience to raise their glasses

SOURCE: (Harrell, 1997)

3. Be Positive and Avoid Clichés.

A toast is upbeat. Look to the future with hope. It is inappropriate to toast a college graduate saying, "If John does as poorly at work as he did at college, we may all be asked to help pay his rent."

Remember that public speaking is a creative activity. Avoid saying things that could be said by anyone, anywhere. Clichés such as, "Down the hatch," "Here's mud in your eye," and "Cheers," are a waste of the moment. Instead, you can say something simple like, "To Ken's future success," or, as is noted in the previous example, "Here's to Ken—the best lawyer in town and the newest partner of our law firm."

12.3 Speeches of Acceptance

speech of acceptance
A speech to expresses gratitude for an award.

The main purpose of an **acceptance speech** is to *express gratitude for the award*. It is personal, gracious, and sincere. Most speakers start out with something like, *"I am genuinely grateful for this award, and I want to express my sincere thanks to everyone here."* It also makes sense to tell your audience what receiving the award means to you.

Most acceptance speeches are brief. In many instances, such as an awards night in high school and departmental recognition in college, several individuals are recognized for their achievements. If acceptance speeches are long, the event will seem interminable. However, in some cases, such as the Nobel Peace Prize ceremony, recipients are asked to do more than express gratitude. These speeches fit within the category of "Keynote Speeches," which are discussed later in this chapter.

Here are four guidelines for the successful speech of acceptance:

1. Thank and Praise the Person or Group Giving the Award.

An acceptance speech is built around the theme of "thank you." You thank the person, group, or organization bestowing the award. You recognize the people who helped you gain it. It is usually helpful to have a list of people you want to thank—you do not want to forget to thank an important person. It is not necessary to give a long list of all the individuals who have influenced you in your lifetime, but you want to acknowledge those who have had an impact on you in some way that relates to your accomplishing this goal

2. Be Sincere.

Your acceptance should be sincere and heartfelt. The audience wants to feel that the individuals bestowing the award have made the right choice. Express genuine appreciation for the award and why this award is important to you. A well-developed and delivered acceptance speech allows the listeners to be part of the moment and share the your joy or amazement.

3. Describe How You Reached This Point of Achievement.

As you are thanking people, you can mention how you reached this point of recognition. If you are a gymnast, you can talk about your training and gymnastic meets. If you are a pianist, you can talk about practice and recitals. The audience wants to know that you worked for this award, and that you deserve it.

At the 83rd Annual Academy Awards ceremony held in 2011, Colin Firth was awarded the Oscar as Best Actor in a Leading Role. This is his acceptance speech.

I have a feeling my career has just peaked. My deepest thanks to the Academy. I'm afraid I have to warn you that I'm experiencing stirrings somewhere in the upper abdominals which are threatening to form themselves into dance moves. Joyous as they may be for me, it would be extremely problematic if they make it to my legs before I get off stage.

So I'm going to do my best to be brief with my gratitude first for being on this extraordinary list of fellow nominees. Something quite formidable and possibly the greatest honor of this. All the crew and my fellow cast members,

Colin Firth backstage after accepting the Academy Award for Best Actor in 2011.

those who are not here, and those who are, Geoffrey, Helena, and Guy, whose virtuosity made it very, very difficult for me to be as bad as I was planning to be. And David Seidler whose own struggles have given so many people the benefit of his very beautiful voice and Tom Hooper for the immense courage and clearsightedness with which he interpreted that. The men who finessed this to the screen, Gareth, Emile, Iain, Xavier, and of course, Harvey, who first took me on 20 years ago when I was a mere child sensation.

And all the people who have been rooting for me back home. Also Jessica Kolstad, my friend, Paul Lyon-Maris, and Chris Andrews for bearing with me through some of the less fortunate moments as well as the good ones and my very fortunate friendship with Tom Ford to whom I owe a very big piece of this. And to the Anglo-Italian-American-Canadian axis, which makes up my family and Livia for putting up with my fleeting delusions of royalty and who I hold responsible for this and for really everything that's good that's happened since I met her. Now if you'll all excuse me, I have some impulses I have to tend to backstage. Thank you very much.

4. Tell a Story or Two.

Select with care the events you want to mention to avoid an endless chronology of your life. Stories about your life, or personal anecdotes, give people a lasting impression of your achievement. Instead of simply telling your listeners, "I am grateful to everyone who supported me in this project," provide your audience with a personal anecdote. For example, when Joanne received an award for being the Most Valuable Player on her soccer team, she provided this story as part of her acceptance speech:

Three events contributed to my success on the soccer field. The first occurred on Christmas four years ago when I found a soccer ball under the tree and a completed registration form to a soccer camp held in my hometown. The second event was our final game during my senior year in high school when we won the city championship and I was fortunate enough to score the winning goal.

I cannot tell you the great sense of satisfaction I felt when my kick took the ball past the goal tender and into the net. The third event was the call I received from our coach inviting me to be part of this college team with its winning tradition and offering me an athletic scholarship.

Helpful Outline for Speeches of Acceptance

1. Expression of gratitude for the award

2. Brief praise of the appropriate people

3. Statement of appreciation to those giving the award

4. Closing of pleasure and thanks

SOURCE: (Harrell, 1997)

12.4 Commemorative Speeches

When we commemorate an event, we mark it through observation and ceremony. Public or private, these ceremonies are often punctuated by speeches appropriate for the occasion. Commencement speeches at college graduation, keynote speeches at banquets, speeches to celebrate the spirit of a special event or a national holiday like the Fourth of July, inaugural speeches, and farewell addresses all fit into this category. In this section, we will overview **commencement addresses** and keynote address. At the end of the chapter, we will provide helpful outlines for other commemorative speeches.

commencement address
A speech delivered at a graduation ceremony to praise the graduates.

Although commemorative speeches may inform, their specific purpose is not informational. Although they may persuade, their primary purpose is not persuasive. They are inspirational messages designed to stir emotions and make listeners reflect on the message through the use of rich language that lifts them to a higher emotional plain. More than in any other special occasion speech, your choice of words in the commemorative address will determine your success.

Many commemorative speeches express the speaker's most profound thoughts. As you talk about what it means to graduate from college, be inaugurated to office, or lose a family member, your goal is to leave a lasting impression on your audience. Although many commemorative speeches are short, they often contain memorable quotations that add strength and validity to the speaker's own emotion-filled message.

12.4.1 Commencement Speeches

Graduation is a time of celebrating the past and thinking about the future. Commencement speakers are selected to help the graduates reflect on their accomplishments and to offer words of wisdom about their next steps. Many graduation ceremonies have multiple speakers—someone from the graduating class and someone especially noteworthy and aspirational (an exemplary alumni, a celebrity, a person of accomplishment). No other speech offers a greater potential to achieve the aims of a ceremonial speech than the commencement address delivered by an honored guest. Though the content of commencement addresses vary, here are some guidelines for organizing an address.

FIGURE 12.4 Shown here at another college speaking engagement, John Grisham adhered to the best practices of commencement addresses when he spoke at The University of North Carolina at Chapel Hill in 2010.

1. Express honor at being selected the commencement speaker.

Being selected as a commencement speaker is a great honor; writing the commencement address is a daunting task. Though we have heard many amazing commencement speeches (Steve Jobs at Stanford; J.K. Rowling at Harvard; Desmond Tutu at Brandeis University, and the speaker at a department-level ceremony at The University of Texas at Austin who spoke about how college is a journey down the yellow brick road, and that it takes brains, courage, and heart to be successful), all speeches should start with an expression about the privilege of speaking at the ceremony. If the authors of this textbook were asked to deliver a commencement address, we would thank those who invited us and include the other graduates in the honor by having them wave to their friends and family members.

Thank you. Thank you for allowing me to share this event with you. As I stand here before you, I am inspired and honored. But perhaps more importantly, you have inspired the people sitting behind you. Your friends and family members are here to share this event with you because they know what this accomplishment means. Graduates, let's start this ceremony off with a short celebration: stand up, turn around, and wave to your loved ones.

Friends and family member, let's start this speech with a cheer for the graduates!

2. Offer praise to the graduating class.

Commencement speakers should pay tribute to the students graduating and to the school as a place of excellence. In our hypothetical speech, we would mention the skills that all the students developed and acknowledge that the graduates are praiseworthy and the college exceptional. We would also include the insight of some of the graduates.

> *You are an exceptional group, graduating from an exceptional university. But, think back to when you started this journey. Did you imagine that you would have learned so much? Your lessons include more than just how to write a research paper, how to survive on four hours of sleep, and how to take five exams in one week.*

> *But more than facts and formulas, each of you developed some insight that should be shared. Yesterday, you each submitted an index card with an insight you've gleaned during the last four years. I want to read you some of these insights....*

3. Offer counsel to the graduates.

A traditional commencement speech provides the graduates advice and insight for the future. In this speech, we would first dispense with some quick advice:

> *Your time here has been filled with laughter, joy, stress, tears, and, of course, the feeling that there is never enough time—not enough time to write the next paper, not enough time to read all the articles and chapters assigned, not enough time to collect and analyze data. But, it's important to know that in life, there is never enough time. Instead, it's how you manage your choices and prioritize your options that determines your success.*

We would then move on to the main point of the speech, which is the power of managing uncertainty.

> *Regardless of where life takes you, remember to be open to the surprises. Don't get so caught up in planning that you forget to explore new options. Sometimes, you should leap into the unknown and embrace uncertainty. Embracing uncertainty is the "ultimate intellectual challenge" because it pushes you to explore your boundaries. You may not know if it's the right choice, but welcoming uncertainty will help you discover what you truly desire in your personal, academic, and professional lives. And when you find what you desire, you will learn and grow.*

Importantly, when you are offering advice and insight about the future, you should focus on the positives and not the negatives. Commencement addresses should be inspirational, motivational, and uplifting.

4. Congratulate the graduates.

Graduations are a time of celebration and the graduates deserve to be congratulated. We would conclude our speech on a positive and celebratory note:

> *So, with all the certainties and uncertainties that you may be feeling right now, know that today is your day to celebrate. Celebrate because today your tears are not driven by stress; your tears are the sign of accomplishment and celebration. Each of you know how hard you have worked to be seated here right now. Celebrate because you went beyond what was expected of you.*

Celebrate because earning an undergraduate or graduate degree is a great accomplishment. Praise yourself for today, you are ending a journey, but you have so much to look forward to. Although you may encounter uncertainties in life, grab hold of those experiences and take a leap into the unknown. Be proud of what you have accomplished and know that this is your day and your celebration and rest on the certainties of your ability. I hope you feel proud of yourself and know that this is the beginning of many more successes.

Graduates, I wish you all the best in everything you do. Thank you and best of luck to all of you!

5. Be conscious of time limit.

Although the commencement address is one of the key parts of a graduation ceremony, the students want to graduate and start their personal celebrations. In her May 20, 2005, commencement address to anthropology majors at University of California, Berkeley, Nancy Scheper-Hughes, a professor of anthropology, addressed her concerns about the length of her speech.

Closer to home, Mario Cuomo, the former governor of New York, compared the role of a commencement speaker to that of a corpse at an Irish wake. Both bodies need to be there in order to have a celebration but no one expects it to say very much. . . . In fact the shortest commencement speech on record was delivered by the late Nels Smith, former governor of Wyoming. When it came to his turn to speak, Smith rose slowly from his chair, approached the podium, surveyed the rows and rows of gowned graduating students and he said slowly: "You done real good." Then he turned and went back to his seat.

Professor Scheper-Hughes was right—commencement speakers should be very conscious of the time limits. Although most commencement speeches last less than fifteen minutes, the strength of the message can endure. In fact, twenty years ago, we heard a commencement speech about the yellow brick road and heart, courage, and brains, and although we forget the speaker's name, we remember the message.

You may have heard the following quote from Winston Churchill, a former Prime Minister of the United Kingdom:

Never give in. Never give in. Never, never, never, never—in nothing,
great or small, large or petty—
never give in, except to convictions
of honor and good sense. Never
yield to force. Never yield to the apparently overwhelming might
of the enemy.

Many people think this was the complete text of his 1941 commencement address to Harrow School, his former preparatory school. However, this was just part of the speech. If you want to see the whole speech, search for it online using your favorite search engine.

Helpful Outline for a Commencement Address

1. Greeting to the graduates and the audience
2. Review of the graduates' successful accomplishments
3. Praise to the graduates for reflecting respected values
4. Prediction and discussion of future challenges
5. Closing inspiration for the graduates to meet these new challenges successfully

SOURCE: (Harrell, 1997)

12.4.2 Keynote Speeches

A keynote speaker is the featured speaker at an event. There may be several people who speak briefly, but the keynote speaker is the focal point of the event. Whatever the setting, whether it is a gathering of members of the American Society of Journalists and Authors or the annual convention of the American Bar Association, the **keynote address** is usually anticipated as a highlight that has the potential to excite the audience to thought and action. Unlike many special occasion speeches, the keynote speech is not brief. You may be called upon to give a keynote speech at some point. We offer the following guidelines.

keynote address
A speech delivered by the featured speaker at a formal event.

1. Your Speech Sets the Tone for the Event.

Think of keynote speakers as cheerleaders and their speeches as the cheers that set the tone for an event. The purpose of the gathering may be to celebrate the group's achievements, to share information with each other, or to give individuals the opportunity to interact with people who are in similar positions or situations. The keynote speaker is there to excite people, to stimulate thought and action.

Keynote addresses motivate people. In 2004, at the Democratic National Convention held in Boston, Massachusetts, Barack Obama, then a relatively unknown state senator from Illinois, was selected to be the keynote speaker. His speech, about improbable dreams and hope, ended with a rousing call to support John Kerry for President:

> *In the end—In the end—In the end, that's what this election is about. Do we participate in a politics of cynicism or do we participate in a politics of hope?*
>
> *John Kerry calls on us to hope. John Edwards calls on us to hope.*
>
> *I'm not talking about blind optimism here—the almost willful ignorance that thinks unemployment will go away if we just don't think about it, or the health care crisis will solve itself if we just ignore it. That's not what I'm talking about. I'm talking about something more substantial. It's the hope of slaves sitting around a fire singing freedom songs; the hope of immigrants setting out for distant shores; the hope of a young naval lieutenant bravely patrolling the Mekong Delta; the hope of a millworker's son who dares to defy the odds; the hope of a skinny kid with a funny name who believes that America has a place for him, too.*
>
> *Hope—Hope in the face of difficulty. Hope in the face of uncertainty. The audacity of hope!*

In the end, that is God's greatest gift to us, the bedrock of this nation. A belief in things not seen. A belief that there are better days ahead.

I believe that we can give our middle class relief and provide working families with a road to opportunity.

I believe we can provide jobs to the jobless, homes to the homeless, and reclaim young people in cities across America from violence and despair.

I believe that we have a righteous wind at our backs and that as we stand on the crossroads of history, we can make the right choices, and meet the challenges that face us.

America! Tonight, if you feel the same energy that I do, if you feel the same urgency that I do, if you feel the same passion that I do, if you feel the same hopefulness that I do—if we do what we must do, then I have no doubt that all across the country, from Florida to Oregon, from Washington to Maine, the people will rise up in November, and John Kerry will be sworn in as President, and John Edwards will be sworn in as Vice President, and this country will reclaim its promise, and out of this long political darkness a brighter day will come.

Thank you very much everybody. God bless you. Thank you.

Barack Obama's speech was very well received. It helped catapult him to national prominence and, four years later, he was again the speaker at the Democratic National Convention. However, this time he was the Democratic nominee for President of the United States.

Although many people associate keynote addresses with political conventions, keynotes can be delivered at a variety of functions. For example, Steve Jobs delivered a keynote to commemorate the launching of Apple's iPad in January, 2010. If you search online for his speech, you will read how his keynote address celebrated Apple's achievements, shared information about the product, and excited people so much that 300,000 iPads were sold the first day (Moren, 2010).

FIGURE 12.5 Shown here in formalwear at the 2010 Academy Awards, Steve Jobs was famous for signaling a more informal tone during his keynote addresses by wearing the casual black turtleneck and jeans he routinely wore to work at Apple.

2. Select Your Topic and Language After Analyzing the Audience and Occasion.

There is a reason you were asked to be the keynote speaker. It may be fame, fortune, or simply achievement based on hard work. You may be provided with some basic guidelines for your speech, such as "motivate them," or "talk about success." How you develop the content of your speech and the words you choose to express yourself should be made after reflecting on the audience and occasion. As one of the keynote speakers at the Global Business Conference in February, 2012, held in Washington, D.C., Secretary of State Hillary Rodham Clinton started her speech by making a specific connection between government and business.

> *And it is in that spirit that we gather today to discuss how America's foreign policy can champion U.S. businesses abroad and drive recovery here at home, and also help provide a strong foundation and effective economic tools that can strengthen and sustain America's global leadership.*
>
> *Now, here at the State Department, we call this Economic Statecraft. And we have worked to position ourselves to lead in a changing world where security is shaped in financial markets and on factory floors, as well as in diplomatic negotiations and on the battlefield. That's why more than 1,000 economic officers on six continents are working with American companies, chambers of commerce, local businesses, and local and national governments to open markets and find new customers. At the same time, we're forming new partnerships with companies, universities, NGOs, and philanthropies to put private sector ingenuity to work solving some of our most difficult global challenges and driving sustainable development.*
>
> *Now, I think it is fair to say, and I see a lot of my very experienced diplomatic colleagues here in the room, this has not always been a traditional focus for us. So why, you might ask, is the Secretary of State now spending as much time thinking about market swings as missile silos?*
>
> *Well, to put it very plainly, Americans need jobs. And every $1 billion of goods we export supports more than 5,000 jobs here at home—even more in industries like telecommunications and aerospace.*

Since her speech was presented to individuals connected with government entities and business organizations, Clinton asserted the importance of business at the very beginning. Throughout the speech, she addressed the importance of promoting American business abroad, attracting investments to the United States, increasing U.S. exports, and, of course, creating more jobs for Americans.

3. Connect with the Audience Very Quickly.

Keynote speakers need to motivate the audience—this speech is the start of an event. Mario Cuomo, then Governor of New York, was the keynote speaker at the 1984 Democratic National Convention. In his first paragraph, he made his speech relevant to the audience.

> *Thank you very much. On behalf of the great Empire State and the whole family of New York, let me thank you for the great privilege of being able to address this convention. Please allow me to skip the stories and the poetry and the temptation to deal in nice but vague rhetoric. Let me instead use this valuable opportunity to deal immediately with the questions that should determine this election and that we all know are vital to the American people.*

4. Pay Attention to Time and Audience Constraints.

Yes, people are gathered to hear you. You are the focus of attention. Say what you need to say, but do not waste their time. Think about what has happened in the time before your speech, and what will happen after your speech. Even if you have what seems to be an unlimited amount of time, realize that your audience may have other things to do. Think about the audience's attention span. Have they been in the same room for the last four hours? An audience can be enthralled for some period of time, but there is a limit as to how long they can pay attention. One of the authors of this textbook attended a ceremony celebrating the university's 100-year anniversary, and slipped out of the room after forty-five minutes of listening to the keynote speaker. (The speech lasted another twenty minutes!) Time is a factor. You do not want to have your audience dreaming of an escape plan.

Helpful Outline for a Keynote Address

1. Orientation of the audience to the mood and theme of the convention
2. Reference to the goals of the organization and their importance
3. Brief description of the convention's major events
4. Closing invitation for active participation in the convention
SOURCE: (Harrell, 1997)

12.4.3 Speeches of Introduction

The purpose of a **speech of introduction** is to introduce the person who will give an important address. Keynote speakers are introduced, as are commencement speakers and speakers delivering inaugural remarks. When you deliver this type of speech, think of yourself as the conduit through which the audience learns something about the speaker. The introduction speech is important because it sets the stage for the speaker and helps to enhance his or her credibility. In other words, you're the opening act and need to set the right tone.

speech of introduction
A brief speech to introduce the person who will give an important address.

It is your job to heighten the anticipation and to prepare your audience for a positive experience. You can accomplish these goals by describing the speaker's accomplishments in an appropriate way. Tell your listeners about the speaker's background and why he or she was invited to address the gathering. This can be accomplished in a brief, but effective, manner as is demonstrated in the following speech of introduction found in an article by Nair (2010) at Buzzle.com:

> *Eight years in office, businessman, environmental activist, Nobel Prize winner, recipient of a Grammy and an Emmy, and runner up for* Time's *Person of the Year; a pretty mean task for one person to achieve. But our chief guest for today is no ordinary person. A politician and a keen environmentalist, what most people do not know about him is that he has politics in his genes; his father was also the Senator of Tennessee for 18 years. He studied at Harvard, graduating in 1969. He volunteered to go to Vietnam as reporter for the Army, after deciding not to find a way to dodge the draft, and forcing someone with lesser privileges to go to war.*

After the war, he attended Vanderbilt University but won a seat in Congress before he got a degree. This started his political life, which we are all familiar with. Without more delay, here he is, former Vice President of the United States, Mr. Al Gore.

FIGURE 12.6 Former Vice President Al Gore has been a popular figure on the public speaking circuit, particularly since winning the Nobel Peace Prize in 2007.

Some of the best advice for public speaking is printed on a coffee mug. The thirty-second President of the United States, Franklin Delano Roosevelt, apparently gave this advice to public speakers—"Be brief, be sincere, be seated." In addition to that bit of wisdom, we will provide you the following guidelines will help you prepare appropriate introductory remarks.

1. Set the Tone, Be Personal, and Be Brief.

An introductory speaker is like an *amuse-bouche*. If you watch the reality television series *Top Chef* (or you are a foodie), you may know what an *amuse-bouche* is—a single bite of food that whets the diner's appetite for more. When you are introducing someone, it is your responsibility to set the focus the audience's attention for the next speaker and prepare them for the speech. If you are introducing a comedian, you should be light-hearted (but don't try to be a comedian). If you are introducing someone running for office, you will probably want to have a more serious style. If your tone does not match the event or the next speaker, the audience may be disoriented and the next speaker will have to adjust to your style.

2. State the Speaker's Name, Qualifications, and Generate Interest in the Talk.

Just like an *amuse-bouche* is a bite of food, when introducing someone, you need to be a very small part of the event. Your key role is to generate interest in the speaker's talk and to get the audience curious. You do this by including some personal information about the speaker. The audience needs to know the next speaker's name and key qualifications.

Recently, one of the authors of this textbook heard a speech introducing a congressman at a U.S. Naval retirement ceremony. The introductory speaker went into great detail introducing the man, detailing his education, military service, activities in community service organizations, campaigns for Congress, and so on. This introductory speech was too long, it was not personal, and the speaker failed to set the appropriate tone for the featured speaker. As a result of this information overload, members of the audience shifted restlessly, coughed, yawned, and even dozed off. In this situation, the main speaker began his speech at a disadvantage.

3. Create Realistic Expectations.

By telling the audience, "This is the funniest speech you'll ever hear," or "This woman is known as a brilliant communicator," you are making it difficult for the speaker to succeed. Few speakers can match these expectations. Instead, the audience may "appreciate the wisdom" of someone's remarks, or "be inspired" or "be entertained fully" by the speaker. Identify what you hope the audience will experience without creating a bar too high for anyone to jump over.

4. Avoid Summarizing the Speaker's Intended Remarks.

Your job is to provide an enticement to listen, not a summary of the remarks to follow. You might tell an audience of college students that you brought a well-known financial advisor to your college to help you make wise financial decisions. Avoid saying, "This speaker will tell you to reduce your spending, save a little money each month, distinguish between wants and needs, and pay your credit card balance on time." This is clearly interfering with the speaker's plan. If you have any questions about how much to include in the introduction, share your proposed comments with the main speaker before your presentation.

5. Invite a Warm Reception for the Speaker and Lead the Applause.

Your job is to get the audience warmed up. You want the speaker to feel welcome, so get the audience to join you in welcoming the speaker. Here are a few examples of how to lead the audience and generate applause (make sure you also clap).

- *Please join me in welcoming our speaker, Karma Chávez.*
- *Put your hands together for our keynote speaker.*
- *And now it's time for the speaker you've been waiting for—let's give a hand to Stephen Littlejohn.*

Although preparing your introduction is important, you also have to be willing to be spontaneous. An unexpected event may have prevented the planned introductory speaker from attending, and you may have to introduce someone. Something may have happened to the speaker, in the audience, or in the world just before the introductory speech, making the planned introduction less effective. In both situations, you need to think on your feet and provide an introduction for the next speaker.

Helpful Outline for a Speech of Introduction

1. Greeting and reference to the occasion

2. Statement of the name of the person to be introduced

3. Brief description of the person's speech topic/company position/role in the organization, and so forth that should generate substantial interest in the speaker and/or message to come

4. Details about the person's qualifications

5. Enthusiastic closing statement

6. Inviting a warm reception for the next speaker

SOURCE: (Harrell, 1997)

12.4.4 After-Dinner Speeches

after-dinner speech
An address after a meal with the purpose to entertain, often with humor, although it may also convey a thoughtful message.

If the keynote address is the meat-and-potatoes speech of a conference, the **after-dinner speech** is the dessert. It is a speech delivered, literally, after the meal is over and after all other substantive business is complete. Its purpose is to entertain, often with humor, although it may also convey a thoughtful message. Keep in mind, a more accurate description of this speech would be "after-meal" as an after-dinner speech can occur after any meal.

1. Focus on the Specific Purpose—to Entertain.

Do not make the mistake of delivering a ponderous speech filled with statistics and complex data. Talking about the national debt would probably be inappropriate, as would a speech on what to do with the tons of garbage Americans produce each day. You can discuss these topics in a humorous way, however, relating, for example, how handling the national debt has become a growth industry for economists or how families are trying to cope with community rules to separate garbage into various recycling categories.

2. Reference the Audience and the Occasion.

What is the purpose of the event? Is it a business function, a fund-raising event, or a social event? Why are the people attending? After-diner speeches should be written for specific events—a speech that is appropriate at a political fund-raiser would likely not work at a corporate marketing convention.

3. Have a Central Idea.

Your audience is relaxed and wants to be entertained, but you need to give them something to think about. Like all speeches, an after-dinner speech needs a central idea—what do you want your audience to think about? Your central theme should also be reflected in the title of your speech. At larger functions, the after-dinner speech will be noted in the program so make sure your title is clear and entertaining.

Courtesy of Michelle Ma, Coastline Community College.

FIGURE 12.7 Delivering an after-dinner speech can be challenging because the audience may not be done eating, and some people will have to turn in their seats.

As is noted in the definition of the after-dinner speech, you do not have to rely solely on humor. You can also be inspirational, filling your speech with stories from personal experiences that have changed your life. This approach is especially effective if you are well known or if the events you relate have meaning to others.

4. Make Your Points with Humor.

You want to entertain your audience. You need to think about your approach and be sure that you're not the only one who finds your material humorous. Your humor needs to be appropriate for the event and all the people in the audience.

The online lesson covers the use of humor in ceremonial and other speeches. The lesson also reviews how to incorporate verbal, nonverbal, and interactive humor strategies into your speech. See Topic 2.

5. End the Speech on an Uplifting Note.

The closing of an after-dinner speech is especially important because it frequently brings the whole event to an end. You want the audience to end the event smiling and laughing so they can leave in a good mood.

After-dinner speeches have a few special challenges that you need to consider. First, consider the time of the event. These speeches may occur late in the evening, so it is important to maintain your energy level. Second, alcohol may be served with dinner. Although you cannot control what the audience drinks, you can control what you drink. Since the successful use of humor in a speech requires you to walk a fine line, you should abstain from drinking any alcohol—one drink may lead you to say something not quite appropriate. Finally, if your speech is the last event, you need to be prepared that some members of your audience may leave during your speech. An after-dinner speech is usually eight to ten minutes—long enough to entertain but not long enough for the audience to get sleepy or distracted. Pay attention to the time limits so the whole audience does not feel compelled to leave.

Helpful Outline for an After-Dinner Speech

1. Statement of reference to the audience and the occasion
2. Humorous transition into the central idea or thesis
3. Presentation of major points developed with humorous supporting materials
4. Closing that is witty and memorable

SOURCE: (Harrell, 1997)

There are some general guidelines for putting your special occasion speech together. The online lesson will help you think about the research you need to do for your occasion, how to outline your speech, and how to prepare your manuscript. See Topic 2.

12.5 Helpful Outlines for Other Special Occasion Speeches

The following sidebar provides various outlines for you to consider. Each commemorates a different event that you may encounter in the future. Each outline spells out both what is expected and the traditional order sequence used.

Helpful Outlines for Other Special Occasion Speeches

Speech of Welcome
1. Expression of honor this person's visit brings to the group
2. Description of the person's background and special achievements
3. Statement of the reason for the visit
4. Greeting and welcome to the person

Speech of Dedication
1. Statement of reason for assembling
2. Brief history of efforts that have led to this event
3. Prediction for the future success of the company, organization, group, or person

Anniversary Speech
1. Statement of reason for assembling
2. Sentimental significance of the event
3. Explanation of how this sentiment can be maintained
4. Appeal for encouraging the sentiment to continue in future years

Speech of Farewell
1. Expression of sorrow about the person's departure
2. Statement of enjoyment for the association with this person
3. Brief description of how the person will be missed
4. Announcement of friendship and best wishes for the future
5. Invitation to return again soon

Speech of Installation
1. Orientation of the audience to the occasion and the theme of this installation
2. Introduction of the current officers
3. Praise of the current officers for the work they have accomplished
4. Announcement for the new officers to come forward
5. Explanation of the responsibilities for each office
6. Recitation of the organization's installation of officers pledge
7. Declaration of the installation of the new officers

Speech of Inauguration
1. Expression of appreciation for being elected or placed in office
2. Declaration of the theme or problem focus while in office
3. Explanation of policy intentions
4. Announcement of goals to achieve while in office
5. Closing appeal for confidence in a successful future

Humorous Speech
1. Humorous attention-getter
2. Preview of the comic theme and intent of the speech
3. Presentation of humorous points and supporting materials that are typical of the audience in terms of events, feelings, experiences, or thoughts
4. Closing that presents a strong punch line

SOURCE: (Harrell, 1997)

Chapter Summary

At some point in your life, chances are you will give a special occasion speech. You may be called upon to toast a member of your family, a colleague, or a good friend. Perhaps you will introduce a guest speaker, or your alma mater may invite you to address the graduating class. All special occasion speeches have certain characteristics in common. When delivering a speech for a special occasion, make sure it meets audience expectations. Tailor your speech to the honoree and the occasion, use personal anecdotes and appropriate humor, and avoid clichés. Be aware that you are speaking for others as well as yourself, be sincere, be humble, and be accurate.

Speeches of tribute honor individuals at important moments—weddings, funerals, birthdays, and other momentous events. These speeches include award presentations, eulogies, and toasts. Speeches of award presentation are delivered as part of special recognition ceremonies. These speeches tell the audience why the award is being given and state the importance of the award. Marked by grace and sincerity, speeches of acceptance express gratitude for an award. Commemorative speeches include commencement addresses and keynote speeches. Commemorative speeches are inspirational messages designed to stir emotions and cause listeners to reflect. Keynote speeches often set the tone for an event through the use of direct language. The purpose of a speech of introduction is to introduce the person who will deliver an important address. Your role is to heighten audience anticipation of the speaker through a brief, personal description of why he or she has been chosen to speak. After-dinner speeches are speeches of entertainment and inspiration, generally delivered at the conclusion of substantive business.

Key Terms

after-dinner speech, 364

award presentation, 344

commencement address, 354

eulogy, 347

keynote address, 358

speech of acceptance, 352

speech of introduction, 361

toast, 351

Questions for Reflection

1. How would you evaluate Colin Firth's acceptance speech in light of what you have learned about this speech form?
2. What are the elements of an effective toast?
3. What are the elements of an effective speech of introduction? What should speakers avoid?
4. Why are brevity and gratitude key elements of an effective acceptance speech?

Activities

1. Select a famous person from the past and prepare a three- to four-minute eulogy in his or her honor. Follow the guidelines presented in this chapter, and deliver the eulogy in front of your classmates. A sincere, thoughtful eulogy is difficult to prepare, so spend time developing and practicing your speech.
2. Locate an individual in your community who is known as an effective special occasions speaker. Interview the speaker about how he or she selects materials, meets audience expectations, adapts to the occasion, and uses language and humor to influence the audience.
3. Team up with a classmate for the purpose of presenting and accepting an award. Toss a coin to determine who will present and who will accept the award. Then join with other teams in your class for a round of speeches involving the presentation and acceptance of awards.
4. Pair up with another classmate and introduce each other. First, introduce each other based on what you already know about the person. The next step is to get to know the person and then develop another introductory speech. The second speech should be more personal than the first because students get to know each other.

References

Afifi, W. A., & Metts, S. (1998). Characteristics and consequences of expectation violations in close relationships. *Journal of Social and Personal Relationships, 15*(5), 365–392.

Bayless, J. (1988). Are you a master of the toast? *The Toastmaster* (November), 11.

Bellow, M. (2010, December 12). *Elizabeth Edwards eulogized by her eldest daughter.* Retrieved from http://www.usatoday.com/news/nation/2010-12-11-edwards_N.htm.

Churchill, W. (1941, October 29). *Never give in.* Retrieved from http://www.winstonchurchill.org/learn/speeches/speeches-of-winston-churchill/103-never-give-in

Clinton, H. R. (2012). Keynote address at the Global Business Conference. Retrieved from the U.S. Department of State website: http://www.state.gov/secretary/rm/2012/02/184284.htm

Cuomo, M. (1984, July 16). Keynote address delivered at the 1984 Democratic National Convention. Retrieved from http://americanrhetoric.com/speeches/mariocuomo1984dnc.htm.

Dimon, J. (2010, May 16). Remarks at Syracuse University's 156th Commencement and the SUNY College of Environmental Science and Forestry's 113th Commencement. Retrieved from syr.edu web site on December 11, 2010.

Firth, C. (2011, February 27). Acceptance speech delivered at the 83rd Academy Awards. Retrieved from http://indiewire.com/article/in_their_own_words_the_complete_2011_oscar_acceptance_speeches#.

Harrell, A. (1997). *Speaking beyond the podium: A public speaking handbook (2nd ed.).* Fort Worth, TX: Harcourt Brace College Publishing.

Heller Anderson, S. (1990). "Chronicle," *New York Times*, January 18, B6. *Interview with Professor Melvin Helitzer, January 17, 1990.*

Kudrow, L. (2010, May 23). Commencement address. Retrieved from commencement.vassar.edu/2010.

Moren, N. (2010, April 5). Apple sells 300,000 iPads in the first day. *Macworld.com.* Retrieved from http://www.macworld.com/article/150417/2010/04/ipad_sales.html

Nair, T. (2010, February 10). *Introduction speech examples.* Retrieved from http://www.buzzle.com/articles/introduction-speech-examples.html

Obama, B. (2004, July 27). Keynote address delivered at 2004 Democratic National Convention. Retrieved from http://www.americanrhetoric.com/speeches/convention2004/barakobama2004dnc.htm.

Olshan, J. (2010, May 17). Protest flops: CEO wins over grads. *New York Post.* Retrieved from http://www.nypost.com/p/news/local/protest_flops_vmCgvBEKNBfEjFv5rGWuMN

Scheper-Hughes, N. (2005, June 5). In a divided nation within a divided world, never more has an anthropology degree been as valuable or as needed. Retrieved from http://berkeley.edu/news/media/releases/2005/06/03_hughes.shtml.

Thompson, K. (2009, July 7). Michael Jackson's daughter speaks: "I love him so much." Retrieved from http://www.huffingtonpost.com/2009/07/07/michael-jacksons-daughter_n_227257.html

Chapter

13

© 2012, imagesolutions, Shutterstock, Inc.

Learning Objectives

After reading this chapter and completing the online activities for this lesson, you will be able to:

1. Describe and apply various technological mediums through which communication and public speaking can take place.

2. Discuss the benefits and caveats of communicating through technological and electronic mediums.

3. Synthesize appropriate strategies for public speaking when using technology and electronic media.

Public Speaking in an Electronic World

At a Glance

INTRODUCTION

It is 6:30 A.M. and your dreaded alarm clock goes off with an annoying shriek that demands you get out of bed now. Upon exiting your warm cocoon, what do you do first? Put on a robe? Brush your teeth? Grab a cup of coffee? For some, these common morning activities may not be the first order of business. According to a 2010 study by Oxygen Media and Lightspeed Research, a startling 34 percent of young women aged 18 to 34 report that they check their Facebook accounts first thing in the morning, *before going to the bathroom*. In a world where the number of Google+ users has risen to nearly five million people mere months after the social networking site's launch in mid-2011, electronics and Internet-based communication are no longer the embodiment of the future—they are the reality of our present. Think about the technological advances made over the last several decades. If you are a recent high school graduate, you probably had access to computers in grade school, and learned to use PowerPoint (or other presentational software) in the first few years of your elementary education. If, however, your graduation from high school was some time ago, then using technology may not come as easily. For many, learning how to design presentational slides, incorporate YouTube videos, navigate the waters of the social networking world, and follow Tweets and blogs may be mysterious and intimidating.

Some of us still watch television or movies in the living room, but a growing number now use computers to access shows through Hulu and Netflix. These popular web sites enable a viewer to access a variety of movies and television series with the click of a mouse. We use our laptops for word processing, entertainment, education, and to continuously connect with others. What's more, we increasingly engage in multitasking. One of the authors of this textbook reported that it is not uncommon for her to be watching a movie on her laptop while returning student emails on her tablet while *simultaneously* reading status updates on Facebook and replying to incoming text messages on her Blackberry **smartphone**. Is this mélange of communication modalities a highly effective use of time or an opportunity for information overload and burnout?

Our **geosocial network**, that is, the short-range and long-distance social ties established through **online social networks** (OSNs) has changed dramatically. The 100 millionth MySpace account was created in August, 2006. However, by July of 2010, Facebook had moved to the second most popular site. MySpace (which recently made a bizarre Prince-like attempt to update its name with a symbol, "My_") has faded in popularity, becoming, in turn, a veritable social networking relic. Consider the number of users for the following social networks as reported in May of 2011 (Lorento, 2011):

- Skype—663 million
- Facebook—629 million
- Qzone—480 million
- Hotmail—364 million
- Yahoo! Mail—273 million
- Twitter—200 million
- Google+—5 million

smartphone
Any cellular device that possesses call making capabilities as well as Internet access, email ability, still and video cameras, MP3 player, video viewing, and built-in applications.

geosocial network
Short-range and long-distance social ties established through online social networks (OSNs) like Facebook, LinkedIn, Flickr, and Twitter.

online social networks (OSNs)
Web sites where one connects with those sharing personal or professional interests, place of origin, education at a particular school, and other identifying characteristics.

Based on these numbers, it is probable that you and most of your friends, family members, coworkers, and acquaintances use one or several of these to communicate on a daily basis. The fact is, whether we like it or not, we cannot put the digital influence back in Pandora's Box. Instead, we must analyze how it affects our lives and learn how to best manage it.

This chapter will examine how technology relates to the public speaking context we have developed in this textbook. First, we will explore the pervasiveness of technology. Then, we will discuss positive and negative aspects of using technology in public speaking. Next, we will identify ways to include technology such as presentation software, video and audio clips, and more in your presentations. Finally, we end the chapter with options and ideas for using technology in a manner that best represents yourself and your communication capabilities.

© 2012 dani3315, Shutterstock, Inc.

FIGURE 13.1　For most of us, technology is a fundamental part of our daily existence.

The online lesson provides links to the latest statistics on Internet usage, so you can learn more about our technological habits. See Topic 1.

13.1 The Pervasive Nature of Technology

Technology is paradoxically ever-present and invisible to most of us. That is, it is such a natural part of our lives that we often fail to acknowledge our frequent usage of it. For example, you do not think about every breath you take each day, you simply breathe; much like this innate process, technology use has become so intrinsic to our everyday experience that we are not cognizant of how it commands our mind. A study featured in the 2011 documentary, *Crackberry'd: The Truth About Information Overload*, revealed that college students do not realize how their constant use of cell phones distracts them from what's taking place in their surroundings. To demonstrate this, researchers had a clown ride a unicycle in circles in a crowded area of a campus quad and found that only 25 percent of the students who were looking at their cellular devices noticed the clown. This means that a whopping 75 percent of the cell phone using students saw *nothing* out of the ordinary, all the while believing that they were sufficiently aware of their surroundings. While innovation undeniably has improved our lives and our ability to communicate, it also poses new challenges to the quality of our communication.

© 2012 Kurt K. Weiss, Shutterstock, Inc.

FIGURE 13.2 Studies show that our habitual cell phone usage can distract us from noticing what is going on around us.

"We cannot *not* communicate" is a communication axiom developed by Paul Watzlawick (1967). This suggests that in face-to-face communication, even when we choose to *not* speak, we are still communicating a message through our silence and our nonverbal communication. Our clothing, hairstyle, posture, eye contact (or lack thereof), scent, and accessories all send messages whether we want them to or not. A similar case can be made for communicating through technology. "We cannot *not* communicate" here, too. Our status updates, tweets, emails, and uploaded pictures convey information about us, but instead of simply being communicative while "in the moment," these entities exist for access online indefinitely. We often do not know when someone is looking, or, in unwanted cases, "lurking," at our profile pictures (unless they choose to leave a comment). What may be meant for an isolated moment is often on the Internet for all time and the Internet has a way of establishing identity, good or bad. On recent dating show, a father asked the potential suitors of his daughter, "If I searched your name on the Internet, what would I find?" This singular question demonstrates the ability for the Internet to shape other's impressions of our selves. If you want to read the tweets of someone you follow, you are not limited to the most recent tweet only; you can go way back to tweets sent months prior, when that person was in a different frame of mind than they currently are. Additionally, while we might choose to unplug our technology, ignore messages, or even deactivate our Facebook account; those decisions clearly send a message or contribute to an undesired result as well. Arguments and hurt feelings can abound when one doesn't text message another back, return a voice mail or send an email reply. Even text messaging someone hours later than their original text can incite irritation ("You took long enough!") Harsher messages are communicated when you "de-friend" a Facebook friend or do not accept another's BlackBerry Messenger (BBM) request. These actions, committed with the instant click of the "ignore" button, say, "I do not want a relationship with you," "I am angry with you," or "You do not matter in my life." Even being in areas without access to technology can communicate messages that incur panic to friends and family. Think back to how many times you may have accidentally left your cell phone at home, been too busy at work to answer a text, or found yourself in a "dead zone" without adequate coverage while a significant other is trying to contact you; often, because they are so used to a quick response, they assume the worst (In an accident? Kidnapped? Facing a life-threatening situation?)

© 2012 Oleksiy Mark, Shutterstock, Inc.

FIGURE 13.3 When is the last time you remember turning off your cell phone for any significant period of time? Because technology is portable, some individuals in our lives expect us to always be available to communicate.

13.1.1 The Impact of the Internet

Because technology is so pervasive in the United States and a great deal of the rest of the world, it is difficult to avoid; those who choose to "turn off and tune out" are also communicating something about themselves, their worldview, and their preferred interaction venues. Many find it odd, or even alarming, when they "Google" someone and find no online presence. One of the authors of this textbook has both a husband and a brother without Facebook profiles; while professional and personable, they simply are not interested in connecting with others through this medium. However, the reactions they get from individuals who hear that they are not "on Facebook" are usually the same—"What, why are you off the grid?" "How do you keep in touch with others?" or "What do you do for fun, then?" Simply stated, our usage *or* avoidance (either intentional or unintentional) of technology possesses the capacity to communicate just as much as our face-to-face interactions do.

The Internet, which serves as the nucleus for most technology-based entities, is such an implicit part of our lives that it is difficult to imagine what we did without it. According to Internet World Stats from June, 2010, more than 77 percent of the people in the United States have home Internet access, as compared to 26 percent of the rest of the world. In the United States, libraries are even quieter these days, as 87 percent of adults use the Internet for their information resource and research needs (pewinternet.org, 2010). We do not, however, just use the Internet for research; studies show we rely on it for other important reasons in our daily lives. Fifty-four percent of adults used the Internet in the 2010 election cycle (Smith, 2011) in one way or another to further political ends or learn more about candidates and issues, and 47 percent of American adults now use their cell phones and tablet computers to get local news and information (Purcell et al., 2011). And this pervasive trend is growing in the United States and abroad.

13.1.2 Technology's Influence in Our Daily Lives

Worldwide, we know that technology has influenced rescue efforts and political action. For example, research shows that in September, 2009, social networking sites facilitated disaster relief operations when Typhoon Ondoy caused destruction and flooding in the Philippines (Morales, 2010). More recently, technology was critical to the Egyptian revolution. Egyptian activist Wael Ghonim, who used Internet social networking sites to spark a revolution in the Spring of 2011, states that, "YouTube, Twitter, and Facebook helped people realize they weren't alone in their frustration and that others shared their dream of freedom. It dawned on them that they could use the Internet to organize" (Zetter, 2011). Internet-based social networking sites not only spark political revolutions, they also help to pass the time. Research by Nielsen reports that U.S. Internet users spend 23 percent of their time using social networking platforms (Hickey, 2010). And it is not just for the young. According to thenextweb.com, some 47 percent of Internet users aged 50 to 64 are social networkers and Twitter users are older than one might expect, with the average age of tweeters at 39 years old. Additionally, **cloud computing**, which allows a user to store and access documents and programs on an Internet based service provider like Amazon, Verizon Terremark, and IBM, (rather than a traditional computer desktop) is also rising in popularity. In fact, research by the Pew Internet Research Center (2010) reveals that the computer desktop may be a thing of the past by 2020, and predicts that most individuals will work mostly through cyberspace-based applications accessed through network devices like laptops and smartphones.

Clearly, technology has its tentacles in business, education, and pleasure. Many meetings that used to take place in a face-to-face setting are being replaced by **videoconferencing**. More and more employees are finding themselves able to avoid a stressful commute by working from their "home office," as long as they have solid connectivity to the Internet as well as access to email and a cell phone. Courses that used to be accessible only in a face-to-face setting are now available in a online distance-learning format that uses web cams, video lectures, interactive Internet-based activities and online drop boxes that often allow for 24/7 accessibility. Tools such as free courses online at iTunes U. offers a lifetime learner the ability to gain knowledge on any subject with the click of a mouse. In many colleges and universities, entire accredited degree programs can be completed without a student ever needing to leave the comfort of his or her own home. Traditional forms of technology, specifically television and radio are being supplanted or supplemented by the Internet. That is, either people are no longer tuning in to their televisions and radios, or they are on the Internet as they watch their televisions and listen to their music. In addition to using computers, the relative affordability of smartphones (like iPhones, BlackBerrys, and Androids) and their accompanying data plans allows individuals to text and receive email on the go, use the Internet to instantly access information, social networking web sites, **blogs**, **webcasts**, and **podcasts,** as

cloud computing
A general term for anything that involves delivering hosted services over the Internet.

videoconferencing
Two-way, real-time transmission of audio and video signals between specialized devices or computers at two or more locations via satellite (wireless) over a network such as a LAN or the Internet.

blog
Short for "weblog," it is a web site that contains an online personal journal with reflections, comments, and often hyperlinks provided by the writer.

webcast
To send live audio or video to the user from a web site. It is the Internet counterpart to traditional radio and television broadcasting.

podcast
A multimedia digital file made available on the Internet for downloading to a portable media player, computer, or other digital device.

well as to fulfill our entertainment needs through YouTube, iTunes, and live television applications. Smartphones have further revolutionized the consumer industry as **QR codes** (*quick response codes*), which are two-dimensional matrix barcodes able to be scanned by a camera-enabled mobile device (such as a smartphone or tablet) and link to additional digital content on the web, have began to pop up everywhere, from magazine advertisements and shelves at the grocery store to church service bulletins and real estate "for sale" signs.

QR codes
Two-dimensional matrix barcodes, also known as *quick response codes*, that, upon scanning with a smartphone camera, link digital content on the Internet to activate a number of phone functions, including email, IM and SMS and connect the mobile device to a web browser.

scan

info...
http://..
text...
data...

© 2012 Artsous, Shutterstock, Inc.

FIGURE 13.4 The rise in popularity of QR codes has further enhanced the utility of our mobile devices, making digital content instantly available after a quick scan.

In sum, technology is ubiquitous. We use technology for all levels of communication—intrapersonal, interpersonal, group communication, mass communication, and public speaking. Technology also changes rapidly, which means we need to adapt. As new technology arrives, we must evaluate how it might aid or hinder the quality and effectiveness of our communication. This next section discusses several benefits and costs related to the use of technology when speaking in public.

The online lesson provides you with an exercise that presents and tests your knowledge of various communication modalities. See Topic 1.

e-learn

13.2 Rewards and Costs of Using Technology in the Public Speaking Arena

Although we live in an electronic age and are disposed to use what is shiny, new, readily available, and dazzling, it is important to keep the *quality* of our communication in mind as we sample all that technology has to offer. As we present ten rewards and ten costs of using technology to communicate and express ourselves in daily life, consider how your own interface with electronics applies. While there is much to be gained by effective use of technology as a speaker, ranging from smartphones to laptops, social networking sites to web cams, we must be mindful to let such mediums enhance, not compromise, the effectiveness of our communication powers.

13.2.1 Ten Rewards Associated with Technology

1. Communication Technology Is Time Effective

"Truth be told, when I am out all day, it is much faster for me to send an email from my smartphone than it is to turn on my computer and send it from my desktop," states one of the authors of this textbook. Sending a text message with relevant details can prove much faster than a long-winded phone call and posting pictures of your vacation on Facebook for your whole family can save you the time of sending them out individually or getting prints made at a local store. Furthermore, preparing some professional slides with presentational software can often take much less time than trying to create the equivalent with a poster board and markers, especially if you are not artistically inclined.

2. Communication Technology Is Portable

One of the authors of this textbook can remember when her cell phone broke in the mid-1990s and she was given a loaner phone while the original was being repaired. The replacement was the size of a brick—it couldn't fit in a purse, much less a pocket, and it had a minimum of features (basically a key pad and a "call" button).

Smartphones in Our Lives: A Blessing or a Curse?

In light of the way in which technology's features are most completely implemented by the power of the Internet-based smartphone, let's take a closer look at this growing trend and how it impacts our relationships, work life, and education.

© 2012 Tyler Boyes, Shutterstock, Inc.

Although smartphones can be a positive force for our productivity and connection with others, overuse of these devices can lead to squandered time and compromised face-to-face relationships.

Smartphones and Relationships

People walk, drive, sit, wait, eat, and sleep with their cell phones. A December 2010 survey revealed that 285 million Americans are mobile subscribers (CTIA—The Wireless Association). Research suggests that 91 percent of all Americans use cell phones (arstechnica.com) and this is not just an American phenomenon. In March, 2009, Reuters reported that a study by the broadband company Bitkom found that Germans in their twenties are typically more willing to give up their current partners or their cars than their mobile devices! Because a smartphone not only allows us to communicate with people but also to create content and surf the Internet with ease, it poses great temptation for most owners. In romantic relationships, a smartphone may be an easy way to cheat on a spouse. Because it is such a personal item, some individuals feel that they can pull off infidelity on their handheld without getting caught.

However, a 2011 article by divorce lawyer Paul Talbert argued that, in his experiences, virtually every cheating spouse is exposed through his or her indiscreet emails, text messages, or their illicit whereabouts confirmed on a smartphone's geotagging feature. Even if it is not used to cheat, a smartphone can still harm our important relationships. A 2011 documentary on Blackberry trends revealed that, on average, smartphone users look at their phones up to

How times have changed! Handheld devices have become so compact that you can carry your entire life around in an object that weighs less than a pound. Whether it is a Blackberry Torch or a MacBook Air, portable technology devices are able to manage our business life, personal life, and even school life with ease. Throw in a 256-gigabyte thumb drive (which is approximately the size of a house key) for good measure, and you have the memory power of 100 computers from the 1970s. As mentioned earlier in this chapter, cloud computing takes this notion of portability to the next level, since all an individual may need to access thousands of personal and work-related files is a Internet-enabled device, cloud service, and an online connection.

3. Communication Technology Is Instantaneous

Firing off a text message from your mobile device, sending an email, posting a status update, or putting forth a tweet takes a matter of moments and then becomes instantly available to your intended audience. This speed is unmatched in traditional formats, since even using the phone requires us to endure ringing and perhaps an answering machine. Technology has fueled our need for speed and anything less feels archaic.

200 times a day and spend between 10 seconds to one minute at a time with each glance. In an effort to "stay connected," the opposite result can occur. This behavior says, "I don't care about you," "I am important and you are not," and "The people with whom I communicate over my phone take priority over the ones sitting right in front of me." Think twice about the messages you may be conveying when you pick up your cell phone—real people have feelings, your smartphone doesn't.

Smartphones and Work Life

Most of us also take for granted our easy access to the net and how it plays into our jobs. The workforce is so entrenched in Internet reliance that when connectivity is down, the business world is virtually paralyzed and productivity dramatically comes to a halt. Smartphones were introduced as a way to maximize productivity, however a Carleton University study featured in the 2011 film *Crackberry'd* revealed that before receiving a Blackberry, employees in the sample size worked an average of 47 hours a week; a month after receiving a Blackberry, the weekly hours of work skyrocketed to just over 70 hours. This study is reflective of the "productivity paradox," which states that the more time we invest tinkering with our smartphones, the less truly productive we are (and the more time we spend working on the same tasks). All

of those "Words with Friends," "Farmville" and Facebook breaks do really add up. Also, since we never quite "get away from work," smartphones can also lead to increased levels of stress, anxiety, sleeplessness, and a general sense of feeling overwhelmed with the inability to "catch up." Smartphones can streamline our efforts at work, but should be carefully let into some areas of our lives, while judiciously barred from others.

Smartphones and Education

In the case of education, smartphones come in second in utility to laptops, which students regularly use in class to take notes, download slide presentations, and search for resources. However, more and more students report ease in using text messaging to take notes or using cell phone programs (like Word to Go) to complete assignments. Starting in 2008, Yale University even implemented a text messaging system called zuku that allows students to use their cell phones to send questions, take brief quizzes, and share comments for a particular class. However, unsolicited texting in class is a problem for many professors. Since it is considered rude, distracting, and disrespectful to both the instructor and fellow students, text messaging should be unequivocally avoided while in the traditional classroom.

4. Communication Technology Is Relatively User-Friendly

One of the authors of this textbook has an eight-year-old cousin who received an Android smartphone for her birthday. Despite the variety of features—Internet capabilities, ability to download music and games, and opportunities for social networking—she had absolutely *no* trouble figuring out how to use it in the first ten minutes that she owned it. Gone are the days of binary code and DOS, most technology is so user-friendly that a young child can handle it with ease.

© 2012 Aliaksei Lasevich, Shutterstock, Inc.

FIGURE 13.5 Did you have a cellular device as a baby? Cell phone usage among small children is on the rise and, for the rest of us, cell phones have become so integrated into our daily experience that it is almost impossible to remember what we ever did without them.

5. Communication Technology Is Creative

Technology has provided the masses with a host of creative outlets. Whether you are a musician with the opportunity to record an entire album in your bedroom using Garage Band or Pro Tools, a photographer who uses a smartphone and Instagram to share your latest vision, a singer who posts an a cappella song on YouTube, or an unemployed writer whose blog receives massive exposure and lands you the job of your dreams, your creative outlets are nearly limitless. Today, the Internet and all of its technical tangents has provided the world with a way to be creative as well as the ability to gain fans, supporters, and notoriety along the way.

6. Communication Technology Is Socially Inclined

It is simple: people keep in touch with other people through technology. Reconnecting with an old friend on Facebook or following the tweets of a cousin allow us to get close to individuals with which we would otherwise have difficulty interacting. Sending emails to friends across the country or the world is free and saves us the expense and complexity of long distance phone calls spanning different time zones. Technology has become the way to connect among people in the younger demographic categories and, in a good number of cases, defines the nature of our relationships. When meeting new people, the age-old sequence of small talk followed by phone number exchange, talking on the phone, hanging out, and becoming "an item" now seems replaced with talking on Facebook followed by text messaging,

Skyping, hanging out, *then* talking on the phone, only if in a committed relationship. One of the authors of this textbook who also works with high school students finds that most of her students do not even consider a romantic relationship official until a the designation of "boyfriend" or "girlfriend" has been posted on Facebook for all to see. In turn, maintaining friendships is difficult at best without texting, social networking, and email upon which to rely.

7. Communication Technology Is Entertaining and Novel

Let's face it; technology is just plain fun sometimes. Whether you are addicted to Angry Birds or eagerly reading about your best friend's proposal on Facebook, the entertainment factor that technology possesses is undeniable. Creating spoof videos to post on YouTube, playing Scrabble in real time with friends across the country, or adding the latest restaurant review to a personal food blog appeals to the desire we have for fresh and novel things. Technology allows us to embrace the new and try the unexpected.

8. Communication Technology Is Accessible

Useful technology is available at every major retailer in the country, to say nothing of the competitive commerce on the World Wide Web. Even if you do not have the funds to purchase the latest laptop or webcam, libraries, Internet cafes, and learning centers abound with free or inexpensive computer and Internet access. Additionally, anyone can set up a free email account with Gmail or Hotmail and, once Internet access is secured, blogging and social networking sites like BlogSpot, Twitter, YouTube, and Facebook are free to use.

© 2012 peruciatti/Shutterstock.com, Shutterstock, Inc.

FIGURE 13.6 Cybercafes and the availability of free Wi-Fi at coffee shops and other businesses have made the Internet, and the world of opportunity that it offers, accessible and inexpensive.

9. Communication Technology Is Appealing to Different Learning Styles

Not everyone learns the same way; while some individuals can hear a lecture and recall all important points a day later, others require visual components for the content to really soak in. Kraus (2008) concluded that mixed modality presentation (auditory and visual) is superior for recall, regardless of whether the presentation is concurrent or sequential or whether materials are presented once or twice. Technology gives you the power to forever etch information and images into the minds of a variety of listeners. Speakers are told that the more senses you engage, the more your audience will remember. Do you recall a television commercial asking you to assist starving children or neglected pets? These pitches are persuasive and memorable because of the tragic and compelling pictures they offer us. Through video sharing web sites like YouTube, bleekr.com, and Yahoo video, you could easily find footage of a tornado in full fury, the war in Pakistan, and police attacking civilians in the latest Middle East revolution. It is important to keep this in mind: visuals should rarely stand alone. When an audience is shown the devastating effects of a tornado via video, the prudent speaker might verbally clarify, elaborate, or refer to the visual images in an effort to create the most effective message.

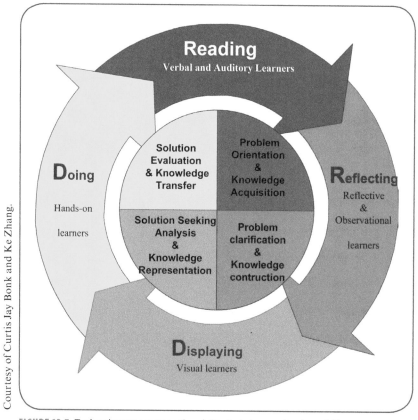

Courtesy of Curtis Jay Bonk and Ke Zhang.

FIGURE 13.7 Technology possesses the ability to bring a mixed modality to your presentation, in turn attracting both visual and auditory learners in your audience.

10. Communication Technology Can Be a Direct Aid for Public Speaking

As noted above, technological elements like presentational software, videos, images, and audio clips can be an excellent addition to a speech presentation. Additionally, smartphones and tablets (like the iPad and BlackBerry Playbook) can serve a very important role in delivery. Many public speaking classrooms across the nation allow students to use their mobile devices as notes during a speech. Putting your speaker's notes or speech outline into a Word document or slide show program on your mobile device allow you to access the content you need in an streamlined package that can be glanced at without much effort or distraction.

13.2.2 Ten Costs Associated with Technology

1. Communication Technology Is Impersonal

When a speaker uses no technology, the audience must focus on the speaker. One of the speaker's tasks is to create a connection with the audience through content, personality, language, and movement. When technology is used, focus often shifts. One fear is that the slides *become the message* rather than *the means* to enrich the message. It is possible that presenters "forego an important opportunity to connect with the audience as human beings" (Alley & Neeley, 2005, p. 418). The concern that technology may hamper the speaker audience connection is echoed by Peter Norvig, Director of Research at Google. He argues that a slide presentation may reduce the speaker's effectiveness because "it makes it harder to have an open exchange between presenter and audience to convey ideas that do not readily fit into outline format" (Norvig, 2003, p. 343). In other formats, there is nothing more personal than a face-to-face greeting, a handwritten note, or a personalized email. Mass texts and forwards, while effective in reaching a large audience instantly, often dehumanize the message and cause receivers to feel distant from the sender. In turn, use technology when it best suits the moment, but don't let it be a stand in for your humanity.

2. Communication Technology Subjugates Face-to-Face Communication and Real Relationships

Although the social aspect to technology is undeniable, it can also be harmful to relationships. An Oxygen Media 2010 study on Facebook behavior found that desperate, negative relational behaviors can prevail. For example, 58 percent of the young women surveyed use Facebook to keep up with "frenemies" and 50 percent are fine with being friends with total strangers. Combine that with the false sense of authentic friendship cultivated by constantly reading status updates and many individuals find that social networking replaces a considerable amount of time spent with actual people. The quality of these relationships is further challenged by the theory of **Dunbar's number**, which posits that the amount of people an individual can maintain stable social relationships with is no more than approximately 150. Instead of a small collection of carefully selected and honed personal relationships, we may instead create a massive network of weak ties with others (socialmediatoday.com, 2010). Throw in the lure of RPG (role playing video games) that allow individuals to create "avatars" and interact with others in a virtual world and, when taken to the extreme, there is little need to leave the house because the line between the virtual world and the real world can test this theory by noting how many people are walking around with their phones in hand, heads cast down transfixed by the glow of the screen. One of the authors of this textbook notes that a decade ago, when one of her classes would have a break, students would head out of the classroom and spend their time speaking with each other. Now, the instant that a break occurs, their hands are reaching for their phones, so that they might read messages or contact others. Here they are, surrounded by humans, not connecting with anyone in their proximity. In turn, human contact skills like nonverbal communication, eye contact, and comfort in social situations will continue to suffer until we reach a healthy balance with technology.

Dunbar's number
A theoretical cognitive limit to the number of people with whom one can maintain stable social relationships in which an individual knows who each person is and how each person relates to every other person. This number is commonly cited at approximately 150.

3. Communication Technology Can Foster Self-Centeredness

An obsession with technology can convey a very self-centered vibe to others. Most technological mediums involve an element of "self"—that is, tweeting, status

© 2012 Yuri Arcurs, Shutterstock, Inc.

FIGURE 13.8 How many relationships can an individual realistically cultivate and maintain? The theory of Dunbar's number states that number is no more than 150, a total much smaller than the average number of "friends" most individuals have through social networking web sites.

updates, text messaging, and blogging usually are about the person doing the posting. While sharing the birth of a new baby or a job promotion might be absolutely appropriate, too much posting about trivial things (like buying new shoes, having a guy flirt with you, or stumbling in drunk one night) can come across as bragging or worse, "too much information" (TMI). Think twice about what you post and understand that everything you share is constructing a salient image of yourself.

4. Communication Technology Offers Little to No Filter

Because there is very little gatekeeping in technological mediums, specious content finds its way into the Internet, social networking sites, and other web sites with ease. Additionally, the speed at which we can transmit unfiltered messages technologically can sometimes land us in trouble. A hastily written text, angry email, or irritated status update or post can have irreversible effects once made public. Also, rumors spread like wildfire on the Internet, and, much like the classic game of telephone where the original message gets twisted, distorted, and downright false as its shared amongst multiple individuals, what gets passed along online can be far from the actual truth. Finally, because anyone can post, upload, or forward anything (Wikipedia!) without any reasonable checks and balances, the credibility of information found online should be assessed before it is accepted as true. If you are unsure about the accuracy of a forwarded email you receive, you can check www.snopes.com (an objective, nonpartisan organization that strives to clear rumors and confirm the truth through research) to see if it is based in logic and reality. Be wise about what you believe and test the veracity of information found though technological mediums.

5. Communication Technology Sometimes Lacks Immediate Feedback

Have you ever sent a text message and waited hours, even days, to receive a response? This period of delay could be the result of a myriad of reasons—the recipient lost her phone, was out of a service area, was tied up at work, *truly* didn't receive the message, or just didn't want to return your missive. Unlike face-to-face conversations that allow us to gauge others and receive feedback immediately (whether we like said feedback or not is another story), technology-mediated communication has unlimited potential for delays. The fact that most of our electronic communication is instantaneous further compounds the issue. In most cases, we are used to getting responses immediately, and when we do not, even if there is a good reason, we are impatient, irritated, and at times, obsessive about not hearing back. This unhealthy fixation with immediate gratification in technological communication puts us at the mercy of electronics and creates a lack of attention span, focus, and discipline on our otherwise adult mentalities. In turn, be patient when sending and receiving technologically mediated communication; there is bound to be something productive you can do to pass time in the meanwhile.

6. Communication Technology Limits Nonverbal Cue Recognition

We are only getting part of the message when engaging in technology-mediated communication. In modalities like tweets, status updates, text messages, and blogs, we may *think* we are getting all that the sender intended to convey, however, we are missing vocal tone, emphasis, articulation, eye contact, body language, and even the sound of the voice. These elements collectively are imperative to send a rich and full-bodied message; without them, we are simply getting a shell. If we are not careful, our constant exposure to these mediums can begin to feel like the norm and, instead of a three-dimensional living, breathing person with many complex dimensions, we settle for the two-dimensional version as authentic enough. While using videoconferencing tools like Skype or the live video feature of an iPhone or other smartphone and add the missing physical dimension (e.g., we can see who we are conversing with), the palpable energy that two people share when in close proximity is still absent. Individuals have tried to combat this issue, especially in text messaging and emails, by incorporating **emoticons**, which are usually derivatives of the "happy face" created by a colon and parentheses mark to communicate happiness, sadness, irritation, humor, or a wink. While these images may help to clarify when someone is joking or upset, they are mere substitutes for the real deal, otherwise known as human facial expressions.

emoticons
Usually derivatives of the "happy face" created by a colon and parentheses mark to communicate emotions like happiness, sadness, irritation, or humor through the use of punctuation marks; typically used in text-based communication such as text messaging or email.

© 2012 Yuri Shchipakin, Shutterstock, Inc.

FIGURE 13.9 Emoticons help us to clarify the various emotions and moods that are generally difficult to convey accurately through our text-based communication, like email and text messaging.

7. Communication Technology Can Be Time Consuming

The hours spent engaged in technological activities can dramatically add up. In the documentary *Crackberry'd* (2011), it was revealed that young adults spend an average of two hours and 41 minutes a day watching television, and 55 percent of young people spend at least nine hours a week (though that number has been known to be higher in other studies) social networking online (either at a computer or on their cell phones) while devoting *only an hour* a week to studying for class. This imbalance can occur without the individual even realizing it; a Facebook check here or a catch up on your favorite show ("Bravo *was* running the entire season of *The Real Housewives of Beverly Hills* all in one afternoon, so I actually *saved* time") there, and, before you know it, major hours have been lost with nothing much to show for them. We've all probably gotten on the Internet to research for an assignment and, before we know it, what should have taken us 20 minutes morphed into two hours because of our "fall down the rabbit hole" comprised of "brief" visits to the Drudge Report, TMZ, and ESPN. It is a dangerous pattern that can only be fought with carefully calibrated time spent with technology—there is a whole world out there!

8. Communication Technology Is Potentially Dangerous

Did you know that technology can be dangerous to your health? In 2008, a twelve-year-old boy underwent leg amputation because of a thrombosis that occurred as a result of inactivity from too many hours spent playing video games. You probably have heard about the young man in China who died in 2007 after playing World of Warcraft (WoW) on his computer for seven days straight. Even text messaging can be hazardous, especially while driving. A 2009 study by the Virginia Technical Institute revealed that at any given moment, 10 percent of drivers are using their cell phones, on average, those who are texting look away from the road for 4.6 seconds (which is translate into driving the length of a football field) and are 23 times more likely to be in an accident from text messaging. Technology has its place, but must be used in the proper context in order to stay healthy and alive.

9. Communication Technology Creates Greater Opportunity for Misunderstandings

As mentioned in item 6 above, because the entire nonverbal element of communication is compromised in this modality, technology-mediated communication is rife for misunderstandings. Information of a dubious nature is posted and passed along so quickly, that drama can ensue in seconds. Factor in the fact that we often do not have the luxury of getting a face-to-face explanation of the content conveyed and anything from an ambiguous status update to precarious posted image can have detrimental and lasting effects of relationships, even when the reality is a misunderstanding, rather than a bona fide problem. So much energy gets expended in these situations and they often require individuals otherwise unrelated to the situation to "take sides" or join in, just because they are in geosocial proximity to the primary people involved. Always try to play the "devil's advocate" when processing technologically communicated content; misunderstandings and drama can be avoided when we give people the benefit of the doubt until they have a chance to clear the air in a face-to-face context.

10. Communication Technology Can Be Unreliable and Crippling

Murphy's Law states, "whatever *can* go wrong *will* go wrong." When relying heavily on technology in your presentations, be sure to double check your files and connections and have a backup plan should your technology fail. Furthermore, sending important messages via text or email should be done with caution because technology can fail; it is difficult to calibrate how many business or personal relationships falter because of technology that "doesn't go through." The only fail-safe way to deliver vital content is face-to-face or via certified mail. Finally, those of you who have left your cell phone at home understand this last point: the absence of your handheld device can be a terrifying and crippling experience. You feel naked or worse, you have the overwhelming need to call everyone to tell them you don't have your phone, except you don't have your phone. We all need a little space from technology and need to see it for what it is—a collection of inanimate objects that can fail us, *not* our life's blood.

Clearly, public speakers must take into the account both the rewards and the costs when negotiating the role that technology will play in their lives. Striking a careful balance that reaps the benefits while avoiding the disadvantages is key when using technological communication in all of its facets.

Internet Addiction: Are You Living Virtually or Virtually Living?

You probably know someone who has struggled with alcohol, tobacco, or drug addiction, but how many individuals do you know with an Internet addiction?

- Generally speaking, the signs of Internet addiction disorder (IAD) include emotional attachment to online friends and activities; preoccupation with the Internet; repeated unsuccessful efforts to control, cut back, or stop Internet use; jeopardized or risked loss of significant relationships, job, educational, or career opportunities because of Internet use; dishonesty or secretiveness with Internet usage; and the use of the Internet as a way to escape problems or relieve a dysphoric (or depressed) mood. Recovery programs exist to help individuals who suffer such symptoms; their primary tactics for addiction reversal include technology deprivation and a focus on the "here and now."

- According to the 2011 documentary *Crackberry'd*," 6 to 10 percent of all people online in the United States meet the criteria for Internet addiction. This, however, is not just an American problem. In fact, South Korea and China have both declared Internet addiction as their number one health threat.

- If you are wondering whether you have an Internet addiction, there are free quizzes that you can access online to assess your symptoms. To meet the needs of those who find themselves suffering from symptoms, the first addiction recovery program for Internet addiction disorder in the United States, called reSTART, opened in 2009 in Fall City, Washington.

- Unlike drug addiction, you probably cannot simply avoid and abstain using the Internet for good even upon recovery; it is too central to our economy, our jobs, our education, and our personal lives to be completely ignored.

13.3 Using Technology Effectively in Public Speaking Situations

Today's technologies provide each of us with a "public" presence never before available. With social websites for fun, career networking, or valued interest, we not only glean information but also create our own public presence—presenting ourselves and our interests in a unique way. Further, videoconferencing with potential employers using a tablet or smartphone gives us a very real presence to them. It is important to know how to clearly show our best self within current technologies.

The effective use of presentation software is expected by today's audiences, who were largely raised in the media era (Cyphert, 2007). When developing visuals for your audience, Professor Edwin Tufte, an expert in the visual representation of technical data, offers a stern warning: "...failure to think clearly about the analysis and the presentation of [visual] evidence opens the door for all sorts of political and other mischief to operate in making decisions" (Tufte, 1997, p. 52). In other words, poorly conceived or executed visuals, PowerPoint or otherwise, opens one to trouble. Clearly, paying attention to the visual message is critical to effective speaking.

You probably learned how to create a slide-oriented presentation well before you reached college. By now, you have probably seen hundreds, if not thousands, of PowerPoint presentations. This rise in use is surely because effective computer-generated graphics can have a great impact on listeners, but not always. Too many slides, coupled with a dry, monotonous delivery, spells disaster. "Some of the world's most satisfying naps, deepest daydreams, and most elaborate notebook doodles are inspired by the following phrase, 'I'll just queue up this PowerPoint presentation,'" states Josh Shaffer, staff writer for the Raleigh, North Carolina *News & Observer* (April 27, 2006).

13.3.1 Choosing Effective Presentational Aids

Some scholars are concerned that when students give speeches with "poorly designed and poorly performed multimedia," they create ineffective presentations; therefore students must learn to "distinguish ineptitude from eloquence" in accompanying multimedia (Cyphert, 2007, p. 187). In other words, beginning speakers typically lack skill in public speaking as well as creating presentational aids. For this reason, we include guidance for using presentational software. Although aimed primarily at computer-generated graphics, much of the following applies to all presentational aids.

1. Choose a presentational aid that fits your purpose, the occasion, and your audience.
Develop a clear specific purpose early in the creative process. If you begin with a specific purpose in mind that fits your goals, the audience's needs, and the requirements of the occasion, you are more likely to find and use relevant technology. Katherine Murray, author of more than 40 books on computers, offers the suggestion, "Start with the end in mind" (www.microsoft.com). Knowing what you are trying to accomplish should guide you in designing accompanying multimedia presentations.

In addition to choosing a presentational aid that suits your purpose, you should also choose aids that are appropriate for the occasion. Certain situations are more serious, professional, intimate, or formal than others. Displaying a cartoon during a congressional hearing, for example, may diminish the credibility of the speaker.

As you determine your purpose, ask yourself whether the visual support is right for your listeners, considering their age, socioeconomic backgrounds, knowledge, and attitudes toward your subject. Consider their sensibilities, as some listeners are offended by visuals that are too graphic. Pictures of abused children, for example, can be offensive to an audience not prepared for what they will see. If you have doubts about the appropriateness of a visual, leave it out of your presentation.

2. Emphasize only relevant points.

Do not be "PowerPointless," a word coined by Barb Jenkins of the South Australia Department of Education Training and Employment. Avoid "any fancy transitions, sounds, and other effects that have no discernible purpose, use, or benefit" (www.wordspy.com). The bells and whistles may be fun, but they can be annoying, or worse, distracting.

We have all seen PowerPointless presentations. One slide has the words "The facts" on it, and that is all. A second slide says "The causes," and a third slide says "The solution." Maybe each slide contains a cute picture, or perhaps there is an elaborate template. Lacking content, they were unnecessary.

In FIGURE 13.10, what features make the PowerPoint slide on the left ineffective? What features make the PowerPoint slide on the right highly effective?

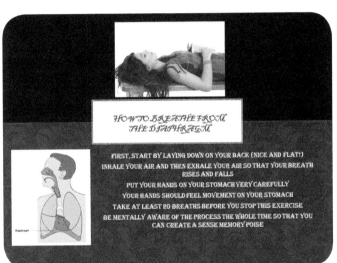
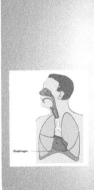

Courtesy of Rachel A. Wegter and Marie Hulett.

FIGURE 13.10 A well-crafted slide can make all the difference. Note how the "good" slide (on the right) abides by the "rule of six," uses an appropriate font, has contrasting colors, uses only one image, reflects correct spelling and grammar, and appears uncluttered. In contrast, the "poor" slide (on the left) does not follow the "rule of six"; it looks cramped and cluttered (packed with unnecessary text and images) and even includes a grammatical error ("laying" vs. the correct "lying"). As an audience member, which one would you want to see?

Implement "The Rule of Six" for Slide Presentations

- Use meaningful titles as content introduction.
- Use no more than six words per line and no more than six lines per slide.
- Avoid using full sentences—it should feel more like an outline than an essay.
- No more than six rows or six columns or six data points of data in a table to make it easier to read.
- The time spent speaking to each slide should be five to six minutes each.

In your desire to create an attractive, professional slide presentation, do not forget the message. It is easy to find tips on general design, the number of words per slide, number of slides, images, transitions, color, and so on. But after you select the presentational aid that meets your purpose most effectively, think about what information needs to be on each slide.

Link *only* the most important points in your speech with a presentational aid. Focus on your thesis statement and main points and decide what words or concepts need to be highlighted graphically.

The online course explores the major differences between effective and ineffective presentational slides. See Lesson 9, Topic 3.

3. Select appropriate design features.

Decisions need to be made regarding template, type of font, and color. The template, which provides color, style, and decorative accents, may be distracting to your audience if you change it regularly, so use one template consistently. One can accidentally waste a great deal of time trying to determine what font-type (typeface) to use. In general, select something simple. While font-types may look fun, intriguing, or dramatic, they may also be hard to read and distracting. Keep your audience focused on the message; they may be distracted from the text if you have moving animations, and slides filled with "special effects." Always use a font size of at least 30 for titles and headings and at least 24 for regular text; any smaller than this and the audience in the back of the room will likely have difficulty reading your slides.

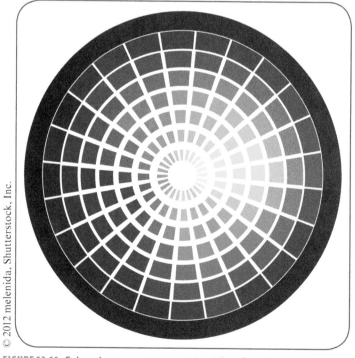

© 2012 melenida. Shutterstock, Inc.

FIGURE 13.11 Colors that appear on opposite sides of a color wheel are complementary colors. When placed next to each other, complementary colors make each other appear brighter and capture an audience's attention.

Make sure the font type and font color complement the template. Rely on strong, bold colors that make your message stand out even in a large auditorium. In their article "About choosing fonts for presentations", Microsoft Office Online suggests, "To ensure readability, choose font colors that stand out sharply against the background" (Microsoft Office PowerPoint, 2003). The words you place on the slide should not melt into the background color. Aim for contrast but keep in mind that the contrast you see on your computer screen may not exist on the projected screen.

Research on college students shows that color aids students' ability to organize and recall information and to solve problems (Kraus, 2008). The color wheel shown in **FIGURE 13.11** will help you choose contrasting colors. You will achieve the strongest contrasts by using colors opposite one another. When these complements are combined, they produce distinct images. Blue and orange make an effective visual combination as do red and green, and so on. Colors opposite each other on this wheel provide the most striking contrasts for visual displays.

4. Avoid allowing your presentational aid to upstage you.

Keep in mind that your audience has come to hear you, not to see your presentational aids. If you create a situation in which the visual support is more important than the speaker or the purpose of the speech, you will have defeated your purpose and disappointed your audience.

Be protective of the beginning and end of your presentation. It is usually prudent to avoid using any presentational aid for the first few moments. After you set the tone of your speech and introduce your main idea, turn to your first aid. Likewise, do not use a presentational aid to end your speech—such a shift in focus risks the

© 2012 Alliance, Shutterstock, Inc.

FIGURE 13.12 If you choose to use a remote during your presentation, practice in advance to ensure that your slides transition with ease.

person-to-person contact you have built to that point. These are merely guidelines and some speakers have both begun and ended speeches effectively with well-selected media.

5. Preview and practice.

An inability to navigate smoothly through your slides limits your effectiveness (Howell, 2008). After creating your slides, run through them. Make sure slides are in the correct order, and that the font types, font colors, and font sizes you have selected are consistent. Proofread and run spell check. Make printouts of your slides. Then practice the speech using your slides. According to a 2009 survey, the most annoying aspect of the PowerPoint presentation is, "The speaker read the slides to us" (Paradi, 2009).

One way to avoid sounding as though you are reading to the audience is through practice. Adding some type of presentational aid makes practicing even more important because you do not want to disrupt the flow of your speech. A reflective pause after displaying a slide can be powerful (Howell, 2008).

During your practice session, focus on your audience, not your presentational aid. Many speakers turn their backs on the audience. They talk to the projection screen or poster instead of looking at the audience. To avoid this tendency, become familiar with your aid so that you have little need to look at it during your talk. Use a remote control, if possible, so you can move more freely in front of your audience.

13.3.2 Considerations for Technology-Mediated Communications

Technology is expanding in the direction of public speaking. Certainly, speeches have been broadcast via radio and television for generations. However, these events were coordinated and executed with a team of individuals connected to radio and television stations. Now, individuals can create and disseminate their own videos over the Internet, and some self-produced work goes "viral" on YouTube. Even text-messaging, tweeting, blogging and social networking, while not traditional public speaking modalities, enable you to express and represent yourself to a larger audience comprised of both individuals that you know and may not know. Understanding how to make these mediums best work for you, then, is imperative.

Although most speakers still work with a live audience, for numerous reasons, you may be required to record your speech. Technology, in this respect is the medium, or the channel through which your speech is presented. In this next section, we provide some suggestions for those specific, technology-mediated occasions ranging from on-camera work to social networking.

Speaking on Camera

You may find yourself facing traditional cameras, such as those associated with television stations, video cameras, or less traditional cameras, such as built-in or remote webcams, phone cameras, and even digital cameras with video capabilities. You may find yourself at times with, and at other times without, a live audience. With a live audience, you still need to follow the basic tenets of public speaking, and adapt your speech to the particular audience and situation. Without a live audience, your primary focus becomes creating a message that is conveyed effectively to your intended audience via your chosen medium. Adapting to the demands of the new channel becomes paramount if you are to succeed.

Think about politicians you've seen on television. Some presented themselves well enough that we listened to their speech, even if we disagreed. Others seemed less polished on television, and some probably pulled your focus off their message and put it squarely on their annoying characteristics. If you have a live audience, give the speech to them, and assume those who record you will do a good job. If you do not have a live audience, you should not "play" to the camera unless directed to do so. This does not mean you should ignore the camera. Treat the camera as another audience member. President Obama has many positive traits as a speaker, but on occasion, he turns his head to audience members on the left and right, and avoids looking forward, toward the camera. The result is the viewer may not feel as connected to the President during that speech. Eye contact should be direct and sustained, and strong speakers avoid moving their head or eyes too quickly.

Posture is important, and the camera may not be as forgiving of imperfections as a live audience. Keep your posture erect. Whether your speech is before a live audience or not, do not forget to gesture naturally. Be sincere and conversational. A recorded speech should be similar to a live audience, but those who are not part of the live audience do not share the same context.

When you know your speech will be recorded, consider the following checklist to help you best prepare.

- **Know your material:** Make sure that you have rehearsed what you plan to say on camera many times over; you should have an understanding of any emotional parts and ultimately, what the content means to you. Imagine that you are speaking to a close group of friends, this way you will come across as more sincere and conversational.

- **Choose your clothes and accessories wisely:** Dark, solid colors such as royal and navy blue and blacks work best on video. Select simple, classic garments (blouses, button-down shirts, slacks, blazers, and sweaters) and avoid anything ill fitting, wrinkled, soiled, low cut, too short, or too tight; when in doubt, err on the side of conservative. While certain light colors can be appropriate (especially pastels), pure white as well as green and red should be avoided as they create problems with lighting. Avoid stripes, intense patterns, clothing with writing on it, shiny fabrics, and sparkles, since they will pose distractions on screen. Footwear should also be chosen with care; consider how much walking you will be doing in front of the camera and select shoes that will not "clunk" in an audible manner (high heels are famous for this). Finally, be mindful of loose jewelry such as large watches or bangle bracelets which can noisily collide when you gesture; in turn, keep it simple.

- **Check "your set" before recording:** Be clear on the area in which you will be recording, make sure that it is a quiet place with a simple background. A short test run should confirm the battery life of the camera, that your microphone is working properly, and that the camera is recording as planned.

© 2012 withGod, Shutterstock, Inc.

FIGURE 13.13 When working with a teleprompter, rehearse your script in advance and aim to be sincere and conversational in tone so that the delivery feels natural and authentic.

- **Strive to be natural:** Try to treat the camera as another audience member; gesture naturally and keep it authentic. While some contexts might require a more professional tone, others will be better served with a casual approach. Analyze the intended audience and the subject matter you will be sharing to determine the tone that is most appropriate.

- **Consider all nonverbal speech elements:** Because when you are on camera, you will both be *seen* and *heard*, make sure to stand up straight, keep your arms free, smile pleasantly, use adequate volume, convey clear articulation (be crisp and avoid lazy speech), correctly pronounce words, and communicate using a relaxed and resonant voice.

teleprompter
A device for displaying prepared text to a speaker or performer.

In certain on-camera situations, you may find yourself getting the opportunity to work with a **teleprompter**. While this will not be a reasonable option for delivering your speeches for the course (they should be well rehearsed and extemporaneous rather than fully scripted), news anchors and television hosts use this format while filming for delivering precise information in a conversational manner. When working with a teleprompter, consider the following tips.

- Practice your script many times in advance so you are familiar with the content and the words become natural.

- Rehearse with your presentational aids in advance and be familiar with how much physical movement, if any, will be necessary to use them before you film. Know that your range of motion might be restricted by how the camera frames you and be aware that the microphone can pick up background noise. In turn, create aids that are portable, easy to read, and quiet (e.g., no jangling or rustling sounds are generated when you handle them).

- Do not be shy about determining the proper speed for your speech with the teleprompter operator; sometimes, experimentation is required at the start to get it right.

- Convey a heightened sense of emotion and energy through vocal variety and authentic facial expressions.
- Maintain eye contact (in most cases, the camera is in the screen of the teleprompter).
- *Think* about the meaning of what you are saying as you say it—do not just read it!
- Do not forget to gesture.
- *Enjoy* yourself—the more you take pleasure in the occasion, the easier teleprompter work becomes.

Radio

A speech on radio may be live or taped. You may have the option to edit your speech. If it is in front of an audience, you can't rewind and start again. Audience analysis is a critical element of public speaking. Unlike national and international politicians and dignitaries who may be heard on most radio stations, speeches you give will be heard locally or regionally. Therefore, it is important to have a basic profile of the listeners within that particular programming market. Establishing common ground is important, no matter the medium.

Once on air, focus on speaking clearly and passionately. Being alone in a room with a microphone may be difficult, but work to energize yourself and deliver your speech enthusiastically. Be aware that pauses seem longer when the listener can't see you, but are powerful tools. Since your audience cannot see you, their aware-ness of your pacing, articulation, and pronunciation becomes even keener. Work to strategically use pauses, and avoid nonfluencies such as "um," "er," "uh," "well uh," and so on.

As you craft your message for the radio audience, special attention to your main points, transitions, and supporting materials will help ensure effectiveness. Gener-ally, radio also requires us to make key points in shorter sentences. Audiences don't have eye contact, gestures, or presentational aids to help them understand your message. Use effective transitions that help your audience track where you are in your message. Phrases like "Now I will turn to my third point," or "To wrap this talk up," help your listeners understand where you are and where you are headed in your message. Further, anticipate audience questions, and structure your support material in a way that addresses them. If, for example, you anticipate many listeners might pose an objection to an idea you forward, you would be wise to articulate the objection yourself and then overcome it with additional support showing how their objection is inconsequential. This is key as your audience will not have the oppor-tunity to ask for clarification, and if not addressed, will surely work against you.

13.3.3 Types of Internet-Based Communication

Teleconferencing is a great way for businesses to conduct meetings when participants are in remote locations. Upon calling into the system at the designated time (begin-ning and ending on time is key), participants should say their first name before speaking to allow all individuals to know who is sharing. Additionally, one should allow for delays in audio transmission by speaking slowly. Because the audio com-ponent is the only element that participants can rely upon, make sure to conduct the call in an area with little to no background noise and use a landline if at all

teleconferencing
The holding of a conference among people remote from one another by means of telecommunication devices such as telephones.

possible. It is important to note that gaps of silence are reasonable to expect, so strive to create a space for everyone to speak and be as polite as possible since visual nonverbals are not present to clarify tone or meaning.

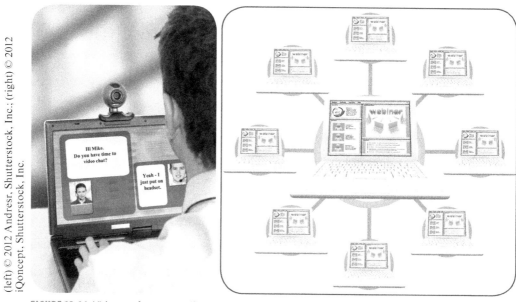

(left) © 2012 Andresr, Shutterstock, Inc.; (right) © 2012 iQoncept, Shutterstock, Inc.

FIGURE 13.14 Videoconferencing offers software has expanded our ability to connect synchronously in a "face-to-face" manner with individuals all over the world.

Unlike teleconferencing, videoconferencing has a visual component and can be set up in three different ways: computer-based system, desktop system, and studio-based system. A computer-based system is often the least expensive method, but its drawback is a lower degree of quality. In its essence, computer-based systems are often simply the combination of a webcam and free software like CUseeMe, iMeet, gotomeeting, Skype, Google Voice, Video Chat, and NetMeeting. A desktop system has dedicated software installed on the computer, which can improve the audio and video quality. The studio-based system offers the best quality, but is also the most expensive.

Videoconferencing is an obvious "green" technology. By communicating over video, organizations can also substantially reduce their carbon footprint. With tools that provide a powerful way to enable conferences and other video content to be streamed live or on demand around the world, we can communicate, engage, and interact with others across distance at any time, from wherever they are (polycom.com). The need to hop in a car or jet in many cases is now circumvented through these technologies. The effects of videoconferencing are evident in the airline industry. Hewlett-Packard, for example, has reduced its global travel by 43 percent (*Travel Weekly*, 2008). Travel management companies predict this trend toward videoconferencing to continue over the next several years.

While videoconferencing is often used for group meetings, the medium is used for public speaking, too. In a videoconference, whether it is a speech or a conference with other participants equally sharing, we encourage you to look into the camera to create eye contact. Avoid sudden abrupt or sweeping movements in order to prevent ghosting (motion blur), be mindful of nonverbal elements like tone and facial expression, turn off your cell phone to avoid potential distractions, and in general, move a little more slowly and deliberately than normal to compensate for audio delays.

Using **Skype** is similar to the computer-based system one would use in videoconferencing, but the major benefit is that it is free when used domestically and is generally less expensive than a long-distance phone call when used internationally. As noted earlier, Skype has more than 663 million current users. While many people use Skype to communicate interpersonally, it has clear public speaking application, and the system provides videoconferencing support.

You may also have an occasion to present at a **webinar**. Generally, a webinar is announced in advance, and people register for it. A date and time for attending via the web is provided. Depending on the situation, those who miss the webinar may be able to access a recording of it later. The audience participating in the webinar may have the opportunity to type questions or comments for the speaker. These questions can be monitored by a third person or by the speaker. This allows the speaker to clarify points, discuss related information, or respond to the audience in some directed manner.

Podcasts and Streaming Audio

Podcasts most generally are audio presentations. Individuals who produce their own podcasts may not edit their speeches. This leads to mixed success. Podcasts connected to organizations are more likely to have equipment and personnel to create a more polished end result. Podcasts such as "Jimmy's no-lose sports picks of the week," broadcast live from his parent's garage, on the other hand, can be quite low in production value.

As a speaker, it is important to remember that your audience may include people who are listening on their iPods, smartphones, tablets, and laptops while working out, sitting at their desk, or driving to work. Listeners may be multitasking. They may choose to skim the podcast and not catch the whole speech. Since they are not listening in real time, listeners may allow for distractions. Keeping in mind your listeners' attention span limitations, it makes sense to remind listeners who you are and what your central idea is more frequently in your podcast than in a traditional speech.

Chris Bjorklund, podcast editor for AllBusiness.com who spent 15 years on radio in the San Francisco Bay Area, offers several suggestions for creating effective podcasts. She emphasized that the quality of the audio is of utmost importance. Listeners will tune out if the podcast sounds as though it's coming from a hollow room or a tunnel. A bad connection, a hiss, or some other irritating sound "is a deal breaker." Her comments speak to the importance of listening to your surroundings while recording (Is the light buzzing or the air conditioner vent hissing?) as well as the quality of sound after you have a finished podcast.

Further, Bjorklund stresses the importance of sounding conversational, and not sounding as though you're lecturing the audience. Communicating energy and enthusiasm is necessary, and she encourages speakers not to "overscript." In other words, the message should not be memorized, and the speaker should focus on creating an effective speaker-audience connection that is less formal than a traditional speech. Striving for a middle ground between an extemporaneous speech and an informal interpersonal conversation can be difficult to get used to at first,

Skype
An IP telephony service provider that offers free calling between subscribers and low-cost calling to people who don't use the service. In addition to standard telephone calls, Skype enables file transfers, texting, video chat, and videoconferencing.

webinar
A workshop or lecture delivered over the Web. Webinars may be a one-way webcast, or there may be interaction between the audience and the presenters.

but is usually best received by audiences. She encourages individuals who podcast regularly to "brand" themselves by using the same, identifiable theme music to "bookend" the beginning and ending of the program. This will help standardize the podcast, enhance listening enjoyment, and create a sense of closure at the conclusion. Many radio talk show hosts use this technique and are identified, in part, by the "bumper" music that has become associated with them.

Email, Text Messaging, and Social Networking

This textbook has certainly made the point that Internet-based and digital communication is an integral part of many of our lives. Despite the fact that these modalities have the ability to shape our persona and create our image, there is very little by way of instruction on how to approach these mediums with prudence and wisdom. In order to make your online presence work for you, consider the following strategies for the effective use of technology-mediated communication:

- **The Internet is forever, so exercise restraint:** Once something is sent or posted online, it has become a part of your virtual irreversible paper trail. Inappropriate content can have extremely negative ramifications for the individual who posts it in a public forum. Take care not to reveal too much information, either in image or text formats and understand the power that your Internet-based sharing has. Currently, there is a trend among educational institutions and employers to monitor public and social networking sites; "crossing the line," whether it be lying about being sick, or picture of you "losing control," can result in expulsion or termination. These instances are more common than you may think. For example, a 2010 study by Oxygen Media concluded that 42 percent of young women think it

(left) © 2012 Joe Seer/Shutterstock.com, Shutterstock, Inc.; (right) © 2012 Left Eyed Photography/Shutterstock.com, Shutterstock, Inc.

FIGURE 13.15 In 2011, actor-comedian Gilbert Gottfried (left) and rapper 50 Cent (right) came under fire for inappropriate tweets that they posted. The fallout from their use of a popular technology modality is a good reminder for us to be careful about what messages we choose to share with the public.

is okay to post photographs of themselves intoxicated, while 54 percent of them do not trust Facebook with their private information. This apparent contradiction is indicative of the type of cavalier behavior going on online. While we may not want viewed by the wrong person, we still post it for most of the world to see. Additionally, what might seem cool or funny to share now, may not seem appropriate down the line. Avoid racist language, sexist words, and language that degrades any religion. YouTube rants and inappropriate tweets intended to "keep it real" or be humorous have landed individuals, both celebrities and noncelebrities, in very hot water. To avoid the need to apologize to the world, ask yourself if there is anyone who you would not like to see what you are about to post, and if the answer is "Yes," then ***do not*** post it.

- **Be mindful of your spelling, grammar, and capitalization choices:** Remember that proper spelling and grammar are a reflection of credibility and perceived intelligence (the ethos factor); in any text-based communication, avoid abbreviations (like TTYL for "talk to you later" or "U" for the word "you"), all capital letters (generally expresses yelling or anger), and slang.

- **Treat emails like a polite conversation:** When you are really furious with someone, you might be tempted to write an angry email (or text message) and press "send." This action can be done easily, from the comfort of our home (or phone), in a matter of seconds. Prior to the Internet, sending an angry letter required much more energy—you had to get a pen, paper, an envelope, an address, a stamp, and *then*, take it to a mailbox. If that letter *actually* got mailed, it is because you wanted it to be sent. Because they provide an irreversible trail, do not send emails in anger; allow some cooldown time. In cases not involving anger, carefully choose your words to reflect a polite and gracious tone that represents you in the best light possible when you cannot be in the room yourself. Use proper English (do not use "text message language" like "R U L8?") and spell words out correctly and completely. Always include a greeting ("Dear Kay" or "Hello David") and do not assume that the receiver knows that the message is from you; in other words, sign your name. Finally, make sure to put something relevant to your overall message in the subject line. If you are writing a note to a professor, for example, put the name of the class and the section number or times when the course meets so that your instructor can best process your question or comment in a swift and personal manner.

- **Adhere to workplace rules on Internet usage:** Do not abuse free Internet access that your job may offer. Limit web browsing to work-related sites only and avoid playing games, engaging in social networking, and forwarding emails that are nonbusiness related to business contacts via a work-provided email address. We all know the type: "Send this to 10 people or you will wake up with a pig's nose," "Forward this to your best girlfriends and if they send it back, then they are really your friends," or, even worse, some mockery of a political figure or the latest collection images of people shopping at Wal-Mart. To close, to establish and maintain a professional image, make sure that your Internet activity at work is completely related to your job responsibilities.

Using Technology to Provide Feedback

Traditionally, when a speaker is finished, the audience applauds. In some cases, listeners have the opportunity to ask questions. Speakers may also find themselves in situations where feedback response sheets are provided to the audience, and the speaker may read those immediately after the speech or when they are received via the mail. In classroom settings, instructors may provide immediate verbal and/or written feedback, and they may solicit immediate verbal and/or written feedback from members of the class. The amount and structure of feedback varies.

As technology advances, becomes less expensive and more readily available, methods for providing feedback are changing. Student and audience response systems such as TurningPoint and clickers are being used in the classroom to engage students. Instructors may include multiple-choice questions during a lecture that tests content comprehension, or they may insert opinion questions to gauge the students' attitudes or beliefs about material presented.

Similarly, a student response system can be used in an academic setting to provide anonymous feedback immediately after the speech. For example, after each speaker, classmates may be asked to identify how effective the speaker's organization was, the extent or which he or she used supporting material, how well the speaker used gestures, movement, eye contact, and so on. Information compiled can be sent immediately to the student.

Positive aspects of the student response system are that all listeners are engaged, and the speaker receives immediate, anonymous, structured feedback from all listeners. Negative aspects include the fact that questions are standardized; responses are a forced-choice of some type, and in-depth, immediate feedback does not occur. In a learning environment, anonymous comments can be negative or positive. The instructor, however, can analyze the data from all speakers and check for trends. Perhaps organization is a problem for most speakers in the class, or maybe most speakers do not include sufficient supporting material, and more time needs to be devoted to those aspects of public speaking.

In online public speaking classes, student speeches are often recorded, posted, and reviewed in an invitation-only discussion board. In these cases, students are often asked to view and then post feedback on colleagues' speeches. Quickly everyone in class gains from the perspectives of their colleagues. These discussions are particularly fruitful when an emphasis is placed on reinforcing speaker strengths, offering suggestions (as opposed to hammering the speaker over a weak area or flaw), and sharing relevant experiences. When discussions are positive and prosocial, feedback greatly assists speakers as they polish their craft.

Whether in a classroom setting or elsewhere, listeners can also use Twitter, Facebook, blogs, and email to provide feedback. For the speaker, immediate feedback is most useful. Using Twitter is a way to provide quick, concise feedback. Through Facebook and blogging, one can engage many members of an audience within a relatively short period of time. In whatever form, if the Internet is used for the purpose of providing feedback to speakers, one needs to remember proper "netiquette." Emails provide an irreversible paper trail. Once the message is sent, it cannot be retrieved.

When providing feedback via email, being polite and somewhat formal is preferable to being perceived as rude, aloof, or uneducated. Constructive criticism is acceptable; slamming a person is not. Avoid writing in all capital letters. Provide feedback as though you are part of the public speaking process too. As such, your credibility is at stake as well. Remember that proper spelling and grammar impacts your credibility, too.

In general, and specifically with social networking sites and blogging, take care not to reveal "too much information." Twitter limits your response length to 144 characters, but blogs and Facebook are very open ended. Focus on the speaker and the speech, not your own issues and personality. Above all, keep in mind that feedback is meant to identify the speaker's strengths, and to foster and encourage improvement.

The online lesson offers additional strategies to consider when using technology to communicate. See Topic 3.

© 2012 Lucky Business, Shutterstock, Inc.

FIGURE 13.16 Because the "Internet is forever," text and post with caution.

Chapter Summary

Technology is undeniably changing how we communicate and these changes, in turn, impact public speaking. The vast majority of Americans use the Internet daily, and most young adults have used computers all of their lives. We are able to write emails, blog, and Tweet, and are connected to various social networks. All these are the hallmarks of the electronic age in which we live. Technology is everywhere and inescapable, and it can be a valuable asset to the trained public speaker.

The advantages of using technology in communication include its time effectiveness, portability, instantaneous nature, relative ease, accessibility, relationship with socialization, entertainment factor, ability to reach different learning styles, and usefulness for public speaking. On the other hand, technology can be impersonal, harm face-to-face communication, cultivate a self-centered perspective, be unfiltered, limit nonverbal cue recognition, be time consuming, be a substitute for real relationships, create misunderstandings, and be unreliable.

For public speakers, choosing a presentational aid that fits the purpose, occasion, and above all is audience-centered is paramount. Presentational technology should be used when it emphasizes relevant points; adheres to the "Rule of Six"; offers appropriate design features; does not upstage; and is used comfortably because it has been well rehearsed.

Typically we give a speech before live audiences, but we may also record that speech for playback later. A speech may be given on camera (with or without a teleprompter), over the radio, during a video-conference, or presented as part of a webinar or podcast. Speakers using technology as a medium for their speeches make important adjustments when an audience is not "live" and face-to-face. These include dressing appropriately for the camera if present, communicating energy, articulating clearly, avoiding meaningless pauses and verbal fillers, and maintaining acceptable audio quality and sound levels.

Feedback is an important part of the speaking process and has also benefited from technology innovation. Listeners can provide immediate feedback through a student response system, or they may provide feedback through emails, blogs, or classroom or web-based discussion boards. Feedback can also be given through Twitter and Facebook. No matter what technology is used, it is important to remember that speakers need constructive feedback. As a listener providing feedback, we strive to acknowledge the speaker's strengths, indicate areas for improvement by offering specific suggestions, and share our own relevant experiences with the speaker. When done right, technology-mediated feedback can be rapid and helpful.

All in all, technology is tightly knit to our day-to-day experience. Understanding its utility and drawbacks can make us stronger communicators and more insightful individuals.

Key Terms

blog, 378

cloud computing, 378

Dunbar's number, 385

emoticons, 387

geosocial network, 374

online social networks, 374

podcast, 378

QR codes, 379

Skype, 398

smartphone, 374

teleconferencing, 397

teleprompter, 396

videoconferencing, 378

webcast, 378

webinar, 399

Questions for Reflection

1. Do you think technology is inherently persuasive? When does it add impact beyond the power of the content of a message? When does it distract from the content of a message?
2. How does technology contribute to the concept of the "global village"?
3. How might technology augment ethos, pathos, and logos?
4. Is the speaker who uses more technology in a speech more credible than one who uses less or no technology?
5. Has increased technology made people more or less connected? Why?
6. Other than the message itself, what do you think is most important for a speaker to remember when speaking in a situation where there is no immediate audience?
7. If you were to provide feedback using some form of new technology, what would you find the easiest? Most helpful to the speaker? Least effective?

Activities

1. Over the course of a week, chart your time spent daily on Internet usage (and make sure to differentiate between moments the Internet is used for work or school and instances that it is used for pleasure and socializing), how many times a day you look at your phone, how many emails you send or respond to, and how many text messages you send or respond to. What are your findings? Are you startled by the results? What, if anything, will you do differently in the future?
2. If you use social networking site (like Facebook, Google+, or LinkedIn), test the theory of Dunbar's number by listing all of your friends or contacts and identifying how you know them, how they relate to your other friends/contacts, and how much time, if any, is spent in interpersonal relationship interaction. How many of your social networking "friends" would you deem true friends? Have you exceed the amount suggested by Dunbar's number? What do your findings reveal about your personal view on friendship?
3. List three important public issues that have what you consider to be high visibility online. In a written analysis, describe the ethos of each cause and how it is portrayed and/or created through media choices.
4. Select a persuasive political speech (in video format) and analyze the production value used in the speech. Consider the choices made regarding lighting and staging, content and style of the speaker, and any media effects used. Present an oral analysis to the class.
5. In groups, develop a list of speeches that would be enhanced by video clips, by clips from YouTube, and by slides.
6. Find two informative student speeches that have appeared on YouTube. One should be an example of a speech that was recorded well, and the other speech should serve as a "bad" example. Support your selections with descriptive observations about their strengths and weaknesses.

7. Choose one of the following specific purpose statements and discuss how you might use technology in your speech to meet your goal.
   a. To convince my audience that driving while texting is more dangerous than driving while drunk.
   b. To persuade my audience that social networking is valuable to the political process in countries experiencing political upheaval.
   c. To persuade my audience to avoid bottled water.

References

Alley, M., & Neeley, K. A . (2005). Rethinking the design of presentation slides: A case for sentence headlines and visual evidence. *Technical Communication, 52*(4), 417–426.

Bonk, C. J., & Zhang, K. (2008). *Empowering online learning: 100+ activities for reading, reflecting, displaying, and doing.* San Francisco, CA: Jossey-Bass.

Business travel: The rise of video-conferencing. *Travel Weekly*, October 16, 2008. Accessed on travelweekly.com.

CTIA Semi-annual wireless industry survey. Retrieved from ctia.org/research on May 17, 2011.

Cyphert, D. (2007). Presentation technology in the age of electronic eloquence: From visual aid to visual rhetoric. *Communication Education, 56*(2), 168–92.

Definition and origin of PowerPointlessness. Retrieved from wordspy.com.

Faxon, H. (2008, February 20). "Text messaging system allows questions, feedback in class." Retrieved on August 9, 2011, from yalenews.com.

Foresman, C. "Wireless survey: 91% of Americans use cell phones." Retrieved on May 17, 2011, from arstechnica.com.

Freeman, S. (July 29, 2009). "Study finds link between text messaging, truck crashes." Retrieved on August 9, 2011, from washingtonpost.com.

"German twenty-somethings prefer Internet to partner." Retrieved from reuters.com web article dated March 2, 2009.

Hickey, A. R. (2010, August 2). Social networking dominates U.S. web use; Facebook leads the way. Retrieved from www.cnn.com.

Howell, D. D. (2008). Four key keys to powerful presentations in PowerPoint: Take your presentation to the next level. *TechTrends, 52*(6), 44–46.

"Internet usage statistics for the Americas." Retrieved from internetworldstats. com data from June 30, 2010. Accessed May 17, 2011.

Jenson-Carr, M. (Producer). (2011). *Crackberry'd: The truth about information overload.* [DVD]. Available from www.Meritmotionpictures.com.

Kraus, R. (2008). Presentation software: Strong medicine or tasty placebo? *Canadian Journal of Science Mathematics and Technology Education, 8*(1), 70–81.

Lorento, D. (2011, June 3). What in the www...does the geosocial universe look like today? *The Westmark KHronicle, 18*(20).

Mayer, R. E. (2001). *Multimedia learning.* New York: Cambridge University Press.

Morales, X.Y.Z.G. (2010). Networks to the rescue: Tweeting relief and aid during Typhoon Ondoy. Thesis abstract retrieved from www.firstsearch.oclc.org.

Norvig, P. (2003, August 2). "PowerPoint: Shot with its own bullets." *The Lancet, 362*(9381), 343–344.

Paradi, D. (2009). Results from the 2009 annoying PowerPoint survey. Retrieved from thinkoutsidetheslide.com.

Parr, B. (2010, July 7). The first thing young women do in the morning: Check Facebook. Retrieved on mashable.com.

Pew Internet and American Life Project Survey December 2010. Retrieved on August 28, 2011, from pewinternet.org.

Purcell, K., Rainie, L. Rosenstiel, T., & Mitchell, A. (2011, March 14). How mobile devices are changing community information environments. Retrieved from pewinternet.org.

Shaffer, J. (2006, April 27). Software can't repair sheer hot air: Yet PowerPoint is trendy way to say little at great length. *News & Observer*, p. A1.

Smith, A. (2011, March 17). The Internet and campaign 2010. Retrieved from pewinternet.org.

Spencer, R. (2011, February 28). Man dies after 7-day computer game session. Retrieved from thetelegraph.com. Accessed on August 9, 2011.

Talbert, P. (2011, February 11). iPhone vs. Blackberry—cheaters beware. Retrieved on August 9, 2011, from huffingtonpost.com.

The top five benefits of video conferencing. A Polycom Fact Sheet accessed on polycom.com/telepresence.

Tufte, E. R. (1997). *Visual explanations: Images and quantities, evidence and narrative.* Cheshire, CT: Graphics Press.

————. (2006). *The cognitive style of PowerPoint: Pitching out corrupts within (2nd ed.).* Cheshire, CT: Graphics Press.

"Twitter users are how old?" Retrieved from thenextweb.com from August 9, 2010. Accessed on August 9, 2011.

Watzlawick, P., Bevelas, J. B., & Jackson, D. D. (1967). *Pragmatics of human communication; a study of interactional patterns, pathologies, and paradoxes.* New York: W. W. Norton.

"Why Dunbar's number is irrelevant." Retrieved from socialmediatoday.com from January 25, 2010. Accessed on August 28, 2011.

Zetter, K. (2011, March 5). TED 2011: Wael Ghonim—Voice of Egypt's Revolution. *Wired.* Retrieved on www.wired.com.

Chapter

14

2012, Daniel Korzeniewski, Shutterstock, Inc.

Learning Objectives

After reading this chapter and completing the online activities for this lesson, you will be able to:

1. Describe the significance of small-group communication and presentations.

2. Discuss and apply small-group member roles and responsibilities.

3. Synthesize appropriate guidelines for group problem-solving and presenting.

Presenting to or Working with Small Groups or Teams

At a Glance

INTRODUCTION

Small groups are a reality in life; you have likely encountered group presentations from your early school years and built on that experience when participating as a member of a team in the workplace or a sport. Small groups have many advantages. In contrast to individuals working alone, small groups tend to make higher quality decisions, generate a greater level of creativity, produce a larger quantity of ideas, engage in better scrutiny of decisions, establish strong feelings of camaraderie, and benefit from the synergy that can only come when a group of individuals work together. Working with others can be a joyful or dreaded experience depending on the skill sets of the group members involved. In this chapter, we will examine both the purpose of small groups and types of small-group presentation formats, consider the roles and responsibilities of group members, and explore useful guidelines for meeting the challenges of presenting in small groups.

14.1 The Significance of Small-Group Communication

Small groups are an inevitable part of our lives. Generally speaking, the family is the first group to which we belong. It is something we're born into, or brought into, but it is not something we choose. The same is true of some of our early groups that develop once our formal education begins. Group-work in school is more popular than ever before and even those who are adverse to group work, the "I'd rather work alone" types, are expected to engage in team-oriented assignments. Sometimes, we take part in an activity not because of a conscious effort to belong to a group, but because of our interests. For example, if you are on the editorial board of your school newspaper or are an organizer of the community blood drive, you are a member of a small group. If you are a member of a church, a musical group, an athletic team, or an academic group, you are a member of a small group. Think about how many groups you have participated in, and realize your membership

FIGURE 14.1 Working with others in a small group can be an energizing and rewarding experience.

in small groups will probably significantly increase, not decrease after you leave college. In business, academic life, government, and civic affairs, tasks are defined and completed through small-group communication.

FIGURE 14.2 When given an option, we tend to choose small groups that contain members interested in the same things that we ourselves find important.

© 2012 Antonio Jorge Nunes, Shutterstock, Inc., modified by Marie Hulett.

As a resident of your city, you may present before a governing board, like a city council. Perhaps you love old buildings and find out that your town has plans to demolish a beautiful and historic hotel to make room for a condominium development. In turn, you make an impassioned plea for the council to consider deeming the hotel a historical landmark. This is an example of a situation where *you asked* to speak before some group. As a student, however, there are occasions where people *ask you* to speak before their group. If you have traveled abroad as a volunteer to work with victims of human trafficking in India, you may receive a request from your cultural anthropology professor to speak before your fellow classmates because of your expertise and experience. While at some point, most of us will find ourselves presenting to a group, we also will likely encounter the need to work *with* others in a small-group setting. Team projects, group work assignments, and committee tasks require us to engage in productive efforts with others and often culminate in some form of presentation to an audience. Unlike individual public speaking, small-group communication requires that we be interdependent with others to achieve a common task. Whether you, as an individual, present to a group or work with additional group members to generate a presentation for an audience, understanding the nature of small groups and how to conduct yourself when speaking to or working with said groups is imperative to the overall quality of your experience.

The Small Group Defined

Every small group has three dimensions in common: size, interaction, and goals.

SIZE

Small groups have at least three and no more than fifteen members—the ideal small-group size is five to seven individuals.

INTERACTION

Small-group members must be able to engage in free and open communication with each of the other group members. These discussions will help generate rules and norms specific to the roles of group members and the climate of the group as a whole. Additionally, small groups are marked by *interdependence* among their members. That is, each group member's actions, choices, behaviors, and attitudes will affect, to some extent, the other group members.

GOALS

Small-group members must be working toward shared goals or purposes; they must work together to achieve the goal, which is, in most cases, the single most powerful entity holding the group together through stress, conflict, and complexities.

14.1.1 The Purpose of Small Groups

To understand the dynamics of small groups, you must understand their purpose. The purpose of any small group varies depending on the type of group. Certainly, all groups share some common experience, which is the interaction and/or work that occurs within the group. Beyond that, we can look at groups as belonging to one of two categories—primary or secondary. According to small-group researcher Beebe (1997), the purpose of a **primary group** is to "fulfill the basic need to associate with others" (p. 15). Included in this first category is your family and best friends. Beebe notes that the main task of the primary group is to "perpetuate the group so that members can continue to enjoy one another's companionship" (p. 16). Tubbs (2008), another small-group researcher, affirms that our primary groups influence both our self-concept and personality as we grow and mature from children into adults (p. 164).

primary group
Fulfills the basic need to associate with others and usually involves your family and close friends.

secondary group
A group focused on accomplishing a task or achieving a goal.

The purpose of a **secondary group** is to accomplish a task or achieve a goal. Groups you belong to in college and in your professional lives fit into this second category. In college, you may want to join a study group in order to do better on a test. You may join a fraternity or sorority in order to engage in social activities. You may be asked to join a committee, or you may volunteer for Habitat for Humanity and participate in problem-solving or decision-making activities. Or, there may be a therapy group you belong to that is designed to help you with personal problems. All of the previous are examples of secondary groups, and as you can argue, there may be multiple purposes to a group. For example, a sorority may be a social group, but in order to do fund-raising, members need to engage in decision-making activities. Also, you may form a sub-group within the sorority that gets together to study for a class.

In public speaking classes, group projects may include, among other possibilities, presenting:

- A chapter or course content
- Results of research on some topic
- A cohesive, informative speech as a group
- The results of a problem-solving activity
- Two sides of an issue (pro-con)
- A mini-lecture on some topic

Regardless of the group project your instructor requires of you, the process is better managed when your group's purpose is clear. This chapter is designed to help make the group experience a positive and productive one. It is important to understand some basics of participating in a small group, including roles and responsibilities, as well as methods of presentation. First, we will discuss the different ways you can be involved in small groups.

© 2012 Petrenko Andriy, Shutterstock, Inc.

FIGURE 14.3 Small groups are a common part of education; understanding how to effectively approach this format will make your experience a more positive one.

Being Involved with Small Groups

One of the authors of this textbook teaches a small-groups dynamics class in which the students are assigned one group to work with on a variety of tasks and assignments for the entire semester. As expected, some of the students approach the course with a level of excitement while others are very apprehensive. Reasons for this apprehension range from shyness around new people or fear of presenting to audiences to negative experiences they may have had with groups in the past. Those less-than-positive outlooks on group work, while unfortunate, are warranted. We can likely all think of a time where we begrudgingly had to take the group project upon ourselves to get the job done properly and within the time constraints. Sometimes, we have to pick up the slack when others do not pull their own weight. This dynamic, however, can be better managed as group members educate themselves about how to operate and communicate effectively in a small-group setting. Research reflects that there is a direct correlation between communication competence and group member satisfaction (Sorenson, 1981). That is, the more you know about how to communicate within a group, the happier you will be with the group interaction and outcome. Conversely, the less instruction you have with communicating in groups, the more likely you will be to experience *group-hate*, a term used to describe the negative feelings one can have toward group work.

Groups, however, can bring us a much needed experience outside of ourselves. Colbeck, Campbell, and Bjorklund (2000) report that working on small-group projects provide students with immediate educational and social benefits as well as exposure to future career skills. Students also gain new perspectives from their group members (Duin, 1990). Just as different groups have varied purposes, there are also three distinct ways to be involved in the small-group setting. You may be a member of a group that meets regularly to discuss issues on campus, for example, or you may be a concerned citizen who wishes to speak before a group. Finally, you may find yourself in a group that is presenting before another group for some reason. Each of these ways will be clarified below.

Participating in the Small Group

The most common way to be involved in groups is to participate in a small group. Groups meet for a variety of purposes. Sometimes the purpose of a small-group meeting is to discuss a current problem. For example, if your organization is low on funds. You must find a way to raise money. A group of individuals wanting to become a recognized group on-campus needs to think of a strategy for presenting their case to the appropriate governing body. Everyone contributes to the discussion, and usually a designated leader facilitates the discussion. In college, you may connect with others through membership in one or more of the following groups:

- Study groups
- Sororities and fraternities
- Performance groups (like bands, theater companies, and dance troupes)
- Residence halls
- Honorary societies
- Academic groups
- Activism and awareness groups
- Athletic groups
- Church groups
- Community service groups
- Cultural groups

Speaking as an *Individual* to a Group

A second way to be involved with a small group is by speaking before one. This is considered public speaking and is the focus of this textbook. Unlike regular public speaking, however, you may have two audiences, not one. The *primary audience* is

FIGURE 14.4 We join groups for a variety of reasons that appeal to our social, artistic, cultural, and community-oriented needs.

the small group, such as a three-member interview panel, a five-member city council, or a sixteen-member academic senate. Your purpose is to provide information, to express a concern, or attempt to persuade. Also in attendance, however, may be a *secondary audience*. This is a collection of individuals who attend the open meeting for any number of reasons, including simply observing its proceedings. It's possible these individuals may have no knowledge or interest in your specific topic, and did not know you were planning to speak.

Situations involving both primary and secondary audiences pose some compelling questions: Do you construct a message for the primary audience, accepting the fact that the secondary audience may not understand the context, concern, or content? Or do you construct a message that takes into account both audiences, knowing that for members of the primary audience, some of the information will be unnecessary or redundant? Complexity of the issue, size of the secondary audience, and time constraint are a few of the factors to consider before developing your message.

Speaking as a *Member of a Group* to a Group
Alternatively, you may find yourself in a third group-oriented situation where you are a member of a small group presenting before another group. This may occur in your communication class when you are part of a group presenting the major concepts of a textbook chapter, in a psychology class when your group relays results of its research project, or in a marketing class when you are asked, as a group, to pitch your new product idea and accompanying campaign. There are many instances in college when you work as a group to accomplish a task and report the results to your classmates. In these cases, the focus is not just on your individual performance, but on your group's overall performance as well.

Being a Member of a *Virtual* or *Online* Group
Finally, the accessibility of the Internet makes it possible for you to engage in web-based group interaction, the likes of which can yield a variety of outcomes and deliverables. This "global village" in which we live allows for people to connect,

correspond, coordinate, and complete tasks at an increasing rate, all without group members needing to be in the same physical place at the same time. You have probably already experienced the informal side of online groups through social networking sites like Google+ or Facebook. However, whether you join a Facebook group that is organizing your five-year high school reunion, or help an online friend recoup their contacts after their cell phone has been lost, social networking groups are often not reflective of true "small-group communication" because they do not create an environment of unobstructed interaction and personalized connection. In fact, many of us might admit that some of our Facebook friends are not authentic friends—they may be "friends of friends" that we never actually meet or interact with. In contrast, like traditional face-to-face small groups, genuine virtual small groups are of a manageable size (no one thousand friend groups here!) and marked by a shared task or goal as well as an environment that necessitates consistent interaction and interdependence. Some group types that fulfill these characteristics include internationally based corporate work teams, those managed by productivity software like Goldmine and even the distance learning course associated with this textbook. Although this small-group format is becoming more common and arguably paves a way for the future, it also poses its own set of complexities including the quality and timeliness of online communication, the potential, for ambiguities, and the lack of direct accountability generally present in the traditional small-group format. For further elaboration this topic, see the "Connect: Strategies for Distance Learning Groups" sidebar later on in this chapter.

With the small-group presentation, you may be the only person who speaks before a small group or you may be one of many individuals who speak before a group. In some instances, you will find yourself on a panel with individuals you have never met, and in others you will participate in significant small-group interaction and preparation before your group presents. Given our interest in helping you become the most effective speaker possible regardless of context, we will now turn the focus to (1) working in small groups, and (2) presenting in small groups. In order to work in a small group, it is helpful to know the characteristics of the group and understand the ground rules, norms, and roles necessary to make the most of the group experience. When presenting in small groups, each person should understand his or her individual role responsibilities, and the members should consider which group format is most appropriate for the purpose and audience. Included in this chapter are suggestions for working in a small group and strategies for small-group presentations.

Characteristics of Small Groups

In an extracurricular club, college class, workplace setting, or carefully constructed online environment, whether or not you were able to choose the members of your group, there are individuals with whom you must interact and cooperate. This dynamic, however, is not always an easy one. Perhaps this is a result of the extreme complexity of interactions that can occur in a group where each person brings his or her own predispositions, attitudes, work ethic, personality, style, knowledge, and ability. You may find your group mates friendly, fascinating, frustrating, or infuriating. Likewise, to be fair, they will have their own perceptions of you and of each other that will play into the interactions to come. Regardless, in all but the direst of circumstances, you will successfully traverse the hills and valleys of group work with these people. While we could discuss small-group characteristics indefinitely, for our purposes, three characteristics seem to be most relevant to the public speaking classroom.

1. **Shared purpose**

   Unlike a collection of individuals who may share the same physical space, otherwise known as a "cohort," true group members share a purpose for communication. Seven people waiting in line for tickets to see the Los Angeles Lakers are not considered members of a small group. Neither are five people sharing a taxi from the Dallas-Fort Worth airport or eight students sitting in a row in a large lecture hall. They lack a communication purpose. But if the individuals waiting in line for tickets interact with each other to form a cooperative so that only one of the seven individuals will wait in line for tickets at subsequent games, they would then have a shared purpose that would guide communication in all future meetings. Additionally, when those eight students must form a group to present their analysis on the assigned reading for the week, they instantly transform from cohorts to a bona fide small group.

2. **Group-oriented and self-oriented goals**

   Second, members of small groups usually have both group-oriented and self-oriented goals. **Group-oriented goals** center around specific tasks to be performed by the group members, whereas **self-oriented goals** relate to individual group members' personal needs and ambitions. For example, as a member of a small group charged with the responsibility of determining policies of a new campus radio station, some of the tasks that you face are developing station operating policies, purchasing equipment, and attracting advertisers. As an individual, however, a self-oriented goal may be to emerge as leader of the group and be liked and respected by all group members. Self-oriented goals may complement group-oriented goals, or they may provide distracting roadblocks. For example, in an attempt to fulfill group-oriented goals, you may request that your fellow group members each be responsible for cold-calling prospective advertisers; this may not be a process that all group members enjoy, and in turn, some decide that your request is unreasonable. At this point, your self-oriented goal of being well liked might be compromised at the expense of your group-oriented goal of generating new revenue. Prioritizing these goals (e.g., "*the financial success of the radio station is more important than how popular I am among group members*") is helpful when navigating these potentially rough waters.

   > **group-oriented goals**
   > Goals that center around specific tasks to be performed.
   >
   > **self-oriented goals**
   > Goals that relate to an individual's personal needs and ambitions.

3. **Size**

   A third characteristic of small groups is group size. A group must have a minimum of three members to be considered a small group and the optimum small-group size appears to be five (Tubbs, 2008). This allows for meaningful interaction and the ability of the group members to generate sufficient ideas. Caution needs to be taken with the minimum number of group members. A group of three can lose effectiveness if one member is left out or if one member withdraws or chooses not to contribute. Also, groups with even numbers need to have some mechanism in place for solving the problem of a potential tie should a majority rules vote take place. As a group's numbers increase, the need for coordination and structure increases.

14.1.2 Small Group Formats

Most of your group work in class occurs before the day you present. You spend time defining your purpose, setting goals, distributing the workload, researching your topic/issues, and organizing your research into significant content.

In a public speaking class, your instructor may suggest a particular small-group format. It is also possible that you and your group members are given the liberty to determine your format. Regardless, there are three main small-group formats in academic and community life: panel discussion, symposium, and forum.

© 2012 Picsfive, Shutterstock, Inc.

FIGURE 14.5 Panels are informal public discussions designed to benefit the learning experience of the audience.

Panel Discussion

panels
Public discussions presented for the benefit of the audience.

Panels are public discussions, and as such are presented for the benefit of the audience (Barker, Wahlers, & Watson, 1995). It involves an informal interchange on some issue(s). The positive and negative features of issues are discussed, just as they were in the closed group meeting, but this time in front of an audience. For example, one of the authors of this textbook found herself on her first panel during college, when students at the college who had been homeschooled were asked by their education professor to share their experiences with an audience on campus. When you are part of a panel discussion, it is important to keep in mind that you are talking for the benefit of the audience rather than for other group members. Although your responses are spontaneous, they should be thought out in advance, just as in any other public speaking presentation.

Panel discussions are directed by a moderator who attempts to elicit a balanced view of the issues and to involve all group members. The role of the moderator is to encourage the discussion—he or she does not take part in the discourse. Moderators coordinate and organize the discussion, ask pertinent questions, summarize conclusions, and keep the discussion moving. Once the discussion is over, the moderator often opens the discussion to audience questions.

As you can tell from the previous description, the critical elements of a panel discussion are: (1) it is an informal discussion moderated or facilitated by someone who is not an active participant, (2) interaction should be distributed equitably among group members with no predetermined time limit for each group member, and (3) generally, there are no prepared remarks.

Symposium

A **symposium** is more formal and predictable than a panel discussion. Instead of focusing on the interaction among group members, it centers on prepared speeches on a specified subject given by group members who have expertise on the subject. A group of medical professionals who discuss the new vaccination requirements for a school district would reflect the spirit of the symposium. The topic and speakers are introduced by a moderator. A symposium is structured, and speakers are generally given a time frame for their comments. After the formal presentation, a panel discussion or forum may follow. This allows for interaction among group members, and for the audience to ask questions of individual speakers.

Forum

In a **forum**, group members respond to audience questions. Someone may provide a prepared statement, but it is also possible to introduce group members and their credentials, and then go straight to audience questions. Unlike a panel discussion or the second half of a symposium, a forum does not include interactions among group members. The forum is very audience centered.

The success of the forum depends on how carefully the audience has thought about the topic (the topic is announced in advance) and the nature of their questions. For example, school boards hold public hearings about their annual budget. In addition to the school board, the superintendent and district financial officer will be present. Generally, the financial officer presents the budget, and anyone present may ask questions. Questions may be asked about transportation, food service, athletics, computer equipment, and so on. If several concerned citizens show up with questions in mind, the meeting could last for hours. If no one in the community attends the meeting, then it will be very short.

A forum also needs a moderator. When the League of Women Voters holds a candidates' forum, selected League members collect questions from the audience and give them to the moderator, who then addresses questions to the appropriate panelists. A forum is not just a random collection of individuals, but a group of people who have been chosen for their interest in the topic/issue or because of their expertise.

Choosing the small-group format may be out of the hands of the group members. Someone may request a "symposium on health care" or a "panel discussion" on immigration policies. If the group *does* have a choice, however, the needs of the audience and the goals of the group should be taken into consideration. Clearly, including a forum of some kind allows for the most audience involvement. However,

symposium
More formal and predictable than a panel discussion, it is centered on prepared speeches on a specific subject given by group members who have expertise on the subject.

forum
A group format where group members respond to audience questions without interacting with each other.

Small-Group Formats: Which One Is Right for You and Your Group?

Panel Discussion

- An informal public discussion
- Benefits the audience
- Speakers share spontaneously, equally, and without specific time constraints
- The moderator keeps the discussion moving and usually ends with a question and answer period

Symposium

- Structured and formal—facilitated by a moderator who introduces the speakers and the topic
- Time constraints imposed for speakers
- Discussion often followed by a question and answer session to allow group members to interact with each other

Forum

- Speakers respond to audience questions
- Speakers do not interact with each other
- Very audience-centered
- The success of the forum depends on the quality of the questions prepared and asked by the audience members present

a forum cannot be as controlled as a panel discussion or symposium. There are instances in which having a panel of experts being questioned by a panel of prepared laypersons may be more informative than allowing audience members to ask questions of the expert panelists. For example, in a live televised town hall meeting, the prepared group of citizens and their questions are selected in advance to make for a smooth and appropriate broadcast.

The online lesson includes examples of the different small-group formats. See Topic 1.

14.2 Small-Group Role Responsibilities

When you become a group member, how you communicate is shaped, in large part, by your role in the group. If you have been appointed leader or have a special expertise that sets you apart from the other members, you may be given more responsibility than the other members. For example, do you find yourself always being the one to take notes when working with a group, or, are you the one that cracks jokes to keep the working environment fun and lighthearted? These tendencies to consistently behave in a certain way when in group settings are reflective of norms or roles.

norms
The often-invisible social structures that group members develop that dictate their behavior; they define the general roles that group members are expected to perform.

According to Kreps (1990), **norms** are often invisible social structures that group members develop that govern behavior. Norms define the general roles that group members are expected to perform. Roles quickly emerge in small groups. While one group member may emerge as the leader, taking the initiative in setting the group's agenda, another one could be uncommunicative and play a minor role in group discussions. Still, other members may try to dominate the discussion, oppose almost every point raised, and close their minds before the discussion begins (Bales, 1953, pp. 111–161). While some groups allow for the roles to develop organically, as described above, others may decide to explicitly assign roles at the start; this choice creates clear expectations and serves as a catalyst for progress within the group.

The role you assume influences how you will communicate in the group, how satisfied you will be in the group experience, and how effective the group will be overall. Although there are many types of roles, we focus on two broad categories: your role as a group leader and your role as a group member.

14.2.1 Leader Responsibilities

The leader of a small group can definitely set the tone for how well the group succeeds in a given task. While some leaders inspire and invite quality interaction and participation, others can squelch the life out the experience by being overbearing or selfishly motivated, causing group members to wish they could work alone. In light of this dynamic, it is important to consider how a group leader can be most effective. You may be elected or appointed as leader of a group, or you may emerge as leader over time. It is also important to note that *not every group requires a leader* to successfully operate (see the sidebar on "Leadership Styles"). However, if you *are* bestowed with the task of being the group leader, you need to be aware of the group's **process** *and the* **relationships** among group members. Behaviors that relate to *process* are designed to help the group complete the task. These include providing direction and purpose, keeping the group on track, and providing clarifying summaries.

Leader Process Roles
- **Provide direction and purpose.** As part of your responsibility to provide direction and purpose, you may choose to open a group gathering with action-directed comments ("We are here to come up with a new product or service that we can pitch to our marketing class next week" "Who has suggestions?") or to examine items on an agenda. Once the discussion begins, others will contribute, but it is the leader's role to focus the meeting at the start.
- **Stay on track.** Staying on track simply means making sure the group does not drift too far from the task at hand. For example, if you are talking about structuring your new product or service presentation like an infomercial, it can be really easy to get off track discussing upside-down tomato plants, towels that can absorb a gallon of spilled soda with a single pass, and ill-fated robes that make you look more like a human sleeping bag than a real person. While *some* extraneous conversation helps build relationships and morale among group members, you as a leader are responsible for making sure time is not wasted and the group does not get sidetracked on irrelevant issues.
- **Provide a clarifying summary.** Information arising from group discussion can become confusing, especially when it is generated by a complex collection of diverse individuals with different perspectives and communication styles. Warning signs include puzzled looks, a battery of questions, and drifting

attention; as soon as people start excessively looking at their cell phones and seeking chances to take breaks, it is safe to assume that group members are getting lost and need clarification. When you as the leader sense this confusion, one of the best ways to move forward is to provide a clarifying summary, which recaps what has just occurred.

For example, after deciding that the marketing class presentation would involve a mock infomercial for an illuminated pet harness and leash, it seemed the group was getting nowhere in terms of determining what props should be used to showcase the innovation. As a leader, you say,

> *We've agreed that we will pitch the idea of an illuminated dog harness and leash but we haven't come to terms with how we will represent this product to our audience. Some of you believe that we should create a slide show that exemplifies what the product could do, while others suggest that we actually construct a harness and leash prototype to show how it would work with a dog. Also, if we decide to go with the prototype, there is dispute about whether to bring a live dog into the classroom, which seems against campus policy, or put the harness and leash on a stuffed toy dog, which could compromise the realistic nature of the product.*

With this type of clarifying summary, you have covered all relevant parts of the discussion thus far and identified the source of confusion or disagreement. Clarifying summaries help bring focus back to the task at hand and propel the group toward productivity.

Leader Relationship Roles

In addition to facilitating the group's *process*, an effective group leader is concerned with *relationship* aspects, which facilitate communication and have the ability to create a safe and positive vibe within a group. It is likely that group members who have an enjoyable experience with each other will also be more successful when it comes to accomplishing their tasks. It is important to note that even if your group

autocratic style
The leadership style that asserts control over group members; it puts greater emphasis on the task rather than maintaining the relationships within the group.

democratic style
The leadership style that encourages participation and responsibility from group members. This style equally balances the emphasis on task and relational dimensions; also known as the *participative style*.

laissez-faire style
A "hands off" approach to leadership that features no defined leader. The group members do not attempt to influence each other and no one "steps up" when important decisions need to be made.

Leadership Styles

When faced with a group situation, the group should consider which type of leadership style is best for its members and the task at hand. Kurt Lewin (1939) identified three leadership styles that take into consideration the varied dynamics and responsibilities that a group can adopt.

The **autocratic style** involves a leader who exerts control over group members; the leader is highly directive, that is, he or she *tells* group members what they should do. There is a greater emphasis on the completion of the task rather than the social and relational dimension of the group.

The **democratic (or participative) style** has a greater focus on participation and aims to establish a sense of individual contribution and responsibility from each group member. Group members have a say in what gets decided, and there is a relatively equal emphasis on both the task and relational dimensions within the group.

The **laissez-faire style** is characterized by the absence or avoidance of leadership. In French, *laissez-faire* literally means "hands off," and so it goes without saying that no one steps up to take the lead and the group functions without influence. As mentioned before, not every group situation requires a leader, and, in those instances, this approach may prevail.

does not have a defined leader, the ability for *all* group members to embrace the roles discussed below is beneficial to the overall health of the group. If you understand this dynamic, you will seek to draw information from all participants, keep group communication respectful and balanced, and try to maintain cohesiveness (or healthy closeness) within the group. Ultimately, the relationship aspects allow the group to move forward in a supportive fashion.

Draw information from participants.

Each person has something to contribute to the group, whether it is in the form of offering specific information, analyzing the issue, or being creative. However, some people are hesitant to speak even when they have something valuable to contribute. Their reasons may range from communication anxiety to uncertainty about their role in the group. As a leader, try to draw information from participants by directing questions to those who remain silent, gently asking each group member to speak, and being supportive when a normally quiet member makes a comment in the hope of encouraging additional responses at a later time. Getting everyone

groupthink
A mode of thinking that people engage in when they are deeply involved in a cohesive in-group, when the members' strivings for unanimity override their motivation to realistically appraise alternative courses of action.

Groupthink—When the "We" Gets Dangerous

While cohesion within a group is essential for achieving a strong and healthy interpersonal dynamic, the closeness that a group may develop can be counterproductive and even destructive. Defined by sociologist Irving Janis in 1982, **groupthink** is "a mode of thinking that people engage in when they are deeply involved in a cohesive in-group, when the members' strivings for unanimity override their motivation to realistically appraise alternative courses of action" (p. 9). When group members excessively bond, the cohesion that is created can cause the group to lose sight of objectivity, resulting in poor decisions, a lack of self-examination, and dangerous like-mindedness. The need to reach agreement at all costs squelches dissenters within the group who might otherwise engage in the critical thinking necessary for the group to operate effectively.

Some signs of the emergence of groupthink of which to be wary include:

- *Arrogance:* When the group gets cocky and acts invincible, groupthink has a chance to flourish.
- *Close-mindedness:* As soon as a group begins to reject information "from the outside" and dismisses those who oppose their philosophy as stupid, or even evil, groupthink has probably set in.
- *The need to conform:* When group members feel a overwhelming pressure to conform to the mindset, behaviors, and language of the group, excessive conformity has run amok and groupthink is developing.

Some strategic steps that a group can take to avoid accidentally slipping into a state of groupthink include:

- *Seeking outside opinions:* Asking for objective assessment of the group and its goals from an individual outside of the group allows for the group to receive neutral and honest criticism.
- *Designating a "devil's advocate":* Bestowing an individual within the group with the responsibility of asking questions and raising critiques regarding the group's process, goals, decisions, and interactions enables the group to thoroughly examine all facets of their actions and come to the best decision or solution.
- *Framing disagreements as acceptable:* Establishing an environment where group members feel comfortable disagreeing with the direction of the group allows for individuals to be honest about their reservations and free to dissent. This antithesis of forced conformity creates a sense of liberty among group members to share their concerns, which can help a group to avoid making flawed or dangerous decisions.

Group Cohesion: Closeness *Can* Be Positive

Although the occurrence of groupthink can negatively impact a group's decision making and overall well being, healthy group cohesion can positively affect a group's experience. Defined as "the degree to which members feel a part of the group, wish to say in the group and are committed to each other and to the group's work (Langfred, 1998; Wech et al., 1998), cohesiveness is produced through a focus and maintenance of social relationships within the group.

Cohesiveness can be cultivated by a variety of actions including:

- Establishing a safe and cooperative environment where working together collaboratively is expected.
- Keeping communication lines open by exchanging contact information with all group members and keeping everyone "in the loop" (e.g., conversationally, via email, text messaging, and so on) when it comes to processes involving the group.
- Extending respect and tolerance to all group members through language and actions.
- Developing a team identity, perhaps by giving your group a name, engaging in "team talk" or "we" statements that acknowledge the group rather than the individuals, or wearing an article of unifying clothing during a presentation.

Research shows that cohesiveness, as long is not overemphasized (thereby making a group susceptible to groupthink) enhances small-group productivity (Beal et al., 2003; Gammage et al., 2001). The more interdependent group members must be when collaborating on a common task, the more the productivity-cohesion connection is pronounced (Gully et al., 1995), therefore making group projects a fantastic way to bolster a healthy sense of cohesiveness within a group.

to contribute is particularly important when one or more members of the group seem to dominate the discussion. It is up to the group leader to model a spirit of participation to make sure the group benefits from the combined wisdom of all its members.

Try to keep group communication respectful and balanced.

A leader should try to prevent group communication from being one-sided and encourage a balanced approach to discussion. We often have preconceived ideas of how something should be done. While dissent is healthy, these ideas may be obstacles to group communication if the leader allows the discussion to become one-sided. The leader needs to recognize when one point of view is dominating the discussion. Inviting others into the discussion or offering varying opinion may open up the discussion for multiple perspectives.

Try to maintain cohesion.

As a leader, you should try to maintain the cohesiveness of the group. You want the group to see themselves as a group and function as a group, not as a collection of individuals with their own agendas. Ideally, everyone needs to work toward the group goal, while not ignoring his or her personal goals. Nothing is inherently wrong with a heated discussion, especially when the issue is controversial. But when the discussion turns into a shouting match or insults are exchanged, it is no longer productive. In a conflict situation, the leader should acknowledge the person's point of view but suggest that the problem be analyzed from other perspectives as well. Conflict is healthy, but unproductive conflict is a major obstacle to task completion. Using "us" and "we" references to perpetuate the notion of the collective group, keeping communication flowing effectively, and making sure members feel their contributions are valued, are essential skills for developing and maintaining the overall cohesiveness of the group.

14.2.2 Member Responsibilities and Roles

Being an active participant is the most important responsibility of each group member. An active participant contributes to the discussion, shares responsibility for task completion, and works effectively with other group members. In light of these actions, group members may want to consider the roles to which they are best suited.

The following list includes the most common **task roles** and **relational roles** a group member can adopt when working with others on a common goal.

Task Roles
1. **The Initiator:** Suggests or proposes new ideas to the group and generally "gets the ball rolling."
2. **The Information Seeker:** Asks for clarification of suggestions made and engages in research regarding content needed for the group to complete its task.
3. **The Opinion Seeker:** Asks for a clarification of values in the group process and seeks feedback from group members.
4. **The Information Giver:** Offers facts, generalizations, and instances of his or her own experience pertinent to the group's task.
5. **The Opinion Giver:** States his or her belief pertinent to a suggestion made by the group.
6. **The Elaborator:** Takes suggestions and offers expansion, examples, and a "fleshing out" of ideas presented to show how they would work in reality
7. **The Energizer:** Prods the group to action or decision and stimulates them to produce a higher quality product.
8. **The Procedural Technician:** Keeps things moving by passing out materials, setting up the meeting room, and keeping the environment satisfactory for productivity.
9. **The Recorder/Note Taker:** Takes minutes of group meetings, writes down suggestions, and serves the role of "group memory."

Relational Roles
1. **The Encourager:** Praises, agrees with, and accepts the contributions of others. Establishes an environment of warmth and tolerance and keeps group members' spirits high.
2. **The Harmonizer:** Mediates differences that arise between group members and attempts to reconcile disagreements and "keep things light."
3. **The Compromiser:** Seeks to find solutions that benefit all group members; may involve admitting fault when necessary, yielding status, and "meeting halfway."
4. **The Gatekeeper:** Regulates the flow of information within the group by facilitating balanced and fair communication from all group members.
5. **The Standard Setter:** Expresses standards for the group in terms of the quality of group interaction and individual behavior within the group.

task roles
Roles that focus on the group job or work to be completed.

relational roles
Roles that focus on the interpersonal communication dynamics within a group.

6. **The Group Observer:** Keeps records of group interaction and offers respectful and honest evaluation when necessary.

7. **The Summarizer:** Clarifies group interactions by recapping what has occurred, points of debate, or the group's direction in general.

8. **The Reality Tester:** Assess the direction of group discussion by testing it for practicality, logic, or interpersonal respect.

The online lesson provides search terms to find links to assessments that will help you determine your leadership style and ideal group member role. See Topic 2.

social loafers
Group members who believe that their participation is unnecessary because others will pick up their slack; also known as *slackers*.

Some group members, however, do not gravitate toward a constructive task or relational role and, in fact, believe that their participation is unnecessary because others will pick up their slack. These individuals are called **social loafers** because they idly blend in to an otherwise productive group environment. Complaining about group members is nothing new. The following is only a partial list of common complaints about other group members organized by both task and relational subcategories:

Task Complaints:

- Doesn't adhere to agreed upon plan or process
- Doesn't work or prepare enough/chronically procrastinates
- Others have to nag group members to get work done
- Doesn't keep group members informed of content of presentation
- Doesn't review and rehearse sufficiently to effectively deliver agreed-upon content
- Information in presentation overlaps too much
- Information is excessive or too brief
- Doesn't proofread PowerPoint or other presentational aids

Relational Complaints:

- Difficult to schedule meetings around/always has a reason why he or she cannot attend
- Pouts when his or her ideas are not selected by the group
- Acts self-centered or put upon
- Gossips about a fellow group members to other group members
- Doesn't return calls or email
- Doesn't attend class on group work days
- Controlling and dominating
- Apathetic
- Doesn't stay after class to check with group

In research on *slackers*, or social loafers, in classroom research, Myers and his colleagues (2009) found that not only are group members frustrated by their lack of participation, the fact that they receive credit for work they do not complete and they make excuses for their behavior is also vexing. Furthermore, group members believe that slackers are aware of their dysfunctional behavior, and that slackers

FIGURE 14.6 Being a social loafer conveys a disrespect for others and contributes to a general feeling of "group-hate" for those left to do all the work.

do not care about the group tasks or group members. Their lack of motivation affects the group in negative ways and can lead to "group-hate." This refers to "feelings of dread that arise when faced with the possibility of having to work in a group" (p. 598).

We understand that students take several academic courses. They have a social and/or work life, and priorities differ among students. But, as you can see by the list of complaints and the research on slackers, once you are part of a group, your actions have an impact on the other people in that group. In a classroom setting, you may not be thrilled with the topic, the assignment, or the other group members. But you do need to work with your group in order to complete the required assignment. Actively working to complete your individual tasks and being available and cooperative will make the situation better for all involved. Fulfill a commitment to the group, no exceptions.

14.2.3 Problem Solving in Groups: The Reflective Thinking Process

As mentioned previously in this chapter, individuals end up in groups for a variety of reasons. In many cases, groups must engage in problem-solving activities, such as how to reduce costs in a school district, how to distribute money equitably to student organizations, or how to raise money for an organization. You may be called upon in a college course or in an organization to work with others on a problem-solving task. The Student Senate needs to find ways to get more students involved in campus events or the campus newspaper is trying to find ways to entice new businesses in the area purchase advertisement space in the publication. Groups are faced with small and large problems on a regular basis. Almost 100 years ago, John Dewey (1910) developed a theory of reflective thinking that is now applied to group communication. One way to proceed through the problem-solving process is to engage in the seven-step **reflective thinking process**. Each of the following steps needs to be completed satisfactorily before moving to the next step:

reflective thinking process
A seven-step problem solving process developed by John Dewey. The steps include: (1) identifying and defining the problem, (2) analyzing the problem, (3) determining criteria for an acceptable solution, (4) generating possible solutions, (5) choosing the solution that best fits the criteria, (6) implementing the solution, and (7) reassessing the solution.

1. Identify and Define the Problem

The first step of this process is to make sure group members understand and agree on what the problem is. Otherwise, the discussion may scatter into many different directions and time will be misused. Suppose a newly elected Student Senate member wants to work with a group to deal with student complaints about residence hall assignments. One problem students identify is that they are not given enough options about where they may live or with whom. A second problem is that the administration does not process complaints effectively. Third, students are unhappy about meal plan options, and fourth, they are frustrated by all the residence hall rules and contracts. Does the group want to take on all of these problems, or to focus on the complaint process? The first thing the group needs to do is identify the problem.

2. Analyze the Problem

This is the information-gathering, sorting, and evaluation stage of the reflective thinking process. In the process of analyzing the problem, group members need to identify what they know about the problem, what they do not know, and what resources are available to help them acquire more information. In this step, group members should find out what caused the problem, how long the problem has been an issue, and the extent of the problem. Creating clear structure for the problem allows for its key elements to be best understood. If only one student has complained about her residence hall assignment, there is not much of a problem. But if significant staff time is devoted to addressing students' complaints, then the problem is significant. Perhaps the problem started when a new administrator took office. Perhaps the problem is ongoing.

3. Determine Criteria for an Acceptable Solution

Many groups skip this step, whether they are newly formed groups in a college classroom or well-established policy groups in a community. However, it is a mistake to come into the problem-solving process with a firm idea of what you think is the best solution. Whatever solution your group suggests must meet agreed-upon criteria or standards. Criteria will differ vastly from situation to situation and should be prioritized based on a clear understanding of the problem. For example, if four students turned in a group paper that was clearly plagiarized, before determining the punishment, an instructor might consider the following criteria:

- Is it (the punishment) fair (to the four students and the rest of the class)?
- Is it appropriate (given the nature of the misconduct)?
- Will it deter future misconduct (on the part of the students who cheated as well as other students who might be contemplating misconduct)?

Criteria related to the residence hall complaints issue might include the following:

- Does the solution consider both the needs of students and college administrators?
- Does the solution apply to all students living in residence halls, not just incoming freshmen?
- Does the solution allow students to change residence halls?
- Does the solution recognize that freshmen do not have cars?

Establishing criteria keeps group members from simply proposing their solution. Any solution presented needs to meet the criteria established by group members.

Courtesy of Rachel A. Wegter.

FIGURE 14.7 Working with others to solve problems requires an open mind, a creative approach, and a commitment to the solution.

4. Generate Possible Solutions

According to Dewey (1910), suspended judgment is critical at this point in the decision-making process. Group members need to identify available options without stifling the process by providing immediate evaluation. Brainstorming, which was mentioned earlier in this textbook, involves generating as many solutions as possible without critical evaluation, and may be useful when trying to generate possible solutions. Be creative. Encourage group members to think "outside the box." Avoid the temptation to say, "that won't work," "that's not possible," or worse, "that's a ridiculous idea." Instead, generate ideas until you agree you have exhausted the possibilities. Ideally, give yourselves time to think about these solutions before evaluating or moving on to the next step. For the teacher who caught the group of students plagiarizing, some of the punishment options include ignoring it, talking to the students, requiring them to give a group presentation on the evils of plagiarism, requiring them to write another paper, lowering their grade on the paper, failing them for the assignment, failing them for the semester, and reporting the students to the Office of Judicial Affairs or the like.

Regarding the problem of residence hall complaints, the group may develop several options, including changing the forms students fill out, suggesting a policy change, providing clearer, more specific information to students, and establishing a committee to hear complaints not resolved between students and administration. The important thing is to *have* alternatives, and not be single-minded in your approach.

5. Choose the Solution That Best Fits the Criteria

Each solution identified in Step 4 needs to be evaluated based on the criteria established in Step 3. In a perfect world, the best solution is one that meets all the established criteria. If that does not happen, the group may need to revisit the possible solutions, and determine whether amending one of the solutions might result in it meeting all of the established criteria. The instructor who caught students plagiarizing needs to evaluate her possible options by the criteria she has set. For example, if she ignores the misconduct, is that fair to those in the class who did not plagiarize? Is failing the students for the course an appropriate punishment for the students' misconduct?

In terms of the residence hall complaints, does changing the form students fill out meet both the needs of students and administrators? Will the form address the issue of changing residence hall assignments? Will a committee be formed to hear complaints from all students in residence halls? An option might not meet each of the criteria perfectly, but the point of this step is to choose the solution that best meets the criteria. If multiple options are acceptable, the group needs to determine how it will decide on which solution to implement.

6. Implement the Solution

Implementing the solution means putting it into effect. It is one thing for a group coming up with ideas for a fund-raiser to decide that a car wash will raise the most money; it is another thing to advertise, staff, supply, and conduct the fund-raiser. The work involved in implementing the solution will vary according to the problem. For example, an instructor dealing with plagiarism can determine the best solution and then communicate that decision to the students and/or administration. If the group dealing with residence hall complaints decides to form a committee to hear complaints, then implementing the solution entails setting up committee structure, policies and procedures, soliciting membership, and informing students about the committee.

expanding the pie
A problem-solving technique that involves finding ways to creatively increase resources as a solution to the issue.

bridging
A problem-solving strategy that aims to identify a solution that satisfies the often-conflicting desires of all parties involved.

Strategies for Thinking Outside of the Box

Expanding the pie involves increasing resources to help solve a problem. When resources seem scarce, individuals tend to get competitive and stressed; when a group can find a constructive way to create more of what they need without self-imploding, good things happen. For example, one of the authors of this textbook ran a high school program in a public school system and wanted to teach a book of which the school did not currently have a supply. In order to gather copies, she got a local book store to order and set aside the most inexpensive version of the book and then asked the students to buy their own copy if they could. Any student who could not afford the book would be able to use a loaner copy that the instructor bought herself. At the end of the year, the students were offered extra credit to donate their book back to the program so students the following year could use the copies. Now the instructor has enough copies for all future classes without tapping the already-stressed school budget, student's wallets, or her own pocketbook!

Bridging offers a way to create an option that satisfies the needs of all parties involved. Instead of a competitive, "I win so you lose" or "you win so I lose," bridging strives to find a solution that allows everyone to win something. For example,

FIGURE 14.8 It takes many pieces to develop a good solution.

In a public speaking class, your group may be involved in determining a solution and suggesting how it could be implemented, but it is possible the group will not be involved with the actual implementation. For example, your group may be given the task of determining how to get students more involved in their department's activities. Your group could work through Step 5 and decide that the best solution is to advertise activities earlier so that students can work them into their schedules. As a group, you may present Steps 1 through 5 to a faculty committee, but ultimately, Step 6 might be the committee's responsibility.

reframing
A problem-solving technique that uses language to break a mindset and create a new perspective.

when going on a road trip with her extended family, one of the authors of this textbook wanted to hit all of the major cities, while her brother wanted to spend time at the national parks along the way. In order to bridge the profound differences in their vacation tastes, they opted to see the national parks on the way up and hit the major cities on the way home. Both parties got some of what they wanted and the trip was a memorable success.

Often we as group members are stuck in a particular mindset about a problem or situation and expending some energy **reframing** reality through our language can make all of the difference in generating viable solutions. For

example, if you and your group have one week to come up with a marketing plan to present to your class, you can gripe about how little time you have (*"We have ONLY one week—how will we ever get this done?"*) and watch the time pass in a negative and foreboding way OR you can reframe the situation in a more positive light (*"We have a WHOLE week to get this done—if everyone works a little bit every day, we will have more than enough time to pull this off."*). Much like seeing the glass half-empty or half-full, reframing is about using our language to create a positive situation that allows group members to achieve more because they are using less negative energy.

Courtesy of Rachel A. Wegter and Marie Hulett.

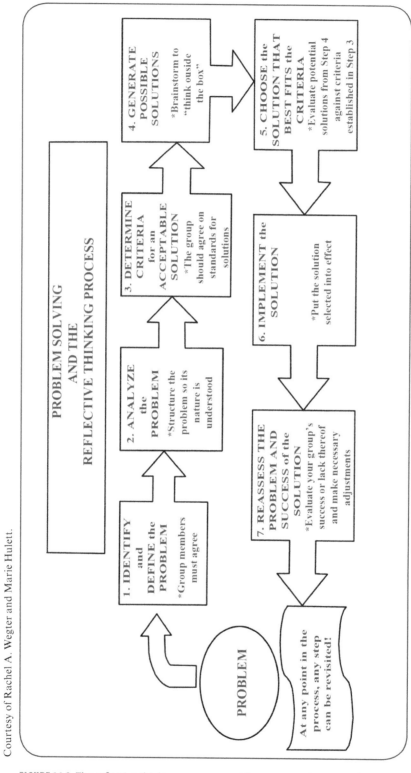

PROBLEM SOLVING
AND THE
REFLECTIVE THINKING PROCESS

1. IDENTIFY and DEFINE the PROBLEM
*Group members must agree

2. ANALYZE the PROBLEM
*Structure the problem so its nature is understood

3. DETERMINE CRITERIA for an ACCEPTABLE SOLUTION
*The group should agree on standards for solutions

4. GENERATE POSSIBLE SOLUTIONS
*Brainstorm to "think outside the box"

5. CHOOSE the SOLUTION THAT BEST FITS the CRITERIA
*Evaluate potential solutions from Step 4 against criteria established in Step 3

6. IMPLEMENT the SOLUTION
*Put the solution selected into effect

7. REASSESS THE PROBLEM AND SUCCESS of the SOLUTION
*Evaluate your group's success or lack thereof and make necessary adjustments

PROBLEM

At any point in the process, any step can be revisited!

FIGURE 14.9 The reflective thinking process provides a systematic approach to problem solving that is suitable for a variety of small-group tasks and situations.

7. Reassess

Reassessing at some point prevents the group from saying "we're done" after implementing the solution. It is an important part of the process because you evaluate your group's success or lack thereof. Fund-raisers are carefully planned and executed, but still may fail. New policies are developed with the best intentions, but may still be ineffective. Do you try the same fund-raiser again? Do you keep the new policy? Before you answer "yes" or "no" to these questions, the group needs to answer some other questions.

Did the fund-raiser fail because it was held at a bad time? Was it advertised sufficiently? Did it ask too much of the people working it or attending the fund-raiser? In other words, the group needs to decide what contributed to the lack of success. Similarly, with the ineffective policy, did administration evaluate its effectiveness too soon? Were students inadequately informed? Was administration insufficiently trained? Those engaged in reassessment need to discuss what factors influenced the lack of success. In a sense, this final step can be the beginning step of a new process, if the solution has not been effective. It is important to note that the group may need to revisit any of the steps along the way if the solution does not seem to be achieving the desired goal.

The seven-step reflective thinking process is one way to help groups move through the problem-solving process. It is certainly not the only way. However, regardless of the approach groups take, it is important that a clear process be established that allows for rational and respectful discussion of all relevant aspects of the problem. A leader should help the group through this process, and group members should contribute productively throughout the process.

14.3 Suggestions for Group Members

As mentioned previously, group work in the college classroom is prevalent. The following eight suggestions are designed to create the most effective small-group experience within the context of your course. Many of these also translate easily to experiences outside the college classroom. This section will close with an overview of strategies specifically designed for virtual groups in the distance learning arena.

The online lesson provides a checklist for you to consider when planning your group presentations. See Topic 3.

1. Know the constraints of the assignment.

Read the syllabus or any other material given to you related to the assignment. Make sure everyone agrees as to the constraints of the assignment. The following are some questions that may guide your group in determining all relevant details:

- When does the group present?
- How much time does the group have to present?
- Does each speaker have the same amount of time?
- Are all group members expected to speak and, if so, equally?
- What information needs to be included in the presentation?

- Are presentational aids required?
- Does each speaker use a set of note cards? Is there a restriction?
- Is there audience involvement at some point during the group presentation?
- Can group members interrupt each other to comment or add insight?
- Is there a paper required? Or an outline?
- How many and what type of sources are required, and should they be cited during the presentation?
- Does the group choose its format, or is there a particular format that is required?
- Are students being graded individually, as a group, or both?
- Will there be any peer evaluations?

2. Work to achieve group goals.

Instructors understand that each individual is concerned about his or her own grade. However, the purpose of a group assignment is to work collectively and collaboratively. Make group goals your top priority. Making a commitment to the group means making a commitment to achieve group goals at each meeting. When you feel strongly about your position, it is legitimate to try to convince the group you are correct. But if others disagree, it is important that you listen to their objections and try to find merit in them. You need an objective detachment from your own proposals to enable you to place the group's goals above your own. A group needs a shared image of the group, in which individual aspirations are subsumed under the group umbrella that strives for the common good.

3. Be responsible for completing your part of the assignment.

Group membership brings with it a set of roles and responsibilities. It may not have been your choice to work in a group or to work with that specific group of individuals. The fact is, the assignment is mandatory. Everyone has a life. Everyone has distractions in their lives. You may be very busy, or you may be uninterested, but your group needs your help. If a group member volunteers to make the PowerPoint presentation consistent from speaker to speaker, you need to make sure that person has your slides when they are requested. If you are supposed to make contact with city officials or individuals who may help with a fund-raising idea, you need to come to the group with that information. Do not be responsible for the group's progress being delayed, or the task not completed. If you cannot attend a meeting, make sure someone knows. Send your work with someone else. If you do get behind, make sure group members know so they have an opportunity to respond in some way.

4. Research sufficiently.

Most group work involves research of some type. When you are finished researching, you should feel confident that you have ample support or that the topic or issue has been covered in enough depth. Depending on the group's purpose or goal, research may involve surfing the Internet, conducting a library search, emailing a web-based questionnaire or posting a survey link on a social media site, calling different social service agencies in town, or interviewing students on campus. Make sure that your research is reasonably exhaustive and, if it involves a survey or questionnaire, has a sufficient and appropriate sample size.

FIGURE 14.10 Clearly assigning tasks within a group project will help take the "guess work" out of preparation and encourages group members to successfully complete their portion of the workload.

© 2012 Yuri Arcurs, Shutterstock, Inc.

5. Communicate effectively and efficiently.

Different people bring to a group a wide range of knowledge and views that help complete the task. Group discussion often produces creative approaches that no one would have thought of alone. Group involvement through communication increases the likelihood that the group's decision will be accepted and supported by all group members and by the broader community. Do not waste time and do not monopolize the group discussions or the presentation.

6. Avoid personal attacks.

Comments like, "You have to be a moron to believe that will work," or "My six-year-old cousin has better ideas than that," accomplish nothing. On the contrary, these comments are so antagonistic that they make it virtually impossible for people to work together. If you do not like an idea, say so directly by focusing on the idea, not the person, such as "It may be difficult to get funds for that project," or "I don't think parents will want to volunteer their time for that." Try not to make your disagreement too negative. Find areas of agreement and commonality, where possible.

7. Go to the source of the problem.

One of the most destructive entities to infect a small group involves gossip and complaints about group members. Often, when one group member is upset with another, they are naturally compelled to discuss their irritation with other group members. This behavior creates factions within the group and can lead to group members feeling embarrassed, defensive, and betrayed. When group members have to "choose sides" between two group members in conflict, the problem can be blown way out of proportion and create drama that no group really wants to endure. If you have a point of contention with another group member, go *directly* to them to discuss your concerns respectfully and discreetly; give them a chance to remedy the situation one-on-one before involving others. Generally speaking, people appreciate the honesty and the ability to explain themselves or clear the air without dealing the complexity that can occur when the whole group is privy to the problem.

8. Leave personal problems at home.

Group conflicts are often the result of personal problems and concerns brought to the group meeting. A fight with a family member, a poor test grade, an alarm clock that failed to go off, a near-accident on the highway, school pressure or work complications can put you in a bad mood for the meeting and lessen your tolerance for other group members. Although an outburst of anger may make you feel better for the moment, it can destroy the relationships you have with other members of the group.

The online lesson includes a form that you can use to evaluate your group members after completing a group presentation. See Topic 3.

14.3.1 Presenting in Small Groups

Whether presenting as a group or as an individual to a group, successful public speaking strategies are necessary. First, consider who you are presenting to; audience analysis, in turn, is essential. Each presentation you prepare should have a clear introduction, body, and conclusion. Your presentation should be well-researched, sufficiently supported, and organized effectively. Delivery should be engaging and extemporaneous. While you should avoid overdependence on notes, it is a good idea for each group member should have notes (or at least a note card) to make sure everyone is presenting content agreed upon by the group in prior meetings. The notes serve as a tangible agreement between group members.

Speaking as a member of a group, however, involves additional review. First, it is important to find a small-group format that best suits your purpose. This was discussed earlier in the chapter. Second, it is important that the speeches all group members give flow as though they were one coherent speech. This last section of

© 2012 Yuri Arcurs, Shutterstock, Inc.

FIGURE 14.11 The preparation that you and your group members put into your presentation should result in a feeling of solidarity as you approach your audience. To some extent, you are dependent on your group members and they are dependent on you; make sure that your rehearsal time takes this dynamic into consideration.

the chapter describes a variety of small-group formats concerns that need to be addressed before the group speaks, and makes suggestions for the presentation.

Preparing to Present as a Group

When you prepare a speech for class, you are responsible for all aspects of the speech. As an individual, you need to prepare, practice, and present. Once you join a group, however, you need to be prepared, but you also need to be aware of how your speech fits into the other speeches, and the group needs to make sure everyone is viewing the presentation from a similar perspective. With this interest in mind, we present the following aspects of the presentation to consider *before* the group speaks. All group members should know and be in agreement with the following:

The Presentation as a Whole

- Speaker order
- Formality of the presentation
- Can group members interrupt each other?
- Can group members wander from their prepared remarks?
- Determine where will the group sit/stand?
- Will all sit and then stand up to speak or will all stand throughout the entire presentation?
- Should the group sit to the side and have the speaker stand in the middle of the front of the class?

Delivery

- Use note cards? Legal pad? Presentation software?
- Prepare individually—think about eye contact (speak to the group, not the instructor), gestures, and vocal aspects
- Time constraints for each speech
- Determine how to signal whether someone is speaking too long or if the group is going too long
- Introduction, body, conclusion
- Who will deliver the group's introduction and conclusion?
- How will each person's introduction and conclusion relate to the group?
- How do you make transitions between speeches so all presentations are connected?

Presentational Aids

- What is available in the classroom?
- Will they benefit the presentation?
- How far away will my audience be from the presentational aids? How will I adjust for this distance?
- Who will be responsible for making them and setting them up?
- Who will handle the transitions?

If you and your group members wait until everyone approaches the front of the room to address these concerns, you will not feel confident and appear unprepared. Deciding where to stand, how to signal each other, and what the speaking order is will reduce awkwardness and uncertainty, and should give a more professional, polished look to the presentation.

Connect: Strategies for Distance Learning Groups

So you've enrolled in a distance learning course and now are assigned to a work group. For generations of the past, this arrangement could seem like a veritable impossibility but the fact is, **virtual groups** do exist and working in one increasingly will become a reality for many of us. By definition, virtual groups are small groups whose members interact by means of electronic technologies (Kozlowski & Ilgen, 2006); additionally, they have three primary characteristics that differentiate them from traditional groups, listed as follows (Schiller & Mandviwalla, 2007):

1. Members are dispersed among multiple locations and various time zones.
2. Group members in virtual groups often possess more diverse backgrounds consisting of a variety of cultures, languages, and affiliations.
3. Membership within the virtual group tends to be less stable and consistent.

Understanding these differences is the first step toward achieving success in virtual groups. Unlike traditional groups, virtual group interaction can take place through a variety of mediums. Conference calls, videoconference calls, live Internet-mediated chats, emails, and text messaging are all modalities that enable the group to communicate, interact, plan, organize, and even present. Whether you find yourself in a group of your choosing, or are thrown together with strangers to complete a common goal, the following strategies should be considered to achieve success in a virtual group format:

1. **Communicate Clearly:** When using text-based channels like email and text messaging, avoid slang, abbreviations, spelling and grammar errors, and technical jargon. Write with precision and clarity so all group members understand the content that you intend to share. When engaging in phone conferences or videoconferencing, review the strategies covered in Chapter 13 to best communicate your ideas in these complex but convenient mediums.
2. **Aim for Personalization:** Getting to know one another through live chats, discussions on everyday interests, and even an exchange or posting of pictures will help to establish the "real person" behind the virtual group member.
3. **Correspond Regularly and Promptly:** Trust and reliability are established through consistency. When the group remains in constant communication and group members respond to correspondences in a timely manner, group members feel safe and productivity flourishes.
4. **Set the Ground Rules Early:** Collectively deciding upon and laying out a set of rules (or norms) to which the group should adhere will help to get everyone on the same page and

virtual group
A small group whose members interact by means of electronic technologies.

14.3.2 General Strategies for Presenting in a Small Group

The following guidelines will help you succeed as a participant in a panel discussion, symposium, or forum. Many of the guidelines apply to all three group formats, but others apply just to one.

1. **Limit the number of points you make.**
   Since you will be given some time constraints, limit the number of points you make. Remember that each person has information to present. Your audience cannot process an overload of material. Aim for brevity, make your point as succinctly and clearly as possible, and do not confuse your listeners with too many details.

prevent group members from frustrating each other unknowingly. Overall deadlines for the group, turn around time for getting back to group members, and protocol when submitting an idea or conducting a virtual group vote should be established in advance to clarify procedures and expedite progress.

5. **Adhere to an Established Agenda and Follow up with Minutes:** Setting an agenda for each virtual group interaction will help to keep group members on track and help to calibrate group progress. The agenda should be typed and emailed to group members before planned interactions and minutes or notes should be disseminated to group members following meetings so everyone knows what was accomplished and what is to come.

6. **Allocate Responsibility Publicly and Explicitly:** Because the virtual group will have to share the workload to achieve the goal, make sure to take inventory of what needs to be accomplished, invite group member preferences for the tasks, and, once the tasks have been assigned, share the complete list with the virtual group so that everyone knows the responsibilities for everyone else involved; this helps the group to avoid confusion and increases transparency.

7. **Consider "Murphy's Law":** Often, whatever *can* go wrong *will* go wrong. In turn, double-check that emails have been received (sometimes, they really do get lost), that presentational software slideshows are compatible for all group members to access, and that technology connections (like Internet, teleconferencing software, and battery life for handheld devices in use) are as they should be.

8. **Embrace Multimedia Elements:** One of the benefits in working in a virtual group is the openness to technology that the group members probably have. The more that a group can harness the power of multimedia elements (like presentational software, video clips, music, and images) in interactions and presentations, the more dynamic the messages being conveyed will be.

9. **Strive for Synchronous Connection as Much as Possible:** The more virtual group members can communicate with each other *simultaneously*, the better. Pursue opportunities for your virtual group to engage in conference calls or use Internet-based videoconferencing software (for example, Skype) to exchange ideas and plan your endeavors; these formats allow for the richest communication exchange (outside of face-to-face interaction), since elements such as vocal tone and nonverbal facial expressions can be perceived through these mediums.

Considering these steps when interacting with your virtual groups will enable you to have the best and most effective experience possible with this expanding world of opportunity.

2. **Avoid repetition.**

   Avoid an overlap in presentation information by determining in advance what the other group members will cover in their speeches. The job of assigning topics should be the responsibility of the presentation organizer. If the organizer is negligent, you may want to get in touch with the other group members yourself. Keep communication channels open with your group members so you do not find yourself giving the same presentation as the person who spoke before you.

3. **Try to meet in advance.**

   Try to meet your fellow group members in advance. When group members meet for the first time on stage, their interaction may sound awkward because they don't know each other. This discomfort may be communicated to the audience.

4. **Restrict your speech to the allotted time.**

   If speakers exceed the time limit, the audience will find it difficult to sit through the entire program, and little opportunity will remain for a panel interchange or a question-and-answer period. In addition, by violating the time constraints, you may cause another speaker to modify his or her speech significantly. Staying within the allotted time frame is a necessary courtesy to the other group members.

5. **Prepare for audience questions.**

   Because the question-and-answer period may be the most important part of the program, spend as much time preparing for questions as you did for your formal remarks. Anticipate the questions you are likely to be asked and frame your answers. During the question-and-answer period, be willing to speak up and add to someone else's response if none of the questions are being directed to you. When a fellow panel member finishes a response, simply say, "I'd like to make one more point that …" If, on the other hand, a question is directed to you that you think would be better handled by another panel member, say, "I think that considering her background, Laura is better able to answer that question."

6. **Consider enhancing your presentation with presentational aids.**

   Simple visual aids are as appropriate in group presentations as they are in single-person public speaking. Coordinate the use of visual aids so information is not repeated by multiple speakers and visual styles are uniform. Be professional and maintain continuity; it is inconsistent to allow one group member to use the blackboard when the rest of the group has PowerPoint slides.

Chapter Summary

We are all involved in small-group activities whether they occur within or outside of the classroom. Opportunities exist for interacting within a group or speaking before a group. As a speaker, consider both primary and secondary audiences. As group members, we share a purpose for communication. Also, group members usually have both group-oriented and self-oriented goals, and group size influences the need for structure and how we communicate.

Each individual has responsibilities within the group setting regardless of the person's role. As leader, you can contribute to the group's process by providing direction and purpose, especially at the beginning of the meeting, keeping the group on track throughout the meeting, and providing a clarifying summary when appropriate. In terms of helping the group communicate effectively, the leader should draw information from participants, try to keep group communication from being one-sided, and try to maintain the cohesiveness of the group.

As a group member, you have several responsibilities, including knowing the constraints of the assignment, working to achieve group goals, being responsible for completing your part of the assignment, researching sufficiently, communicating effectively and efficiently, avoiding personal attacks, and leaving your personal problems at home. Following the seven-step reflective process helps to keep the group organized and focused and helps to make sure that members do not jump to quick solutions without sufficient analysis and deliberation.

When the occasion arises for you to present as a group member before an audience, it is important to determine whether a panel discussion, symposium, or forum best suits your needs and the needs of your audience. Your knowledge of public speaking and your individual skills come into play as you present before the group. However, it is important to meet as a group beforehand to determine such things as speaker order, amount of speaking time allotted for each individual, whether or not presentational aids will be useful, and who will be responsible for preparing such aids. Each person's presentation should cover only a few points. The presentations should not overlap, and group members should be prepared for audience questions. An effective presentation involves preparation on the part of all group members as well as attention to detail regarding content connection, transitions from speaker to speaker, and overall professional performance.

Key Terms

autocratic style, 422

bridging, 430

democratic style, 422

expanding the pie, 430

forum, 419

group-oriented goals, 417

groupthink, 423

laissez-faire style, 422

norms, 420

panels, 418

primary group, 412

reflective thinking process, 427

reframing, 431

relational roles, 425

secondary group, 412

self-oriented goals, 417

social loafers, 426

symposium, 419

task roles, 425

virtual group, 438

Questions for Reflection

1. What is the difference between being a member of a small group that works together and then presents before another group and being a member of a panel that never meets before it presents before another group?

2. How would your presentation differ if you had a primary audience only or you had both a primary and a secondary audience?

3. Your group members disagree on the best way to approach an assignment involving community service and the elderly. While you and some additional group members want to volunteer at a convalescent home, other group members express fear and discomfort at the idea. Apply the techniques of expanding the pie, bridging, and reframing to generate possible solutions to the problem.

4. When you work with others to accomplish tasks in college, can you usually identify who the leader is? How? What seems to be the most difficult aspect of being a leader in a college classroom project?

5. Can you think of a situation when your fellow group members did not fulfill their group responsibilities? If so, how did you react? How did other group members react?

6. Under what circumstances would it make sense to present as a member of a panel? When would a symposium be used? When is a forum appropriate?

7. If you were giving advice to a friend who had not participated in a small-group presentation, what would you tell your friend about speaking as a member of a group before another group?

8. Describe a time when you observed or experienced groupthink. What happened as a result?

Activities

1. Select an actual small group on campus or in your community and obtain permission to observe several meetings. Take field notes on what you observe and identify which roles task and maintenance roles were adopted by group members. Prepare a presentation or reflection on your observations. Pay particular attention to how the group approaches problem solving.
2. Think of some disagreements you have been in and apply the reflective thinking process to see how the problem could have been solved.
3. Write a description of an ideal small-group member. Then honestly reflect on how closely you personally align with your description.
4. Create a list of rules that you think could and should be applied to most small groups to lend to their successes.
5. Join with three or four other class members to work on a common problem. Use a panel or symposium to present your analysis and recommendations. The group should move through all steps of the reflective thinking process. Present the process and your solution to the class.

References

Bales, R. F. (1953). "The equilibrium problems in small groups," in T. Parson, R. F. Bales, & E. A. Shils (Eds.), *Working papers in the theory of action*. Glencoe, IL: Free Press.

Barker, L. L, Wahlers, K. J., & Watson, K. W. (1995). *Groups in process: An introduction to small group communication*. Boston: Allyn & Bacon.

Beal, D. J., Cohen, R. R., Burke, M. J., & McLendon, C. L. (2003). Cohesion and performance in groups: A meta-analytic clarification of construct relations. *Journal of Applied Psychology, 88*(6), 989–1004.

Beebe, S. A., & Masterson, J. T. (1997). *Communicating in small groups: Principles & practices (5th ed.)*. New York: Longman.

Colbeck, C. L., Campbell, S. E., & Bjorklund, S. A. (2000). Grouping in the dark: What college students learn from group projects. *Journal of Higher Education, 71*(1), 60–83.

Dewey, J. (1910). *How we think*. Boston: D. C. Heath.

Duin, A. H. (1990). Terms and tools: A theory and research-based approach to collaborative writing. *The Bulletin for the Association for Business Communication, 53*(2), 45–50.

Ehrlich, E., & Hawes, G. R. (1984). *Speak for success*. New York: Bantam Books.

Gammage, K. L., Carron, A. V., & Estabrooks, P. A. (2001). Team cohesion and individual productivity: The influence of the norm for productivity and the identifiability of individual effort. *Small group Research, 32*(1), 3–18.

Gully, S. M., Devine, D. J., & Whitney, D. J. (1995). A meta-analysis of cohesion and performance: Effects of level of analysis and task interdependence. *Small Group Research, 26*(4), 497-520.

Janis, I. (1982). *Groupthink: Psychological studies of policy decisions and fiascos.* Boston: Houghton Mifflin.

Kozlowski, W. J., & Ilgen, D. R. (2006). Enhancing the effectiveness of work groups and teams. *Psychological Science in the Public Interest, 7*(3), 77–124.

Kreps, G. L. (1990). *Organizational communication (2nd ed.).* New York: McGraw-Hill.

Langfred, C. W. (1998). Is group cohesiveness a double-edged sword? *Small group Research, 29*(1), 124–143.

Lewin, K., Lippitt, R., & White, R. (1939). Patterns of aggressive behavior in experimentally created social climates. *Journal of Social Psychology, 10*(2), 271–299.

Myers, S. A., Smith, N. A., Eidsness, M. A., Bogdan, L. M., Zackery, B. A., Thompson, M. R., Schoo, M. E., & Johnson, A. N. (2009). Dealing with slackers in college classroom work groups. *College Student Journal, 43*(2) 592–598.

Schiller, S. Z., & Mandviwalla, M. (2007). Virtual team research: An analysis of theory use and a framework for theory appropriation. *Small group Research, 38*(1) 12–59.

Sorenson, S. (1981). "Grouphate." Paper presented at the International Communication Association, Minneapolis, MN.

Tubbs, S. L. (2008). *A systems approach to small group interaction (10th ed.).* New York: McGraw-Hill.

Wech, B. A., Mossholder, K. W., Steel, R. P., & Bennett, N. (1998). Does work group cohesiveness affect individuals' performance and organizational commitment? *Small group Research, 29*(4), 472–494

Glossary

A

abstract topics
Topics that are not grounded in tangible element, but instead are ideas, theories, principles, and beliefs.

academic journal
Published collections of research articles and essays written by scholarly experts.

active listening
Type of listening where a person focuses exclusively on the speaker and the message.

active voice
When the subject of the sentence performs the action.

adequacy
Reflects the need to have a sufficient amount of distinct main points in your speech, typically no fewer than two and no more than five.

after-dinner speech
An address after a meal with the purpose to entertain, often with humor, although it may also convey a thoughtful message.

alliteration
The repetition of the initial consonant or initial sounds in series of words.

analogy
A comparison made to show similarity.

anaphora
The repetition of the same word or phrase at the *beginning* of successive clauses or sentences.

anecdote
Usually a short narrative of interesting, amusing, or biographical incident.

antithesis
The use of contrast, within a parallel grammatical structure, to make a rhetorical point.

appearance
Your physical nonverbal presence established through clothing choice, accessories, piercings, tattoos, and hairstyle.

argot
A collective term that encompasses the specialized vocabulary of all subgroups.

articulation
The act of speaking clearly, precisely, and intelligibly; your verbalization of distinct sounds.

asynchronous messages
Content delivered with a time gap that prevents real-time delivery or immediate feedbacks.

attitudes
Predispositions to act in a particular way that influence our response to objects, events, and situations.

autocratic style
The leadership style that asserts control over group members; it puts greater emphasis on the task rather than maintaining the relationships within the group.

award presentation
A speech delivered as part of a ceremony to recognize an individual or group chosen for special honors.

B

beliefs
A mental and emotional acceptance of information; judgments about the truth or the probability that a statement is correct.

blog
Short for "weblog," it is a web site that contains an online personal journal with reflections, comments, and often hyperlinks provided by the writer.

brainstorming
A group activity intended to generate a large quantity of topics. Contributions are not judged while being generated.

bridging
A problem-solving strategy that aims to identify a solution that satisfies the often-conflicting desires of all parties involved.

C

calculated ambiguity
A speaker's planned effort to be vague, sketchy, and considerably abstract.

cant
Refers to the specialized vocabulary of nonprofessional groups, such as truck drivers and construction workers.

cause-and-effect organization
Focuses on arranging main points into causes and effects.

channel
The medium through which the message is sent.

chronological organization
Information in a speech organized chronologically is focused on relationships in time; events are presented in the order in which they occur.

citation
Evidence of the source used to support a claim. May be provided verbally and in a reference sheet.

cloud computing
A general term for anything that involves delivering hosted services over the Internet.

co-culture
Conveys the idea that no one culture is inherently superior to other coexisting cultures.

cognitive dissonance
The psychological theory by Leon Festinger that argues that we seek internal consistency between attitudes and behaviors.

cognitive restructuring (CR)
A cognitive therapy to help people cope with anxiety by redefining what they are afraid of; this therapy has successfully reduced people's fears of public speaking.

commencement address
A speech delivered at a graduation ceremony to praise the graduates.

communication
The creation of shared meaning through symbolic processes.

communication apprehension
The natural fear or anxiety of communicating in various settings.

comparative advantage organizational pattern
A speech organization pattern that compares the pros and cons of choices.

conclusion
The final part of the speech, which includes a summary of main points, the final take-away message, and provides closure for the audience. Usually, the conclusion comprises 5 to 10 percent of the entire speech.

consistency
The continuity and well-organized pattern of coordinate and subordinate points within your outline.

coordinate points
Main points on an outline, often supported by subordinate points.

correctness
The accuracy of the material (Is it error free?); one of the three "Cs" of informative speaking.

CR. *See* **cognitive restructuring (CR).**

credibility
The reliability of the material (Does the information come from a trustworthy source?); one of the three "Cs" of informative speaking.

criteria satisfaction organizational pattern
A speech organization pattern that uses established criteria to evaluate options or actions.

critical listening
Listening with the need to assess, evaluate, and judge the merits of the ideas and propositions.

critical thinking
Type of thinking that enables you to evaluate your world and make choices based upon what you have learned.

critique
To provide a detailed analysis and evaluation of the strengths and weakness of something.

culture
A society's shared and socially transmitted ideas and perceptions of the world as defined in terms of norms, the rules people follow in their relationships with one another; values, the feelings people share about what is right or wrong, good or bad, desirable or undesirable; customs accepted by the community of institutional practices and expressions; institutions; and language.

currency
The timeliness of the material (Is the information up to date?); one of the three "Cs" of informative speaking.

D

decoding
The act of unwrapping the message and assigning meaning to it.

delayed feedback
Type of feedback that is time-lapsed and may come in the form of letters, emails, phone calls, formal evaluation, or votes.

delivery
The verbal and nonverbal strategies a speaker can use when conveying his or her message to the audience.

democratic style
The leadership style that encourages participation and responsibility from group members. This style equally balances the emphasis on task and relational dimensions; also known as the *participative style*.

demographics
Used to describe the sociological categories of your audience.

dialogic communication
Communication that demonstrates an honest concern for a listener's interests.

dramatic story
A narrative that incorporates elements of suspense, adventure, or perilous circumstances to gain the audience's attention at the start of a speech.

Dunbar's number
A theoretical cognitive limit to the number of people with whom one can maintain stable social relationships in which an individual knows who each person is and how each person relates to every other person. This number is commonly cited at approximately 150.

dynamic variables
Variables that are subject to change, like the decision you make about a particular speech, your appearance and word choice.

E

emoticons
Usually derivatives of the "happy face" created by a colon and parentheses mark to communicate emotions like happiness, sadness, irritation, or humor through the use of punctuation marks; typically used in text-based communication such as text messaging or email.

emphasis
Stressing certain words or phrases to draw attention.

encoding
The way in which a message is packaged so that it is best received.

epistrophe
The repetition of a word or expression at the *end* of phrases, clauses, or sentences.

equality pattern
An organizational pattern that involves giving approximately the same amount of time to each point.

ethics
The rules we use to determine good and evil, right and wrong. These rules may be grounded in religious principles, democratic values, codes of conduct, and bases of values derived from a variety of sources.

ethnicity
The fact or state of belonging to a social group that has a common national or cultural tradition, heritage, and even language.

ethnocentrism
Belief in the superiority of one's own ethnic group.

ethos
The characteristic spirit of a culture, era, or community as seen in its beliefs and aspirations.

eulogy
A speech that honors someone who has passed away.

euphemisms
Substituting a mild or vague term or phrase in place of a blunt or harsh word or phrase.

example
Support that helps illustrate a point or claim.

exemplar definitions
Definitions that help explain a complex concept by providing familiar examples.

expanding the pie
A problem-solving technique that involves finding ways to creatively increase resources as a solution to the issue.

extemporaneous speaking
A method of delivery that involves a combination of speech practice and the use of carefully prepared notes to guide the presentation.

extrinsic ethos
A speaker's image in the mind of the audience. Extrinsic aspects include perceived knowledge and expertise, perceived trustworthiness, and speaker confidence and enthusiasm.

eye contact
The connection you form with listeners through your gaze.

F

facial expressions
The movement of the eyes, eyebrows, cheeks, and mouth to communicate affect or feelings.

facts
Pieces of information that are verifiable and irrefutable.

fallacy
An argument that seems plausible but turns out on close examination to be misleading.

feedback
In public speaking, this refers to the messages the audience sends back to the speaker.

filled pauses. *See* **verbal fillers.**

fixed-alternative questions
Questions with limited responses to specific choices, such as age, education, and income. Fixed-alternative questions can offer many different responses, or they can offer only two alternatives, such as yes/no. Such questions help you analyze the attitudes and knowledge of your prospective listeners.

forum
A group format where group members respond to audience questions without interacting with each other.

four-step process
The way in which to organize a speech, which involves selecting the main points, supporting the main points, choosing the best organizational pattern, and creating unity throughout the speech.

full-content outline. *See* **planning outline.**

G

general index
A comprehensive and cross-referenced collection of sources.

general purpose
In a speech, the general purposes are to inform, persuade, and entertain or inspire.

geosocial network
Short-range and long-distance social ties established through online social networks (OSNs) like Facebook, LinkedIn, Flickr, and Twitter.

gestures
Using your arms and hands to illustrate, emphasize, or provide a visual experience that accompanies your thoughts.

glossophobia
The fear specific to speaking in public.

group-oriented goals
Goals that center around specific tasks to be performed.

groupthink
A mode of thinking that people engage in when they are deeply involved in a cohesive in-group, when the members' strivings for unanimity override their motivation to realistically appraise alternative courses of action.

H

heterogeneous
Diverse in character or content (e.g., "a large and *heterogeneous* collection").

homogeneous
Of the same or similar nature or kind (e.g., "a tight-knit, *homogeneous* society").

I

illusion of transparency
A speaker's sense that their anxiety is more apparent than it really is.

illustration
A story that engages the listeners on an emotional level and usually details a situation or instance; can be used during the introduction or conclusion of a speech.

imagery
Creating a vivid description through the use of one or more of our five senses.

immediate feedback
Feedback that is instantaneous and may range from laughter, nods, and applause to verbal comments, the rolling of eyes, and yawns.

impromptu speaking
Usually a short speech delivered at the spur of the moment with little preparation time.

infinitive phrase
Expresses an action in its simplest form.

information literacy
The ability to recognize when information is needed and have the ability to locate, evaluate, and use it effectively.

informative speech
Type of speech that communicates information and ideas in a way that an audience will understand and remember.

innuendo
Made up of hints or remarks that something is what it is not. Essentially, they are veiled lies.

interest chart
A visual display of possible topics.

interest map. *See* **topic map.**

internal previews
Extended transitions that tell the audience, in general terms, what you will say next.

internal summaries
Follow a main point and act as reminders; useful to clarify or emphasize what you have just said.

intrinsic ethos
Ethical appeal found in the actual speech, including such aspects as supporting material, argument flow, and source citation.

introduction
The first part of the speech, which includes the attention getter, preview, and frequently allows the speaker to establish credibility. Generally, the introduction comprises 10 to 15 percent of the entire speech.

J

jargon
The technical language of professional subgroups like doctors and lawyers.

K

keynote address
A speech delivered by the featured speaker at a formal event.

kinesthetic learner
One who learns best through opportunities to engage in physical activity and interactive experience.

L

laissez-faire style
A "hands-off" approach to leadership that features no defined leader. The group members do not attempt to influence each other and no one "steps up" when important decisions need to be made.

linguistic relativity
A theory that proposes that language shapes the way we see the world; also known as the *Sapir-Whorf hypothesis*.

listener
One who perceives through sensory levels and interprets, evaluates, and responds to what her or she hears.

loci method
Involves a speaker assigning/associating each main idea (from the speech) to a part of a place they know well (like their house).

logos
Rational appeals or appeals based on facts and logic.

M

mean
Calculated by adding all the numbers in a group and dividing by the number of items. It is the most widely used statistical measure and is commonly referred to as the *average*.

median
The middle score in the group.

message
The content being conveyed by the sender.

message credibility
The extent to which the speech is considered to be factual and well supported through documentation.

metaphor
A mental equation when something is compared to something else.

mode
The value that occurs most frequently.

monologic communication
A form of communication in which the audience is viewed as an object to be manipulated and, in the process, the speaker displays such qualities as deception, superiority, exploitation, dogmatism, domination, insincerity, pretense, coercion, distrust, and defensiveness.

mood
The overall feeling you hope to evoke in your audience.

motivated sequence
A five-step speech organization pattern that leads to action.

movement
The physical shifts from place to place.

N

narrative
A short story, either truth-based or fictitious, presented to gain or hold attention and usually intended to convey deeper meaning.

noise
Anything that interferes with the communication process. Noise can be physical, physiological, psychological, or semantic.

nonfluencies. *See* **verbal fillers.**

norms
The often-invisible social structures that group members develop that dictate their behavior; they define the general roles that group members are expected to perform.

O

occasion
The situation for public speaking comprised of the time, place, event, and traditions that define the moment.

online social networks (OSNs)
Web sites where one connects with those sharing personal or professional interests, place of origin, education at a particular school, and other identifying characteristics.

open-ended questions
Questions that let audience members respond however they wish.

operational definitions
Definitions that specify procedures for observing and measuring concepts.

opinions
Points of view that may or may not be supported in fact.

organization of ideas
The placement of lines of reasoning and supporting materials in a pattern that helps to achieve your specific purpose.

OSNs. *See* **online social networks (OSNs).**

P

panels
Public discussions presented for the benefit of the audience.

parallelism
An organizational tool that relates your introduction to your conclusion.

participative style. *See* **democratic style.**

passive voice
When speakers or writers make the object of an action into the subject of a sentence.

past-present-future
A form of the chronological pattern that allows a speaker to provide perspective for a topic or issue that has relevant history and future direction or potential.

pathos
Emotional appeals or appeals designed to get the audience to feel a certain way.

pauses
Intervals of silence between or within words, phrases, or sentences.

persuasion
Any attempt to influence the thoughts, feelings, or behavior of another.

physical noise
Anything within the environment that distracts the speaker or listeners, including cell phones ringing, a loud truck driving by, or a buzzing light fixture.

physiological noise
Interference with the communication process that occurs when our senses fail us in some way, like poor vision or hearing loss.

pitch
The frequency of sound waves in a particular sound—specifically, level, range, and variation.

planning outline
Also known as the *full-content outline*, it includes most of the information you will present in your speech without including every word you plan to say.

podcast
A multimedia digital file made available on the Internet for downloading to a portable media player, computer, or other digital device.

posture
The relative relaxation or rigidity and vertical position of the body.

primacy effect
The belief that it is the first point in your speech that listeners will most likely remember.

primary group
Fulfills the basic need to associate with others and usually involves your family and close friends.

primary research
Collecting original data for the purpose of answering a question or questions.

problem-solution organization
Especially common in persuasive speeches, the goal is to present an audience with a problem and then examine one or more likely solutions.

progressive pattern
Using your least important point first and your most important point last.

pronunciation
Involves saying a word in an acceptable manner.

proposition of fact
A proposition of fact suggests the existence of something.

proposition of policy
A proposition that proposes a course of action.

proposition of value
Assertion rooted in judgments based on deep-seated ideals.

psychographic analysis
An analysis that provides a profile of an audience based on individual characteristics rather than group characteristics. Psychographics identify behaviors, such as lifestyle choices, attitudes, beliefs, and values.

psychographics
The study and classification of listeners/audiences according to their behaviors, interests, aspirations, attitudes, beliefs, and values.

psychological noise
Interference with the communication process that occurs within an individual's mind, including stress about a relationship, a poor exam score, or financial worries.

Q

QR codes
Two-dimensional matrix barcodes, also known as *quick response codes*, that, upon scanning with a smartphone camera, link digital content on the Internet to activate a number of phone functions, including email, IM, and SMS, and connect the mobile device to a web browser.

questionnaire
A compilation of questions used to conduct survey research.

quick response codes. *See* **QR codes.**

quotation
A saying, presented verbatim, of an individual, usually placed at the beginning or end of a speech to establish emotional tone and get the audience thinking about an important concept.

R

race
Major division of humankind, having distinct shared biology and understanding.

rate
The number of words spoken per minute.

reasoning
The process of using known and believed information to explain or prove other statements less well understood or accepted.

receiver
The target of the message.

recency effect
The belief that it is the last point in your speech that listeners will most likely remember.

reflective thinking process
A seven-step problem solving process developed by John Dewey. The steps include: (1) identifying and defining the problem, (2) analyzing the problem, (3) determining criteria for an acceptable solution, (4) generating possible solutions, (5) choosing the solution that best fits the criteria, (6) implementing the solution, and (7) reassessing the solution.

reframing
The cognitive process of reinterpreting the meaning of an event, resulting in the creation of a new perspective.

relational roles
Roles that focus on the interpersonal communication dynamics within a group.

rhetorical question
A question asked to spark audience contemplation of the speech topic; however, an answer is not desired nor expected.

rhetorical sensitivity
The speaker's ability to be aware of the speech setting and audience reactions and adjust accordingly.

rhythm
The systematic and regular arrangement of sounds.

S

sampling
The act, process, or technique of selecting a representative part of a population for the purpose of determining parameters or characteristics of the whole population.

Sapir-Whorf hypothesis. *See* **linguistic relativity.**

scale questions
A type of fixed-alternative question that asks people to respond to questions set up along a continuum.

secondary group
A group focused on accomplishing a task or achieving a goal.

secondary research
Reviewing information someone else collected, analyzed, and presented.

self-oriented goals
Goals that relate to an individual's personal needs and ambitions.

semantic noise
The disconnect that can exist between the speaker's words and the listener's interpretation.

sender
The one who conveys a message to an intended audience.

signposting
Using oral lists, such as "first, second, third," to help your audience understand the structure of your speech.

similes
Create images as they compare the characteristics of two things that are not alike using the words "like" or "as."

singularity
The need for each main point to reflect a distinct area of the chosen topic.

situational apprehension
The perspective that apprehension is a short-term reaction to specific contexts.

Skype
An IP telephony service provider that offers free calling between subscribers and low-cost calling to people who don't use the service. In addition to standard telephone calls, Skype enables file transfers, texting, video chat, and videoconferencing.

slackers. *See* **social loafers.**

slang
The specialized vocabulary of "stigmatized" groups, such as criminals or teenagers.

smartphone
Any cellular device that possesses call making capabilities as well as Internet access, email ability, still and video cameras, MP3 player, video viewing, and built-in applications.

social loafers
Group members who believe that their participation is unnecessary because others will pick up their slack; also known as *slackers*.

spatial organization
An organization pattern in which the sequence of ideas moves from one physical point to another.

speaker credibility
The extent to which a speaker is perceived as competent is considered.

speaker's notes
An abbreviated key-word outline, lacking much of the detail of the planning outline. Although in a condensed format, these notes function as a reminder of what you plan to say and the order in which you plan to say it.

speaking from manuscript
Reading the speech verbatim.

speaking from memory
Committing the entire speech to memory and delivering it without the aid of notes.

specific purpose
The precise response a speaker desires from his or her audience.

speech of acceptance
A speech to expresses gratitude for an award.

speech of demonstration
Type of speech that focuses on *how* something is done.

speech of description
Type of speech that helps an audience understand *what* something is.

speech of explanation
Type of speech that helps an audience understand *why* something is so.

speech of introduction
A brief speech to introduce the person who will give an important address.

speed differential
The difference in the rate of normal speech and the speed with which we can process information.

static variables
Those things that remain stable from speaking situation to speaking situation.

statistics
The collection, analysis, interpretation, and presentation of information in numerical form.

step-by-step
A form of the chronological pattern that is used to describe the steps, in order, of a process.

striking images principle
Idea that speakers should assign vivid characteristics to ideas they wish to convey in their speeches.

strongest point pattern
You spend the most time in your speech on the first point, less time on the second point, and even less time on the last point of your speech.

subordinate points
Supporting facts, examples, or evidence that fortify the coordinate points.

supporting material
Sources used to substantiate a claim or support a thesis.

survey
A data collection method in which information or opinions are gathered for the purpose of analysis.

symposium
More formal and predictable than a panel discussion, it is centered on prepared speeches on a specific subject given by group members who have expertise on the subject.

synchronous messages
Content relayed in real time, allowing receivers to respond immediately.

T

task roles
Roles that focus on the group job or work to be completed.

teleconferencing
The holding of a conference among people remote from one another by means of telecommunication devices such as telephones.

teleprompter
A device for displaying prepared text to a speaker or performer.

testimony
Statements by someone who has experienced an event.

thesis statement
Premise that focuses on what you want to say and generally includes your speech direction as well as your main points.

three "Cs" of informative speaking. *See* **correctness, credibility,** and **currency.**

toast
A brief message of good will and congratulations.

tone
The emotional disposition of the speaker as the speech is being delivered.

topic map
A graphic organizer or diagram (also known as an *interest map*) that allows you to represent the connections between topics as ideas, images, or words. Such maps provide a visual framework for organizing information in terms of a line of argument or a train of thought.

topical organization
The most frequently used organizational system tied to the unique needs of your topic; the nature and scope of your topic dictate the pattern of your approach.

trait apprehension
The perspective that some people are generally more anxious about public speaking than others.

transactional communication
The process of simultaneously both sending and receiving messages.

transitional sentences
Phrases and sentences that help the speaker move from one major part of the speech to the next.

transitions
Verbal bridges between ideas, words, phrases, or sentences that tell your audience how ideas relate.

V

values
Socially shared ideas about what is good, right, and desirable. They are deep-seated, abstract judgments about what is important to us.

verbal fillers
"Nonwords" and phrases like "um," "uh," "like," and "you know" that disrupt the flow of speech and challenge speaker credibility; also known as *nonfluencies, filled pauses*, or *vocal fillers*.

videoconferencing
Two-way, real-time transmission of audio and video signals between specialized devices or computers at two or more locations via satellite (wireless) over a network such as a LAN or the Internet.

virtual group
A small group whose members interact by means of electronic technologies.

visual learner
One who learns best thorough visual mediums including pictures, colors, film clips, and presentational slides.

visualization
A technique by which a person creates powerful mental images of successful performances in order to reduce nervousness.

vocal fillers. *See* **verbal fillers.**

volume
How loudly or softly you talk.

W

webcast
To send live audio or video to the user from a web site. It is the Internet counterpart to traditional radio and television broadcasting.

webinar
A workshop or lecture delivered over the Web. Webinars may be a one-way webcast, or there may be interaction between the audience and the presenters.

weblog. *See* **blog.**

Index

G